Law
&
Economics

Law
&
Economics

JEFFREY L. HARRISON
University of Florida

JULES THEEUWES
University of Amsterdam

W. W. NORTON & COMPANY
New York · London

Editor: Jack Repcheck
Director of manufacturing, College: Roy Tedoff
Managing editor, college: Marian Johnson
Project editor: Rebecca A. Homiski
Editorial assistant: Mikael Awake
Manuscript editor: Patterson Lamb
Book design: Charlotte Staub
Illustrations: John McAusland
Composition: Matrix Publishing Services
Index: WordCo Indexing Services, Inc.
Manufacturing: Courier, Westford

Library of Congress Cataloging-in-Publication Data

Harrison, Jeffrey L., 1946–
  Law and economics / Jeffrey L. Harrison, Jules Theeuwes. — 1st ed.
      p. cm.
  Includes bibliographical references and index.
  ISBN 978-0-393-93053-5 (hardcover)
  1. Law and economics. I. Theeuwes, Jules. II. Title.
  K487.E3H369 2008
  340′.11—dc22

                                                    2007050461

W. W. Norton & Company, Inc., 500 Fifth Avenue, New York, N.Y. 10110
                       www.wwnorton.com

W. W. Norton & Company Ltd., Castle House, 75/76 Wells Street,
London W1T 3QT

1 2 3 4 5 6 7 8 9 0

To *Sarah*

To *Veerle*

Brief Contents

Contents

UNIT FOUR · ECONOMICS OF TORT LAW

UNIT SEVEN · **BEHAVIORAL ISSUES**

Preface

BARON CHARLES PERCY SNOW WAS BOTH A MOLECULAR PHYSI-
cist and a literary man, and knew about the cultures of the sciences
and the humanities. In 1959 he published an essay making a strong
case that a big divide exists between these two cultures and that practitioners on both sides know little of each other's disciplines. Snow
noted that well-educated people in the literary world could not
answer the most basic questions from the sciences. Communication
between the two worlds was difficult if not impossible. His essay was
hotly discussed on both sides of the Atlantic and on both sides of
the intellectual divide.

One of the few success stories in combining two very different
worlds is law and economics. The legal and economic disciplines are
distinct in terms of methodology and scientific approach. In large
measure this stems from different objectives. Economics is a *positive*
science, while law is essentially *normative*. Yet the mixture of the two
is appealing and exciting and gives way to a completely new discipline. Alfred Marshall (1842–1924), the great Cambridge economist,
defined economics as the study of mankind in the ordinary business
of life. It is the study of "what is." One could see law as the study of
the rules that regulate mankind in the ordinary business of life. It is
a study of man's reaction to his environment.

This book is an examination of law from the point of view of economic theory. The point is not that law should comply with economic

rules—even economics does not claim that. Instead, it is an effort to both assess the economic impact of laws and to compare that impact with laws that are guided by goals of efficiency. When economics is applied to law a necessary central theme is internalization as a means of achieving efficient outcomes. Consequently, in large measure what follows is a close look at how law requires people and firms to internalize negative externalities and to assist them in internalizing positive externalities.

This book is divided into seven units. The first one is designed to help you review some of the basic economics principles and terms that will be used throughout the book. Some basic tools will, therefore, be discussed in Chapter 2. Others will be addressed when they are relevant to a specific issue. Unit 2 is about property law and related concepts. Your first impression may be that economics and property law seem unrelated. As you will see, however, economics actually provides a powerful rationale for the existence of private property and helps to explain why there are disputes about the uses of property. In Unit 2, you will learn much more about the Coase theorem. This unit includes an economic analysis of intellectual property law, rent control, and a variety of other topics. For example, you will analyze, from an economic perspective, why laws against downloading music from the Internet may or may not make sense.

Unit 3 is devoted to an economic analysis of contract law. Is there an economic reason to even enforce contracts? More interestingly, suppose someone makes a simple promise of a gift and then reneges? Is there an economic reason for enforcing that promise? Contract law also gets into the concept of the "efficient breach" of contract and the question of whether courts should refuse to enforce contracts that seem to be lopsided or unfair. It may surprise to you to find that it may not be efficient for parties to enter into and draft contracts in which all possible eventualities are fully treated. It just may not be worth the effort to draft contracts that are as thick as an encyclopedia. Incomplete contracts are the norm, and there is an important role for economics in such an imperfect world.

Unit 4 will introduce you to tort law. This term may not be familiar to you, but actually you already have heard a great deal about tort law. Tort law comes into play when one person harms another person or his or her property. The standard example is when someone is careless and crashes into another car. But there are also, perhaps bizarre, cases like the suit against McDonald's by someone who burned herself on hot coffee or against the owner of a wild animal by someone whose fingers were bitten off when he put them in the animal's mouth. An important part of the study of torts concerns damages when a wrong is committed. Suppose someone is severely injured. It makes sense that he or she should be compensated for medical bills and for the salary lost while recuperating. Suppose he or she was an avid skier. Should there be compensation if skiing is now impossible or is not as fun as it once was? If so, how would you calculate this?

Maybe the most controversial application of economics to law is covered in Unit 5. The issues in that unit concern the application of economics to criminal law. Does it make sense to think in terms of efficient levels of crime and to treat criminals as though they make "rational decisions"? The issues in this unit are guaranteed to make you think about the possibility of applying concepts of efficiency in the context of laws that seem to be about moral issues.

Unit 6 is more narrowly focused. You may be surprised by the degree to which economists have analyzed the litigation process itself—including the economics of settlement. This unit will introduce you to this fascinating and sometimes complex area of study. Included in this analysis is the more general question of whether economic factors determine how law changes.

Unit 7 focuses on the most rapidly growing area of economic scholarship—behavioral economics. Do people actually behave the way economists assume they do?

Bonus material on the economics of antitrust and other selected issues is available through a Harrison/Theeuwes link on the W. W. Norton website. Go to *www.wwnorton.com* for the following chapters: "The Goals of Antitrust Law"; "Market Definition, Market Power, and Collusion"; "Economic Regulation: Monnopolies"; "Marriage, Divorce, and Contract"; and "Intrafamily Transfers of Income: Inheritance and Related Issues."

As you can see, the underlying message here is that potential applications of economics to law is pervasive, interesting, and extremely useful. Have fun!

We would like to thank those who have assisted in this project. Sarah Harrison was in many respects the manager of this enterprise: bridging language differences, organizing, editing, and reacting. McCabe Harrison provided able research assistance. Roger Blair, an early participant in this effort, generously contributed comments and materials. Finally, much of what is contained here reflects the suggestions of Jack Repcheck, our editor at Norton, and several unidentified commentators, all of whom enriched the analysis.

Jeffrey L. Harrison
University of Florida

Jules Theeuves
University of Amsterdam

Introduction

CHAPTER ONE

Introducing Law and Economics

BRINGING LAW AND ECONOMICS TOGETHER

A T FIRST GLANCE, YOU MAY WONDER WHAT LAW AND economics have in common and even why there is an area of study called "law and economics." Economics is about allocating scarce resources, whereas law seems to be about resolving disputes in ways that are fair or just.[1] Put in familiar terms, economists are interested in putting scarce resources to their highest and best uses while lawyers and judges are interested in settling disputes that, more often than not, are about dividing whatever wealth has been produced. Take a look at a few examples and you will soon get a feel for how they are combined.

In 1997, a court in Alaska considered the validity of a new law passed by the Alaska legislature that raised the fee prisoners must pay in order to file lawsuits. Within the court's consideration of the increase in the fee is the impact on the number of lawsuits. As part

---

1. Although we will discuss "law," you should know that "the law" does not consist of a list of settled rules. The "law" changes over time and may vary from state to state and country to country. For example, in the United States, each state is free to determine its own rules with respect to contracts and many other areas. Although the law tends to be similar from state to state, you would have to research the law in each state to know the rule in a particular state.

of its consideration, the court noted the following: "the cost of litigation acts as a mechanism to screen out meritless lawsuits; people must weigh this cost against the importance of the dispute and the likelihood of success in court."[2] In fact, the court referred directly to the idea that when prices go up, the quantity demanded (in this case for lawsuits) goes down.

In 2003, a court in Colorado reviewed the damages awarded to one party when the other party breached a contract. In a passage that will likely surprise you (and most people), the court noted that the law is designed to *encourage* breaching under some circumstances:

> There are . . . occasions where the breach of a contract is thought to be economically efficient and socially beneficial. The theory of the "efficient breach" posits that the purpose of contract law is not to discourage all breaches. To the contrary, certain breaches, such as those where the breaching party's gains exceed the injured party's losses are thought to be desirable.[3]

Third, take a look at this passage that appears in a decision addressing how much those who have violated the law should be punished:

> Many years ago, in an influential article that was in part responsible for his receipt of the Nobel Memorial Prize in economics, Professor Becker pointed out that charging a thief the cost of what he had stolen would not adequately deter theft unless the thief was caught every time. Since thieves will not always be caught, they must be penalized by more than the cost of the items stolen on the occasions on which they are caught. This "multiplier" is essential to render theft unprofitable and properly to deter it.[4]

Remember, these excerpts are not from economics texts. All of them are from actual opinions written by judges in the course of deciding cases.

The joining of law and economics does not end, though, with judges' opinions. Consider this language found in a study by the Food

---

2. *George v. Alaska,* 944 P.2d 1181 (1997).

3. *Gioacchino v. American Family Mutual Insurance Company,* 64 P.3d 230 (Colo. 2003).

4. *Ciaraolo v. City of New York,* 216 F.3d 236 (2d Cir. 2000).

and Drug Administration designed to assess the impact of limiting the sales of cigarettes to minors:

> In sum, the FDA finds that compliance with this proposed rule would impose some economic costs on the tobacco industry and short-term costs on several industry sectors. With regard to small businesses, most impacts would be small or transitory. For a small retail convenience store not currently complying with this proposal, the additional first year costs could reach $320. For those convenience stores that already check customer identification, these costs fall to $35. Moreover the proposed rule would not produce significant economic problems at the national level, as the gradual displacement in tobacco-oriented sectors would be largely offset by increased output in other areas.[5]

The question is not whether law and economics should be joined. In effect, like it or not, the joining of law and economics has already occurred. Indeed, there are some areas of law, like antitrust and regulation, that one cannot hope to understand without a firm backing in economics.

It is likely that you see a trend running through these excerpts. In all of these cases, the judges or regulatory agencies creating law or interpreting it have drawn on economic analysis to make the process more complete. Thus, when the term *law and economics* is used, in almost all instances it means the application of economic tools and analysis to legal issues as opposed to the application of law to the discipline of economics.

THE BREADTH OF THE APPLICATION OF ECONOMICS TO LAW

Now that you have a taste of what the term *law and economics* means, you may want to know just how far the application of economics to law has gone. In two words: very far. Consider this: In 1960, a University of Chicago economist and eventual Nobel Prize winner,

---

5. U.S. Food and Drug Administration, "Proposed Rule Restricting the Sale and Distribution of Cigarettes and Smokeless Tobacco Products to Protect Children and Adolescents," 60 FR 41314.

Ronald Coase, published an article titled "The Problem of Social Cost." That short article is currently the single item of scholarship—from any discipline—that is most frequently relied upon by legal scholars. Yes, the most relied-upon article by legal scholars was penned by an economist. Richard Posner, a judge at the second highest level of federal courts, wrote *An Economic Analysis of Law* in 1973, which is now in its seventh edition. In addition, Steven Breyer, a current member of the U.S. Supreme Court, is the author of an important book entitled *Breaking the Vicious Circle: Toward Effective Risk Regulation,* published in 1991.

If you have seen the movie *A Beautiful Mind* (or read the book), you know about John Nash, and you probably addressed the concept of a Nash equilibrium in prior courses. The concept of a Nash equilibrium and a great deal more of game theory (which is the theory of strategic interaction) are standard fare in law courses ranging from antitrust law to negotiation. Also, in antitrust law and other courses devoted to the management and regulation of markets, it is crucial to have a basic understanding of industrial organization, which is the part of economics that concerns itself with the structure and performance of sectors and markets and with the conduct of suppliers and demanders in those markets. In fact, in today's legal opinions, it is not uncommon to find references to demand, supply, elasticity, marginal cost, marginal revenue, market share, market power, monopoly, oligopoly, allocative efficiency, productive efficiency, externalities, and even Pareto optimality.

Another indication of the pervasiveness of the application of economics to law is that many law schools currently employ one or more faculty with advanced degrees in economics. In many instances, these professors hold degrees in both economics and law, but that is not always the case. There are some law professors at very prestigious law schools who have not attended law school at all.

This is not to suggest that the application of economics to law is new. In fact, in 1897, the famed jurist Oliver Wendell Holmes wrote in a very influential legal journal that "the man of the future is the man of statistics and economics."[6] The writings of Adam Smith

6. Oliver Wendell Holmes, "The Path of the Law," *Harvard Law Review* 10 (1897): 457.

(1723–1790), Karl Marx (1818–1883), and John R. Commons (1862–1945) are also marked by early efforts to apply economic teachings to matters of law and policy. Economic tools have been implicitly applied to law since organized society began.

Even though law always has been the subject of economic analysis, you may think that it only applies to certain types of law—antitrust or securities regulation, for example. Actually, some of the more interesting and at times controversial applications of economics to law are in areas of law that may seem completely detached from economics. For example, one major unit in this book is devoted to criminal law. This may seem strange. Take the idea of stealing a car. Obviously it is against the law, but we do not treat it in the same way as a murder. Why not? One reason may be that a car theft does not make us as angry as murder and so we do not think car thieves should be punished as severely. On the other hand, perhaps we actually want people to steal cars once in a while, and a very severe punishment might discourage even the occasional car theft. To understand why this could be the case, assume you are caught in a flood or are being pursued by someone with a knife and you see a car, not your own, that you can use to escape. Your likelihood of doing this may turn on what you think the legal consequences will be. When economics is applied to law, one begins to think in terms of "efficient" levels of criminal behavior. In fact, there are very few, if any, areas of law that are untouched by economic analysis.

LAW, ECONOMICS, AND VALUES

Despite the pervasiveness of economic analysis in the field of law, the two disciplines can also be viewed separately. Sometimes they complement each other perfectly and at other times they are contradictory. Consider the following example which actually happened to one of your authors.

A university constructed a new building consisting of thirty offices for the thirty-person math department. The offices in the building varied in size, floor plan, and view so that some were very desirable and others were not so desirable. The math professors were stumped on how to decide who should get which office and called on members of the economics faculty and the law faculty as consultants.

The economics faculty felt the offices should be allocated to maximize something. The best possibility would be to allocate them to maximize utility. As you know, it is hard to make comparisons of utility from person to person, so the economists suggested the alternative of allocating the offices on the basis of who would pay the most for them. In other words, by auctioning each office, the person who placed the highest value on a particular space would get it. Although not a perfect gauge of utility, willingness and ability to pay seemed like an acceptable substitute.

The law professors had a completely different perspective. Their discussion was about how to assign offices in a "fair and equitable" manner. The suggestions ranged from a lottery to assigning offices on the basis of seniority with the most senior member of the department getting the first choice. The law professors spoke more in terms of what "should" be done—"should" meaning "morally correct." If you had been one of the mathematicians, whose advice would you have followed?

LAW AND ECONOMICS IN ACTION 1.1

(MAYBE) THE MOST IMPORTANT QUESTION

The text describes two ways of determining how to allocate the new offices to the mathematicians. In fact, the two ways could be applied to any scarce resource. One way relies on the market and the other on virtually any other standard. It could be height, weight, seniority, a lottery, or any other value. The question is whether the initial allocation makes any difference with respect to who actually ends up with the offices or any other scarce resource. Think about it. Suppose the offices were initially allocated by lottery but that the recipients could then do whatever they wanted with them including selling them to other mathematicians. If you are beginning to think that the professors who value specific offices the most will buy them from those to whom they were initially assigned, you have hit on something that is critical to the study of law and economics—the Coase theorem. There is much, much more on this throughout the book, but even at this level you should begin to consider the power of market transactions to ultimately determine how resources are allocated.

These two perspectives differ in at least two important ways. First, the economists, coming from a discipline that has at its heart how to get the most out of scarce resources, were looking to squeeze the most utility out of the limited number of offices. In short, given that there were thirty offices, how could they be used to maximize social welfare? The legal perspective is far less concerned with allocating resources in a manner that maximizes anything. Instead, the focus is more on social norms and what is fair.

Another difference is that the economist, at least while in the role of an economist, will not tell you what you *should* do in terms of the overall objective. If the mathematicians decided they wanted an efficient allocation, the economists could guide them on how to achieve that outcome. Economists, acting within the confines of their discipline, however, do not claim to be able to instruct people on what is "fair" or "moral." On the one hand, law is brimming with theories and ideas about what is fair, just, and moral. And the truth is that those who work with law cannot avoid making moral judgments. On the other hand, the discipline of law does not provide a single rule of moral guidance with which all would agree.

These fundamental distinctions between law and economics have led to some resistance—by judges, attorneys, and law professors—to the application of economics to law. For some people involved in law at one level or another, economics has little or nothing to offer. In fact, its perspective is to be avoided. This view and the controversies that follow typically can be traced to one of two problems. To understand these problems, first think back to our car theft example. Suppose a group of economists were able to determine how many car thefts would take place in a certain state as a function of levels of punishment. For example, using an econometric model, they may project that if the punishment were instant electrocution, there may be only 10 thefts per year. On the other hand, if the punishment were a mild caning, there might be 10,000 thefts. There are costs and benefits associated with these and every other possible level of punishment, and in an ideal setting, the economists could tell you the level of punishment that is consistent with the most favorable cost-benefit trade-off and hence with the efficient level of car theft.

You may follow and feel comfortable with the car theft example, but not everyone does. The first problem that some would point out is that the cost-benefit analysis is applying apples and oranges. Suppose instead of car theft, the crime were murder or rape. Is there an efficient level of rape and murder? You may say that economics still works and that the efficient level is zero. Or you may say that you are not willing to apply what is ultimately a cost-benefit analysis to considerations of life, death, and property interests because the values involved cannot be expressed in dollars and cents. One way of putting this would be to say that even though no murder should be tolerated, it is not because it is inefficient but because it is morally wrong.

The question here is whether it makes sense in these circumstances to adopt the view that economics is irrelevant. Many would argue that it does and this is a hard question to answer. Still, there are at least two arguments that economics is a valuable tool. First, although some may think that they would never engage in a cost-benefit analysis when it comes to important moral values or a sense of duty, sometimes even these irreducible values come into conflict and a comparison that draws on economic methodologies may be useful. Cost-benefit analysis is nothing more than a methodology for making reasoned choices. Choices are usually unavoidable. Even the staunchest opponent of abortion will sometimes be forced to compare the alternative of keeping the mother or the child alive and use arguments before or against one or the other. Second, even when values are irreducible, it does not mean there are no costs of adhering to certain principles. For example, even an absolute adherence to a rule of no abortion imposes costs on others. An awareness of these costs is required by basic notions of responsibility.

The other source of controversy is closely related to the irreducibility issue but is a bit more practical. Often this controversy comes into play when those applying economics claim too much. Again, going back to the car theft example, suppose the economists you hired tell you the efficient level of car theft and the degree of punishment that will achieve that level. If you are in charge of enacting laws that cover car theft, should you then adopt that level of punishment? The answer is that maybe you should, but it is not economics that leads to that answer. Whether you want to adopt a policy encouraging "efficient" car theft is a separate question that economics does not answer. Although this is not something to be concerned with in your first course on law and economics, it may be that some of the tension between law and economics stems from instances in which people who do not know much about economics have tried to claim it provides the answers to all difficult questions. It clearly does not, but in most instances it can provide crucial information.

QUESTIONS FOR DISCUSSION

1. There are two legal traditions in Western society: the Common Law tradition such as in the United States and the United Kingdom and the Civil Law tradition such as in France and other countries that were once conquered and occupied by Napoleon Bonaparte. In the Common Law tradition, disputes are decided on the basis of rules that courts have established and modified over generations. Novel disputes are the occasion for altering the law. In the Civil Law tradition, disputes are decided on the basis of the Civil Law Code book and changes in the law have to pass through the parliament.
   a. Can you say that one tradition is better than the other?
   b. Can you identify differences in societal costs or benefits comparing these two traditions?
   c. Are these two traditions really that different?

2. Discuss: The existence of a legal system is economically very valuable for society.

CHAPTER TWO

Tools for the Economic Analysis of Law

I N 1997, THE ALASKA SUPREME COURT WAS ASKED TO DECIDE whether it was legal for the state to have a law requiring prisoners to pay a fee in order to sue the state itself.[1] Critical to the decision was the reasoning for enacting the new law. According to the court:

> One of the axioms of economic theory is that people are generally more likely to purchase goods and services, or to purchase more of them, as the price of those goods or services goes down. . . . As many experienced lawyers might attest, this rule applies to lawsuits. Although some people can afford to litigate endlessly, and other people are by temperament inclined to litigate regardless of expense, most people will consider the cost of litigation . . . when deciding whether to initiate or continue a lawsuit. In effect, the cost of litigation acts as a mechanism to screen out meritless lawsuits: people must weigh this cost against the importance of the dispute and the likelihood of success in court.

In effect, the court determined that the increase was likely to reduce the number of baseless suits against the state. As you will see throughout the pages of this book, the application of demand, supply, and many other economic concepts by lawyers and courts is far from unusual. You probably already understand the mechanics of supply and demand from

1. *George v. Alaska*, 944 P.2d 1181 (1997).

your prior study. This chapter provides a review of these most essential tools. In addition, you will be introduced to some concepts that may be new but which are crucial in the economic analysis of law.

DEMAND, SUPPLY, AND COMPETITIVE EQUILIBRIUM

Demand

The concept of demand is confusing to some people because it is actually a schedule of prices for a good or service and the quantities of that good or service that would be purchased at each price in a given market during a given time period. In other words, demand is a series of possibilities. It is important to note that need not backed by purchasing power does not register as part of demand; demand is composed only of those both willing and able to pay. The term used for a point on the schedule corresponding to a specific price is quantity demanded. When demand is plotted on a graph, price is found on the *y*-axis and quantity is on the *x*-axis. Take a look at Figure 2.1, in which the demand for soccer balls is plotted.

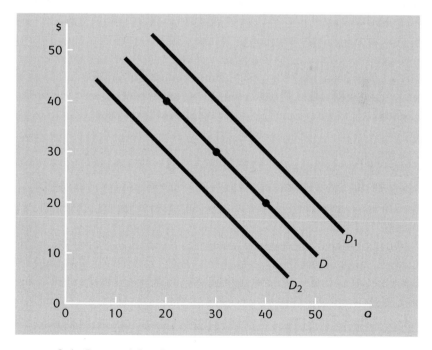

FIGURE 2.1 Demand for Soccer Balls

In theory, demand could be determined by surveying a group of people. Each person would be given a list of prices and asked how many soccer balls he or she would purchase at each price. The quantities of these individual demands would then be summed up at each price to get the total quantity demanded in the market for soccer balls at each price. This is the number that actually appears on the graph. In actuality, when economists examine the relationship between prices and quantities, they are often dealing with a great deal of data and complex mathematical models that include a number of variables in addition to price. The key in those models is to hold the impact of all other variables constant—including tastes and preferences—in order to focus on the price/quantity relationship. Whether using a simple or more complex way of determining demand, there is almost always an inverse relationship between price and quantity. On the graph, this means the demand curve slopes downward. For example, at a price of $40, the quantity demanded is twenty balls and at $20 the quantity demanded is forty balls. In terms of the opening example of the Alaska law raising the price of filing a lawsuit, the Alaska legislature hoped that the higher price would make a lower quantity of lawsuits "demanded."[2]

It is important to distinguish changes in quantity demanded from changes in demand. A change in quantity demanded means that a change has occurred along the same demand curve in response to a price change. A change in demand occurs when the entire curve shifts to the left or right. Changes in demand are the result of changes in tastes and preferences, income, or the prices of substitute or complementary goods. For example, in the United States when the World Cup games are played, soccer tends to become very popular and demand for soccer balls might increase to D_1. On the other hand, at the midpoint between World Cups, the demand might shift all the way to D_2.

One additional important characteristic of demand is the extent to which quantity demanded reacts to price changes. When the percentage change in prices is exceeded by the percentage change in quan-

---

2. Obviously, demand can also be expressed algebraically. For example, $q^d = a - bP$ where q is the quantity demanded, a is a constant, P is the price, and b is the slope of a linear demand curve. Do you understand why the slope is negative?

tity demanded, demand is said to be elastic. This would be the case for a good that has many acceptable substitutes. Even a small price increase would cause buyers to immediately shift to the substitutes. When the percentage change in prices is greater than the percentage change in quantity demanded, demand is said to be inelastic. For certain goods, even large changes in price may mean only small changes in the quantity demanded. This might be the case when the good is a necessity and there are few or no substitutes. For example, a person needing heart surgery is likely to be very unresponsive to price changes associated with the surgery. When the percentage change in price and quantity demanded are the same, demand is said to be unit elastic.

Elasticity of demand may seem to have limited relevance when economics is applied to law, but quite the opposite is true. Think back to the example of the Alaskan law raising the price of filing a lawsuit against the state. Obviously, a higher price will lead to fewer lawsuits, but how many fewer? If the demand to file those suits is inelastic, then the increase in the filing fee may not give the state the relief it was seeking from meritless lawsuits. On the other hand, if demand is elastic, the state may find that it has discouraged both lawsuits with merit and those without. In short, policymakers need to know not just that price and quantity demanded are inversely related but also to understand how responsive quantity demanded is to price changes.[3]

Supply

The other half of the analysis is, of course, supply. Supply is a schedule of prices and the quantities sellers would offer for sale at each price in a given market at a given time. As with demand, supply could be determined by asking possible sellers how many units each would offer to sell at each price and then adding the quantities to get the total quantity supplied at each price. The term *supply* refers to the whole schedule and *quantity supplied* is a specific amount at a specified price. When plotted on a graph, supply is usually depicted

---

3. Although a knowledge of elasticity would assist lawmakers in determining how much to raise filing fees, you should understand that an elastic demand does not mean that suits with merit would be discouraged. Similarly, an elastic demand would not mean that only meritless suits are discouraged. Do you see why?

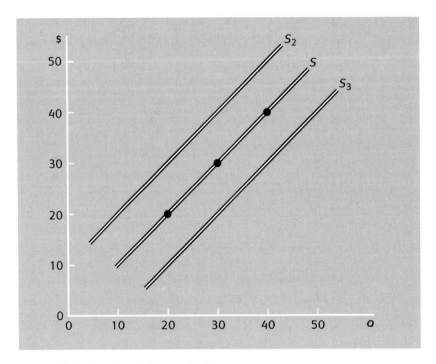

FIGURE 2.2 Supply of Soccer Balls

as sloping upward, but as a technical matter, this may not always be the case. *S* in Figure 2.2 might be the supply of soccer balls in our hypothetical market.[4]

It is important to understand how a firm determines its supply. If you are a producer and are asked how many units you would offer for sale at a certain price, you would compare that price to your costs of production. As long as the cost of producing an additional unit is less than the price offered, you would be willing to sell that unit and make a profit. Suppose it costs you $1 to produce one more soccer ball, $2 to produce a second soccer ball, and $3 to add a third soccer ball. In other words, the marginal cost of the first unit is $1, for the second it is $2 and so on. If you are asked what quantity you would offer at $1, the answer would be one; at $2, the most you would

---

4. Like demand, supply can also be expressed algebraically. For example, a linear supply curve such as in Figure 2.2 might be expressed as $q^s = c + dP$ where q is the quantity supplied, c is a constant, P is the price, and d is the slope or the relationship between quantity supplied and price.

offer would be two and at \$3, the most you would be willing to offer is three. If you think about it, you have just given the points along your marginal cost curve and, as you can see, this is the same as your supply curve.

In addition to movements up and down the supply curve, sometimes the entire curve shifts. For example, if you use leather in your soccer balls and the cost of leather increases, the least you would take for the balls, regardless of the level of production, would increase. This would mean a shift in the curve to the left as illustrated by S_2. If the cost of an input (such as leather) decreases, supply would increase. This would be a movement of the curve to the right to S_3.

CASE 2.1 Supply and Demand Working Together in Law:
United States v. Richardson, 238 F.3d 837 (7th Cir. 2001)

As you know from Chapter 1, one of the most influential law and economics scholars is Richard Posner. Posner was a law professor at the University of Chicago before becoming a federal court judge. In *United States v. Richardson*, Judge Posner was asked to consider the legality of the sentence given to a person who acquired child pornography through the use of a computer. The law itself penalized those possessing pornography when "a computer was used for the transmission" of the illegal material. The law did not specify whether it was the sender's or the receiver's computer that was relevant. Thus, the defendant argued that the law did not apply to him because he did not use a computer to transmit the material. Judge Posner held that the law did apply to the defendant, reasoning that by not specifying which computer, the law was designed to have an impact on both the demand and supply side of the child pornography market. Do you see how this could be true? The rationale would be like this: A law against receiving pornography that was transmitted by a computer has an impact on the demand for that material. On the other hand, punishing those who transmit by computer is on the supply side of the market, and the penalty is a cost that will have an impact on the supply.

Competitive Market Equilibrium

Supply and demand alone are only lists of possibilities. You cannot know what will happen in the actual market until the demanders and suppliers begin to interact. The interaction in our soccer ball market is shown in Figure 2.3. You will notice that demand and supply intersect at thirty balls and $30 per ball. When demand equals supply, the market for soccer balls is in equilibrium. In this market, the equilibrium price is $30 and the equilibrium quantity is thirty balls. This does not mean the market will simply go to that point and stick there. Instead, it will tend to move toward that point.

In order to understand why, consider the price of $40. At that price, the graph shows that the quantity demanded will be twenty balls and the quantity supplied will be forty. There are more balls than people are willing to buy, which is called a surplus. Surpluses will cause prices to fall because sellers must lower prices to find buyers. In this case prices will tend to fall toward $30. Now look at what would happen at a price of $20. The quantity demanded would be forty and the quantity supplied would be twenty. There are not enough balls for all who want them; there is a shortage. When this happens, prices tend to climb. In fact, at every price other than $30, there will be a tendency for the market to "correct" itself by eliminating either a surplus or a shortage.

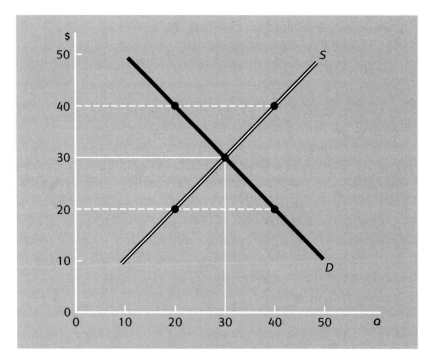

FIGURE 2.3 Market Equilibrium

IMPERFECT COMPETITION

The model presented so far assumes that the market is competitive. In other words, neither consumers nor firms have market power and are more or less at the mercy of the market to determine price. When buyers have market power—the power to raise prices above competitive levels and keep them there—we say that the markets are imperfectly competitive. The extreme example of this is monopoly, which means an entire industry is served by one firm. As you will see later in this book, antitrust law and some regulation are direct responses to markets that are not competitive. In addition, a great deal of the application of economics to law occurs in markets that are imperfectly competitive. It is important therefore to review price and output determination under imperfect market conditions, one example of which would be monopoly. A useful way to understand the impact is to begin with a competitive market as depicted by the intersection of supply (S) and demand (D) in Figure 2.4. The equilibrium price P_c and

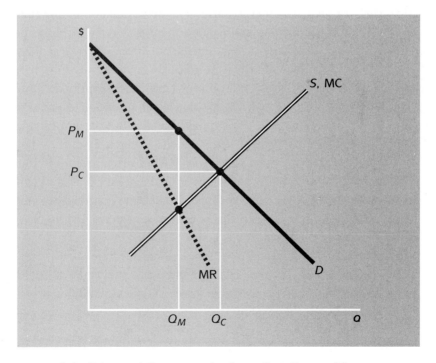

FIGURE 2.4 Price and Output under Imperfect Competition

quantity Q_c are set by the intersection of the curves. The demand is the summation of the demand of a great number of buyers, and the supply is the summation of a great number of competing sellers. No seller or buyer can individually determine the price. They all simply react to the market price. This is not to say they could not actually attempt to sell output at a higher price than the market price. If they did, they would sell nothing.

Now assume that through a massive, and admittedly unlikely, merger all the sellers are combined into one firm. The big change is that the firm now can set price. It will not lose sales to competitors because it has no competitor. The firm must make a decision about the profit-maximizing price. A profit-maximizing firm will produce additional units of output as long as each one is profitable. A unit is profitable as long as the marginal (additional) revenue gained from selling it exceeds the marginal (additional) cost of producing it.

As already discussed, the supply curve is the summation of the individual firms' supply curves, each of which is the same as the firm's marginal cost curve. Thus, in Figure 2.4, supply is also the marginal cost (MC) for the newly merged firm. The determination of marginal revenue is a bit more complex. Because there is only one firm in the market, the price it charges will have an impact on the units demanded. To sell more it will have to decrease prices. For example, if the firm is selling six units at $10 per unit, it may have to lower price to $9 to sell seven units. In other words, it must lower price for all units in order to sell one more unit.[5] The implications of this are critical and can be understood by noting what happens to total revenue. When the firm sold six units, total revenue was $60. At seven units, it is $63. Revenue does not increase as the price charged drops because the revenue for the other six units declined. In fact, the marginal revenue for the seventh unit is $3, and this is the amount that must be compared to the marginal cost.

In Figure 2.4, this means that the marginal revenue curve (MR) lies under the demand curve. The demand curve shows the price the unit sells for, and the marginal cost curve shows the additional revenue generated by selling that unit. A unit adds to profit as long as

---

5. If the firm can engage in price discrimination it will escape the necessity of reducing price to all in order to sell one more unit.

marginal revenue exceeds marginal cost. Thus, in Figure 2.4, all units to the right of the intersection of MR and MC will increase profit. The firm will not produce beyond that intersection. The profit-maximizing level of output will be Q_m, because it is at that unit that marginal revenue stops exceeding marginal cost. Already, you will note that the monopolist sells less than would be produced if the industry were competitive.

What about the price? Having determined the profit-maximizing quantity, the question for the monopolist is this: What is the highest price for which that output can be sold? The answer can be read off the demand curve. In Figure 2.4, the price that is consistent with selling Q_m units of output is P_m. As you can see, P_m is above P_c. Thus, under imperfect—in this case monopoly—conditions, prices are higher and output lower than they would be under perfectly competitive conditions. Another important impact of monopolization should also be noted. Under competitive conditions, price is determined where demand and supply intersect. Consequently, price is equal to marginal cost. This is not the case, however, when the industry is characterized by monopoly conditions.

MARGINAL ANALYSIS AND OPPORTUNITY COSTS

Two basic concepts in economics generally are no less important when economics is applied to law. The first is marginal analysis. Rational economic decisions are made by considering the *change* in costs and benefits resulting from a change in levels of output or a change in policy. As you have just seen, a business firm may consider increasing output and will compare the marginal cost of that increase with the marginal revenue from selling the extra output. In law and economics, the comparison might be between the increased costs of enforcing a ten-mile-an-hour decrease in the speed limit and the increase in benefits in the form of fewer accidents and injuries. The important thing is that past commitments are of limited, if any, relevance. For example, reasoning such as "I should go to the play because I have already paid for the ticket" is not economically rational. Marginal analysis would go more like this: "What is the additional cost of going to the play and how much will I enjoy the play?"

Another critical concept is opportunity cost. Opportunity cost is the value of the option foregone when another option is chosen. For example, the opportunity cost of spending, say, $6 on a movie ticket is the utility foregone when the movie ticket is selected over the next most utility-producing or profit-increasing alternative. In economics, the opportunity cost of a decision, although not an out-of-pocket cost, is critical in determining whether the best or optimal choice is the one selected.

CONCEPTS OF EFFICIENCY

When economics is applied to law, several different concepts of efficiency are employed. Some of these terms may be new to you, but they are used throughout the study of the economic analysis of law. A concept that does *not* come up very often, but which is probably most familiar to you, is that of *productive efficiency*. Productive efficiency refers to producing a certain level of output at the lowest possible cost per unit. For example, if you refer to a particular method of making pizzas as efficient, you are probably referring to productive efficiency. In law and economics, four other types of efficiency tend to be at least as important as productive efficiency.

Allocative Efficiency

One of the aspects of competitive markets that make them attractive is that they are consistent with allocative efficiency. Very generally, allocative efficiency refers to the drawing of resources into the manufacture of goods and services that are most valued by society. You can get a better understanding of this by reconsidering what demand and supply tell us. When demand was discussed, it was defined as a schedule of prices and the quantities that would be purchased at each price. If you start from the point of view of quantities, demand tells you the most that would be paid in order for each quantity to be bought. In other words, one can determine the *value* of each quantity by looking at the demand curve.

Supply can be viewed from the same perspective. At each quantity, one can determine the least the seller would accept in order to manufacture and sell that quantity. That price, as you have seen, is equal to marginal cost. To take it one more step, what determines marginal cost? It is the cost of outbidding competing buyers of the inputs used to produce the good or service. In a very real sense, the marginal cost of producing one good is the cost to society in terms of the *other* goods that will not be produced with those same inputs (i.e., it is the opportunity cost).

If demand shows the value attributed to a good or service and supply shows the cost to society of producing that good or service, it makes sense from a broad social perspective to produce that good or service at the point where the two curves intersect. Back in Figure 2.3, you can see that as long as demand is above supply, the value attributed by buyers is higher than the cost to produce them. When supply is above demand, the opposite is true—buyers value the goods less than the cost to produce them. At the equilibrium point, the value attributed to the good is equal to the social cost of producing the good, thus achieving the allocatively efficient level of output. As you will see, a great deal of antitrust policy and government regulation is influenced by the concept of allocative efficiency.

Maximizing Social Welfare

Economics is often applied to determine how to maximize social welfare. This is the second of the four additional views of efficiency. It can be tied into supply and demand and is in many respects another way to visualize allocative efficiency. To understand why, examine Figure 2.5, which includes supply and demand curves that produce an equilibrium price and quantity of P and Q, respectively. The graph also includes two triangles. One is labeled consumer surplus and the other producer surplus. As the labels imply, the areas of these triangles are equal to the gains or benefits to buyers and sellers due to interacting in the market.

First take a look at the consumer surplus in this market. The price is P, but the demand curve tells you that until quantity Q is reached, all consumers valued the item more than P and were willing to pay more than P for it. In effect, every time they paid less than the most they were willing to pay, they received consumer surplus. The amount of consumer surplus for each item is the difference between the amount consumers paid and the amount they would have been willing to pay. For example, take a look at unit 3 in Figure 2.5. The price

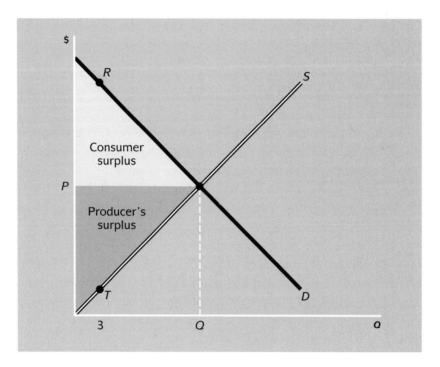

FIGURE 2.5 Social Welfare

is P, but the amount someone would be willing to pay for that unit is R. The consumer surplus for that unit is $R - P$. The consumer surplus triangle is the aggregation (sum) of all the individual consumer surpluses.

The same analysis applies to producers. The supply or marginal cost curve indicates the lowest amount producers are willing to take for any particular unit. P is the price they receive; for all units out to Q, sellers receive more than the least acceptable. Again focus on unit 3. The price again is P, but the cost of producing the unit is T. The producer's surplus is $P - T$. The producer's surplus triangle is the aggregation (sum) of all the producers' surpluses from individual items.

If we sum producer surplus and consumer surplus we get the overall social welfare generated in the market. Suppose, as is depicted in Figure 2.6, that we have the same demand and supply but for some reason the price is at P_1, meaning that the quantity is at Q_1. This

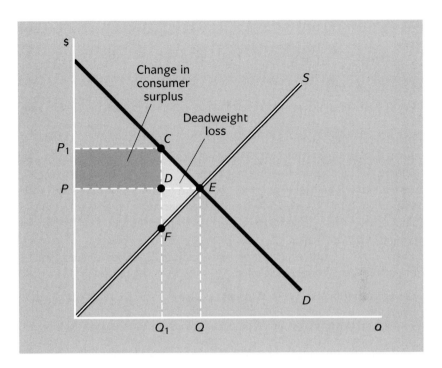

FIGURE 2.6 Welfare Loss

would be the case if the firm were a monopoly or operated under imperfectly competitive conditions as described above. Several things have changed. First, the new consumer surplus triangle is smaller. Some consumers will still experience a surplus but it will not be as great as it was. Some consumers, because of the higher price, have dropped out of the market. This is why quantity decreased from Q to Q_1. Producer surplus has increased because some of what was consumer surplus has been captured by producers due to the higher price. This is the area of rectangle PP_1CD. Finally, some of what was consumer and producer surplus has disappeared completely. Overall social welfare has decreased. This is called the deadweight loss and is equal to triangle CFE. Again, this was a measure of well-being that existed in the market and is now extinguished. The point is that when economists speak in terms of social welfare, they mean the sum of both consumer and producer surplus. It is at its maximum when markets are competitive.

SUPPLY, DEMAND, ALLOCATIVE EFFICIENCY, AND ANTITRUST LAW

As noted in the text, allocative efficiency is achieved and consumer welfare maximized under competitive conditions. When a firm can raise price above competitive levels, as illustrated in Figure 2.6, consumer welfare is reduced. This will be the outcome when two or more firms agree not to compete for customers by lowering price. As you will see in Chapter 20, in the United States and other countries, there is a body of law called antitrust law that is specifically designed to encourage markets to behave competitively. Thus, it should not surprise you to find out that the courts deciding antitrust cases are keenly aware of the concepts of supply, demand, and allocative efficiency. For example, consider this statement from a relatively recent decision:

> Consumer welfare is maximized when economic resources are allocated to their best use . . . and when consumers are assured competitive price and quality. . . . Accordingly, an act is deemed *anticompetitive* under the Sherman Act only when it harms both allocative efficiency *and* raises the prices of goods above competitive levels or diminishes their quality.[6]

Clearly, no area of law has been influenced more greatly by economic analysis than antitrust law. On the other hand, as you go through this book, you will see that most areas of law have also been influenced by economics to one extent or another, and nearly all of them can be assessed in terms of whether they promote allocative efficiency.

Pareto Efficiency

Italian economist Vilfredo Pareto (1848–1923) is generally credited with originating the baseline standard of efficiency in the context of welfare economics. It is also one of the concepts of efficiency most frequently relied upon by those who apply economic analysis to law. Pareto's standard can be understood in terms of set allocations of resources and the impact on society if those allocations are altered. If a change can be made that makes at least one person better off and no one worse off, then the change is Pareto superior. A change that

---

6. *Rebel Oil Co., Inc. v. Atlantic Richfield Co.*, 51 F.3d 1421 (9th Cir. 1995).

leaves at least one person worse off, regardless of the beneficial effects on others, is called Pareto inferior. Finally, if no change can be made from a given allocation without making at least one person worse off, the allocation is Pareto optimal.

What you will note right away about "Paretian" standards is that gains and losses are not weighed against each other. Even if one party is made much better off by a reallocation and another is only a little worse off, the change is Pareto inferior. This requirement is tied to the idea that it is impossible to compare the utility—the sense of feeling better off—of one person with that of another. More technically, it is impossible to make interpersonal comparisons of utility. What an economist can be sure of is that, if no one is made worse off and someone is made better off, overall utility has increased. This means that Pareto "efficiency" is not really about maximizing utility. It also means that a government relying on Paretian standards can do very little because it is hard to define policies in which there are only winners and no losers.

This may seem somewhat impractical to you, but in fact Pareto standards characterize a great deal of what goes on in the world. The best examples are exchanges or the formation of contracts. One can view a great deal of contract law and its related doctrines as being linked to Paretian standards of welfare. For example, if you walk into a restaurant and buy a sandwich, it is because you feel better off eating the sandwich than spending the money on anything else and because the restaurant owner would rather have your money than keep the sandwich. The outcome is Pareto superior. The same is true if you buy a car or even contribute to a charity. The key is that the exchange or contribution be voluntary. As you will see in the chapters on contract law, a great deal of that body of law is designed to encourage the formation of contracts under circumstances that will promote Pareto superior outcomes. For example, contracts are often not enforced if the contract is entered into mistakenly or when one party has misrepresented the quality of what he or she is selling.

CASE 2.2 Pareto in the Courts: *Watson v. Pietranton,* 364 S.W.2d 812 (W.Va. 1988)

When courts make decisions, they are very often seeking a fair outcome. "Fairness" is, however, a very slippery concept. A good candidate for what is fair is whether an outcome is consistent with

Pareto standards of efficiency. In effect, a change that makes at least one person better off and leaves no one worse off is hard to classify as "unfair." Thus, it should not surprise you that Paretian concepts of efficiency have found their way into judicial opinions. For example, a court in West Virginia was asked to consider the legality of a fee-splitting agreement between attorneys. In this case, one attorney had become too ill to continue work on a case and contracted with another to carry on. They agreed to split whatever fee was collected. These agreements are generally frowned upon because the client may be paying more and for services that were not actually performed. Here the court enforced the agreement using the following reasoning:

> Mr. Pietranton [the ailing attorney] did a lot of work for his fee. There is no evidence that the client paid a higher fee because of the fee-splitting arrangement, which means that under established custom and usage a Pareto optimum is achieved: everyone is made better off without anyone's being made worse off. And this is the system that we should not only condone, but encourage.

In effect, the court found that the arrangement was beneficial to the attorneys and did not result in any harm to the client. From a broader perspective, most contracts people make can be viewed as efforts to achieve Pareto superior outcomes. Once a contract is made, it is not Pareto superior for one person to breach it. Do you see why? We will return to this in Chapter 8.

Kaldor-Hicks Efficiency

A final standard of efficiency is Kaldor-Hicks efficiency, or wealth maximization.[7] In large measure, wealth maximization is a reaction to the confining nature of Paretian standards. It is also the standard that tends to be relied upon most by economists when they apply economics to law. Wealth maximization permits involuntary transfers when those gaining by the reallocation could have fully compensated those who lose. For example, suppose you have a rare autographed copy of *Crime and Punishment,* and you would be willing to sell it for $20,000. On the other side of the world is a person who would like to buy an autographed copy of *Crime and Punishment* and is willing to pay

---

7. Nicolas Kaldor (1908–1986) and John Hicks (1904–1989) were two famous British economists. John Hicks won the Nobel Prize in 1972.

$25,000. Further suppose that these two people will never find each other, or that it would cost more than $5,000 in search costs to do so. If you do not see why the $5,000 is crucial, you will after a few more chapters.

In this context, if you were the "reallocation Czar" it would be efficient for you to simply take the book from its current owner and give it to the person willing to pay $25,000. Wealth is said to have increased because the book is now owned by a person who values it more. Another way of saying this is that the new owner could have compensated the old owner if necessary. The Kaldor-Hicks or wealth maximization standard does not, however, require compensation. The key is to insure that resources end up in the possession of those who value them most. If compensation were paid, the outcome would be Pareto superior.

THE EVOLUTION OF ECONOMICS

For years in the nineteenth and twentieth centuries, economic analysis was unquestioningly used as a basis for policy suggestions. However, during the 1930s, a split emerged between positivist economists and welfare economists over this very issue. Positivist economics concerned itself with prices and facts and sought to give predictions for the future and increase efficiency when doing so was clearly Pareto superior—it made some people better off without making anyone worse off. Positivist economists argued that in changes that are not Pareto superior, someone will be made worse off, and to analyze whether this change should take place, we must make an interpersonal comparison of utility. Such a comparison cannot be scientific and will always be based on some arbitrary standard. Thus, economics should avoid any prescriptions about policy when the proposed policy would not be Pareto superior. The welfare economists were more concerned with economics as a means for measuring welfare and creating positive social change, and acceptance of the positivist position would have rendered their field rather boring and useless. This is where Nicholas Kaldor and J. R. Hicks came to the rescue. In their 1939 articles, they agree with the positivist position that interpersonal comparisons of utility are unscientific and arbitrary. However, in the September 1939 issue of the *Economic Journal*, Kaldor explained a way to get around this problem by looking at policies or transfers as though they are Pareto superior. For example, imagine that a new policy makes one group of people better off and another group worse off. We can then find out how much money it would take to fully compensate the losers. If there is still a net gain from the transfer, then economics can recommend it as sound policy. Four months later, in the same journal, Hicks brought together a number of different theories to create a sounder basis for welfare economics' policy evaluations. He also tackled the question of whether the hypothetical transfers ought to actually take place when a policy is enacted. He admits there is no decent answer, as the question is distributive and is based on moral and political concerns. Mainly, he points out that distributive questions should not hamper policies that clearly increase efficiency.

Wealth maximization may seem harsh to you. Is it really fair to simply take something from one person and give it to someone else? Maybe not, but it is ultimately the way governments work. For example, a law may be passed that raises the drinking or driving age and, thereby, lowers the value of your business. Supposedly, the idea is that your losses are more than offset by the gains to others. Similarly, do you voluntarily send money into the government each year to support education, road building, and the military? Probably not. The money is taken from you and then used for programs that may or may not be of any benefit to you. One hopes, however, that when the money is spent, those benefiting from government services gain more than you sacrifice. In fact, it would be extremely hard for a government to function if all reallocations had to be voluntary.[8]

One of the things that you will note throughout this book is that the concept of "resources" takes on a very broad meaning that includes an array of rights not generally thought of in the same way as more conventional resources. For example, who should have the right to use a specific beach, or to play loud music, or even to break a promise? In a sense all these rights are resources. A wealth maximization approach to decisions of allocation would require that even these

8. It is important to note that there is an argument that you actually do consent to these "involuntary" measures by a decision to participate within the system at all, knowing that from time to time the system may work to your disadvantage.

rights/resources should go to those who attribute the greatest value to them.

Maximizing wealth is not the same as maximizing utility. The first reason is rather obvious. Utility refers to psychological satisfaction, but wealth maximization requires that desire be expressed as a willingness and ability to pay. As a consequence, those who cannot pay for something, even though they might derive great utility from it, will not be regarded as valuing it. The second reason relates to the fact that compensation is not required. The book example provides a good illustration of this point. Recall that the buyer would have paid up to $25,000 and the seller would have accepted $20,000. If the book is simply transferred and nothing is paid, the "buyer" keeps the money. In order to know whether utility has increased, we would have to compare the utility of the selling price for the buyer and seller. This would require an interpersonal comparison of utility, which is impossible. While utility maximization is certainly superior to wealth maximization, this goal is usually out of reach, and some law and economics scholars regard wealth as an acceptable substitute for utility.

This chapter does not exhaust the tools that you will need to apply economics to law, but it is enough to get you started. Additional tools will be discussed in the context of specific issues where they are relevant. In particular, keep in mind that "prices" in the context of law are not always expressed in monetary funds. For example, criminal penalties are the price of some undesirable activities. Also, remember that economics can be used to understand the behavior of people in the context of legal relationships. More important, it can be employed to refine and improve laws and policy generally.

QUESTIONS FOR DISCUSSION

1. Do you understand why, from an economic perspective, it can be said that there is a demand for exceeding the speed limit in an automobile? If so, how might you construct a price and quantity schedule for speeding? How might a concept be put to use by lawmakers?

2. The Alaska law discussed in the text was designed to raise the price of suing the state in hopes of reducing the number of lawsuits. Is this a good idea? Are there any dangers of making access to the courts more expensive?

3. Several states have laws that prohibit price increases above a certain level immediately after a natural disaster like a hurricane or tornado. The idea is to prevent "price gouging." Can the laws result in surpluses or shortages? Explain. Do you think these laws are a good idea?

4. Explain, using Figure 2.5 in the text, why the situation where the market is in equilibrium (i.e., when price is equal to P and quantity is equal to Q) is a Pareto optimal situation. Show that for transactions to the left of quantity Q both the buyer and the seller can increase their utility (and achieve a Pareto superior situation), whereas to the right of quantity Q this is no longer possible.

5. What happens to the demand for soccer balls in the following situations: baseball bats become less expensive; soccer moms become convinced that playing soccer is very healthy for kids; membership fees for soccer clubs increase substantially; soccer-playing kids get a higher weekly allowance from their parents?

6. What happens to the supply of soccer balls if the wages of workers sewing soccer balls increase? If the government subsidizes the production of soccer balls?

7. Suppose the demand schedule is specified as:
$$Q_d = 10 - P$$
And the supply schedule is
$$Q_s = 2 + P$$
   a. What is the equilibrium price in this market? What is the equilibrium quantity?
   b. More difficult, how big is consumer surplus, producer surplus, and total surplus at equilibrium?
   c. Suppose at some point the market price equals $5. Is there a shortage or a surplus in this market? What will happen to the price?

Economics of Property & Related Concepts

CHAPTER THREE

Private Property and Public Goods: An Introduction

"*LA PROPRIÉTÉ C'EST LE VOL*" (PROPERTY IS THEFT) was the battle cry of Pierre Joseph Proudhon (France, 1809–1865), one of the intellectual fathers of socialism. He took an extreme position in the ongoing discussion of what can be privately owned and what belongs to society. This question may seem foreign to you now, but why should anyone be able to lay claim to exclusive use of a parcel of land or a herd of animals or even a computer program? After all, in the past, exclusive use was often just an arbitrary matter determined by who was strongest, had the biggest army, or was chummy with the king. Given all of this, are there arguments for the existence of private property that are compelling from the standpoint of economic efficiency? The answer is yes, and part of this chapter is devoted to one of the most powerful arguments for private property: the "tragedy of the commons." The basic theory is laid out below, as are alternative responses to the "tragedy." As you will see, however, some of the assumptions underlying the need for private property do not always hold. Following the description of that argument, we discuss the important distinction between public and private goods. Finally, we introduce the way that law protects private property.

TRAGEDY OF THE COMMONS

"The Tragedy of the Commons," an article written by Garrett Hardin in 1968 in *Science,* has had a profound effect on the present discussion of private and public property.[1] The "tragedy" plays out in earlier times but is just as relevant today. The "common" property in his article is a pasture open to all, something that was typical in most towns and villages. Each user of the commons—herdsman—is expected to keep as many cattle as possible on the commons. In the beginning, when there are few cattle, there is no problem. But as the number of cattle grows, there will be less grass available in the pasture for each cow. In the end, the pasture will be overgrazed and completely ruined.

A simple example, presented in Table 3.1, shows this mechanism at work. Column A shows the number of herdsmen using the common pasture for their cattle. Their number is increasing from one to eleven. For simplicity, assume that each herdsman has only one cow. The herdsmen are interested in the number of gallons of milk their cows are producing. Column B shows the costs of maintaining a cow (e.g., the herdsman imputes to himself a wage to milk the cow and he has to feed her in the winter). Again we assume this cost to be fixed per cow and equal to $1. The third column (Column C) gives the number of gallons of milk produced by each cow. Assume that each gallon of milk is worth $1. Thus, the denomination of the third column is both in gallons and in dollars. The basic assumption we make is that the greater the number of cows grazing on the pasture, the less grass will be available for each individual cow. When a cow gets less to eat, she will give less milk; as the number of herdsmen and their cows increase, the individual yield in gallons of milk per cow decreases.

The crucial question to be asked now is this: Why do herdsmen keep adding cows to the pasture? The answer is straightforward: because they profit from it. They will go on adding cows as long as they continue making a profit. Private profit is defined as net return; that is, return minus costs. This is given in the fourth column where

1. Garrett Hardin, "The Tragedy of the Commons," *Science* 162 (1968): 1243–1248. Retrieved from http://dieoff.org/page95.htm.

TABLE 3.1 Tragedy of the Commons Illustrated

NUMBER OF HERDSMEN (a)	COST PER COW (b)	GALLONS OF MILK PER COW (c)	NET RETURN TO HERDSMAN (c − b)	NET RETURN TO SOCIETY (a(c − b))
1	1	10	9	9
2	1	9	8	16
3	1	8	7	21
4	1	7	6	24
5	1	6	5	25
6	1	5	4	24
7	1	4	3	21
8	1	3	2	16
9	1	2	1	9
10	1	1	0	0
11	1	0.5	−0.5	−5.5

we calculate the difference between return (Column C) and costs (Column B). If there is only one herdsman (Row 1), his cow will yield $10-worth of milk. His costs are $1. His net return (profit) is $9. When there are two herdsmen, each of them will have $9-worth of milk. Subtracting $1 costs gives each of them $8 profit. Compared to the previous situation, the first herdsman's profit will have gone down from $9 to $8, but he is still making a positive net return, so he will still send his cow to the common pasture. As more herdsmen send their cows to the pasture, the net return will go down but stay positive until there are ten herdsmen using the pasture. At that point, each of them is making zero profit. As each herdsman is going for a positive profit, each has an incentive to use the common pasture until there are at most ten of them. By that time, the pasture is used so much that each cow yields only one gallon of milk. This is the overgrazing result. If an eleventh herdsman joins, all the herdsmen will be operating at a loss. At that point, a cow will cost more than the value of the milk she yields.

The "tragedy of the commons" is that each of the individual herdsmen has an incentive to keep on using the common land beyond its optimal use from society's point of view. This optimal use of the pasture is illustrated in the fifth column, in which we calculated the total net return to society for the use of the common pasture. This is the difference between the sum of the returns of all the herdsmen (number of herdsmen times value of milk production per herdsman—$a \times c$) and the sum of the costs of all the herdsmen (number of herdsmen times cost per herdsman—$a \times b$). The net return to society is maximized when there are five herdsmen (and five cows) using the common pasture. At that point, total net return to society is $25, which is the highest possible return in the column.

The numbers used in the example in Table 3.1 are specific, but the mechanism it illustrates is general. What the example in Table 3.1 should make clear is that the individual herdsman has no incentive to avoid overusing the common property. As long as a herdsman can make a private profit, he will send a cow to the pasture, and the collective behavior of all herdsmen will cause overgrazing. The private incentives of the individual herdsman are not in line with the best social outcome. This would completely change if the pasture became the private property of one farmer. How many cows would a farmer who privately owned the land put in his pasture? Using the cost and yield figures of Table 3.1 and assuming that the dairy farmer was deciding on how many of his own cows he should put on the pasture, the answer would be five cows.[2] He would maximize his profit at $25 and would have an incentive not to overgraze his pasture. Thus, giving the property right to the pasture to an individual would align private incentives with the best social outcome.

Does the tragedy of the commons seem like ancient history to you? It should not. A modern version of the tragedy of the commons is the overfishing of the sea. For example, fishermen now need to go farther and farther out to sea to find cod. The result is that the cost to all fishermen of bringing the fish to market and the price to ultimate consumers increases. Another example of the tragedy of the commons problem is the traffic jam at rush hours. The highways are like a common property for all to travel on by car. At rush hour, highways will be overused and congested, and traffic jams and longer travel time

2. We don't actually have to assume that he uses the pasture for his own cows. He could also rent the land to the other herdsmen for grazing. The total rent he could maximally charge is equal to the total net return of all the herdsmen (the last column in Table 3.1). He would then cream off all of the profit of all the herdsmen. Even in this maximum rent case, he still would allow only five cows in the pasture because at that point he would maximize his rental income.

will result. At its extreme, the tragedy can even result in the extinction of a species. As you probably know from high school history, massive herds of buffalo once roamed the Great Plains. Buffalo were killed for their hides, for food, and just for "fun" resulting in their near-extinction. The same process has greatly affected the whale population. At bottom, you can see that the overall problem is that individuals think about their own welfare only and not about the most efficient use of the commons by all.

CASE 3.1 **What Can Be Property?** *G. S. Rasmussen & Associates, Inc. v. Kalitta Flying Service,* 958 F.2d 896 (9th Cir. 1992)

Most people think that the concept of "property" refers to land and tangible items. This is true, but it also includes "intellectual property," the subject of Chapter 8, and more difficult-to-define "property." In a relatively recent case, a court was asked to answer the basic question of when something is property. George Rasmussen, an aeronautical engineer, worked out a series of modifications to DC-8 cargo planes that would enable them to carry thousands of pounds of cargo beyond the designed capacity. In order to actually fly a plane with these modifications, the Federal Aeronautics Administration (FAA) must approve them and issue a certificate, called a Supplemental Type Certificate (STC). Rasmussen applied for and got the certificate as anyone would who went through the same procedure.

Kalitta wanted a modified DC-8 but did not want to pay Rasmussen for the use of his certificate. So he made the necessary modifications and in his application to begin flying, he typed in the number of Rasmussen's STC and included a photocopy of it. The FAA gave Kalitta permission to begin flying. Rasmussen sued, claiming that Kalitta had taken his property. In legal terms this is called "conversion." The problem was that it was not clear that the certificate was the property of Rasmussen or anyone else. Here is part of the court's discussion.

IS THERE A PROPERTY RIGHT?

How property rights in new goods and services are established and defined is a question of considerable significance in a society, such as ours, where private ownership is the principal incentive for the creation and maintenance of commodities, and for their efficient allocation. The failure or inability to recognize private property rights in certain types of goods often leads to a variety of adverse effects. One phenomenon, known as the tragedy of the commons, is the over-use of public goods because individual users do not suffer the full cost of their consumption. A related phenomenon is the free-rider problem [to be discussed later], where third parties enjoy the benefits of a good without having invested the time, money and effort of creating it. While the tragedy of the commons results in the overconsumption of existing goods, the free-rider problem discourages the creation of new goods. In order to avoid such inefficiencies, the law generally favors the establishment of property rights. . . .

Giving innovators the exclusive right to reap the benefits of their efforts compensates them for the costs of innovation, the risk. . . .

To the extent we can distil a principle on the basis of this somewhat amorphous body of law, three criteria must be met before the law will recognize a property right: First, there must be an interest capable of precise definition; second, it must be capable of exclusive possession or control; and third, the putative owner must have established a legitimate claim to exclusivity. The interest Rasmussen asserts here easily meets these criteria.

The nature and extent of the rights afforded by an STC are capable of precise definition: It enables an airplane owner to obtain an airworthiness certificate for a particular design modification without the delay, burden and expense of proving to the FAA that a plane so modified will be safe. Federal law also limits the interest in a significant way: The rights created by an STC are only applicable to airplanes within the safety jurisdiction of the FAA— "civil aircraft in air commerce." Thus, Kalitta is free to make Rasmussen's modification on airplanes it flies entirely outside the United States. Nor are there any conceptual or practical difficulties in restricting the right to the holder of the STC, or to someone who is a transferee or licensee. In fact, the federal regulations contemplate exactly that. Rasmussen's interest is thus precisely defined and capable of exclusive possession. The final requirement—that Rasmussen have established a legitimate claim to exclusivity—is also amply met here. Rasmussen expended considerable time and effort in research and design; he conducted the appropriate tests and compiled the necessary data; he prepared an operations manual and lined up an instrument manufacturer; he convinced the FAA that the modification is safe; and he obtained a certificate which results in preferential rights in the issuance of airworthiness certificates by the FAA. Without Rasmussen's efforts, the STC Kalitta relied on simply would not exist. Rasmussen has the type of reasonable investment-backed expectations that give rise to a legitimate claim of exclusive control over the STC. We therefore hold that Rasmussen has a property interest in his STC under California law.

Think about the way the court made its decision. For most people, something is either property or it is not. Here the court seems to ask the question of whether it makes economic sense to call the certificate "property." Does this seem backward to you?

LESSONS LEARNED

The example of the herdsmen is a simplification; the issues surrounding property in real life are far more complicated. Nevertheless, the tragedy of the commons is a compelling rationale for the assignment of private property rights. There are, however, other lessons to be learned and alternatives to private property as a way to preserve the "commons."

First, in the early stages when there are not too many users, a common property does not raise any problems. The common resource can be so abundant and the users so few that the world is far away from a tragedy of the commons. Take the moon. At this moment the moon belongs to nobody. In fact, no one—at least that we know of—has gone there in thirty years! The moon could be said to belong to everybody. But suppose moon travel becomes technologically feasible and cheap, and we discover valuable minerals beneath the surface of the moon. In the beginning, there still might not be much of a problem because there will be enough to go around for the few countries and companies that invest in digging up the minerals and hauling them back to earth. But after a while, with more miners flying to the moon, property rights would have to be assigned and parcels of the moon would have to be allocated. A similar situation arose with airplanes. In the beginning, with few airplanes, it did not matter where they flew because there was plenty of airspace. After a while it got crowded and flying routes had to be established and allocated. Flight control has now become a very complicated matter. The same thing happened with satellites in outer space; there are now so many of them that they have to circle the earth in allocated paths (the geosynchronous zone for communications satellites). In effect, the costs of designating and enforcing property rights are not always justified until there really are competing users and uses of the property.

Second, private ownership is a "solution" to the tragedy of the commons, but it is not the only solution and is often not a feasible one.[3] Take the case of outer space. Nobody really "owns" outer space; it belongs to us all (until the day aliens turn up and claim property of the universe). In a very weak sense one could say that the owner of a satellite owns a certain property right in the sense that he is allowed to fly his satellite in that orbit and nobody else can fly one there. Similarly, the oceans of the world are in some sense the common property of us all. Some part of the oceans "belongs" to the countries that border these oceans; a zone of twelve miles out from the coast is part of the national territory of the country. A further "economic zone" of two hundred miles out gives the country certain mining rights (such as for oil and gas). Farther out, the high seas belong to everybody, and the tragedy of the commons can be seen there at full force. There is the general problem of overfishing and more specific problems such as the disappearance of whales and other sea animals. Although it might be possible to assign property rights to the oceans, actually enforcing those property rights might prove impossible.

This leads to the possibility of contractual agreements among parties not to overuse a resource. When multiple parties are involved, negotiation and enforcement expenses can be very high. Still, the use of agreements to solve the problem is more widespread than you would probably think. In the case of the oceans, for example, international conferences are organized and international agreements are drawn up allowing each country certain fishing rights. A fishing right is a quota giving the citizens of different countries a specified amount of fish (so many tons of cod, herring, etc.) in a certain area of the ocean. Within the European Union, for instance, fishing rights are allocated among the member states and monitored. Countries fishing more than they are allowed are fined. In the case of whales, certain countries (Japan, Norway) are allowed a limited number of catches over a given period. Similarly, many countries—but not the United States—have agreed to curb emissions that result in global warming and the "greenhouse" effect. If you think back to the herdsmen and the commons, this suggests that one possible solution is not to assign parts of the common to each herdsman but for each to simply agree not to increase their individual herds beyond a certain level.

3. See Michael Taylor, "The Economics and Politics of Property Rights and Common Pool Resources," *Natural Resources Journal* 32 (1992): 633.

Another possible solution involves limited-use permits. For example, before industrial production expanded to its present scale, and before large sections of the world population became prosperous enough to drive cars and heat or cool their houses and offices, the air and waters around us were plentiful and there was no problem of air or water pollution. Air and water were common goods enjoyed by all. But as the wealth of nations increased enormously and the world population grew to exceedingly large numbers, clean air and water became scarce. With our levels of production and consumption came environmental pollution and a "tragedy of the commons" effect on clean air and water. Environmental pollution is an "externality" caused by our production and consumption. A solution to the environmental problem is to issue "polluting rights" (e.g., CO_2 emission rights) or to issue "rights to a clean environment." These rights can again be seen as a form of property right, but they actually are licenses to engage in a certain activity for a defined period.

This raises another possible solution that does not require formal measures. First, however, it is necessary to consider what is called the "prisoner's dilemma." The standard formulation is that two people are caught committing a crime and are questioned about it before they can confer. Each prisoner is then approached by the prosecutor with a deal. If one confesses and the other prisoner does not, the first one will go free and the other will go to prison for twenty years. If they both confess, both will go to jail for 10 years, and if neither confesses, they both will escape with three-year sentences. The possibilities are illustrated in Figure 3.1, which shows the years of prison time for each prisoner depending on the strategy taken.

| | | Prisoner 1 | |
		Confess	Do not confess
Prisoner 2	Confess	10 / 10	20 / 0
	Do not confess	0 / 20	3 / 3

FIGURE 3.1 **The Prisoner's Dilemma**

	Farmer	
	Conserve	Do not conserve
Factory Conserve	1,000 / 1,000	0 / 6,000
Do not conserve	6,000 / 0	12,000 / 12,000

FIGURE 3.2 **Expenses Associated with Conserving and Not Conserving**

The best outcome would be for both parties to refuse to bargain, resulting in a three-year sentence for each. On the other hand, if one prisoner takes the risk of not confessing and her counterpart does confess, then this strategy backfires and the nonconfessor goes to prison for twenty years. Given this outcome, the choice is likely to be to confess, and when both parties do this, they receive sentences of ten years each. In fact, this is the rational outcome for each prisoner if she is acting independently. On the other hand, if there were some way to solve the dilemma, the prisoners could cooperate in order to arrive at the three-year sentence.[4] Unfortunately, there is no way to have a formal enforceable agreement, so the parties must learn to simply trust each other.

The problem the prisoners have can be converted into an instance in which individuals are using a common resource. In this case, suppose it is a lake that is used by a farmer for irrigation and a factory disposing of its waste. The lake is capable of accommodating both uses indefinitely as long as both exercise some restraint. If the lake is used too intensely, the farmer will have to install a well at considerable expense, and the factory owner will have to have the waste hauled away, also at considerable expense. Each party would be willing to limit its use of the lake and incur some expense in doing so, but such an effort will be a waste unless the other party does the same thing.

Figure 3.2 will help you understand the dilemma. Each party has a choice of whether to incur conservation expenses or not. If they

4. See Amartya Sen, "Behavior and the Concept of Preference," *Econometrica* 40 (1973): 241.

both do, the expense will remain modest—say, $1,000 a year—as they can both continue to use the lake. If each one decides to ignore its impact on the lake, the lake will eventually be useless to both and the cost per year will be $12,000. If either party alone attempts to take conservation measures while the other does nothing, the lake will survive—but at a cost of $6,000 to that party. Obviously, the best outcome is for the parties to both take conservation measures. The question is whether they are able to overcome the dilemma with which they are faced. The answer is yes if they can make an enforceable agreement that mutually limits their use of the lake. But suppose they cannot?

There is, in fact, a great deal of empirical evidence that individuals are able to solve the prisoner's dilemma, especially if only two people are involved and they are able to play the game repeatedly (i.e., they have to decide about cooperation or noncooperation repeatedly over time). In these instances, one party may take a cooperative action and wait to see whether the other party responds by cooperating also. In the context of the tragedy of the commons, one herdsman might see the long-term consequences of overgrazing and limit his use of the commons. Perhaps another herdsman will note that action and duplicate it. Norms may evolve over time that actually mean that parties cooperate and the commons are preserved without the assignment of property rights or formal contracts. As the number of people increases, however, this type of outcome is less likely.

LAW AND ECONOMICS IN ACTION 3.1

ACHIEVING COOPERATION

One of the most important explorations of the prisoner's dilemma is Robert Axelrod's *The Evolution of Cooperation*. Axelrod describes the best strategies to employ when playing the game and the implications this has for cooperation in real-world settings. Axelrod argues that individuals acting in their own self-interest will learn to use and benefit from cooperative behaviors emphasizing reciprocity so long as they have many chances to interact and, therefore, a reason to maintain cooperative behavior. He applies this theory to the development of altruistic behavior in animals and evolution, but he also shows how the prisoner's dilemma model, and the same reasoning, can be applied to everything from politics to social structures. One interesting example of cooperation in a seemingly impossible setting is the "live and let live" system that occurred in the trenches in World War I, in which soldiers on both sides would often intentionally miss their targets so long as the other side continued to do so as well. Axelrod also gives advice to players of the prisoner's dilemma game as well as policymakers and reformers who want to create an environment of reciprocity to maximize benefits for everyone.

As all these examples show, property or property-like entitlements come in a variety of forms. Maybe it is a license, or it can be the absolute right to use land in any way one desires and to transfer those rights to others. In law, property is described as including a "bundle of rights." The bundle can be fairly small or virtually unlimited.

CASE 3.2 A Not-So-Simple Solution to Overfishing:
New York v. Evans, 162 F.Supp.2d 161 (E.D.N.Y. 2001)

Unless you live in New England, the word "scup" probably does not sound like something you would like to eat. As it turns out, however, scup (also known as porgy) is a fish that is so popular the supply is dwindling as fishermen catch and sell as much as possible. In *New York v. Evans*, a federal court labeled the overfishing a "tragedy of the commons" and reviewed a plan by the government to solve the problem. At first, the federal government totaled the number of pounds of scup that could be caught without endangering the long-term supply and assigned a quota to each state where scup-fishing takes place on a large scale. This plan was challenged by Massachusetts claiming its allocation was too small. That challenge was successful, so the federal government tried again. This time, rather than dealing with the state-by-state bickering, it simply announced a coastal-wide total. When the total was reached in a fishing season, fishing was to be halted. This too was challenged because, among other things, it was said to encourage "derby-style" fishing. Derby-style fishing occurs when fishing is a race to catch as many fish as possible before the quota is reached. This time the court said the plan was valid.

Can you think of another solution? Think about this. Suppose a study reveals that one million pounds of scup can be harvested each fishing season without destroying the "commons." The government then auctions off "rights" or licenses that permit the holder to catch no more that 1,000 points of scup per license. It sells only 1,000 of these licenses. Individuals caught fishing without licenses or exceeding the permitted amount are heavily fined or even imprisoned. Is this plan better than the coastal-wide quota? Does it take care of the "derby-fishing" problem? Which do you prefer? Which do you think fishermen would prefer?

A final lesson that can be learned from our simplified example of the tragedy of the commons is that changing something that was common property (such as the common pasture) into private property leads to a better solution. What this tells us is that the way we structure property in society (in the example, private rather than common property) creates different behavioral incentives. When property is common, people may not be concerned about overgrazing. If property is private, the owner has an incentive to keep his pasture green and plentiful. If he neglects his property, he will end up a poor farmer. Private property leads to a more efficient solution than common property in the example we discussed. We will come back to the efficiency aspects of property and the way it is allocated in later chapters.

The advantage of a regime of private property rights, subject to the exceptions described above, is pretty obvious. There are complications, however. Having a system of property rights means nothing if they are not enforced. Enforcement is not free. Typically ownership is formally recorded somewhere and recording gives rise to some costs. Lawsuits arise when one person takes or uses the private property of someone else. Again the cost increases. Consequently, one overriding consideration is whether it is worthwhile from the standpoint of society to have and enforce property rights in every context. As an economic matter, it makes little sense to incur the expense of creating and enforcing property rights unless the resource protected can then be exploited sufficiently to offset those costs.

LAW AND ECONOMICS IN ACTION 3.2

SURF AND TURF: A COOPERATIVE SOLUTION TO THE TRAGEDY OF UNINTENDED CONSEQUENCES

At one time lobster was the equivalent of roadkill. It could be found just about anywhere in the Northeast on the beaches at low tide and it was a staple for prison food. Now, of course, it is something of a delicacy and, with over three million traps set, a replay of the tragedy of the commons seems like a real possibility. The relationship between the government and lobster fishermen is a complex one sometimes marked by threats of regulation and other times seeming to involve cooperative efforts. In recent years, it appears that the tragedy has been avoided through a process under which the government sets goals and lobster fishermen cooperate in order to achieve those goals. A number of practices have evolved. The first is to release any lobster with eggs and to cut a notch in the tail fin so that other fishermen will know that the lobster is a breeder. The second is to release males over a certain size on the theory that these are also the best breeders. As it turns out, observation of the norm appears to be working as lobsters are now relatively plentiful. In 2003, for example, about 50 million pounds of lobster were harvested in Maine alone.

Could it be that lobster fishermen have avoided the tragedy of the commons without direct outside intervention? Not so fast! Scientists now think the tragedy may have been avoided as a result of other tragedies. As it turns out, cod were predators of lobster and sea urchin. Overfishing of cod has now made them relatively scarce, allowing sea urchin to flourish. Sea urchin eat kelp, which is used by lobster for cover, and the lobster population did not keep pace. Then came the sushi craze and Japanese fishermen overfished the urchins. The kelp grew back and lobster flourished. Does this suggest to you that the tragedy of the commons is not always something to be avoided? Or does it mean that we are just beginning to learn about the consequences of our actions?

Reference: "Claws! Have Maine's Lobsters Become Plentiful through Judgment or Luck?"
  The Economist, August 19, 2004.

PRIVATE AND PUBLIC GOODS

Private property is critical to the working of the market economy. Exchange in our market economy can only take place between a seller who is the private owner of a good and a buyer who is willing to buy that good. The sale is a transfer of ownership from the buyer to the seller. Private ownership is a well-defined concept, and the laws governing private property are the basis of most of the economic activities and exchanges that take place. Critical to the analysis thus far, however, is the idea of not permitting people to impose costs on others through the use of property. By making the property "private," they are required to consider the costs and benefits of their economic activity.

Suppose the problem is not that people can use property and impose costs on others but that they use their property to create *benefits* that others may take without paying. This problem can give rise to a number of government reactions, one of which is the creation of a body of laws governing intellectual property.[5] You will learn about this in Chapter 8. But suppose it simply is not feasible—through the definitions of private property or conventional laws as to what constitutes property rights—to keep others from enjoying the benefits of someone else's productive efforts. This is where the distinction between public and private goods comes in.

First, think about the main characteristics of private goods. These are *exclusiveness* and *rivalry*. A private good is *exclusive* if the owner can exclude others from using it or from benefiting from it. The pasture becomes a private good when the farmer puts a fence around it and even more important, when that piece of land is officially registered to his name. From that moment on, he can legally exclude the other herdsmen from using it (or charge them for the use) and he can sell this property and the exclusiveness that comes with it to another farmer. A laptop, an apple, and a pair of jeans are all private goods. Public goods are nonexclusive. The favorite example of a public good is a dike like those in Holland or a levee like those along the Mississippi river. Once a dike is built to protect the farmers living behind it from floods, it is impossible to exclude any of the farmers behind the dike from benefiting from it. The dike protects everybody who lives in and travels through the area behind the dike. Material goods are not the only things that can be thought of as private and public.

---

5. Intellectual property rights were developed to allow the creator or inventor to exclude others from copying and to charge for its use. Text, music, pictures, movies, and computer codes are goods that, with the help of modern technology, can be coded into bits (electronic zeroes and ones). Inventions are products of the human mind that are valuable for consumption or production purposes. Information goods and inventions can be easily copied, and it is sometimes impossible or very hard to exclude others: Gifted people who hear a song can play it immediately back on the piano; another author can easily copy the storyline of somebody else's book; once the mechanism of an invention has been explained, others can use it for themselves.

Shaving a customer is a private service that a barber can exclusively sell to each individual client. A shave is a private good in this sense. But police protection against crime and the protection the army provides against foreign invasion are services that benefit all the citizens of a city or of a country. Nobody will be excluded from these services.

Rivalry means that using a good for one purpose excludes using it for another purpose. Private goods have this property of rivalry. An apple can be used either for eating or for making apple juice or for apple pie, but not for all of these uses at the same time. When I eat the apple, somebody else cannot eat it. It is important to decide what is the best use for the apple and who benefits the most from owning the apple. In the market economy apples are private goods; somebody owns them and they carry a price. The price will be instrumental in directing the apple to its best use and to allocating it to the user who values it the most.

Compare this concept of private goods with a decision you may make to buy a watchdog or have your front yard beautifully landscaped. If the dog barks and generally frightens prowlers in the neighborhood or people who walk by your house to enjoy your flowers, the good is not private. In fact, the watchdog and the landscaping in these circumstances fail both the exclusivity and rivalry tests. These are public goods. Now think in broader terms. Would it be possible to have police protection and national defense if all we had was a system of private property and private goods? It is unlikely. Again the exclusivity and rivalry tests are failed. Often it becomes necessary for the government to produce public goods if they are to exist at all or in order to make them available in desirable quantities. The money for doing this is typically generated by taxing people.

The following two figures illustrate the problem in greater detail. Figure 3.3 shows the market for beef, a private good. Figure 3.4 shows the provision of police protection, a public good. The vertical axis of Figure 3.3 depicts the price of beef per pound in dollars. The horizontal axis has the quantity of beef in pounds. The demand curve for consumers A (D_A) and B (D_B) shows how many pounds of beef each consumer wants to buy at each given price. At the price of $5 per pound, consumer A wants to buy five pounds of beef and consumer B wants to buy ten pounds. Suppose there are only two consumers in the market. Market demand is the sum of the quantity demanded

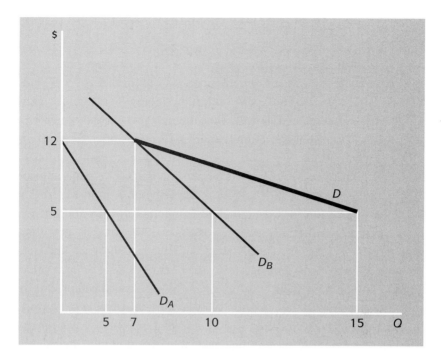

FIGURE 3.3 The Market for Beef

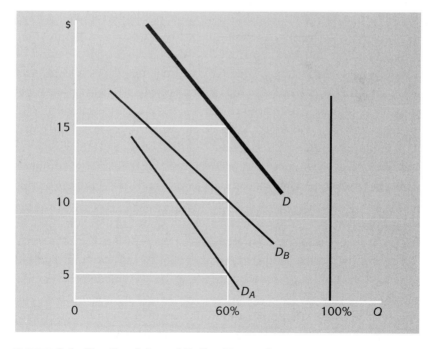

FIGURE 3.4 The Provision of Police Protection

of both consumer A and consumer B at each price. At a price of $5 per pound, the total quantity demanded on the market is 15 pounds (5 + 10). At a price of $12 per pound (and at any higher price), consumer A is not interested in beef. This might represent a shopper who uses the beef in a stew for a family dinner. But consumer B still wants to buy seven pounds. This could be a fast-food restaurant that has to have beef almost regardless of the price. The market demand at price $12 is seven pounds (0 + 7). The market demand, D in Figure 3.4 is the *horizontal* sum of the individual demands (D_A and D_B) of each consumer. The demand side is only one side of the market. The other side of the market is the supply side (which is not shown). The supply side is derived in a similar way as the demand side. For each price, the individual supply curve of each of the different beef producers will show us how many pounds of beef they are willing to supply. When we add the individual supply curves horizontally, we get the market supply curve in a similar way that we obtained the market demand curve. As explained in Chapter 2, the market clears at the intersection of market demand and supply. The same holds true for the market for beef, and at that intersection the market price is established. Suppose the market demand and supply intersect at a market price of $5. At this price, consumer A would buy five pounds and consumer B would buy ten pounds. Suppose it becomes harder to produce beef (for instance, Mad Cow disease means costly extra testing); then the supply curve would shift upward and the market would clear at a higher price. Suppose the market clears at a price of $12. In that situation, consumer A would no longer buy beef. Consumer B would still buy seven pounds. In this way, private goods are exchanged on the market. In this example, as the price gets higher, only the consumer who values beef very much will end up buying beef.

A different story unfolds in the case of police protection. Like all goods and services, some citizens value police protection more than others and are, thus, willing to pay more for it. On the other hand, if police protection is provided, it tends to be provided for everyone, since police protection is not subject to exclusivity and rivalry. This means it is useful to adopt a different perspective in order to determine the demand. In effect, we want to know how much people value different levels of protection. For this purpose, the quantity of police protection is measured on a scale from zero protection (no police) to 100 percent protection (a police officer at every street corner).

To derive the demand, we might ask citizen A how much she is willing to pay for each level of police protection. For example, for 60 percent she answers that she is willing to pay $5 a year for that level. Citizen B says that he is willing to pay $10 a year. When there are only two citizens, the total willingness to pay is $15 dollars (5 + 10) for a 60 percent level of police protection. All of this is reflected in Figure 3.5. Comparable to the individual demand curves for private goods, consumers have individual demand curves—or rather individual willingness-to-pay curves (D_A and D_B)—for public goods such as police protection. These curves are downward-sloping, because we assume that citizens are willing to pay more to move from zero protection to 5 percent protection than they are willing to pay to move from 55 percent to 60 percent. The total demand curve or willingness-to-pay curve (D) for a public good is derived from *vertically* adding up the individual demand or willingness-to-pay curves.

The total willingness-to-pay curve tells the government how much in taxes citizens are willing to pay for different levels of police protection. How high a level of police protection the government will provide depends on the cost of providing police protection or the supply curve of police protection. The intersection of demand and supply defines the amount of police protection. In the private good case (beef), the consumers end up paying the same (market) price for a pound of beef, but they consume different quantities of beef. Interestingly, in the public good case, the citizens consume the same amount of police protection but would pay a different price in the form of taxes.

Under the assumptions we have made here, the quantity of police protection will be determined by the intersection of supply and demand and will be at an allocatively efficient level. There is, however, a very big problem when it comes to matching the model with reality. The way we derived the provision of the public good until now hinges on the assumption that citizens are honestly willing to divulge their willingness to pay. This is not realistic. For example, would you say how much you value a good or service if it means that you will be charged that amount *and* you knew that you would get the same amount if you claimed it was worthless to you? If you think you might not, then you can understand the problem when it comes to public goods like police protection. Citizens may reason that they will profit from police protection even if they don't tell the truth as long as the other citizens tell the truth and pay for the police. When citizens attempt to enjoy the benefits produced by others without paying, we say they are "free riding."

The outcome of free riding can be illustrated in Figure 3.5. Again, D is the demand assuming no free riding, and it actually does reflect the value attributed to police protection. We have now added a supply curve S that intersects the demand curve at a 60 percent level of police protection. This is the "full truth" equilibrium for police protection. If, however, free riding occurs and people conceal their demand, the effective demand in the market will be lower. Suppose citizen A claims (untruthfully) that she does not care about police protection at all and is not willing to pay one cent for it. Suppose citizen B still truthfully reveals his willingness to pay. In this case, the demand curve of citizen B will become the total demand curve (as

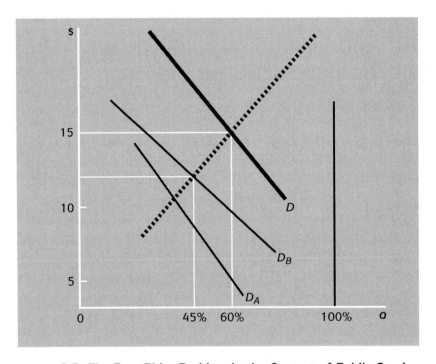

FIGURE 3.5 The Free-Rider Problem in the Context of Public Goods

citizen A has claimed she has no demand at all). The intersection between supply and demand occurs now at a lower point and only a 45 percent level of police protection will be provided for. This 45 percent is lower than the allocatively efficient level of 60 percent and occurs because of the free riding by citizen A.

Because of this free-rider effect, governments will usually not adopt this method of surveying citizens. The election process is used instead to establish the appropriate level of police protection in an approximate way. Some political parties stress the law-and-order issue and higher police protection, and citizens express their preference for the public good of police protection by voting for these parties.

HOW IS PRIVATE PROPERTY PROTECTED?

The fact that there are powerful economic arguments for the existence of private property does not automatically mean that a claim to ownership is respected by all. That is, in fact, where law comes in. The question is, What happens to those who take, use, destroy, or otherwise violate the private property of others? In this context, you should understand that property rights are just one type of right. Other rights—like the right to have someone perform a contract or to vote— are also treated very much like property in the eyes of the law.

The law reacts in a variety of ways when rights—including traditional property rights—are violated. This is spelled out in an important article by Yale law professor and Federal Judge Guido Calabresi and coauthor A. Douglas Melamed.[6] According to Calabresi and Melamed, property and rights more generally tend to be protected in one of three ways: "property" rules, liability rules, and inalienability.

In the case of a property rule, a person may not make use of or interfere with your property without permission. If someone violates the rule, he or she is likely to be penalized by a court in some way. In the case of a liability rule, the person interfering does not need permission but will be required to compensate you for any damage. In effect, he or she is "liable" for damages. Finally, and perhaps strangely,

---

6. Guido Calabresi and A. Douglas Melamed, "Property Rules, Liability Rules and Inalienability: One View of the Cathedral," *Harvard Law Review* 85 (1972): 1089.

there are instances in which rights may not be transferred or taken with or without your permission. This is the concept of inalienability.

The type of rule employed in any particular case has important economic consequences and we will return to this in Chapter 6. For now, it is enough to understand how the rules might work in particular circumstances. First, suppose someone sees this book in a bookstore and takes it without paying. The bookstore's ownership in the book is protected by a property rule and the culprit, if caught, may be jailed or fined. Second, as so often happens, imagine that someone driving a car accidentally runs into your car. Unless the person is driving while intoxicated, it is likely that the only thing that will happen is that he or she will have to pay to have your car repaired. This would involve a liability rule. Finally, there are laws that prohibit sales of certain rights, like the right to vote or to have sexual relations. In effect, these rights are inalienable. As already noted, as an economic matter, it makes sense to protect some rights in one way and others in another way.

QUESTIONS FOR DISCUSSION

1. Can you think of a "tragedy of the commons" that affects you? Would roadside litter be an example? A public restroom? A college library? How so? Would any of the responses discussed in this chapter solve the problem?

2. The chapter notes that the assignment and enforcement of property rights can be expensive. How so? Can you think of instances in which the cost is not worth the benefits?

3. One solution to the tragedy of the commons is to form agreements. If one pictures the earth as a giant commons and the tragedy as global warming, why would any one country refuse to participate in the agreement? Does it make any sense for the others to agree if all countries do not participate in the agreement?

4. Suppose you go into a plush store with well-trained staff that sells stereo equipment. You question the sales personnel and get all the information you need and then buy the stereo from a mail-order discount store. Are you "free riding?" If so, does this mean infor-

mation about stereos should be provided by the government? Why isn't every good that is subject to free riding produced by the government? Can you think of a way the upscale stereo store could make sure stereo information is subject to exclusivity?

5. Three students want to watch a video together. Renting the video will cost $3. Would you consider watching the video to be a private good or a public good? The students decide that everyone should chip in $1 to cover the rental. This might be fair, but is it always efficient?

6. Go to Table 3.1 on the "tragedy of the commons" and assume that the cost per cow (column b) is now $3 rather than $1. If the grassland is still a commons, how many cows will be grazing on the commons? If the grassland is private property, how many cows will the owner keep?

CHAPTER FOUR

Externalities

M Y UPSTAIRS NEIGHBOR'S VIOLIN PRACTICE SESSIONS ARE painful to my ears. My downstairs neighbor has a beautiful rose garden behind the house. I enjoy looking at it. In both examples, my neighbors' actions have an effect on my level of utility. My upstairs neighbor does not compensate me for my suffering. On the other hand, I do not compensate my downstairs neighbor for the pleasure his rose garden is giving me. Both instances are examples of externalities. My upstairs neighbor creates a negative externality, my downstairs neighbor a positive one. These are fairly simple examples of everyday externalities. More traditional examples of serious externalites include a factory polluting the air or water—poisoning fish caught by downstream fisherman—or the noise and exhaust of heavy vehicle traffic.

This chapter deals with externalities. The reaction of the law to externalities helps to define what it means to own "private property." In the first section, we examine externalities more closely and describe how they relate to property rights. Externalities can introduce inefficiencies into the economy. This is explained in the second section. The third section presents the remedies used to correct the inefficiencies caused by externalities.[1]

---

1. Note that many externalities are so minor that it is not worthwhile to correct the inefficiency. I will usually and within limits bear my upstairs neighbor's violin practice and I will compliment my downstairs neighbor on his beautiful roses and leave it at that.

AN INTRODUCTION TO EXTERNALITIES

The Basics

Externalities are said to arise when individuals or firms are favorably or unfavorably affected by decisions of another individual or firm. Within this general context, it is important to be aware of an important distinction. Some researchers define externalities very broadly as *any* positive or negative effect. Other researchers—among them economists—define externalities more narrowly and restrict the label "externality" to only those positive or negative effects that are neither rewarded nor compensated.

A critical term in this distinction is *internalization*. If someone produces a positive externality and is not compensated for it, we say he or she has not internalized the benefit. Conversely, if that person is paid, he or she *does* internalize the benefit. The same is true of negative externalities. If you cause others to suffer—financially or psychologically—and then pay them an amount that offsets their disutility, we say that you have internalized the *externality*. Thus, the narrow interpretation described above refers to situations in which internalization has not occurred.

In this chapter, we will use this more narrow definition of an externality. In other words, an externality occurs when one is harmed or benefited by the actions of another *and* there is no offsetting payment. For example, if I buy flowers at the florist because I like to look at the flowers and enjoy the smell, the florist produces a benefit but internalizes the benefit because I pay for the flowers. This interaction between the florist and me is a market transaction and does not involve an externality as defined in this chapter. On the other hand, if I just hang around outside the shop enjoying the colors and fragrances, there is no market transaction and the florist has not internalized the benefit. By the definition used in this chapter, an externality exists.

Similarly, suppose my neighbor begins to build a tennis court in his back yard. This causes all kinds of noise and stirs up the dusty soil. Each day my car is coated with dirt and dust. If that is all there is to it, the construction has created an externality. On the other hand, if the construction firm or my neighbor pays for me to have my car cleaned and for the inconvenience of the noise, there may technically be an externality; but, since the construction firm itself internalizes the cost, it makes little sense to worry about it or even to view it as an externality for any practical economic purposes.

For economists, an externality is a market failure. It is a positive or negative effect that has no price and for which there is no market. In the case of air pollution, an economist would say there is no market for air because nobody "owns" the air and can offer it for sale; therefore, there is no price at which a firm can buy air to use for production purposes. As we will see below, the reason there is no market for "air" is because there are no property rights for air, but this can be solved.

CASE 4.1 Externalities Come in Many Forms: *City of Los Angeles v. Alameda Books, Inc.,* 535 U.S. 425 (2002)

Air and water pollution are classic externalities—the ones you are likely to hear about most often. It is important to remember, though, that externalities can come in a variety of forms. In the following excerpt, the United States Supreme Court describes an externality and the City of Los Angeles' response:

> In 1977, the city of Los Angeles conducted a comprehensive study of adult establishments and concluded that concentrations of adult businesses are associated with higher rates of prostitution, robbery, assaults, and thefts in surrounding communities. . . . Accordingly, the city enacted an ordinance prohibiting the establishment, substantial enlargement, or transfer of ownership of an adult arcade, bookstore, cabaret, motel, theater, or massage parlor or a place for sexual encounters within 1,000 feet of another such enterprise or within 500 feet of any religious institution, school, or public park.
>
> ★★★
>
> Concerned that allowing an adult-oriented department store to replace a strip of adult establishments could defeat the goal of the original ordinance, the city council amended § 12.70(C) by adding a prohibition on "the establishment or maintenance of more than one adult entertainment business in the same building, structure or portion thereof."
>
> Alameda Books, Inc., and Highland Books, Inc., are two adult establishments operating in Los Angeles. Neither is located within 1,000 feet of another adult establishment or 500 feet of any religious institution, public park, or school. Each establishment occupies less than 3,000 square feet. Both . . . rent and sell sexually oriented products, including videocassettes.

Additionally, both provide booths where patrons can view videocassettes for a fee. Although respondents are located in different buildings, each operates its retail sales and rental operations in the same commercial space in which its video booths are located. There are no physical distinctions between the different operations within each establishment and each establishment has only one entrance.

After a city building inspector found in 1995 that Alameda Books, Inc., was operating both as an adult bookstore and an adult arcade in violation of the city's adult zoning regulations, respondents joined as plaintiffs and sued under 1983 for declaratory and injunctive relief to prevent enforcement of the ordinance. At issue in this case is count I of the complaint, which alleges a facial violation of the First Amendment.

As you can see, here a government response to an externality may violate the First Amendment, which guarantees a right of free speech. What follows is Justice Kennedy's analysis of the problem:

Speech can produce tangible consequences. It can change minds. It can prompt actions. These primary effects signify the power and the necessity of free speech. Speech can also cause secondary effects, however, unrelated to the impact of the speech on its audience. A newspaper factory may cause pollution, and a billboard may obstruct a view. These secondary consequences are not always immune from regulation by zoning laws even though they are produced by speech.

Municipal governments know that high concentrations of adult businesses can damage the value and the integrity of a neighborhood. The damage is measurable; it is all too real. The law does not require a city to ignore these consequences if it uses its zoning power in a reasonable way to ameliorate them without suppressing speech.

The question in this case is whether Los Angeles can seek to reduce these tangible, adverse consequences by separating adult speech businesses from one another—even two businesses that have always been under the same roof. In my view our precedents may allow the city to impose its regulation in the exercise of the zoning authority. . . .

A zoning measure can be consistent with the First Amendment if it is likely to cause a significant decrease in secondary effects and a trivial decrease in the quantity of speech. It is well documented that multiple adult businesses in close proximity may change the character of a neighborhood for the worse. Those same businesses spread across the city may not have the same deleterious effects. At least in theory, a dispersal ordinance causes these businesses to separate rather than to close, so negative externalities are diminished but speech is not.

The calculus is a familiar one to city planners, for many enterprises other than adult businesses also cause undesirable externalities. Factories, for example, may cause pollution, so a city may seek to reduce the cost of that externality by restricting factories to areas far from residential neighborhoods. With careful urban planning a city in this way may reduce the costs of pollution for communities, while at the same time allowing the productive work of the factories to continue. The challenge is to protect the activity inside while controlling side effects outside.

Externalities and Property Rights

You may already have a sense for how critical externalities and internalization are to understanding what it means to own something. Think back to the example of the construction site next door to my house. Suppose the construction firm makes no effort to compensate me for the dust and noise. Now I am faced with a fundamental question. Does my ownership mean that I have a right to stop others from causing dirt and dust to land on my land? Does it mean I have a right to be free of excessive construction noise? If the answer is "yes," the construction firm has violated my property rights and will be required to compensate me for my loss.

Suppose instead of the construction site we go back to my neighbor with the screeching violin. It is very annoying and eventually I call the police. The response is "too bad." In other words, my rights do not include a guarantee that I will be free of annoying violin-practicing neighbors or be compensated by them.

You should note a number of things. First, ultimately, property rights are defined in terms of the rights you possess with respect to others. Second, property rights are whatever the law says they are. In other words, they do not exist in the absence of some defining legal structure. Third, property rights can be broad or narrow. For example, the most basic property right is that people cannot take your property without permission. On the other hand, what if they just want to use it from time to time? It may be that your property rights do not include the right to stop them.[2] Fourth, since the limits of one's prop-

---

2. The ability of others to use your property for limited purposes is sometimes called an *easement*.

erty rights are defined by law, what is or is not an externality is also ultimately a function of the law. This leads to a new question, one that will be addressed in the next chapter: Can economics guide the law in how it defines property rights?

CASE 4.2 Where Does an Externality Originate? *Spur Industries, Inc. v. Del E. Webb Development Company,* 494 P.2d 700 (1972)

From the text, you may have the impression that there is a circularity to identifying externalities. For example, if you need clean air for breathing, a factory may have to use costly air filters to avoid polluting the air. Is your need for clean air creating an externality for the factory or is the factory's use of the air creating the externality? It all depends on who the law says has a right to use the air.

A well-known case illustrating the complementary nature of externalities involved a feedlot for cattle (Spur) and a developer (Del E. Webb) of residential housing. This was known as Sun City. The feedlot was established first. It is a fact that a head of cattle in a feedlot can produce about thirty-five pounds of manure a day. Manure means odors, flies, and generally unhealthy conditions. Of course, unless people are around, this is not a problem and, in some respects, not even an externality.

A few years after the feedlot started business, Webb decided to develop the area for residential use. At first, home sites were developed and sold that were unaffected by the feedlot. As time passed, however, the home sites got closer to the lot and became difficult to sell. In addition, some residents who had bought land from Webb began to complain about the feedlot's externalities. Eventually, Webb asked a court to enjoin (stop) the operation of the feedlot.

Technically, the case involves what is called "coming to the nuisance." From an economic perspective, you might call it "coming to the externality." The standard rule is that the law will not assist a person who comes to the nuisance. Typically, people know what they are doing and the price they pay for the land reflects that it may not end up being protected from all annoyances. In effect, you could argue that they were compensated for the externality because the price for the land was lower than what it would have been if there had been no potential externalities.

How would you decide this case if you were the judge? As it turns out, the court decided not to follow the "coming to the nuisance" rule. Instead, it ordered the feedlot to stop operating. According to the court, it was deviating from the standard rule because "of the damage to the people who have been encouraged to purchase homes in Sun City." This may seem unconvincing to you, but consider the rest of what the court said:

> It does not equitably or legally follow, however, that Webb, being entitled to the injunction, is then free of any liability to Spur if Webb has in fact been the cause of the damage Spur has sustained. It does not seem harsh to require a developer, who has taken advantage of the lesser land values in a rural area as well as the availability of large tracts of land on which to build and develop a new town or city in the area, to indemnify those who are forced to leave as a result.
>
> Having brought people to the nuisance to the foreseeable detriment of Spur, Webb must indemnify Spur for a reasonable amount of the cost of moving or shutting down. It should be noted that this relief to Spur is limited to a case wherein a developer has, with foreseeability, brought into a previously agricultural or industrial area the population which makes necessary the granting of an injunction against a lawful business and for which the business has no adequate relief.

Doesn't this sound like Del Webb was, in fact, the cause of the externality? The reasoning would go like this. One consequence of Del Webb's action was that Spur was required to move its feedlot. This is costly to Spur and Del Webb must internalize the cost. You probably see that the process a court goes through is the assignment of property rights. In this case, it is as if the court decided that Spur "owned" the right to use the air. Of course, Spur was then forced to sell it to Del Webb.

Types of Externalities

The affected party in an externality can either be an individual or a firm. When an individual is affected, it usually means that his utility has been reduced (or increased in the case of a positive externality) in an involuntary way. An individual's utility can be reduced by a stranger smoking on the train, the stench of the neighbor's pigsty, the noise of airplanes passing overhead. These externalities are called *consumption externalities* because they reduce an individual's ability to "consume" clean and fresh air or a silent and quiet environment.

Restriction of consumption possibilities reduces the quality of life and the level of utility.

When a firm is affected by an externality, it usually means that its production possibilities are either hampered (negative externality) or stimulated (positive externality). These are called *production externalities*. A classic example of a negative production externality is that of a steel mill emitting dirty smoke and making it harder for a laundry nearby to clean clothes. The laundry has to use more detergent and a longer washing cycle to clean the clothes. Hence, the laundry's production is more difficult and expensive. A classic example of a positive production externality is that of the beekeeper and the orchard owner. The production of honey by a beekeeper might directly affect the level of output of the orchard next door. The concentration of bees close to the orchard has a positive influence on how many apples and cherries the orchard owner will produce.

In the examples given, the externalities are mostly *unidirectional*. A firm or an individual creates a positive or negative effect for another firm or individual. But externalities can also be *reciprocal*. Congestion on the highway is an example of a negative reciprocal externality. As I join the traffic jam during rush hour, I create a negative externality for the other drivers (it takes them longer to get to work or to the shopping mall). But their presence also creates a similar externality for me. Farmers in a marshy area who drain their own land make it easier for each other to lower water levels and, in this way, reciprocally improve each other's productivity. This is a positive reciprocal production externality.

The externality can be *one on one* (as in the beekeeper and the orchard owner example), *one on many* (as when somebody builds a huge and ugly building in a beautiful part of the old city, causing an eyesore for everybody), or *many on many* (as in the thousands of car drivers causing air pollution and smog for the thousands of inhabitants of a city).[3] It should be obvious that when there are very few parties involved (such as in the two neighbors case), it will be easier for the parties to find a solution to the externality than when there are thousands of people involved. We come back to this obvious point in Chapter 5 when discussing the Coase theorem.

---

3. It is hard to find an example whereby many parties create an externality for one individual or firm.

When many agents are involved—or even the whole world, as is the case with carbon dioxide and the greenhouse effect—the externalities become like a public good. As we explained in Chapter 3, the main characteristics of a public good are nonexclusiveness and nonrivalry. Take the example of the greenhouse effect or of traffic smog in a city. It is clear that nobody can be excluded from the harm (this is the nonexclusiveness property), and my suffering from air pollution does not diminish your suffering, or my reduction in well-being does not diminish yours (this is the nonrivalry property). In the case of positive externalities, think about my neighbor's rose garden. For the most part, he will be unable to exclude people who live nearby from seeing and smelling the roses. Moreover, when they do, it does not decrease his own or anyone else's enjoyment.

In the case of public goods, free-riding behavior occurs frequently. Some of the parties causing the environmental externality might do less or nothing at all to avoid the externality and hope that others will solve the problem. Some of the parties affected by the externality might claim that they are not bothered by it and hence refuse any contribution to a solution.

LAW AND ECONOMICS IN ACTION 4.1

NETWORK EXTERNALITIES

An externality that is discussed much in this age of information and communication technology is a network externality. Networks have a fundamental economic characteristic: The value of connecting to a network depends on the number of other people already connected to it. It is better to be connected to a bigger network than to a smaller one. At one time, the most basic example of a network was a fax network. If one person had a fax machine, it was worthless. If two did, each one became more valuable and so on. Now the type of network externality that is most frequently discussed is related to computer operating systems and programs. For example, if more people use Microsoft Windows their computers may be better able to communicate. Similarly, the more people who use MS Word as a word processing program, the more valuable it is for all MS Word users because it increases the opportunity to exchange MS Word files. In fact, in the recent antitrust lawsuit against Microsoft, one of the defenses raised was that the widespread use of Windows led to network externalities.

It is said that markets with network externalities are "tippy" markets. These markets tend to go from one extreme to another. They are described as winner-take-all-markets. In these markets, the bigger-is-better characteristic gives rise to positive feedback. Positive feedback makes the strong get stronger and the weak get weaker, leading to extreme outcomes. Think about MS Word and WordPerfect. At some point in time, WordPerfect was the dominant word processing program. Then came MS Word. As more and more people switched from WP to Word, the latter became stronger and the former weakened. Now MS Word dominates.

Reference: Carl Shapiro and Hal R. Varian, *Information Rules* (Cambridge: Harvard Business School Press, 1999), Chapter 7. "Networks and Positive Feedback."

In Table 4.1, we summarize the different kinds of externalities. It is clear that externalities occur very frequently. But of course not all of them are worrisome or need the attention of policymakers and lawmakers.

As we stressed above, an important characteristic of an economic definition of an externality is that it affects third parties other *than by affecting prices*. Put differently, people and firms affect each other very frequently through the market and hence through price changes. But these price effects are not externalities. Externalities are problematic because there is no market in which clean and fresh air and water or a quiet environment can be traded. Third-party effects running through prices are sometimes called *pecuniary externalities* to distinguish them from the *direct externalities* discussed in this Section. Consider the following example of such a pecuniary externality.

In April 1980, Fidel Castro decided to allow Cuban common law criminals (quite a number of them) imprisoned in Cuba to immigrate to the United States. The exodus out of Cuba started from Mariel, a

TABLE 4.1 Types of Externality

Beneficial (positive)	Harmful (negative)
Unidirectional (upstream to downstream)	Reciprocal (traffic congestion)
Two person (neighbors)	Many persons (traffic air pollution)
Affecting utility (noisy neighbor)	Affecting production (overfishing)
Public (greenhouse effect)	Private (smoking in a restaurant)

Cuban harbor, and it became known as the Mariel boat lift. In only a few months, approximately 125,000 Cubans flowed into the urban labor market of Miami. Miami's labor force increased by about 7 percent in a very short time. Most of the new immigrants were unschooled and unskilled, and they competed in the Miami labor market with the unschooled and unskilled American workers. The extra inflow of unschooled and unskilled Cubans drove down the wage for this group of workers. The unschooled and unskilled American workers were affected by this pecuniary externality. On the other hand, the loss to the American workers (lower wage received) was balanced by and exactly equivalent to the gain by the firms employing them (higher profits because of lower wages).

Pecuniary externalities cancel each other out. They are redistributive because they do not affect the size of the pie, just how it is shared. The American workers suffer and the American employers gain. Pecuniary externalities fall under the heading of equity rather than efficiency. To stress this point, it is interesting to look at how the story developed. David Card studied the long-term effect of the Mariel boat lift on employment and wages in the urban labor market of Miami and found that five years later the wage levels for unschooled and unskilled workers in Miami were comparable to wage levels in other large urban areas of the United States.[4] The effects of the boat lift on the labor market were only temporary. The initial reduction in wages for unschooled and unskilled workers and the higher profits for firms employing them in the Miami area attracted more firms to the Miami area and, through this process, wages rose again until they were at par with other urban areas. Pecuniary externalities are a result of how the market system works. They create winners and losers, but they are useful in the sense that they signal shortages or abundance. These signals are necessary for the efficient functioning of the market. Direct externalities, on the other hand, create inefficiencies.

EXTERNALITIES CREATE INEFFICIENCIES

We will illustrate the inefficiency caused by an externality using the example of a harmful externality. In Figure 4.1, we look at the situa-

---

4. D. Card, "The Impact of the Mariel Boatlift on the Miami Labor Market," *Industrial and Labor Relations Review* 43, no. 2 (1990): 245–257.

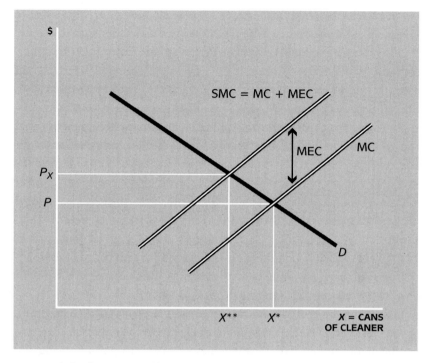

FIGURE 4.1 Costs Including Externalities

tion of a producer located upstream who discharges pollutants into a river.[5] The polluted water kills off the fish and creates a negative consumption externality for individuals who enjoy fishing from the river on a Sunday afternoon. It also creates production externalities for the downstream firm that needs clean water for its production (e.g., it might need it to make soda pop). The problem is that the polluting producer who produces product X—say, kitchen sink cleaner—disregards this external effect in his production decision. He will maximize his profit setting his marginal cost (MC) of producing one more

5. A real-life example of this that shocked the world in the 1950s occurred in Japan. Methylmercury was used in a chemical production process in an upriver plant and discharged into the water system. Methylmercury accumulated in fish and shellfish, and people who ate them were poisoned. This was first discovered in Minamata City and the illness was later called Minamata Disease. This disease caused severe sensory disturbances such as hearing and balance abnormalities and constriction of the visual field. For more information see http://www.einap.org/envdis/Minamata.html.

bottle of kitchen sink cleaner equal to the demand for such a bottle (D_x), the associated output being $X^\star$ bottles of kitchen sink cleaner.[6]

Suppose the externality cost to society of the last bottle of kitchen sink cleaner produced is equal to MEC. MEC stands for marginal externality cost and represents the monetary equivalent of the loss of utility for the consumers and of the reduction of the production possibilities for the downstream producers. MC stands for the marginal cost of capital and labor used in producing kitchen sink cleaner. If we add the marginal externality cost to the marginal cost for all production levels X, we obtain the MC + MEC curve. We call this the social marginal cost curve or SMC. This SMC curve is, from a societal point of view, the correct marginal cost curve. The SMC curve reflects all the costs to society—the true opportunity cost—of producing kitchen sink cleaner. The efficient level of production would thus be where the market price P_x equals social marginal cost. Hence the efficient level of production is $X^{\star\star}$.

Production level $X^\star$ is an inefficient level of production. Compared to the efficient level $X^{\star\star}$, production level $X^\star$ is too high because the producer of kitchen sink cleaner does not have to pay for using the river to discharge his pollutant. The river is part of his production process just like labor and capital, but he does not pay for the use of the river. Because he does not have to pay all of the costs associated with producing cleaner, he produces too cheaply and hence too much. The market system fails in this case.

The difference between $X^\star$ and $X^{\star\star}$ is inefficient production. For that part of the production, the buyers of kitchen sink cleaner pay a price P which is lower than the cost to society of producing kitchen sink cleaner (the SMC is above the price line corresponding to P for all levels of production between $X^\star$ and $X^{\star\star}$). Intuitively, it is easy to see that the solution to this inefficiency must be to confront the producer with the cost of using the river in his production of kitchen sink cleaner. This is in economic terms what it means when we say "the polluter pays." Using the river has an opportunity cost that is equal to the monetary value of the harmful consumption and production externalities for the downstream consumers and producers, which in the figure is MEC. So, intuitively, if we make the polluter pay MEC

---

6. Recall that the demand shows the value attributed by buyers to the product.

as a price for using the river, then the relevant marginal cost for his profit-maximizing production decision would shift from the MC curve to the SMC curve. If this happens, he has internalized the cost of pollution. He will equate SMC to the market price P_x and produce the efficient amount $X^{\star\star}$. We will turn to remedies for environmental problems in the next section.

LAW AND ECONOMICS IN ACTION 4.2

THE COST OF REDUCING GREENHOUSE GAS EMISSIONS

Imposing a carbon tax is a way of charging the marginal externality cost (MEC) to the polluter and making him internalize the cost of the externality. But how high should the carbon tax be? A variety of studies have been done, most focusing on near-term costs—through 2010 or 2020—of one of two policies reducing emissions to 1990 levels or implementing the 1997 Kyoto Protocol. The studies typically determine the marginal cost of reducing emissions by calculating the carbon tax—a tax levied on fossil fuels in proportion to their carbon content—that would be needed to drive emissions down to a specified level. A ton of coal contains 0.65 tons of carbon, so a $1 per ton carbon tax would translate into a tax of $0.65 per ton of coal; the same tax would add $0.14 to the price of a barrel of crude oil and $0.02 to the price of a thousand cubic feet of natural gas. The aim of the Kyoto Protocol is to reduce greenhouse gas emissions. If the carbon tax per ton of carbon emitted is sufficiently high, less carbon will be emitted. A tax high enough to reduce carbon emissions in the United States to levels agreed by the Kyoto Protocol is estimated to range from $94 to $400 (in 2000 U.S. dollars) per ton of carbon.

Reference: Warwick J. McKibbin and Peter J. Wilcoxen, "The Role of Economics in Climate Change Policy," *Journal of Economic Perspectives* 16, no. 2 (Spring 2002): 107–129.

The case of positive externalities is illustrated in Figure 4.2. Take the example of the tulip fields in Holland. If you take the train between the Hague and Amsterdam on an April or May day, you will travel through large stretches filled with blooming tulips in all the colors of the rainbow. This is the region in which a huge number of tulip bulbs are produced. Most travelers on the train enjoy the sight of the tulip

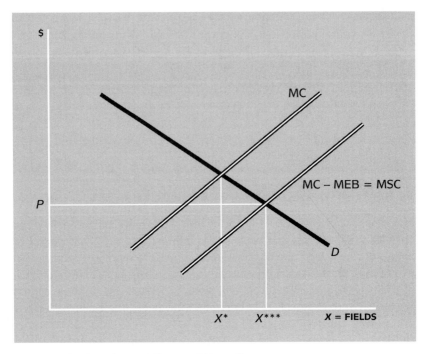

FIGURE 4.2 Supply and External Benefits

fields. The travelers do not pay the tulip bulb farmers for their increase in utility. If the tulip bulb farmers were compensated for this beneficial externality—for instance, through a subsidy from the railroad company—their net marginal cost of producing tulip bulbs would decrease and they would extend their tulip fields. In Figure 4.2, the MSC curve lies below the MC curve. The distance between the curves is the marginal external benefit (MEB). An amount equal to MEB is paid to the farmers, lowering the marginal cost curve and resulting in an increase in output from X^* to X^{***}.

Another way of looking at the tulip case is that it means people can enjoy the benefits of tulips in bloom without going into the market and buying them. The tulip fields in bloom are a public good and hence train travelers can free ride on them and consume them without paying for them. The demand for tulips on the market understates the social benefits of growing tulips and tulip bulbs and they are, therefore, underproduced. If the true utility that tulips provide were translated into demand, demand would be higher and output higher.

REMEDIES

How can the inefficiencies caused by externalities be addressed? Here we address remedies for negative externalities. By remedies, we mean specific ways to reduce the inefficient, high level of production and the concomitant high level of the negative externality (e.g., pollution). There are two groups of remedies used to adjust production and pollution to efficient levels. A first group uses the price mechanism. The basic idea is that the polluter is confronted with the cost or "price" of pollution and takes this price into account when making his production decisions (and internalizes the externality costs). The cost of pollution increases his production costs and subsequently he will produce less. If we confront him with a price exactly equal to the marginal externality cost, he will produce the optimal amount ($X^{\star\star}$ in the figure above).

The second group of remedies consists of command and control instruments. In this case, the government or a regulatory agency such as the U.S. Environmental Protection Agency delineates actions the polluting firm must take or emission limits that it must observe.

There are three basic forms of *pricing remedies* for negative externalities:

- Environmental taxes
- Tradable emission permits
- Abatement subsidies

There are also three basic forms of *command and control remedies*:

- Abatement technology; for example, "Install flue gas desulphurisation equipment"
- Emission rate; for example, "Effluents can contain no more than 10 mg of pollutant X per 1000 gallons discharged"
- Emissions level; for example, "Plant Y can emit no more than z tons of pollutant X in any month"

It is instructive to compare the two groups of remedies.

Pricing Remedies

Suppose, for simplicity, that there is a constant marginal environmental cost for each bottle of kitchen sink cleaner equal to $0.50.

Suppose also that $0.50 is the correct estimate of the monetary value of the loss of utility and of reduction of production possibilities of the amount of pollution caused by producing one bottle of cleaner. If the government decides that all producers of kitchen sink cleaner have to pay an environmental tax of $0.50 per bottle produced, then this environmental tax provides a perfect remedy.

Because of the tax, the marginal cost curve in Figure 4.1 increases by $0.50. It shifts upward and the relevant marginal cost curve becomes equal to

$$MC + \text{Environmental Tax } (= \$0.50)$$

If $0.50 is the correct monetary estimate of the marginal externality cost, then

$$MC + \text{Environmental Tax} = MC + MEC = SMC$$

Through the environmental tax, the producer of the cleaner will internalize the externality cost and will decide to produce $X^{\star\star}$ bottles, which is the efficient amount. By reducing his production level from $X^{\star}$ to $X^{\star\star}$ after the tax is imposed, he also reduces the level of pollution. He will still pollute when producing the efficient amount $X^{\star\star}$, but the level of pollution that comes with production level $X^{\star\star}$ is an efficient level in that the price consumers are willing to pay for a bottle of kitchen sink cleaner P_x (and which in some sense represents the utility value that consumers attach to this bottle of kitchen sink cleaner) is higher than (or at least as high as) the marginal social cost of producing the cleaner (MC + MEC). In other words, the level of production is now allocatively efficient.

There are two problems with environmental taxes as a remedy for negative externalities. First, there is a huge information problem for the government imposing the tax. For the tax to achieve the efficient levels of production and pollution, it has to be equal to the marginal externality cost. In most cases this will be impossible to measure. So the government is likely to either impose too high a level of tax, overshooting its objective, or impose too low a tax level and underachieve. In addition, the public will be required to pay the cost of administering the tax. Still, the tax, although not precisely correct, is likely to produce a more efficient outcome than no tax at all.

MONETIZING ENVIRONMENTAL VALUES

According to a 2005 article in *The Economist,* banks, firms, and govern-ments are beginning to find ways to place monetary values on the envi-ronment and environmental goods and services. This allows for a scientifically sound method to let the market, at least partially, help us deal with the externalities created by pollution and land use. One exam-ple is finding how fresh water, which is running out in Panama, can best be supplied to the Panama Canal, which requires massive amounts in order to operate its lock system. The most efficient way of doing this would be to replant forests throughout the area, which would create a natural sys-tem for filtering and gradually supplying water, as well as reducing runoff and erosion into the canal that creates a need for expensive maintenance.

The problem with such a solution, even if someone believed it could be done, has always been who will pay for it. An insurance firm known as Forestre believes it has a solution in this situation. Chairman John Forgach plans to work with other insurance companies and firms to underwrite a twenty-five-year bond to pay for the reforestation. The bond would then be sold to the canal's biggest customers, all of whom pay heavy premi-ums for insurance in case of the canal's closure. In return, their premiums would be less expensive since they have made the canal less likely to close, and both sides, as well as Panamanians, would benefit or profit.

Forgach's plan might also work elsewhere, since companies already buy expensive environmental insurance in case of lawsuits or other prob-lems and could be given cheaper premiums if they found cheap ways to reduce pollution. This transformation is aided by the ability of scientists to begin to put a price on the goods and services provided by ecosystems and a better understanding of how they work and what they do.

Reference: "The Growing Importance of Environmental Economics," *The Economist,* April 21, 2005.

A second problem is that a uniform environmental tax rate is not appropriate if the different firms each producing their brand of kitchen sink cleaner have their own level of marginal externality cost; that is, the production of some brands creates more pollution than is pro-duced with other brands. If the government imposes an environmen-tal tax equal to the average marginal externality cost over all firms, then this tax level will be too high for low-polluting brands and too low for the high-polluting brands. A better solution would be to differentiate the tax levels, but this would complicate the information problem even further.

A possible solution to this information problem is achieved when the government issues tradable emission permits to the polluting firm. Assume that the government or the environmental agency has established that, at most, ten thousand tons of pollutant can be discharged into a river without endangering the quality of the water. Then it could decide that it would issue ten thousand permits for one ton of pollutant each. A permit would allow the owner to discharge one ton of pollutant in the river per year, say. Discharging without a permit would carry a stiff fine.

The government would then offer these permits for sale and allow the firms to trade in the permits (after they have bought them, they can use them in their production process or sell them).[7] The price for a market for permits will be determined by supply and demand. Firms that can at very low cost reduce their discharge level—by, for instance, installing cleaning equipment—will offer the permits for sale. If they can get a price for their permits that is higher than the cost of reducing their level of discharge, they will make money.

Who will buy the permits? Firms for whom it is rather expensive to install cleaning devices and reduce discharge levels. They are better off buying a permit and discharging. The price will reflect the technical cost of cleaning up and avoiding pollution. The government does not have to figure out how much to charge the firms for polluting; the market determines the price of a permit and hence the cost of discharging. If, through innovative cleaning methods, the cost of cleaning rather than discharging pollutants diminishes for some firms, then the supply of permits will increase and the price of a permit will decrease on the market for permits. The market for tradable permits also provides the firms with

7. It is not essential that the government offer the permits for sale. The government could also distribute them free among the firms. What is essential is that the permits can be resold among the firms. If the government sells the permits, this will raise income for the government. If the government gives them to the firms, the latter will receive income from selling them. The income distribution between government and firms is different in the two cases, but the efficiency is not affected by it.

an incentive to invest in research and development of improved cleaning techniques. If they can come up with a new technique that is cheaper than the permit, they do not need to buy a permit and can even sell the permits they have. Thus, in the long run, tradable permits will stimulate innovation in environmental techniques.

A third price-related remedy is when the government subsidizes firms for installing abatement or cleaning equipment to reduce pollution. When would a government give subsidies to firms if it also can raise a tax and hence tax revenue? Possibly when the goods that cause the pollution are also important for the export revenues of a country. If other countries that compete on the same international market do not worry about pollution externalities, then taxing the home firm would increase its international price and hence it might lose substantial market share, which would reduce export revenues. By subsidizing the abatement equipment, the government solves the externality problem without creating a necessity for a price increase of its home firm on the international market.

Command and Control Remedies

In the three command and control remedies listed above, the government is very specific in the way it determines what is allowed and what is forbidden. The information problem in determining the allowed levels is huge. Command and control remedies have an advantage over pricing remedies in that they are precise and certain in their effects, but at the same time they can be very inefficient. If the government commands firms to install a certain piece of equipment to clean up exhaust pipes, that might not always be the most cost-efficient piece of equipment available. If, on the other hand, the government works with, say, a tradable permit, it provides polluting firms with an incentive to install the most cost-efficient equipment.

LAW AND ECONOMICS IN ACTION 4.4

SULFUR DIOXIDE EMISSIONS TRADING

Title IV of the 1990 Clean Air Act Amendments established an interesting way for firms to internalize the costs they impose on others when they emit sulfur dioxide (SO_2). The act established the first large-scale, long-term environmental program to rely on tradeable emissions permits. Under the act, the total amount of sulfur dioxide that can be emitted has been decreased. The government sells, through an auction, "allowances" that permit the holders to emit one ton of sulfur dioxide in the year in which the allowance was purchased or in the future. The allowances can also be traded like a commodity. In some instances, environmentalists have purchased allowances to ensure that they will not be used. For example, the University of Southern Maine is home to an "Acid Rain Retirement Fund." The program was designed to cut acid rain by reducing sulfur dioxide emissions from electric generating plants to about half their 1980 level, beginning in 1995. It is of interest both as a response to an important environmental issue and as a landmark experiment in environmental policy.

The program allows a firm to determine how it will internalize the externality of sulfur dioxide by comparing the cost of allowances with the cost of decreasing emissions and choosing the less expensive strategy. At the time the act was passed, it was thought that an allowance might sell for as much as $1,500. At times, however, the price has dipped as low as $150.

The U.S. acid rain program illustrates that where the tradeable permit approach can be used, it is superior to command and control environmental regulation. Title IV more than achieved the SO_2 emission goal and did so on time, without extensive litigation, and at a cost lower than had been projected.

Reference: Richard Schmalensee, Paul L. Joskow, A. Denny Ellerman, Juan Pablo Montero, and Elizabeth M. Bailey, "An Interim Evaluation of Sulfur Dioxide Emission Trading," *Journal of Economic Perspectives* 12, no. 3 (Summer 1998): 53–68.

Apart from the price and control and command remedies, there are other solutions available to the negative externality problem. One of these solutions is unitization. A realistic example of this is adjacent oil fields belonging to different owners. Pumping at any well will draw away oil from the neighboring oil fields. Each individual owner will be motivated to pump faster to capture the oil under the neighbor's field and to prevent the neighbor from capturing the oil under his. Each individual owner also has an incentive to drill more wells and to locate them along the boundaries of his or her tract. The result is overdrilling and overpumping. Unitization of the entire oil field is a solution; the owners decide collectively where to drill wells and how fast to pump, and each owner gets a pro-rated share of the total amount of oil that is brought up. This eliminates the motivation to overpump and overdrill.

Finally, it is often said that the core problem of an externality is that property rights are not assigned. Nobody "owns" the air or "owns" the river. If property rights were assigned to individual owners, then markets could develop and this would also provide a solution to the externality problem. We will come back to this property rights arrangement in the next chapter when we discuss the Coase theorem.

QUESTIONS FOR DISCUSSION

1. In effect, externalities are defined as uncompensated costs or benefits affecting secondary parties. Suppose the sight of someone wearing a New York Yankees T-shirt annoys you—even makes you angry. Is this an externality? Is there a principled distinction between this and your neighbor playing music too loudly?

2. From the reading, you may get the impression that there is a certain "making it up as you go along" quality to the law's reaction to externalities. For example, suppose you buy a house in the country for the serenity. Someone buys land nearby and starts operating an amusement park. Can economic analysis guide a court in determining whether you should be entitled to your serenity and the amusement park prohibited from operating?

3. Do you see how the concept of externalities is related to the tragedy of the commons discussed in Chapter 3? Explain.

4. In the chapter, a number of reactions to negative externalities were discussed. In some instances, the goal was to force a firm to recognize and make its decisions on the basis of MEC. This represents a cost to someone else. Is it necessary that the amount paid by the firm actually go to those who are harmed by the externality?

5. The sulfur dioxide allowances program has been a success but has resulted in one interesting lawsuit. The State of New York, in order to protect its parks and rivers from acid rain, prohibited the firms in the state that owned allowances from selling them to any state that was upwind from New York. A federal court ruled that this prohibition was illegal. How would the prohibition affect the value of the allowances?

6. In this chapter, we discuss price and command and control remedies to alleviate or solve the inefficiencies caused by negative externalities. Positive externalities also create inefficiencies. For example, students who invest in their own education will personally benefit in terms of better job opportunities and the personal satisfaction of possessing knowledge. Society will benefit as well—because sophisticated means of production, higher economic growth rates, and more innovation is possible with a more educated populace. Students do not internalize these marginal externality benefits and hence will invest less in education than is optimal for society. Draw a figure similar to the ones in this chapter to illustrate the underinvestment in education. Discuss possible price and command and control remedies to solve the inefficiency of insufficient investment in education.

CHAPTER FIVE

The Coase Theorem

LL OF US KNOW THE STORY ABOUT ARCHIMEDES who, while sitting in his bathtub, suddenly has a flash of insight into a problem he has been struggling with, shouts "Eureka!," jumps out of his bath and runs naked into the street (to the surprise of none of his neighbors as they had probably seen this happen before). In his autobiography, the Chicago economist George J. Stigler writes that although he has spent all of his professional life in the company of first-class scholars, only once did he encounter something like the Archimedean revelation, and it was as an observer.[1] He goes on to tell about a presentation that Ronald Coase gave at the University of Chicago in 1960. During his presentation, Coase presented a completely new approach to the theory of externalities. The implications of the paper, which Coase presented at that Chicago seminar and later published in the *Journal of Law and Economics*,[2] have been concisely formulated as the Coase theorem and are central to the analysis of law and economics. In his book, George Stigler says that at the beginning of the workshop, after Coase had stated that he was planning to overhaul the economic theory of external effects, the audience was very skeptical, but by the end of two hours of argument

1. George J. Stigler, *Memoirs of an Unregulated Economist* (New York: Basic Books, 1988).
2. R. H. Coase, "The Problem of Social Cost," *Journal of Law and Economics* 3 (1960): 1–44.

Ronald Coase had won them all over. His seminal article is entitled "The Problem of Social Cost," and it has become one of the most cited articles in the economics and legal literature.

This chapter takes a close look at the Coase theorem. Initially, in the first section we discuss how the Coase theorem fits into the material you have studied so far. In the next two sections the specific ways in which the theory was a departure from the orthodoxy of the time are examined. For the theory and its implications to hold, certain assumptions must be made. These critical assumptions are discussed in the fourth and fifth sections. In the sixth we return to the ideas of property rules, liability rules, and inalienability to explain their economic significance, with conclusions in the final section.

WHERE DOES THE COASE THEOREM FIT IN?

As we saw in Chapter 4, in an efficient economic system, goods worth more than they cost to produce get produced; goods worth less than they cost to produce do not. But with external effects such as pollution, whereby the actions of one person impose costs on another person, some goods get produced even though their cost is greater than their value. In this sense, externalities lead to inefficiencies. In Chapter 4, we discussed two types of remedies to restore efficiency to the economic system. In the first group of remedies, the price system is used to confront the polluter with the "price" of his pollution activities. Remedies in this group are environmental taxes or subsidies and tradable emission permits. These remedies can be seen as applications of "the polluter pays" principle. The second group consists of command and control instruments, whereby the government specifically indicates what the polluter cannot do or what he is obliged to do. Economists usually favor the remedies using the price system.

In the early 1960s, when Ronald Coase was presenting his theory, tradable emission permits had not come to central stage, and environmental taxes were the economists' most favored remedy to "solve" negative externalities and to make the polluter pay. These environmental taxes were initially introduced into economics by Arthur Pigou and hence they are also known as "Pigouvian taxes."[3] According to con-

---

3. A. C. Pigou, *The Economics of Welfare*, 4th ed. (London: Macmillan, 1932).

ventional economic theory before Coase, Pigouvian taxes would bring back efficiency to an economy plagued by harmful external effects.

In this historical context, Coase made three innovative points, renewing not only the economic analysis of harmful effects but also our view on the economic analysis of legal rules:[4]

1. "The polluter pays" principle and the application of Pigouvian taxes to make the polluter pay do not always lead to an efficient result.
2. The existence of externalities does not necessarily lead to an inefficient result.
3. The problem is not really externalities but transaction costs.

His first two points go against what was accepted economic theory in the 1950s.

ENVIRONMENTAL TAXES ARE NOT NECESSARILY EFFICIENT

Coase's contribution starts with noting that the traditional approach to externalities has obscured the nature of the problem. In the traditional approach according to Coase:

> The question is commonly thought of as one in which A inflicts harm on B and what has to be decided is: how should we restrain A? But this is wrong. We are dealing with a problem of a reciprocal nature. To avoid the harm to B would inflict harm on A. The real question that has to be decided is: should A be allowed to harm B or should B be allowed to harm A?[5]

To illustrate this insight that an externality is a problem of a reciprocal nature, take the following example of a confectioner using two mortars and pestles in connection with his business, thereby making noise that bothers and harms a doctor whose consulting room is next to the confectioner.[6] Assume for simplicity that the noise pollution causes $100

---

4. Coase was awarded the Nobel Prize for Economics in 1991 for these innovations. See David Friedman, "The Swedes Get It Right," *Liberty,* March 4, 1997. http://daviddfriedman.com/Libertarian/The_Swedes.html.

5. Coase, "The Problem of Social Cost," 1.

6. This example is a rude schematic representation of the case of *Sturges v. Bridgeman*, 11 Ch. D. 852 [1879]), which is also used by Coase in his article to illustrate the general problem.

worth of damage. Moving the confectioner's production site away from the doctor's consulting room would cost $80. The other solution is that the "victim"—in this case, the doctor—move his consulting room elsewhere in his house or garden. This will cost $50. If we impose a Pigouvian tax of $100 on the polluter, he will move his production unit, but at $80 this is not the cheapest solution. The problem can be avoided at a lower cost and hence the Pigouvian tax is not efficient.

Coase's first point is that pollution is the joint production of polluter and victim. A legal rule defining property rights is required to determine which is which. On the other hand, a legal rule that *arbitrarily* assigns blame to one of the parties gives the right result only if that party happens to be the one who can avoid the problem at the lower cost. So the government or agency that is imposing the pollution tax has to know who is the least-cost-avoider in order to achieve the economically efficient solution. In the example, it is efficient to impose a tax on the doctor or to order the doctor to move his consulting room.

Looking at pollution as a two-sided, reciprocal effect of polluter and victim requires a complete change in one's frame of mind when thinking about harmful effects. The instinctive reaction of almost everybody is to blame the polluter and to make him pay for the damage done. The innovative insight of Coase is that the polluter is not necessarily the one who can solve the externality problem with the least cost. Making the polluter pay is not always the most efficient solution. In fact, it may be premature to label either of the parties a "polluter." If the doctor is really the "victim" in the example, then the efficient solution of making him move his consulting room seems unfair. However, our view of what is fair would change completely if we add that the confectioner's machinery caused the doctor no harm until, eight years after he had first occupied the premises, he built a new consulting room right next to the confectioner's workshop.[7] In that case, the doctor "came to the pollution" and hence it would seem fair to ask him to move back to where he came from. In effect, what we have is a case of competing uses in which one person's use of a resource makes it impossible for the other person to use it.

---

7. Which is precisely what happened in the *Sturges v. Bridgeman* case on which Coase based his example.

The most interesting aspect of Coase's contribution is that it does not really matter whether we "blame" the confectioner or the doctor, whether we give the confectioner the right to make the noise or give the doctor the right to a quiet consulting room. As long as they both can make a deal, it will always be possible to bargain between them and achieve the efficient solution. This is explained in the next section.

EXTERNALITIES ARE NOT NECESSARILY INEFFICIENT

In his article, Coase made the following observation: As long as people can make and enforce contracts in their interest, environmental taxes and other forms of governmental intervention are not necessary to get an efficient outcome. What the government has to do is to assign the "right to pollute" to the person who originally was called "the polluter" or the right to be "pollution free" to the person who originally was called "the victim." Applying this to our example, it does not matter whether the government assigns the right to the confectioner to make the noise or to the doctor to have quiet. The two parties, doctor and confectioner, will bargain with these rights and achieve the efficient solution.

This is how this principle works in the example of the confectioner and the doctor. Remember, it costs the doctor $50 to avoid the noise and the confectioner $80 to move. There are two possible legal rules in this case:

Legal rule number 1: The original polluter has the "right to pollute"; that is, the confectioner is allowed to make the noise.

Legal rule number 2: The original victim now has the right to a "pollution-free environment"; that is, the doctor has the right to silence.

What happens under legal rule number 1? Very simply, the doctor will move his consulting room to another part of the house, which is the efficient (least-cost) solution. In order to avoid moving himself, the doctor would be willing to offer the confectioner up to $50 to move his mortars and pestles, but the confectioner will obviously say no to that since his moving costs would be $80.

What happens under legal rule number 2? Now the doctor has the right to silence. The confectioner knows it will cost the doctor $50 to move his consulting room. On the other hand, it will cost the confectioner $80 to move his production side. The confectioner will go to the doctor and offer him more than $50 to move his consulting room. The confectioner is willing to pay any amount between $50 and $80 to make the doctor move. If the doctor gets more than $50, he makes money on moving his consulting room. They both will be better off. Under legal rule number 2 the outcome will be the same as under legal rule number 1: The doctor will move. This is always the efficient solution because it means the least expensive response to the externality is adopted.

The main conclusion is that whatever the legal rule, whatever the initial distribution of rights, the parties will bargain and always end up with the most efficient solution to the external effect. To appreciate this point even more, assume that through technological progress, cheap noise-free murmur-only mortars come onto the market and the confectioner can have these installed for $40. The doctor's moving costs are still $50. Under the new situation, the efficient solution is for the confectioner to install the new murmur-only mortars. Let's see if this is the outcome under each legal rule.

What happens now under legal rule number 1? The confectioner has the right to make the noise and, in principle, the doctor should move. However, the doctor knows the problem can be solved with new mortars for $40, which is less than his $50 moving costs. So he goes to the confectioner and offers him anything between $40 and $50. The confectioner accepts and installs the new mortars. Both are better off and the outcome of their bargaining is efficient.

What happens now under legal rule number 2? The doctor has a right to quiet. The confectioner will only offer up to $40 for the physician's right to silence, which the doctor will reject. So the confectioner will spend $40 for the new mortars, which is the efficient solution.

CASE 5.1 **Rights to the Sun:** *Fountainbleau Hotel Corp. v. Forty-Five Twenty-Five, Inc.,* 114 So.2d 357 (1959)

A case that is used very frequently to describe the implications of the Coase theorem involved the Fountainbleau and the Eden Roc, two neighboring resort hotels on Miami Beach. The Fountainbleau is just south of the Eden Roc—a fact that turned out to be critical when the owners of the Fountainbleau decided to construct a fourteen-story tower very close to its north property line. The problem was that the tower would cast a shadow over the Eden Roc's pool area. In response to this threat, the Eden Roc appealed to a Florida court to stop (enjoin) the construction of the Fountainbleau's tower. In effect, the Eden Roc was claiming that its property right included the right to have access to the rays of the sun even though they passed over the Fontainebleau's property before landing on the Eden Roc pool. The court ruled that there is no such right and that the Fountainbleu's construction could proceed. Think about the issue. According to the Coase theorem, does the construction of the tower really depend on the court's decision? Suppose the tower would have increased the profit of the Fountainbleau by $20 million and resulted in losses to the Eden Roc of $30 million. Would the tower be built? Or suppose the court had decided to enjoin the Fountainbleau and the profit from the tower would have been $30 million for the Fountainbleau and the loss to the Eden Roc $20 million. Again, would the tower be built?

So again, the conclusion is that whatever the initial definition of rights, the final outcome is always the same and efficient. The basic point that Coase was making is the following: In the case of external harms, all the government or the legal system has to do is assign "property rights" and the parties will take care of the rest. This insight of Coase extended our view of property rights. The rights to pollute or to a pollution-free environment are part of the bundle of property rights. If you own a factory, these rights to pollute or not to pollute are an essential part of the way you can dispose of your property. Coase made us realize that property can be defined as a bundle of rights, a set of rules about what one can or cannot do with the things one owns and that it is possible to sell or buy rights from that bundle to shape one's property rights in an optimal way. See the textbox on the fable of the bees for an interesting illustration of harmful effects, property rights, and contracts.

LAW AND ECONOMICS IN ACTION 5.1

THE FABLE OF THE BEES

Some economists have long been unconvinced by Coase's analysis and have argued that it is merely a theoretical curiosity of little or no practical importance in a world where transaction costs are never zero. James Meade, another Nobel Prize winner, suggested that Coase's approach offered no practical solution for the sort of externality problem associated with honeybees. Bees graze on flowers from various crops, so a farmer who grows crops that produce nectar benefits the beekeepers in the area. This is a positive externality. The farmer does not get any of the benefit, so he has no incentive to grow more crops to increase the production of honey. Since bees cannot be convinced to keep contracts there is no practical way to apply Coase's approach. We must either subsidize farmers to grow more nectar-rich crops (a Pigouvian subsidy) or accept the inefficiency created by the positive externality. It turns out that Meade is wrong. Steve Cheung showed in an article on the honey industry that contracts between beekeepers and farmers do exist and have existed for the longest time. When the crops were producing nectar and did not need pollenization, beekeepers paid farmers for permission to put their hives close to the farmers' fields. When the crops were producing little nectar but needed pollenization (to increase yields), farmers paid beekeepers. Bees do not keep contracts, but bees, like people, are lazy and prefer to forage close to the hives.

References: Meade, James E. "External Economies and Diseconomies in a Competitive Situation, *Economic Journal* 62(1952): 54–67; Cheung, Steven N.S. "The Fable of the Bees: An Economic Investigation," *Journal of Law and Economics,* 16(1973): 11–33.

THE CRITICAL ASSUMPTIONS

While establishing this very important point, we have been making two implicit assumptions. The first assumption is that there are no transaction costs, and the second is that there are no wealth effects.

To start with the latter first, what do we mean by "no wealth effects?" As you must have realized by now, the different legal rules lead to the same (efficient) solution, but in the end the parties involved have different financial consequences. In the first example about the confectioner and the doctor, the confectioner bargained with the doctor and paid—depending on the outcome of their bargain—between $50 and $80 to make him move his consulting room. In the second example, the doctor ended up paying between $40 and $50 to the confectioner to make him install the new mortars. In the first example, the confectioner pays money; in the second he gets money. The reverse holds for the doctor. So the legal rules affect the money flows and the financial position of the parties involved. These differences in financial consequences have, in the end, different effects on the wealth of the parties (they get richer or poorer depending upon the legal rule). When people's wealth position changes, this may affect their consumption or savings behavior or their working behavior (they might, for instance, work harder to gain back the money they have paid to the other party, and the other party might work less after the deal). These wealth effects on consumption, savings, and labor supply are economic effects and the economic outcome will differ between legal rules if these wealth effects are substantial.

It is not only the wealth position after the property rights have been assigned that has economic effects. Initial wealth holdings—or to put it more simply, whether people are rich or poor to start with—can have an influence on the final outcome of an assignment of property rights. For example, suppose you have a house on the coast across the street from a vacant lot that is on the beach. You have a beautiful view of the beach as long as no one builds on the lot across from you or builds only one floor. According to the Coase theorem, whether the person across the street has the right to build the second floor or you have the right to block it will not determine whether the floor will be constructed. Suppose you really do not want the second floor to be built but have only $10,000. The neighbor values building the floor at $20,000. If your neighbor is assigned the right, you will not be able to buy the right away and it will stay with the neighbor. On the other hand, suppose it is assigned to you. Your neighbor may offer you $20,000, but you say no. Why is this? The problem is that you must have wealth to buy, but you need no wealth to decline an offer. In effect, the assignment of the right may influence its ultimate allocation. The impact may mean that initial allocations are "sticky" in that they are not always undone by the parties even when it seems as though they should be.

Does this mean the Coase theorem is wrong? Not really. What the Coase theorem says is that the right ends up in the hands of the party who values it most. Value in this context means willingness and ability to pay. In the example, this is the case. When it was assigned to your neighbor, you could offer only $10,000 and so that is the measure of how much you valued the right. On the other hand, the Coase theorem does not rule out the possibility that the assignment itself will have an impact on its eventual allocation. Still, you should know that one criticism of the Coase theorem is that the outcome is indeterminate. By this, the critics mean that the "efficient" allocation cannot be known until the allocation is actually made.

COASIAN EXPERIMENTS

Economists and law professors frequently perform experiments to determine whether the Coase theorem "works." Some of the earliest experiments were performed by Matthew Spitzer and Elizabeth Hoffman. One of their first efforts involved an exercise like the following. Teams of two were given a list of possible payoffs for Player A and Player B. It would look something like this:

PAYOFF	PLAYER A	PLAYER B
1	$8	$6
2	$9	$2
3	$10	$0

Player A was assigned the role of controller and could select an option and the payoff would be distributed as indicated in the chart. The other player could attempt to influence that decision. As you can see, Player A would be tempted to select option 3 and maximize his payoff. In terms of property rights, you could say that A is assigned the right to select that option. On the other hand, you can also see that, if a deal could be struck, it would be better for the "team" for Player A to select option 1. It would mean a total payoff of $14 instead of $10. The question is whether Player B can negotiate with A to influence him to select option 1. What Hoffman and Spitzer found was that in the vast majority of instances, the controller did give up the right to select option 3 in favor of option 1. In other words, the players overcame the initial allocation. This is comparable to the confectioner and the doctor in the text negotiating to the point of treating the noise externality at the lowest cost.

The Hoffman and Spitzer experiments suggest the Coase theorem does work. There was an interesting wrinkle, however. It probably occurred to you, looking at the payoff matrix, that the way to get to the total payoff of $14 was for Player B to pay Player A. In other words, B could give A enough of his share that A would still get at least $10, as he would have if he had chosen option 3. In fact, the participants demonstrated a far greater propensity to divide the total income of the payoff evenly. In short, controllers were generally willing to move to the joint income-maximizing outcome while not maximizing their personal income. We return to the implications of this in Chapter 30.

Reference: Mark Hoffman and Elizabeth Spitzer, "The Coase Theorem: Some Empirical Tests," *Journal of Law and Economics* 25, no. 73 (1982).

The other implicit assumption, which is certainly not innocuous, concerns transaction costs. In all our examples so far, we have assumed that both parties involved could effortlessly and without any costs conclude a bargain about how to deal with the external effect and draw up a contract that stipulated their terms of agreement. In real life, bargaining and making deals and drawing up contracts involves costs. These costs are called transaction costs.

IT ALL DEPENDS ON TRANSACTION COSTS

Although we are introducing transaction costs here in the context of externalities transaction costs, they are obviously an integral part of all market transactions (buying, selling, lending, leasing, renting, hiring, etc.). Transaction costs are the costs of running an economic system such as a market system. The core activity of a market system is that the supplier and the demander make a contract (for the sale, the lease, the hire, etc.). In order to get to a contract, you first have to incur costs in order to find a partner with whom to make a contract (find somebody who is willing to sell, lend, or rent you something you want or find an employer who is willing to hire you). These search and information costs involve buying a newspaper and checking the advertisements, phoning around, traveling to the other party, checking the goods, and so on. Next, you have to bargain about the terms of the contract (date of delivery, payment, after-sale service). These are the costs of drawing up a contract. Finally, there are the costs of monitoring the execution of a contract (Does the other party deliver on time? Is the quality satisfactory? Does he pay on time?), and there are the costs of dealing with noncompliance and, if worse comes to worse, there are costs related to breach of contract. All of these costs are elements of transaction costs. In the examples above, we assumed them away; we assumed that parties could reach an agreement without effort or costs. Real life, however, is different and transaction costs do affect the outcome of a legal rule, as we will see in the next section.

LAW AND ECONOMICS IN ACTION 5.3

THE ENDOWMENT EFFECT

The most interesting aspect of the wealth effect is that it can be unrelated to actual wealth. In other words, individuals do change valuation depending on the reference point, but the reference point has nothing to do with differences in ability to pay. As an example, think about this experiment. A group of people were gathered together and brought into a room. As each one entered he or she was given either $3.00 or a ticket to a raffle. The terms of the raffle were explained to the group. It was for coupons redeemable for books worth $70 or $50 in cash. At that point, the participants were permitted to exchange what they were given. Those who received $3.00 were permitted to buy raffle tickets for that amount. Those who possessed raffle tickets could sell them for $3.00. Since they all heard the same information about the raffle, you would expect that a consensus would have formed about whether the raffle was a good gamble based on the expected value of winning. This would be the probability of winning times the value of the prize. Thus, in the experiment, if the expected benefit were $4.00 one would expect all those receiving $3.00 to trade it for a ticket, and if it were worth less than $3.00 one would expect people to sell their raffle tickets.

In fact, 82 percent of the participants who received tickets elected to keep them. And, 64 percent of those who had received $3.00 elected to keep the money rather than trade it for a ticket. In other words, whatever objective value the raffle had, it was perceived differently by the participants. This effect is very much like the wealth effect but receiving the $3.00 or the raffle ticket in the initial allocation seems very unlikely to determine the ability of the participants to pay. Instead, what seems to be at work is something more like an "endowment effect"—meaning that simple possession of something determines how much one values it. More generally, one's perception of value was a function of a reference point that had little to do with wealth per se.

Reference: Jack L. Knetsch and J. A. Sinden, "Willingness to Pay and Compensation Demanded: Experimental Evidence of Disparity in Measures of Value," *Quarterly Journal of Economics* 99 (1984): 507.

In the previous section, we presented examples involving two neighbors and one pollution problem. In the first example, the cost to move the confectioner was $80. The cost to move the doctor was $50. The difference between these two amounts is substantial enough to cover transaction costs and still leave enough room for a deal that benefits both parties. Even if it had taken them some time and effort to reach an agreement, the cost involved in drawing up a contract would still have been small compared with the costs of the externalities and the difference in costs to solve the harmful effect. But suppose the cost of contracting exceeded $30. Then the contract would not be made because the cost of the reallocation exceeds the gain. In other words, the benefit of the transaction is the difference between the costs of avoiding the harm, and this is compared with the transaction cost.

But take the example of noise pollution created by an airplane. Anyone who has taken an airplane to Hong Kong and landed at its international airport knows that the plane passes so close to high-rise apartments that it is almost possible to see from the plane what the inhabitants are having for breakfast. The noise pollution is substantial. Why is it not eliminated? Transaction costs can make Coasian bargaining contracts impossible to make. Suppose the legal rule was that the people of Hong Kong have the right to silence. In that case, the airline companies landing in Hong Kong would have to conclude contracts with the many million inhabitants of Hong Kong who are affected by airplane noise in a small or a big way. The transaction costs of finding all the victims, establishing how much they are affected, negotiating with them, and drawing up contracts are large and preclude any solution in this way.

Suppose the airplanes have the right to pollute and to make the noise. Then all the million inhabitants of Hong Kong have each individually to bribe the polluter to stop making the noise. The individual cost for each person in Hong Kong to track down the airline company and to sit down and conclude a contract and to monitor the contract afterward might be larger than the individual harm one is experiencing from the noise. If these prohibitively high transaction costs do not stop individuals from taking action, there is also the "free rider" aspect because of the public good character of noise pollution.[8]

---

8. You may want to go back to Chapter 3 to review what it means to be a free rider.

The noise pollution affects everybody. If there are a million victims and 900,000 get together to buy off the polluter, then 100,000 other victims are free riding. Knowing this will reduce the willingness of the first 900,000 to pay off the airline companies. Because of possible free riding, each victim has an incentive not to pay, and the attempt to bribe the sound polluter to stop the sound will fail. The problem becomes harder the more people get involved.

In this case, individual bargaining will not lead to the efficient solution of the externality because high transaction costs make it impossible; therefore, it will not suffice for the government to issue a property right and leave it to the parties concerned to bargain their way to an efficient outcome. It may be preferable for the government to gather all the necessary information on the costs and the benefits of air travel and the location of the airport if it wants to enact an efficient rule. Based on this, it might conclude that the benefits outweigh the costs but that the airplane noise has to be constrained in some way. As explained in the previous chapter, this can be done by command and control rules (for instance, limit landing and taking off to between 8:00 A.M. and 8:00 P.M.) or by imposing an environmental tax on each decibel of noise emitted by the airplane landing or taking off.

A final factor that is sometimes equated with transaction costs arises not when there are many potential parties but when there are few. For example, go back to our example of the confectioner and the doctor. Again, it costs the confectioner $80 to move and the doctor $50. Further suppose the doctor has the legal right to have the noise reduced. As already discussed, the confectioner will want to buy that right for anything less than $80, and the doctor would presumably sell it for anything over $50. If you think about the situation as a market for the right, there is one demander—the confectioner—and one seller—the doctor. This is known as a bilateral monopoly. As the seller knows the buyer cannot buy the right from anyone else, he may demand $79. As the buyer knows that there are no competing buyers, he may offer only $51. At that point, the parties may be tempted to stall, bluff, and maneuver so extensively that the exchange is delayed or may not happen at all.

SOME IMPLICATIONS OF TRANSACTION COSTS

Back in Chapter 3 when you were learning the basics of property, you also learned that property and rights more generally tend to be protected through the use of property rules, liability rules, and inalienability. Under a property rule, the party taking or damaging your property without permission may be punished. Liability rules require only that the interfering party compensate you for your loss. Inalienability means that the property or right cannot be sold.

The existence of transaction costs has important implications for how and when these rules may be applied.[9] First, take a case of low transaction costs: someone drives by your apartment and sees an old motorcycle that you are restoring. It would be very easy for the person to find you and attempt to negotiate a price and draw up a simple sales contract. In short, the transaction costs of a change in ownership would be low and it makes sense to require—through the use of a property rule—the potential buyer to negotiate with you about the price you are willing to take. In fact, unless that negotiation takes place, it is hard to be sure that the exchange would be efficient or Pareto superior.

In other instances, transaction costs are high. For example, suppose you are walking down a country road when a thunderstorm breaks out. Lightning strikes are all around and you look for shelter. The only thing you see is a barn on the property of a farmer and you would like to go in the barn but that would violate the rights of the farmer and you cannot find him or her. In effect, you would like to rent the barn until the storm passes but transaction costs are high. In this and other high transaction costs instances, it makes sense to apply liability rules. More specifically, liability rules are attractive when an exchange would be likely to take place if it were not prevented by high transaction costs. In effect, the law allows you to use the barn but you may have to compensate the farmer at the fair market value. You should note that this involuntary transaction is not necessarily efficient because we cannot know if the farmer would have been willing to accept the fair market value.

The final rule—inalienability—can also be connected to transaction costs although it is not clear that economic considerations alone can explain every rule of inalienability. For example, in the United States

---

9. Guido Calabresi and A. Douglas Melamed, "Property Rules. Liability Rules and Inalienability: One View of the Cathedral," *Harvard Law Review* 85 (1972): 1089.

it is illegal to sell human organs. One way to square this with a transaction costs analysis is to realize that to many people the selling of organs is reprehensible. The idea of people buying and selling kidneys, for example, is deeply disturbing to them. It is so disturbing that they are willing to pay to know that they live in a society in which organ sales are prohibited. Obviously, transaction costs are so high that those opposing organ sales could not possibly find all potential sellers and negotiate with them not to sell. In addition, there are likely to be free-rider problems. In these instances, prohibiting sales may actually be efficient but such a prohibition would not be an outcome the market could produce.

CONCLUSIONS

The main point that Ronald Coase made in his article is that the market system will take care of externalities automatically and in an efficient way as long as property rights are well defined. This insight has been dubbed the Coase theorem:

> If transaction costs are zero—if in other words, any agreement that is to the mutual benefit of the parties concerned gets made—then any initial definition of property rights leads to an efficient outcome.[10]

The Coase theorem is powerful: When two parties can bargain without transaction costs, the resulting outcome will be economically efficient. One extreme interpretation of the Coase theorem is that the legal system does not matter. Whatever the allocation of initial property rights, individuals and businesses will reallocate these rights through private bargaining and market transactions. They will reallocate until the distribution of property rights is efficient. In the text box on the economics of a prisoner-of-war (POW) camp, we illustrate reallocation of an initial distribution of Red Cross aid packages in World War II prisoner-of-war camps whereby at the end an efficient allocation was achieved. What happened in this special world is similar to what one could imagine happening in another special world with zero transaction costs.

10. Coase, "The Problem of Social Cost," 23.

THE ECONOMICS OF THE POW CAMP

During the Second World War, allied prisoners in German war camps would regularly receive packages with food and toiletries from the Red Cross. All packages had the same content: coffee, tea, chocolate, can of baked beans, can of fruit, soap, shaving cream, shaving blades, and of course cigarettes. In terms of our discussion of the Coase theorem, this was the initial distribution of property (rights). Of course, preferences varied from prisoner to prisoner. The British preferred tea to coffee whereas the French preferred coffee to tea. Bearded men did not really want the shaving stuff, but might desire cigarettes, which nonsmokers wanted to get rid of. Very soon, and spontaneously, a market opened in which these initial articles were traded among the prisoners. In the end, the contents of the Red Cross packages had been reallocated among the prisoners and the result was that everyone was happier. In terms of our discussion in this chapter, an efficient solution was achieved.

Reference: R. A. Radford, "The Economics of the POW Camp," *Economica* 12 (1945): 189–201.

If the implications of the Coase theorem for the economics of externalities are substantial, those for law in general are even more revolutionary, for the theorem tells us that the content of a legal rule does not matter as much as one might think. There has to be a clear legal rule, but what it says is hardly relevant. We will have the same amount of pollution (clean air, silence, clean water) regardless of whether polluters or victims are liable. We can extend these conclusions to other areas of the law. The same amount of effort will be devoted to precaution against causing tortious injury independent of whether injurers or victims are held liable for the harm caused.[11] The parties will bargain among themselves and the party with the lowest cost of precaution will always end up taking the precaution. Or as Medema and Zerba put it: "Attempts of judges to engage in social engineering from the bench will be fruitless, apart from distributional (as opposed to

---

11. As you will see in Unit 4, "tortious" conduct is usually a reference to accidents.

allocational) effects. Assuming that rights are alienable, the allocation of resources will be the same regardless of the rule of law, and that allocation will be efficient."[12] The "distributional" effects that Medema and Zerba refer to are similar to what we defined as "wealth effects."

The interpretation we just discussed rests very much on the assumption that transaction costs are zero (or are, in any case, negligible). Transaction costs almost always are not zero and are often substantial. In those cases, the initial distribution of property rights matters immensely. If these property rights are not allocated in an efficient way, then transaction costs will prohibit the parties involved achieving efficiency afterward. In those cases, whenever governments are assigning property rights (to pollute or to be pollution free) or when courts have to decide who has the right (to do something or not), they could consider the efficiency effects of their decision. If we think that economic efficiency is the criterion to go by, then when transaction costs are positive, rights should be assigned to those who would possess them in the end-state when transaction costs are zero; that is, the legal system should "mimic the market." Note that this last statement is valid only if economic efficiency (or what is otherwise known in the law and economics literature as "wealth maximization") is the norm, and this is a normative assumption that surpasses the simple message about the presence or absence of efficiency that Ronald Coase was making in his famous article.

CASE 5.2 **Separated and Living Together:** *Coltman v. Commissioner of Internal Revenue,* 980 F.2d 1134 (7th Cir. 1992)

> One of the bedrock implications of the Coase theorem is that markets work best when rights and rules are clearly assigned. It may surprise you to find that the Coase theorem has influenced some court opinions, including the one described here dealing with taxation. To understand it, you only have to know—if you do not already—that taxpayers are permitted to deduct certain expenses from their income before paying federal income tax. Also, you

12. Steven G. Medema and R. O. Zerba, "The Coase Theorem," in *Encyclopedia of Law and Economics,* ed. Boudewijn Bouckaert and Gerrit de Geest (Cheltenham: Edward Elgar, 2000) 5:839.

should know that a taxpayer's nonpayment of taxes is something that is determined by a commissioner. When the taxpayer challenges that decision, the commissioner becomes the defendant in the lawsuit. With that information, consider the following:

SHADUR, SENIOR DISTRICT JUDGE

This . . . dispute involves the income tax deductibility or nondeductibility of payments made by a husband to his estranged wife pursuant to a court order during taxable years in which, though they were actively engaged in divorce proceedings, he had not removed himself entirely from the family residence. Bertram Coltman, Jr. ("Bertram") disputes the assertion by the Commissioner of Internal Revenue of a tax deficiency stemming from Bertram's deduction of those payments in 1982 and 1983. . . .

Before the Tax Court Bertram lost and the Commissioner won. . . . [Bertram then appealed.]

During the tax years at issue the relevant provisions of the Internal Revenue [were as follows]:

Section 71(a)(3):

Decree for Support. If a wife is separated from her husband, the wife's gross income includes periodic payments (whether or not made at regular intervals) received by her after the date of the enactment of this title from her husband under a decree entered after March 1, 1954, requiring the husband to make the payments for her support or maintenance. This paragraph shall not apply if the husband and wife make a single return jointly.

Section 215(a):

General Rule. In the case of a husband described in section 71, there shall be allowed as a deduction amounts includible under section 71 in the gross income of his wife, payment of which is made within the husband's taxable year.

Section 71 was fleshed out by [the following Treasury Regulation]:

(3) Decree for support. (i) Where the husband and wife are separated and living apart and do not file a joint income tax return for the taxable year, paragraph (3) of section 71(a) requires the inclusion in the gross income of the wife of periodic payments . . . received by her . . . from her husband under any type of court order or decree . . . requiring the husband to make the payments for her support or

maintenance. It is necessary for the wife to be legally separated or divorced from her husband under a court order or decree; nor is it necessary for the order or decree for support to be for the purpose of enforcing a written separation agreement.

Before the Tax Court the battle lines formed over the question whether the fact of the parties' living (at least part-time) under the same roof automatically rendered Bertram's payments nondeductible. . . .

During the taxable years at issue, which included the time of the Coltmans' divorce trial, Bertram used the family residence in suburban Winnetka, Illinois as a part-time waystation between his real residence in Kenosha (where he was living with a "significant other" for most of the week) and his business in Chicago. We will not dwell as the parties have on the details of Bertram's living arrangements, for we view the matter as controlled by . . . Section 71.

To be sure, the statutory word "separated" could arguably be read either (1) as demanding only the spouses' total marital estrangement (something that could coincide with their living separate lives under the same roof) or (2) as also requiring at least the spouses' physical separation by their not sharing the same home at all. But the Commissioner certainly made a rational choice by opting for the latter requirement in the course of construing the statute via the regulation. "Separated and living apart" is thus a valid reading of the congressional term "separated," and we reject Bertram's effort to invoke a skewed reading of "living apart" that would encompass the lifestyle that he and Michelle followed in 1982 and 1983.

One related final observation may be made, not as a reason for the result that we have reached based on the regulation's reading of Section 71, but as to the effect of that result. This is certainly an area in which a bright-line rule affords a real advantage to taxpayers, who can negotiate (or who can obtain judicial rulings as to) their financial arrangements during the unpleasantness of the pre-divorce-decree period, with full knowledge as to whether they are dealing in pre-tax or post-tax dollars. It provides a classic illustration of the Coase Theorem, which has earned Professor Ronald Coase a long-belated but much-deserved Nobel Prize: So long as the rule of law is known when parties act, the ultimate economic result is the same no matter which way the law has resolved the issue. That of course provides cold comfort for Bertram, who has had the misfortune to negotiate without that degree of legal certainty.

QUESTIONS FOR DISCUSSION

1. In Chapter 1, you were told the true story of the mathematicians with new offices who were not sure how to allocate them. One approach to allocation was an auction. Others could be by seniority, or even height, weight, or the flip of a coin. What does the Coase theorem tell you about the final distribution?

2. Suppose a factory is dumping waste into a river. Downstream there are ten residents who like to use the river for fishing and boating, but the pollution is impairing the usefulness of the river for these purposes. In fact, an appraiser estimates that each resident's property would be worth $60,000 if the river were clean. It would cost the factory $500,000 to dispose of the waste in a way that does not harm the river. The residents ask a court to enjoin the factory from polluting but lose. In a transaction-cost-free environment, what do you think would happen? In this actual situation, do you see factors that may prevent that from happening?

3. Think back to the confectioner and the doctor in the text. Suppose the confectioner could install insulation that would eliminate the noise for $100 and that the doctor could eliminate the noise for $50. They get into an argument, with the confectioner maintaining that he has a right to make noise and the doctor claiming he has the right to be free of the noise. They go to court about the issue. If you were the judge, who would win? Why? Would it make a difference if the doctor was there first?

CHAPTER SIX

Government Takings and Compensation

THE PREVIOUS CHAPTERS HAVE DEMONSTRATED THAT WHAT it means to "own" something is largely a governmental or political decision. This actually understates the role of the government and courts in defining property rights. As it turns out, what the government creates—property rights—it can also take away or limit. For example, suppose you own land that is perfect for connecting two sections of highway and the government would like to use it for that purpose. Or suppose you enjoy playing loud music in a bar you own and the city you live in wants to pass a law that will prohibit loud music; as a result, you would have fewer customers and your profits would decrease. These examples raise the issue of the government's power to either take or regulate your property. This power is called "takings," and this chapter explores its workings and implications.

Takings are necessary for public goods that a competitive market doesn't supply, such as roads, parks, dikes, canals, power lines. They are also sometimes necessary to remedy externalities such as noise and air pollution. Most countries, including the United States, have a requirement that the government not be able to take the property of private individuals without some form of compensation. There are good reasons for this. A policy that would permit governments to freely take property would reduce the incentive of the government to be careful about what it takes. In addition, it would fundamentally alter what it means to "own" something. The rule would be more along the lines of "you own it but only if the government does not want it." This would certainly reduce the incentive of the "owner" to invest in his property: Why try to improve or expand if the government can always take it away tomorrow? Thus, in most countries, the government may "take" property under certain conditions, but it must compensate the owner. The first section of the chapter summarizes the legal issues that arise when the government takes property.

The potential for government takings raises many challenging economic questions, not all of which can be answered.[1] First, why should the government have a right to take at all? Why not require the government, like other buyers, to go into the market and pay what is necessary to acquire the rights? These issues are discussed in the second section. Second, if the government does take, why should it be required to provide compensation? This is discussed in the third section. It may seem like a strange question, but remember that under the Kaldor-Hicks standard of efficiency, compensation is not required. All that would be required in a takings context would be that the public value the land for its use more than the owner values it for private use.[2] Obviously, the owners from whom the land is taken would experience this as grossly unfair. Third, if compensation is required, at what level? This question is the focus of the fourth section. The last part of the chapter considers whether the law of takings is consistent with sound economics.

1. For a more detailed analysis of the law, see William A. Fischel, *Regulatory Takings: Law, Economics, and Politics* (Cambridge: Harvard University Press, 1995).

2. Note also that the Kaldor-Hicks standard of efficiency is about static efficiency. The property that is taken has a given value both in its private use and in its public use. If at this moment in time the value in public use is higher than the value in private use, it is obviously efficient to reallocate the property from the private owner to the public. Compensation does not enter this efficiency comparison. However, from a dynamic efficiency perspective, taking without compensation could be worrisome. As we said in the beginning, if the government can take property without due consideration then we take away the incentive for owners to maintain and invest in property.

TAKINGS ISSUES

In the United States, protection from government "taking" is found in the Takings Clause of the Fifth Amendment to the U.S. Constitution, which prohibits taking "private property . . . for public use without just compensation."[3] As a historical matter, the clause was a reaction to a period during which state governments freely took property from individuals without compensation. Specifically, in the years leading up to the writing of the Constitution, land and other property was frequently taken for military use during time of war. It was felt that citizens needed some assurance that this would no longer happen.

It is important to note that the takings clause gives governments permission to take, yet it limits them at the same time.[4] In effect, the government may take without permission as long as it does so for a "public" use. If it is a permissible taking, then the government must pay for the property. Cases that arise deal with one of three issues. First, has the government engaged in a taking? The preferred position of the government would be to influence the use of property but not have it ruled as a taking. Under these circumstances, the government is not required to pay. Second, the government concedes that it has taken property and is willing to pay fair market value, but the owners argue that the government may not take the property at all because it is not for "public use." Note that the government may still obtain the property by buying it. Finally, even if it is a taking for public use, the issue of what is fair compensation remains.

This may seem straightforward, and in some instances it is. If the federal government takes your land—under a power called "eminent domain"—in order to build a road, there is obviously a taking for "public use" and you must be given "just compensation"—which means fair market value. On the other hand, questions of what is a "taking," "a public use," and "just compensation" have all been repeatedly litigated and the issues can be complicated. This is espe-

---

3. The Fifth Amendment applies to action by the federal government. The Fourteenth Amendment extends the prohibitions of the Fifth Amendment to actions by state governments.

4. The limitation applies to the federal government and to state and local governments as well.

cially the case when the government does not want physically to possess the land but regulates in a way that causes it to decline in value.

For example, in a well-known case, the state of South Carolina prohibited a beachfront landowner from building residences on his property.[5] The state did not want to possess or occupy the land but argued that the regulation was necessary to preserve South Carolina's beaches. In another case, the owner of property in Washington, D.C., was prohibited from building on some recently subdivided lots because the parcel of land as a whole was viewed as a historical landmark.[6] Again, the government did not want physically to possess the land but wanted to limit what the owners could do. An even more perplexing issue arose in Hawaii in the early 1980s.[7] Hawaii was originally settled by Polynesians who developed an economy based on a feudal land system. Until the early 1980s, approximately 50 percent of Hawaii's land was owned by seventy-two families. Interestingly, the remaining 50 percent was owned by the state and federal government. In order to undo what was an oligopoly in land ownership, the Hawaiian government developed a complex procedure that would permit those leasing land to buy the land from owners at fair market value. Those forced to sell land protested and based their argument on the Constitutional requirement that government takings be for "public use." In this instance, the land would end up privately owned and used.

In the aftermath of these and many other cases, the United States law of "takings" can only be very generally summarized. First, in the Hawaii case, the Supreme Court held that the taking was for public use, the public use being the need to end the feudal-land system. This obviously means that governments have broad discretion to "take" property for "public use." Second, when the government permanently physically occupies the land or makes it possible for someone else to do so, there is a taking, and compensation is required. The compensation must be at fair market value, which is determined by the

5. *Lucas v. South Carolina Coastal Council*, 505 U.S. 1003 (1992).

6. *District Intown Properties Limited Partnership v. District of Columbia*, 198 F.3d 874, cert. denied, 531 U.S. 812 (2000). "Cert. denied," which means "certiorari denied," is a notation meaning that the losing party in the case asked the U.S. Supreme Court to consider its appeal but the Court refused.

7. *Hawaii Housing Authority v. Midkiff*, 467 U.S. 229 (1984).

average price at which similar properties have sold. Third, when the use of the land is regulated and the impact is only economic, it is only a taking if the economic impact is so great that the value of the land is eliminated or virtually so. Finally, when the regulation has a partial economic impact, compensation will be required on a case-by-case basis depending upon the economic impact to the owner, the reasonable expectations of the owner when the land was acquired, and the type of government action. Figure 6.1 summarizes this, but keep in mind that these are broad generalizations and it is not always easy to predict the outcome of a takings case.

Action	Taking?	Example
1. Physical occupation by government.	Yes	Land is taken to build a highway.
2. Regulation rendering property nearly worthless to owners.	Yes	Livestock are banned from land suited primarily for cattle.
3. Regulation partially reducing value of property to owner.	Depends on type of action, expectations of owner when property acquired, and economic impact.	Beachfront property cannot be used for dwellings.

FIGURE 6.1 Is It a Taking?

CASE 6.1 Smoking: *D.A.B.E., Inc. v. City of Toledo*, 393 F.3d 692 (Fed. App. 2005)

It is one thing to say that the Fifth Amendment protects individuals from government takings with compensation and quite another to know when it occurs. One thing that is clear is that it is not a taking merely because the government action makes property worth less. For example, suppose you own a bar or restaurant and people come there to drink and smoke. In fact, for some smoking and drinking are complementary activities—the more they do of one, the more they do of the other. Now the city says "no smoking" unless you construct within your establishment an area that completely isolates smokers from nonsmokers. You have a choice of incurring the expense or losing sales, which may happen anyway if you reconfigure your floor plan. Quite literally, the government has taken an element of your property rights. This was what happened in *D.A.B.E.* D.A.B.E. ran Arnie's saloon and complained that the regulation amounted to a taking. The court's reasoning will provide further insight into the complexity of takings.

> The Supreme Court has recognized two categories of takings: regulatory and physical. . . . Appellants allege the former. Furthermore, their attack on the ordinance is limited to a facial challenge, which requires them to prove that the "mere enactment" of the ordinance constitutes a taking of their property. According to the Supreme Court, the test to be applied in considering facial challenges such as this one is "fairly straightforward." Under that test, "[a] statute regulating the uses that can be made of property effects a taking if it denies an owner economically viable use of his land. . . .
>
> The evidence presented in this case fails to establish that, on its face, the Clean Indoor Air Ordinance denies appellants "economically viable use" of their respective properties. Appellants have submitted affidavits alleging that they have lost—or fear they will lose—customers as a result of the ordinance, because smoking is an activity in which many customers wish to engage while patronizing their establishments. Even if true, however, those allegations are simply not enough to satisfy appellants' burden of proof.
>
> In [*Hodel v. Va. Surface Mining & Reclamation Ass'n*, 452 U.S. 264] the Supreme Court held that the Surface Mining Control and Reclamation Act did not, on its face, effect a regulatory taking because of three features of the Act: first, it did not, "on its face, prevent beneficial use of coal-bearing lands;" second, it did not "categorically prohibit surface coal mining" but "merely regulate[d] the conditions under which such operations may be conducted;" and third, it did not "purport to regulate alternative uses to which coal-bearing lands may be put." The same factors that compelled the Court's conclusion in *Hodel* apply in this case. First, there is nothing on the face of the Clean Indoor Air Ordinance that prevents the "beneficial use" of appellants' property. To the contrary, the ordinance has absolutely no effect on any aspect of appellants' businesses other than to restrict the areas in which appellants' patrons may smoke. Second, the ordinance does not "categorically prohibit" smoking inside appellants' establishments; it "merely regulates

the conditions under which" smoking is permitted. We recognize that the construction of separate smoking lounges in most cases will require some financial investment, but an ordinance does not effect a taking merely because compliance with it "requires the expenditure of money." Finally, for obvious reasons, the ordinance does not "purport to regulate alternative uses" of appellants' respective properties. Therefore, pursuant to *Hodel*, it is clear that appellants have failed to establish that the Clean Indoor Air Ordinance, on its face, effects a regulatory taking of their property.

WHY SHOULD THE GOVERNMENT BE PERMITTED TO TAKE AT ALL? ECONOMIC JUSTIFICATIONS

A taking by the government is basically a forced sale. In effect, it allows the government to change what would be a property rule to a liability rule. (Recall from Chapter 5 that a property rule means that if you take something from someone without permission, you get penalized; a liability rule means that you can take something without permission, but you have to pay for it.) That is, usually a buyer must negotiate with a seller and attempt to find a mutually agreeable price. The government's position is more like someone who has accidentally collided with your car and can simply pay you the fair market value.

This raises the question of whether there is any economic reason for allowing the government to bypass the process that you or I would have to observe. In other words, why shouldn't the government have to go into the market like any other buyer and pay the price required in order to obtain what it needs or wants? In many ways, this would reduce a great deal of controversy. For example, in the South Carolina case, it is almost certainly true that for the right amount of money the landowner would have happily abandoned his "right" to build residences on his beachfront lots. Similarly, in the Hawaii case, the same outcome could have been achieved had the state of Hawaii simply bought the land from the landowners and then auctioned it off or even given it away. This sounds like a simple solution, but as will be explained below, it conceals the fact that when the government enters the market, it may be at a disadvantage compared to other buyers. What the empowering part of the Takings Clause does is to allow the government to purchase land at market value—the price other buyers would have been required to pay.

A JUDGE LOOKS AT THE ECONOMICS OF TAKINGS

If you think all judges are unaware of the economic implications of their decisions, consider the reasoning of Judge Stephen F. Williams in a recent case.[8]

> The economist's justification for the Takings Clause is that it provides a check on government's likely tendency to waste resources by treating private property as a free good. . . . This is just an application of the general principle that if a firm can externalize costs (e.g., the health costs of polluting the air), it will use more of the unpriced resource (in this example, air as a waste sink) than it would if required to pay. And it will tend to overproduce the goods or services whose production uses the superficially "free" good—i.e. it will produce them at a level where the true value of the extra inputs exceeds the true value of the extra output. . . . As applied to government regulation, similar oversupply can be expected—here, production of regulations that impose more costs than they afford benefits, that do more harm than good.

Judge Williams wrote a concurring opinion, which means he agreed with other members of the court with respect to the outcome of the case but wanted to express some reasoning that was not found in the opinion written by the other judges.

Because the government must still pay what other purchasers would have to pay, why is the Takings Clause of any benefit? There are instances in which taking, even at the fair market price, would be better for the government than it would be in the absence of the Takings Clause and, therefore, ultimately to taxpayers who must finance these forced purchases. This is easy to understand when you consider the nature of the type of need a government exhibits when it goes into the market for land.

---

8. Judge Williams serves on the U.S. Court of Appeals for the District of Columbia. The case was *District Intown Properties Limited Partnership v. District of Columbia*, 198 F.3d 874 (1999).

First, consider the construction of a highway. There will obviously be an economical route for the highway to take—probably one that goes near population centers and avoids especially expensive construction problems. These parcels of land will be contiguous. The point is that as soon as the route of the highway becomes clear, each landowner may gain a significant amount of monopoly power with respect to the government. Interestingly, this power generally will extend only to a single purchaser—the government—because buyers for other purposes will likely have many other choices. In these instances, the government escapes paying the premium as the government's great need for the land is not reflected in the fair market value.

Second, consider the case in which the government wants to regulate the activity taking place on certain land. For example, suppose several businesses along a coastal area are polluting in a way that harms the people living in adjacent areas, and the only solution is to close the businesses. The fair market value of the businesses is equal to the present value of future profits, but the owners can ask for more because the property is uniquely valuable to the government—because there are no substitute parcels of land for the government to buy in order to achieve a decrease in pollution. Because taking is permitted, the government can avoid paying the premium associated with its particular need and pay the fair market value (which equals the opportunity cost for the business owners).

A third possibility arises when the state wishes to carry out a project for which it needs a large parcel of land. Suppose the land is subdivided and owned by a variety of people. Further suppose that unless all parcels are acquired, the entire parcel is worthless. If the state must negotiate to acquire each parcel, not only will each landowner have power with respect to the state but those who hold out also have power over the other landowners—because each one has veto power with respect to whether the entire parcel will be acquired.

In all three examples, the structure of the negotiation would take the shape of a bilateral monopoly (where there is only one buyer and one seller) and leads to transaction costs, which are not productive from an economic standpoint. Negotiations are one-on-one in a bilateral monopoly and proceed through bargaining. Bargaining strength depends on the threats a bargainer can make to walk away from the bargaining table. This threat to walk away is convincing if there are alternatives to the object one is bargaining about. In the situations discussed earlier, the government can exert hardly any threat at all; as it does not have any alternative, it cannot walk away. This would give the owner of the land tremendous bargaining power. First, the state will pay more than the seller's opportunity cost to acquire the property. For example, suppose there is a parcel of farmland that is worth $10,000 based on the present value of the crops that can be grown there. In addition, suppose farming is the most valued use of the land. Now the government would like the land in order to build a highway that the public values at $30,000, and to reroute the highway the government would have to spend $20,000. The landowner can hold out for a price up to $20,000, the amount needed to reroute. The eventual price will exceed the opportunity cost of the farmer. A requirement that the government pay more than fair market value would probably alter the state's decision making so that projects that are efficient are not undertaken, and this is detrimental to society as a whole. Second, bilateral monopoly is typically associated with high transaction costs—meaning that the process of the exchange itself is burdensome. Here again, there is a risk that a project that taxpayers value more than its cost would not be taken on by the government.

In the three examples above, the amount above the fair market value demanded by the sellers is the result of the opportunity presented when the government wanted the land. A fourth example would save the government money but has consequences that are not as desirable. Suppose the state wants to purchase a parcel of land that has been owned by a certain family for some time. The fair market value is $50,000 but the owners refuse to sell, as a result of sentimental attachments, for less than $75,000. This has nothing to do with the nature of the potential purchaser—the owners would not take less than $75,000 from anyone. Here a taking at $50,000 is permitted, and it does mean less of a burden on taxpayers. On the other hand, the forced exchange may be inefficient. To understand why, think of two of the forms of efficiency we discussed in Chapter 2. Exchanges are Pareto efficient if at least one party is better off and no one is worse off. Exchanges—even involuntary ones—are Kaldor-Hicks efficient, or allocatively efficient, if the party gaining from the exchange (in the case of a taking—the public) is better off by more than the disadvantaged party is made worse off.

Now go back to the landowners who value the land at $75,000 but who are forced to accept $50,000. Obviously the exchange is inefficient from a Paretian standpoint. It may be allocatively inefficient as well unless the government is certain that the property would be put to a use that is valued by the public by more than $75,000. Because the government is permitted to pay fair market value—basically an average—and not the actual value of the land to its current owners, there is a risk that the land will be put to a less valued use.

THE GOVERNMENT CAN TAKE, SO WHY SHOULD IT PAY COMPENSATION? MORE ECONOMIC REASONING

If there are some good reasons for allowing the government to take land and pay "just compensation" (although less than the owners might like), why force the government to pay at all? This would not be unprecedented: In the United States, the government may take the labor of people through the draft and pay less than market value for those services.[9] In addition, taxation itself involves an involuntary transfer.

The most fundamental case for compensation is that it makes inefficient takings less likely. Consider an economic system having a number of possible demanders of land, labor, and capital. Suppose further that one of those possible demanders (i.e., the government) can take the resources it needs (e.g., land) and determine the price it wants to pay or even pay no price at all.

In Figure 6.2, we start with the market for land before there are any government takings. There is a private demand for land and a supply of land. The competitive market price equals P^* and an equilibrium quantity transacted on this market Q_p. As we saw earlier, at market equilibrium consumer and producer surplus are maximized and hence social welfare is at its maximum. Now the government steps in. It needs land to build a road. In Figure 6.2, we introduce the government by shifting the demand curve to the right. (It is a shift because the presence of a major potential buyer like the government actually changes the market.) The new demand curve now represents private plus governmental demand. The shift of the demand curve is deter-

---

9. The practice of drafting people for military service, unlike the taking of land without payment, has been held to be constitutionally permissible.

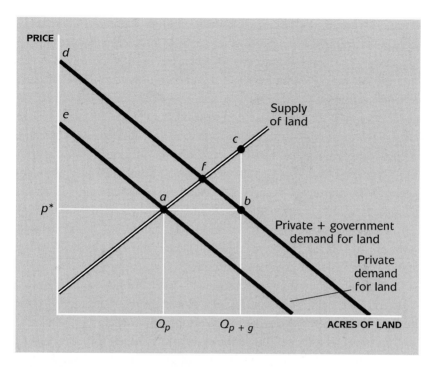

FIGURE 6.2 Social Welfare Effect of Takings

mined by both the number of acres the government needs for road-building and by the price it is willing to pay for the land it needs. The price the government is willing to pay is determined by the extra welfare the new road generates for society. (We will come back to the case in which the road does not raise welfare as much as we assume in Figure 6.2.) The landowners in whose property the government is interested are on that part of the supply curve that is immediately to the right of Q_p.[10]

The government is able to set its own price for the takings. Suppose the government sets the price at which it takes the land at the

10. For convenience of exposition, we have assumed that the suppliers who own the land the government wants to take are on the supply curve immediately to the right of Q_p. This need not be the case, of course. They could be even further out on the supply curve, which would imply they have a higher reservation than those we consider in our discussion and would need a higher price to be fully compensated.

competitive market price P^* that existed before it entered the market. The government takes a number of acres of land, equal to the $Q_{p+g} - Q_p$, and pays P^*. What happens to social welfare? Some suppliers sitting on the supply curve between a and c are forced to sell their land at a price that is below their reservation price. These suppliers lose surplus (producer surplus) equal to the triangle abc. By building the road, society gains surplus (consumer surplus) equal to the trapezoid $edba$. Comparing gains and losses of surplus for society as a whole, the triangle afb is both a producer loss and a consumer gain and cancels out. In net terms, society gains the trapezoid $edfa$ and loses the triangle fcb. The gains are higher than the losses, and the taking and compensation at the previous market price increases social surplus. This is an application of the Kaldor-Hicks or wealth maximization standard of efficiency. The government could, of course, also pay a price that is higher than the market price P^*. When increasing the compensation it pays for its takings above the market price P^*, the government will shift surplus to the suppliers of land.

What happens to welfare if the government does not compensate at all for its takings (i.e., pays a price of zero)? In that case, the loss of surplus for the sellers is equal to the trapezoid $acQ_{p+g}Q_p$. The gain in consumer surplus for society is equal to the trapezoid $abed$ plus (because it gets the land free) the rectangle $abQ_{p+g}Q_p$. The area $afbQ_{p+g}Q_p$ now represents both a gain of consumer surplus and a loss of producer surplus. On the one hand, society has gained more because it gets the land for nothing, but the suppliers lose more because they get no compensation whatsoever. Yet in net terms, society still gains the trapezoid $edba$ and loses the triangle fcb. In Kaldor-Hicks terms, nothing really has changed; there is still more to gain than to lose for society. It terms of redistribution of welfare, the situation is drastically different.

The Kaldor-Hicks balance of winners and losers does not always need to go the way we just analyzed. Suppose, for instance, that the road the government is building contributes only minutely to social welfare. To take this to an extreme, let's take the example of a road that goes from nowhere to nowhere and has no social value. The government still takes the land and pays the market price P^*. Now there is only loss of welfare. The loss is equal to the triangle abc plus the rectangle $abQ_{p+g}Q_p$. The triangle abc is lost because the government pays less for the land than the reservation price of the owners. The rectangle $abQ_{p+g}Q_p$ is lost because the government subsequently uses the land for a road that has no value.

The analysis we just presented requires, of course, that the government know the value of its projects and the costs of those projects. Obviously, there are myriad problems with such a comparison. As a practical matter, whether a compensation requirement makes government decision making more efficient is an empirical question. There are arguments either way. At the very least, the compensation requirement forces the government to focus on the costs of its actions.

Another argument stems from a general preference that taxes be administered in order to be as close as possible to a neutral effect. This usually means spreading tax liability over as great a population as possible. A no-compensation policy would mean that "taxation" would fall disproportionately on a few individuals and create distortions that a neutral policy would not. For example, all government activities that required the use of land would amount to a tax on owning land. This, in turn, would make landowning less attractive than other forms of investment. In addition, power to impose disproportionate taxes increases the threat of arbitrary and punitive actions by public officials.

An additional argument in favor of compensation is that it lessens or avoids costs resulting from demoralization.[11] In other words, the fact of living in a society in which the state may take and not pay for property imposes psychological costs on citizens.[12] This is above and beyond the losses incurred by actually experiencing the taking.

---

11. This possibility was put forth in Frank I. Michelman, "Property, Utility and Fairness: Comments on the Ethical Foundations of 'Just Compensation' Law," *Harvard Law Review* 80 (1967): 1165.

12. An enormous amount of empirical research has been conducted on the relationship between stable private property rights and economic performance. A general consensus has emerged that a system to private property rights is often a requirement for economic development to occur. See Douglass North, "Economic Performance Through History," *American Economic Review* 84 (Summer 1994): 358; Anthony Scott, "The Fishery: The Objective of Sole Ownership," *Journal of Political Economy* (April 1955): 116; Frederick Bell, "Mitigating the Tragedy of the Commons," *Southern Economic Journal* 52 (January 1986): 653.

Obviously, demoralization is a hard factor to quantify, but it seems likely that people would be willing to pay something to escape the fear of uncompensated takings.

Finally, no compensation is likely to create distortions in the decision making of private businesses, which must choose the most efficient combination of land, labor, and capital to produce their output. For example, it might be possible to employ a production process that is labor intensive but uses less land or one that uses less labor and more land. Of the three basic factors of production, all other things being equal, there will be a tendency to avoid those that are riskiest.[13] A system under which land could be taken without compensation would create enormous incentives to substitute away from land as a factor of production because land would become relatively more costly. Similarly, for all investment and savings purposes, land would become relatively unattractive when compared to financial instruments, art, and other appreciating assets. Indeed, it would have the effect of making all land acquisition conditional—like having a co-owner.

There are also arguments against compensation. First, compensation may mean the decision makers focus only on out-of-pocket costs. For example, if the government acquires property for a highway, it may cause the value of adjacent parcels to decline or it may decrease the well-being of nearby homeowners who will hear traffic noises. If these costs are ignored, there will be overinvestment in public projects.[14] Ideally, though, when the government decides whether or not to build a road, it would draw up a cost-benefit analysis of this project. Acquiring the land through takings is one cost component. Depreciating neighboring housing values and creating noise pollution are two other cost components. The point is that the government should do a complete cost and benefit analysis including all relevant components and not just the ones that have a market value.

13. The Takings Clause of the U.S. Constitution applies to all property, not just to land. In practice, the more controversial cases and, therefore, the greatest risk have arisen in the context of land.

14. This problem is referred to as "fiscal illusion." See Thomas J. Miceli and Kathleen Sergerson, "Regulatory Takings: When Should Compensation Be Paid?" *Journal of Legal Studies* 23 (June 1994): 749.

Second, a no-compensation scheme would also seem to avoid another problem, the moral hazard.[15] The idea of moral hazard is taken from a concept usually considered in the context of insurance. The problem is that people who are fully insured against losses may take more risks than they would if they were not insured. The extreme version of this would be to make claims when there is no loss at all. In the case of land use, it could mean the pursuit of riskier improvements to land in anticipation of being "insured" by the government if it is the action of the government that makes the improvement unprofitable. The crucial assumption here is that the government gives complete and full compensation for all ameliorations and improvements. And there has to be a substantial probability of taking. The probability that a random landowner would be involved in a taking must be very small. It would be irrational to overinvest in property on this negligible chance. If, however, you know that there is a more than even probability that your land will be the subject of a taking, the point is more valid.

THE CIRCULARITY OF EFFICIENT COMPENSATION

As the discussion suggests, there is an array of compensation possibilities ranging from no compensation at all to compensation resulting from individualized negotiations. Each possibility carries with it the potential for suboptimal decisions either by the government or by individuals or both. The problem is that the unintended effects of any compensation scheme mean that the determination of efficient levels of takings and compensation is a bit like hitting a moving target. For example, consider a policy of no compensation. In theory, the government could determine all costs—including demoralization costs and third-party effects—associated with such a policy and only undertake projects that result in benefits at least as great. The problem is that some of the relevant costs are those associated with the policy of no compensation itself. These are costs other than those associated with the value of the property actually taken. Depending on the value of these costs, the same project could be undertaken at a lower cost by

15. Lawrence E. Blume, Daniel L. Rubinfeld, and Perry Shapiro, "The Taking of Land: When Should Compensation Be Paid?" *Quarterly Journal of Economics* 99 (1984): 71.

actually offering compensation. The problem here is that by offering compensation at market levels, the government may unintentionally cause costs to go up as a result of the moral hazard. Moreover, even market price compensation may result in demoralization among those who value property at higher than fair market prices. This cost could be avoided by a policy of paying negotiated prices, but this would revive the moral hazard as well as bilateral monopoly problems.

This search for efficiency focuses only on the cost side of the equation. At least as difficult to assess are the benefits of public programs. Not only are these benefits diffuse but, as you saw in Chapter 3, the propensity in these markets may be for individuals to free ride and purposely disguise the extent of their demand. Free riders are unwilling to disclose the exact amount of their benefits for fear they will be charged for an amount equal to their benefits. This free-riding problem is solved by requiring everyone to pay taxes and by financing public goods through the government budget. In fact, the need for takings in the first place is the consequence of so-called market failures. Public goods such as roads, dikes, canals, and parks are not supplied by the competitive market system. The government has to step in. But whether the government provision of public goods ultimately benefits the general public more than it costs is an empirical question.

MODERN TAKINGS ANALYSIS

From a general economic perspective, the proper application of takings law seems fairly straightforward: A taking is efficient as long as all the costs imposed by the government are offset by the benefits to the public. As the preceding analysis suggests, this is an elusive standard in practice. In fact, the law falls well short of exhibiting a consistent economic philosophy. The truth is that sometimes the government must internalize the costs it imposes on others and sometimes it doesn't have to, and it is difficult to predict when internalization will be required and when it will not be.

CASE 6.2 The Complexity of Takings Analysis: *Kelo v. New London*, 125 S.Ct. 2655 (2005)

The difficulty inherent in the economic analysis of takings law is demonstrated by a recent—and surprising to many—decision by the U.S. Supreme Court. First, it is important to note that even if the government wants to "take," it can do so only for a public purpose. In *Kelo*, the city of New London, Connecticut, was looking for ways to revitalize its economy. It was able to attract a global drug research center. The center was expected to generate "approximately between: (1) 518 and 867 construction jobs; (2) 718 and 1362 direct jobs; and (3) 500 and 940 indirect jobs," in addition to generating "sizable property tax revenues." The problem was that much of the land that was to be used for the research center was privately owned. The city attempted to use its power of eminent domain to acquire the land and then to transfer it to Pfizer, the company that would own and operate the research center. The question was whether the city was permitted to take property when the use was exclusively for economic purposes. The objection by the landowners was that the taking was not for a "public purpose."

By the narrowest possible margin (5–4) the Court held that the taking was permissible. It noted the limited scope of its inquiry. It could only decide whether the Constitution permitted the taking. This did not mean, however, that individual states could not enact their own laws limiting the power of governmental units to take property. The Court was divided precisely along political lines, with the relatively liberal members of the Court voting that the taking was for a public purpose and the conservative members of the Court holding the position that taking for economic development purposes was not within the definition of "public purpose." Do you suppose this represents a disagreement about economics or politics? Does economic analysis tell you how to decide this case?

As noted at the outset, there are some very general guidelines. An actual taking—meaning the state physically possesses the property or allows someone else to—will result in compensation at fair market values. The more difficult cases are the "regulation" cases—those in which the government seeks to determine what the owner of the property may do with that property. The issue of when a regulation results in compensation is a difficult one that even the most sophisticated analyses are unable to solve. The problem ultimately comes down to defining the rights of the property owner. A property owner who had a reasonable expectation that the regulations would not occur and whose investment reflected that expectation is more likely to claim successfully that a taking has occurred. Conversely, regulations that a reasonable person might expect and which were arguably allowed for and reflected in the initial investment are not as likely to be regarded as a taking. This division makes economic sense because the person who did not reasonably expect the absence of the regulation was arguably compensated in advance by virtue of a diminished purchase price.

Unfortunately, an examination of what courts actually do reveals an inconsistent application of these guidelines. Two important decisions of the U.S. Supreme Court illustrate this. The first case, decided in 1887, involved brewers of beer who had invested in property used specifically for that purpose. A few years after the investment, the state of Kansas passed a law prohibiting the manufacture and sale of intoxicating beverages. The brewers argued that the new law reduced the value of their property from $10,000 to $2,500 and was a taking without "due compensation."[16] The Supreme Court ruled that there was not a taking because all property "in this country is held under the implied obligation that the owner's use of it shall not be injurious to the community." Moreover, it was within the power of the state of Kansas to define what was injurious. In effect, when the land was purchased it was always subject to the regulation that was eventually enacted. In theory, this possibility was reflected in the price paid for the land.

In 1922, the Supreme Court considered a similar issue. This time landowners had purchased land from a coal company. The actual purchase was for the surface of the land with the coal company keeping the right to remove the coal from the land. In 1921, however, Pennsylvania passed a law forbidding the mining of coal in any way that would have an impact on homes on the surface of the land.[17] Pennsylvania Coal Company complained that this was a taking without due compensation. This time the Court ruled that the regulation had gone so far that it amounted to a taking.

From an economic perspective, it is not easy to reconcile these cases. In the Kansas case, the principle would seem to be that all land is acquired with the knowledge that government regulation for the

16. *Mugler v. Kansas*, 123 U.S. 623 (1887).
17. *Pennsylvania Coal Co. v. Mahon*, 260 U.S. 393 (1922).

benefit of citizens may occur. If so, then one can argue that the Pennsylvania Coal Company was equally on notice that the state of Pennsylvania may take action to protect those living on the surface of the land.

In actuality, the outcomes in takings cases probably have little to do with a consistent economic policy. For example, with respect to the Kansas and Pennsylvania cases, one legal scholar has suggested that the difference may be explained by the fact that Kansas was attempting to protect the public generally while Pennsylvania actually shifted property rights from one identifiable group to another.[18] Another scholar has argued that the Court wanted to benefit the coal company because there was a shortage of coal.[19]

What you have seen is that it is not only difficult to explain the law of takings in terms of economic principles, but it is also hard to find consistent legal standards. This too, however, is relevant for the economic analysis of law. The absence of clear standards has economic implications because the uncertainty surrounding when the government may legally take property and what will be paid is itself a cost.

QUESTIONS FOR DISCUSSION

1. When the government takes land it must pay. When it takes money through taxes, it does not pay. In fact, the idea is absurd. So why is there a distinction? Why not treat taking land as a form of taxation?

2. The argument is made in the chapter that even when the government pays the fair market value for property, it takes and even when the value of the benefit of public use of that property exceeds the fair market value, the outcome may not be efficient. Explain why.

3. Imagine a city that depends for its income and employment on the fortunes of one company. Almost everyone living in the city works for the company. Most small businesses supply the company or its workers. Now compare the following two cases. When the

18. Carol Rose, "Planning and Dealing: Piecemeal Land Controls as a Problem of Local Legitimacy," *California Law Review* 71 (1983): 837.

19. Fischel, *Regulatory Takings*, 24n6.

municipality needs to build a new (urgently needed) city hall in the center of town, it is considered a taking and the municipality pays fair market value for the property. When the company needs to build a new (urgently needed) head office in the center of town, it pays what the present property owners charge. In both cases, the situation is one of bilateral monopoly as explained in this chapter. The municipality is protected against the owner's exploiting the situation and cashing in on the scarcity premium. The company will have to bargain the best it can but will probably end up paying a scarcity rent to the present owners. Should the company be given the same deal as the municipality?

4. a. Refer to Figure 6.2 in the text. Assume that the government knows the reservation prices of the landowners who own the land between Q_p and Q_{p+g}. That is, the government knows exactly what the supply curve looks like between points a and c. It pays each of these owners exactly what his or her reservation price is. Does that make the taking efficient—that is, does it increase welfare?

   b. Of course, the government does not know the reservation prices and landowners have good reasons to hide their real reservation prices from the government. If the government does not know these reservation prices, does that mean that the taking will always be inefficient?

5. Takings obviously involve instances in which the government is engaged in a forced purchase. The government is also involved in givings. For example, property may be rezoned so that is it more valuable. Similarly, think back to the Kelo case discussed in the case note. There Pfizer, the drug company, could have purchased the land itself. The way it works out, the company is likely to acquire the land on more favorable terms. This chapter has discussed the economics of takings. Do you think "givings" can be subject to the same analysis?[20]

---

20. See Abraham Bell and Gideon Parchomovsky, "Givings," *Yale Law Journal* 111 (2001): 547.

CHAPTER SEVEN

"Price" Regulation

Y OU HAVE ALREADY SEEN THAT GOVERNMENT PLAYS a role in defining property rights and how they are protected. You have also seen that what the government creates it can take away. In this chapter, the "taking away" is a bit more subtle because it takes the form of controlling prices. For example, in some cases maximum prices are set. This is what happens when there is rent control. Related to this are instances in which minimum prices are set. An example of this is the minimum wage. You should note two things. First, whether controlling rent or wages, the impact is similar in effect, although not in form, to the taking you read about in Chapter 6: The value of an asset, your rental property, or the business in general is reduced because the stream of income from using that asset is reduced. Second, a ceiling on the rent and a floor on wages are irrelevant unless these are set below or above, respectively, the level that would be set in the market.

The first section is devoted to the economic impact of rent control. The government is also involved in other efforts to regulate prices, such as minimum and maximum prices one may pay. These forms of price regulation are discussed in the last two sections of the chapter.

REGULATION OF MAXIMUM PRICES: RENT CONTROL

Rent controls have existed in New York, London, Paris, and many other large cities at least since World War II. In Sweden and Britain, where rent control on furnished apartments has existed for decades, shortages of rental accommodation are chronic. Over time, the quality of rental housing usually worsens because apartment owners are not motivated to maintain their housing stock. To study these economic effects of rent control, it is instructive to see what rent control does to the market for rental housing. First, the impact in a competitive market is illustrated and then the impact in an imperfectly competitive market in which owners possess monopoly power.

THE COMPETITIVE CASE

Figure 7.1 shows the demand and supply of rental housing measured in, say, square feet for rent (Q) as a function of the rent R per square foot for rent. Supply depends on the stock of rental housing available, composed mainly of buildings built in the past. Increases in the supply of rental housing will either come from conversions (from owner-occupied to rental housing) or by construction of new buildings.

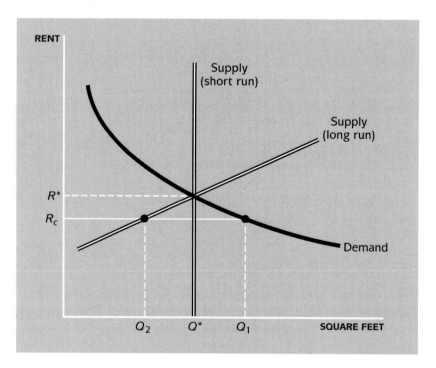

FIGURE 7.1 Effects of Rent Control on Market for Rental Housing

Decreases occur by conversions to other uses and by demolition or abandonment. Reactions take time, so we need to distinguish short- and long-run supply. In the short run, the supply of rental housing is quite inelastic; that is, the amount of houses for rent will change only marginally in the short run. Price increases and decreases will generate only small reactions from homeowners. In Figure 7.1, we have drawn the short-run supply curve as a straight vertical line, assuming that the amount of rental housing is fixed in the short run. It might be more realistic to make the short-run supply curve slope just a little bit, but that does not affect our argument below. We have assumed that there is $Q^\star$ square feet available for rent in the short run.

The long run is a different story. Given enough time, the supply of rental housing will react to the expected return on the investment in rental housing. If the expected return falls significantly below what can be earned on comparable investments, funds will go elsewhere and the supply of rental housing will decrease. If the expected return is higher than comparable investments, funds will move into rental housing and the supply will increase. Long-run supply is elastic. In Figure 7.1, the positive slope of the long-run supply curve captures this higher price sensitivity over time. Quantity supplied adapts to market conditions given enough time.

CASE 7.1 Rent Control as a Taking: *Yee v. City of Escondido,* 503 U.S. 519 (1992)

In the previous chapter, we noted that the U.S. Constitution forbids taking of "private property . . . for public use without just compensation." In the case of rent control, the government also takes away property—or at least a part of the value of the property, but in this case there is no compensation for the property loss of the owner. Two legal issues arise. First, is there a taking at all? Second, is the taking for a "public use?" Rent control does not involve a physical taking. Thus, as you know from Chapter 6, the regulation must be so pervasive that it completely or nearly completely eliminates the value of the property to the owner. Obviously, this is where a challenge to rent control is likely to fail. As it turns out, there are no Supreme Court cases that directly address the constitutionality of rent control.

A case with a novel argument with respect to rent control is *Yee v. City of Escondido,* in which mobile home parks were subject to rent controls and to restrictions on when the mobile home owners could be evicted. The park owners claimed that the combination of regulations amounted to a physical taking. Their logic was that that homeowners could stay indefinitely and even sell their homes and right to occupy space in the park to others. Moreover, when selling, they received a premium because the new occupants were able to rent at below-market levels. This, they claimed, was comparable to a physical taking. The U.S. Supreme Court ruled that the combination of regulations was not a "taking." According to the Court, park owners could, with sufficient notice, change the use of their property to something other than mobile home parks. Thus, the relationship entered into with mobile home owners was voluntary and not a "taking." Given the layering of regulations in *Yee* that were not viewed as a taking, it is very unlikely that a conventional rent control regulation would be viewed as a taking.

Demand per square foot of rental housing is quite elastic. If the rental price increases, fewer people will want to rent, people who do rent will rent smaller apartments to keep monthly rental burdens down, people will share more or move to lower-grade rental housing. Some people will prefer to buy instead. On the other hand, if the price of rental housing decreases demand will go up. In Figure 7.1, the demand for rental housing has a negative slope, expressing the sensitivity of the square feet of housing to the level of rent.

In Figure 7.1, the equilibrium rental rate is $R^\star$. It is the rental rate for which the amount of rental housing demanded equals the amount of rental housing supplied in the short run and the long run. The market clears at the amount of square feet of rental housing demanded and supplied equal to $Q^\star$. Now suppose the city decides that the equilibrium rental rate $R^\star$ is too high because many low-income people cannot afford decent rental housing in this way. The city stipulates that the rent cannot exceed the controlled rental rate R_c, which is of course lower than the equilibrium rent $R^\star$. The whole purpose of rent control is to fix a rent that is lower than the going rent.

R_c is a disequilibrium rental rate. The market does not clear at that rate. In fact, at rental rate R_c the amount demanded (Q_1 in Figure 7.1) is larger than the amount of rental housing supplied. We have to distinguish between short-run and long-run supply. In the short run (this is what happens immediately after the introduction of rent control), the amount supplied is still $Q^\star$. The amount demanded is Q_1, which is larger than the amount supplied $Q^\star$. In a disequilibrium situation such as the one occurring with rent control, the quantity exchanged is determined at the lesser of quantity demanded or quantity supplied. The quantity of rental housing exchanged is $Q^\star$. Hence, there will be a housing shortage equal to $Q_1 - Q^\star$ in the short run.

This is not the end of the story. In the longer run, because rent control has decreased income earned on housing compared to what can be earned on other investments, funds will move out of the rental housing sector and the amount of rental housing supplied will decrease over time to Q_2. As time goes on, housing shortages will worsen and will eventually be equal (in the figure) to $Q_1 - Q_2$. Note also that in the long run the available quantity of rental housing will be less than if free market rents had been charged. If free market equilibrium rents ($R^\star$) had been charged rather than the controlled rent (R_c), the amount of housing supplied in the long run would still have been $Q^\star$ rather than the smaller amount Q_2. Such control-induced shortage led University of Chicago professors George Stigler and Milton Friedman to talk about "ceilings created by controls" as opposed to "roofs provided by housing."

Another way to bring the return on the investment in rental housing more in line with other investments is to save on maintenance and upkeep. Less maintenance and upkeep reduces the cost to the owner of supplying rental housing, and this will increase his profit margin. The result over time is urban blight. An alternative possibility is that tenants themselves will spend money to offset landlord neglect. For example, tenants may replace lighting and undertake small repairs that landlords would ordinarily be expected to do. It is possible that tenants, or some of them at least, will actually end up spending more than they would have if the rent been set in the market. In addition, landlords may institute various fees for "moving in," "maintenance," or "routine repainting" all of which effectively raise the price of housing. The problem is that "rent" is but one element of the contract between the landlord and the tenant. Other terms of the contract may offset whatever gain the tenant seems to have made by virtue of rent control.

Given the shortage in the rental housing market, the "power" shifts to the suppliers of rental housing. As there are more demanders than

there are rental houses available, the suppliers of the available rental
housing can pick and choose whom they want to rent their housing
units to. The preferences of the owners of rental housing will determine who can rent and who cannot. When the rental lease ends, owners will evict tenants they do not like and replace them with tenants
who are more to their liking. This in itself may result in a social cost.
For example, a landlord may attempt to choose tenants on the basis
of age or race. To reduce this power of the suppliers of rental housing, rent control is often paired with security-of-tenure laws protecting tenants from eviction and giving them priority over prospective
new tenants. But this has a flip side. The combination of rent control
and security-of-tenure laws implies that existing tenants gain from the
rent control (they have cheap rental housing and they have no incentive to give this up), whereas newcomers cannot find rental housing.
Rent control also provides incentives for black markets and has all
kinds of other undesirable side effects. The incentives for these undesirable effects can be seen clearly in Figure 7.2.

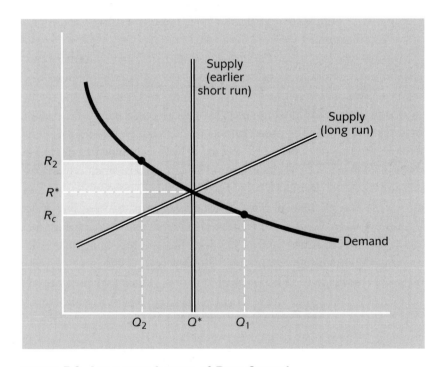

FIGURE 7.2 Long-term Impact of Rent Control

SOME RENT CONTROL COMPLEXITIES

Rent control can actually take a variety of forms. It may mean an absolute ceiling on the rent charged for a particular housing unit. Or it can allow for increases only when tenants change or for small percentage increases on a yearly basis. The idea here is to allow landlords to earn a "fair" return on their investment. Each form, as you would expect, results in different market reactions and then regulatory reactions designed to prop up the rent control regime. For example, if a landlord can raise the rent when a new tenant moves in, this is likely to encourage short-term leases. Landlords may choose relatively transient tenants, elderly tenants, or look for excuses to evict those who stay "too long." This in turn may result in the need to control not just rents but the terms for terminating a lease. Also, if you recall the Coase theroem, landlords and tenants are likely to bargain in ways that decrease the impact of law. The same can be true of rent control. For example, the rent may be controlled, but the tenant may have to make a one-time "moving in" fee. This possibility may be met with restrictions on side payments.

Further complicating the rent control issue is the question of how the benefits of rent control are distributed. It is tempting to think that rent control means that relatively poor people can afford housing that would otherwise be unavailable to them. Rent control alone, however, will not achieve what may seem to be a redistribution from the relatively rich (landlords) to the poor tenants. Unless there are income limits on the types of people who take advantage of rent-controlled housing, landlords may choose to rent to the relatively well-to-do. In effect, whatever redistribution occurs takes place within the same socioeconomic class. On the other hand, efforts to make sure rent-controlled housing goes only to those in need raises new issues (and costs) related to the process of allocating that housing.

Figure 7.2 follows the same setup as Figure 7.1, but concentrates on the long-run situation whereby the supply of rental housing is equal to Q_2 and the controlled rental rate is equal to R_c. We have now arrived at a situation where (in what is now the short run) the stock of rental housing is equal to Q_2. If all the available supply of Q_2 were rented on the black market, then the rental price would rise to R_2 with black marketeers earning receipts above the controlled rate R_c. The shaded area shows these extra earning receipts. This shaded area is an indication of how much tenants are willing to pay above the controlled rate to black market landlords.

Landlords have used clever devices such as large "entrance fees" that they charge to each new tenant. In charging high entrance fees, landlords are trying to capture part of the earnings in the shaded area. When there are no security-of-tenure laws, landlords may force tenants out when leases expire to extract more entrance fees from new tenants.

Price ceilings are often used to allocate a product in short supply. If in a free market a shortage develops, the market reaction is to increase the price substantially to allocate the scarce supply among customers who are willing to pay a high price. But huge prices are often considered morally repulsive and politically unacceptable. For instance, in a war situation, shortages in necessities (food, clothes, shelter, and heating) develop and a free market would react to that by immense price increases. Governments usually step in and use other methods to allocate the scarce supplies. Rationing is often used in wartime with, for instance, food stamps, but it is also well known that black markets are endemic in situations of shortages.

Closer in time, the 1970s oil crisis created a shortage of gasoline, which was rationed by long waiting lines. During this oil crisis, the importance of sellers' preferences in shortage situations became clear as sellers often sold only to regular customers. The possibility of caps on fuel is a good illustration of the difficulties in deciding whether price caps are good policy. Price ceilings are obviously reactions to high prices, but think of some other reactions to high gasoline prices. One would be to conserve fuel. People who use cars, especially gas guzzlers, might begin to think twice about how much they drive. The next time they have a choice, they may buy more fuel-efficient cars. In effect, no one likes high gasoline prices but in some ways they steer consumers to make choices that most would support.

LAW AND ECONOMICS IN ACTION 7.2

RENT CONTROL: WHAT THE RESEARCH SHOWS

The economic theory of rent control is fairly clear. If the rent is set at below market clearing levels, there will be shortages, investment in housing will decline, and landlords will allow the condition of rental property to deteriorate. On the other hand, some tenants will be better off, and allocating housing on the basis of something other than income may increase diversity within neighborhoods. What do the numbers show? This is actually a more complicated question than it may seem.

One complication arises from the different forms of rent control. We tend to think of rent control meaning a fixed rent, but it may actually mean a "controlled" rent that is allowed to change with conditions. In determining the impact it is not appropriate to compare the controlled regime with one that is perfectly competitive. The better comparison is between the controlled regime and what the market would look like in the absence of control. The "free market" is likely to be imperfectly competitive.

Nevertheless, many studies are of interest. One such study examined the impact of the elimination of rent control in Cambridge, Massachusetts.[1] According to the report, when rent control was eliminated, investment in housing increased by 20 percent above what it would have otherwise been. In addition, the increase was felt in both affluent and modest income areas.

Yet another study confirmed the impact of rent control on the willingness of landlords to maintain the quality of housing.[2] The authors compared the rent-controlled units in New York City with those that were not controlled and determined that the rent-controlled units deteriorated faster.

Another study examined the impact of rent control in segregation.[3] The idea is that rent control enables poor families to live in expensive neighborhoods. The results were mixed. Rent control did enable relatively poor people to live in more expensive neighborhoods. On the other hand, rent control favored older residents more than younger renters. There was scant evidence that rent control advanced racial integration. All in all, the author concluded that there were better ways to achieve integration.

Finally, there is the critical question of whether those living in rent-controlled housing are better off than they would be without rent control. Here the relevant comparison is between the rent-controlled price and the price that would exist if the market had not been regulated. This

1. Henry O. Pollakowski, "Rent Control and Housing Investment: Evidence from Deregulation in Cambridge, Massachusetts," Civic Report, No. 36 (May 2003), Center for Civic Innovation at the Manhattan Institute.

2. C. Moon and J. Stitsky, "The Effect of Rent Control on Housing Quality Change: A Longitudinal Analysis," *Journal of Political Economy* 101 (1993): 1114.

3. Edward L. Glaeser, "Does Rent Control Reduce Segregation?" Harvard Institute of Economic Research, November 2002, Discussion Paper No. 1985.

is a different question from how much lower today's controlled prices are than today's uncontrolled prices. At least one study indicates that rent-control rents are higher now than they would have been if the market had been permitted to work.[4]

The Imperfectly Competitive Case

The rent control market analyzed thus far is competitive. Suppose, instead, the rental market is controlled by a few large landlords. In other words, each owner possesses monopoly power. This is illustrated in Figure 7.3 in which price and output determination under monopoly conditions is illustrated. The intersection of marginal cost (MC) and marginal revenue (MR) determines the profit-maximizing quantity (X). The profit-maximizing price is P minus the highest

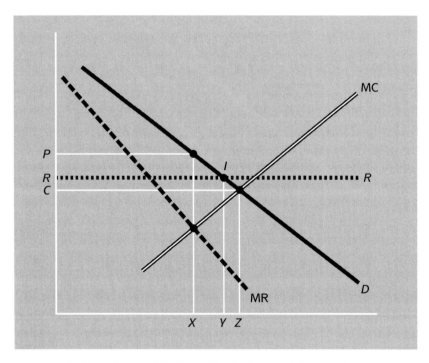

FIGURE 7.3 Rent Control in Imperfectly Competitive Markets

4. Dirk W. Early, "Rent Control, Rental Housing Supply, and the Distribution of Tenant Benefits," *Journal of Urban Economics* 48 (2000): 185.

price, as determined by the demand curve (*D*)—at which quantity *X* can be sold. If the market were competitive, assuming the same cost of production, the equilibrium price would be *C* and the quantity bought and sold would be *Z*.

Suppose that government regulation results in a price ceiling of *R*. At that price, the monopolist would still determine the level of output at the intersection of marginal cost and marginal revenue. The marginal revenue curve, however, is now horizontal at the regulated price out to the point at which it intersects with the demand curve. Then it drops straight downward (is discontinuous) to the original marginal revenue curve. It is flat because selling additional units does not require lowering the price. The reason is that out to the intersection with the demand curve, all buyers are willing to pay even more than the regulated price. The intersection of the new marginal revenue curve and the marginal cost curve is at output level *Y*. In effect, price controls mean more production, not less.

Does this mean that rent control is always desirable when there is monopoly power in housing markets? In the short run, maybe so. On the other hand, the degree of monopoly can vary. Particularly important are barriers to entry. Unless entry barriers are prohibitively high, high housing prices, if associated with high profits, would ordinarily draw investors into the market. Rent control could actually discourage this development. On the other hand, if entry barriers are high, rent control could mean that monopolists will offer more housing for sale at a lower price.

OTHER REGULATED "PRICES"

The converse of a price ceiling is a price floor. A regulated price floor is a minimum permissible price that can be charged. In this case the market price cannot go beneath the floor. The minimum wage is a prime example. In this case, the government does not permit the wage paid to be below a certain level. Price floors are also common for agricultural products. For instance, the common agricultural program of the European Union has, among others, a price floor for milk. Here again, we consider "price" controls under competitive and imperfectly competitive conditions.

Minimum Wages and Prices under Competitive Conditions

As can be seen in Figure 7.4, a price floor W_{min} is binding or effective if it is higher than the equilibrium price. For the labor market, the equilibrium wage rate is $W^\star$. At this equilibrium wage, the supply of labor equals demand and the labor market clears. This equilibrium wage rate might be so low that working people still end up below the poverty line. The government, in order to avoid poverty, will often decide to introduce a legal minimum wage higher than the equilibrium wage. Effective price floors lead to excess supply. The excess supply is equal to the difference between the quantity supplied at the minimum wage rate (Q_1) and the quantity demanded (Q_2). The difference $Q_1 - Q_2$ will show up as unemployment in the labor market.

In the case of price floors for agricultural products, an effective price floor will result in excess supply (overproduction) of agricultural products. In the European Union, excess supply of milk has accumulated over time, and this is referred to as the "milk lake."

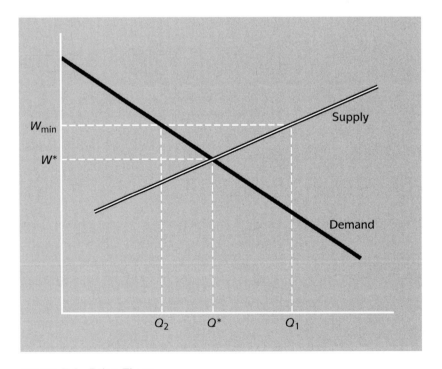

FIGURE 7.4 Price Floor

Excess supply of milk has also been transformed into butter. Europeans also talk about "butter mountains."

Workers and farmers often have politically active groups who argue that government should have price floors to combat poverty among unskilled workers and small farmers. Workers finding work at the minimum wage and farmers being able to sell their produce at higher prices are the winners of this price floor policy. Losers are consumers and unemployed workers. Minimum wages and agricultural price floors increase the price of products for consumers. These losses are spread across a large and diverse set of consumers who each individually experience only a small loss, although the total loss might be considerable.

Wage and Price Floors under Imperfectly Competitive Conditions

In some instances, labor markets and the markets for goods are characterized by monopsony conditions. Monopsony is the flip side of monopoly. Instead of one seller with market power (monopoly), in the monopsony case, there is only one buyer with market power, who is able to force wages or prices to levels that are lower than would exist under competitive conditions. Figure 7.5 illustrates the basic model. First, D and S are the demand and supply for labor under competitive conditions. As in Figure 7.4, the equilibrium wages is $W^\star$ and the level of employment is $Q^\star$.

Under monopsonistic conditions, however, the wage and level of employment are not determined by the intersection of supply and demand. Instead, the monopsonist equates its demand curve with the marginal factor cost curve (MFC) in order to determine the quantity hired.[5] The demand curve reflects the extra revenue the additional unit of labor generates for the employer, and the MFC reflects the additional cost of that unit of labor. The profit-maximizing level of labor is X. The wage will be determined by finding the lowest wage on the supply curve consistent with that level of labor supplied. Thus,

---

5. MFC lies above the supply curve because the monopsonist cannot merely react to the wage set in the competitive market. Instead, the monopsonist must pay higher wages in order to purchase additional labor. The marginal factor cost is higher than the wage paid to each additional worker because each worker—even those who could have been hired at lower wages—also receives the higher wage.

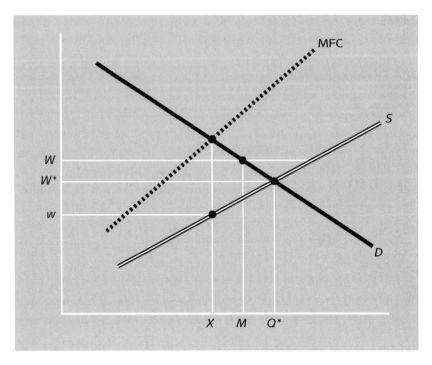

FIGURE 7.5 Price Floors under Monopsony Conditions

in the monopsony market, the quantity hired will be X and the wage will be w.

Suppose government regulation sets the minimum wages at W. The new MFC curve is now horizontal out to the point at which it intersects with the supply curve. You can reason through why this would be the case. If the minimum wage is fixed at W, all workers who were willing to work at a lower wage will be willing to sell their labor. As long as that wage is below the demand curve, they will be hired. Once the minimum wage intersects with the labor supply curve, the new MFC continues as the original MFC curve. Under these conditions, the intersection of MFC and demand is at employment level M and the wage is the minimum wage. In effect, under monopsony conditions, employment is actually higher and the wage is higher as well.

As with rent control in monopoly markets, minimum wage requirements may retard market developments that would have solved the problem. For example, the typical case of monopsony labor markets is a single employer in an isolated geographic market. If the monopsonist is able to pay less-than-competitive wages, other firms attracted by low labor costs would be inclined to relocate to the low-wage area. There will begin to be a higher demand for labor and competition, both of which will raise wages. A set minimum wage could retard this development.

ACCESS PRICING

A recent economic concern for the governments in North America and Europe is access to networks such as telephone lines, power lines, railroads, and even postal services. Take, for instance, a telephone company that owns the copper telephone wiring connecting all houses and businesses in an area. The company also provides telephone service to the households and businesses connected to this essential facility. Other firms would like to have access to the network to provide their own telephone services to consumers (e.g., mobile telephone companies want to be able to connect phone calls from their customers owning cell phones to customers connected to the copper telephone line). Internet service providers would like to access the network to provide Internet services. If the network owner charges to those requesting access monopoly prices that are too high, he can create a situation in the market for telephone services or in the market for Internet access (often indicated as the "downstream markets") that makes competition very difficult, if not impossible. He can even refuse access to all competitors and keep the downstream market for telephone and Internet services all to himself.

Sometimes such a network is called an essential facility. An essential facility is necessary to supply customers. In order to stimulate competition, the government might require the owner of the essential facility to provide access to his competitors. The issue then becomes this: What is the price of access?

CASE 7.2 **What Is a Fair Access Rate?** *Verizon Communications, Inc. v. FCC*, 535 U.S. 467 (2002)

In 1996, the U.S. Congress passed the Telecommunications Act of 1996, a very complex piece of legislation. One element of the act states that the owners of local telephone facilities must allow competitors to have access to those facilities. The problem, as you see already, is what the incumbents can charge for that access. If they are allowed to charge whatever they want, they can effectively block access. On the other hand, access can amount to a taking if the access rate is set too low. In the United States, the Federal Communications Commission (FCC) has devised various formulas and then the party or parties unhappy with the formula appeal to the courts. Naturally, incumbents would like to charge rates that allow them to make a profit on the investment they have made in their facilities. The problem is that the facilities may be outdated, inefficient, and expensive. In short, the newcomer may find he is paying rates based on obsolete technology. The FCC decided that rates could be set on a "forward-looking" basis. Forward-looking is defined as "the most efficient telecommunications technology currently available." In a sense this will then allow newcomers to reflect in their rates to consumers the current technology. On the other hand, it may mean that incumbents are charging rates to their competitors that make it difficult for newcomers to compete. In 2002, the U.S. Supreme Court was asked to rule on the constitutionality of this rate and found that it was permitted. You should note that in cases like this, the Court will not examine the rate in great detail. Instead, it asks whether the action of the commission setting the rate is supported by the evidence.

Regulating access price is very tricky. If access prices are set too high, competition will not be stimulated. The high cost of access will stop new entrants in the telephone and Internet services markets from offering their products to make a profit. If access prices are set too low, there will be plenty of new entrants requesting access, but the essential facility owner (just like the owner of a rental apartment) may be insufficiently compensated for the investment in his facility. With access prices set too low, he might also lose incentive to maintain the quality of his network and certainly will have little desire to innovate his network. Too low an access price will reduce the capital value of his essential facility and, in this sense, it could be considered a regulatory taking comparable to what happens with rent control.

QUESTIONS FOR DISCUSSION

1. Suppose a law is passed that freezes all rents at current levels for as long as the current tenants remain in the property. When prop-

erty is rented to new lessees, owners may raise the rent. What do you think the result would be?

2. As noted in the text, access rates are often set not at the lessor's cost but at the lessor's marginal cost had it made the most efficient decisions with respect to the design of its system. Is this consistent with any notion of efficiency?

3. The prices of prescription drugs tend to increase at a rate that is higher than the rate of inflation. From time to time, there are legislative proposals to limit these price increases. Would this result in a scarcity of prescription drugs?

4. In some markets, it is possible for a minimum wage to actually increase employment. In which market is this more likely to be the case? The market for economics professors? The market for professional football players? The market for factory workers?

5. Minimum wages are seen as instruments to fight poverty among working families. Empirical research has shown that a lot of minimum wage earners (youngsters doing temporary jobs, secondary income earners) belong to households having combined income above the poverty thresholds.
   a. What are other policy instruments to fight poverty among the working poor?
   b. If these other instruments are more effective than minimum wages to attack poverty, could we abolish minimum wages?

6. In the rent control case we showed that landlords have an incentive to profit from rent control by charging entrance fees. Also landlords are less inclined to maintain their apartments in the long run. To "solve" these problems, municipalities in some cities have stepped in and become the owners of these rental apartments and then rented them out at subsidized rents to lower-income people. Does governmental ownership solve all the problems discussed in this chapter?

CHAPTER EIGHT

Intellectual Property

TYPICALLY WE THINK OF PROPERTY AS CONSISTING OF LAND or physical possessions, but a substantial body of law is designed to protect property rights in ideas.[1] "Intellectual property" includes copyright and patents, trademarks, industrial design, and geographic indication of source. Just as property rights extending to more conventional types of property are necessary to encourage their efficient use, intellectual property rights are necessary to promote inventions and creations. In fact, the protection of intellectual property is clearly linked to economic growth. At the same time, these property rights restrict the free and unlimited use of creative ideas and inventions by others, which limits opportunities to extend existing ideas and inventions into even newer and even more creative ideas. This tension of intellectual property rights is the central theme of this chapter. It is discussed in greater detail in the first section. The next section details the specific forms of intellectual property. The last part describes a general economic theory of intellectual property.

---

1. This does not mean that all ideas are protected; copyright protection extends only to the *expression* of ideas. In other cases, ideas may not be sufficiently novel to be protected. For example, even if you invent something completely on your own, you cannot patent it if someone else already has done so.

THE INHERENT TENSION IN PROTECTING INTELLECTUAL PROPERTY

In early 1999, Shawn Fanning, only eighteen at that time, wrote a computer program that allowed anyone with a computer and an Internet connection to download music without paying for it. The computer program made peer-to-peer (or P2P) sharing possible. It allowed anyone to download music from another person's computer, and that other person could be a next-door neighbor or somebody on the other side of the world. This computer program was the basis of Napster (Napster was Fanning's nickname in high school, because of his hair). Napster was an Internet service that allowed its users to swap music files free. At one point, thousands and thousands of people were making copies of copyrighted songs through Napster, and neither the music industry nor the artists received any money for those copies. Many people loved Napster because it allowed them to get music free instead of paying $15 or more for a CD. The music industry and the artists did not love it and asked the court to shut down this "free (down) loading" service. It took a while, but on February 12, 2001, a U.S. appeals court upheld an earlier court injunction and ordered Napster to stop the service or face huge fines. Since then, Napster has redefined itself and is now a successful website where one can listen to or download music tracks legally after paying a fee. These modest fees, whether paid to iTunes or Napster or through compulsory licensing arrangements, add up and are soon likely to be the principal way artists internalize the gains from their efforts.

At this moment, there are still web sites where music can be illegally downloaded free. Downloading without due payment is an infringement of copyright law. It is called piracy and it still raises controversy. On one side are the music writers, performers, and record companies correctly claiming that they are not compensated for the creative effort and the costs they put into producing the music. On the other side are people making the argument that music should be freely available because it increases the welfare of society. This controversy illustrates the basic tension not only in copyrighted music but also in intellectual property rights in general.

Intellectual property rights are hotly contested outside the realm of music and some of the issues range from the silly to those with the potential to create a long-run impact on entire industries. For example, in one case a designer of a hat with black and white splotches—like a Holstein cow—claimed that Ben and Jerry's ice cream had infringed on his copyright by selling baseball caps with similar splotches. In another (very important) case, the owner of rights to motion pictures sued Sony for making video recording equipment. The recording of movies that appeared on television, it was argued, constituted a copyright infringement. The Supreme Court held that it was not, but you might think about how your life would be different had the case been decided differently.

To understand the tension inherent in intellectual property law, first consider the point of view of creative people. Ideas lead to new forms of music, thrilling plots for books, and exciting movies that we can enjoy. Ideas lead to new products such as wireless communication, new sources of energy, and new medicines that can improve our lives. Ideas can improve the way we produce virtually anything, make it possible to make more with less effort, increase our productivity so that we end up with more income and more free time to spend it. To enhance creativity in society, property rights in ideas are needed to enable a creator to benefit from her creation so she will create more. Once the property right is established, the author or inventor can exploit her creative output by charging others to use it. In other words, she can internalize the benefits of her creativity. This is often done by licensing someone else to use the idea.

On the other hand, there are very commendable arguments that ideas should be made available to the public as widely as possible. There are two reasons for this. First, compositions and patented products are ultimately useful only if there is wide dissemination. That is ultimately the way social welfare is increased. Second, ideas build on other ideas. Inventions do not usually fall out of the sky but grow out of already existing knowledge. To invent the electric motor, we had to understand how electricity worked. The first electric motors were huge and clumsy machines, but we had to go through that awkward stage before we could engineer the tiny wonders we can build now. The same is true for artistic creations. Elvis did not invent rock music all by himself but built on artists who came before him, as did the Beatles and the Rolling Stones. Creativity breeds creativity and that is why wide access and availability are necessary. Access and availability are also essential for training new scientists and artists. Einstein had to be able to study Newton before he could write articles that completely revolutionized physics. Students in universities and in art schools need access to books and art works to learn their skills. If intellectual property rights implied that society had to pay *too* much for access to existing ideas, the production of new creations and the generation of new ideas would be hindered. If intellectual property rights implied that creators could withhold the use of their ideas, that would even be worse.

There will always be a basic tension between the right to compensation to stimulate creative people and the need of society to have wide access to creations to build and expand on them. This trade-off has both long-term and short-term consequences. For example, suppose a drug company were told that its patent was going to be shorter or that it could charge only a certain price for its patented drug. In the short run, this looks like a great idea. That particular drug will be available at a lower cost. On the other hand, to the extent a drug company undertakes research based on the expected returns and these returns are determined by the length of the patent, the long-run impact may be to slow drug research.

Obviously a balance needs to be struck. A world with no property rights in ideas would likely be a poorer one. Creativity would be undersupplied. That is not to say there would be no creativity. Great works of art, such as the ceiling of the Sistine Chapel by Michelangelo, and great books, such as Dante's *Divina Commedia* or Newton's *Principia,* were created in times when there were no intellectual property rights. In those days artists often had a patron—Michelangelo Buonaratti was commissioned by Pope Julius II in 1508 to repaint the ceiling of his chapel—or they had other ways to support themselves—Isaac Newton got a fellowship at Trinity College at the University of Cambridge, which allowed him to dine at the Fellow's Table. Artists seem to be driven to be creative. But it is likely that creativity would exist at suboptimal levels. In other words, a great deal of creativity would not take place that would benefit society by more than it costs.

On the other hand, a system of intellectual property rights is not costless. There are costs of administering the system, and there are costs of allowing some people to have exclusive access to the resources—ideas—that are created. The economic approach to intellectual property is one that seeks to find the efficient balance by comparing the costs and benefits of protecting ideas.

THE INTERNALIZATION OF INTELLECTUAL PROPERTY

Each country typically has a system of protection for intellectual property rights. New questions emerge all the time, and many of them have international implications. Thus, over time, the system of intellectual copyrights has extended enormously. At present, an international organization, the World Intellectual Property Organization (WIPO), based in Geneva, Switzerland, is mandated to administer intellectual property matters worldwide. Founded in 1974, it is a specialized agency of the United Nations. At present, 90 percent of the world's countries belong to WIPO and adhere to international agreements on intellectual property rights. New countries are added every day. The growing importance of the Internet is one of the many examples of why new intellectual property issues emerge regularly.

One such issue is cybersquatting. Cybersquatting is a dispute about domain names. A domain name is the address of a website that is intended to be easily identifiable and easy to remember, such as google.com or amazon.com. These are user-friendly addresses for easy connection between people and the Internet. Hence, they are valuable for providing information and for doing business through the Internet. Cybersquatting involves the preemptive registration of domain names. Cybersquatters exploit the first-come, first-served nature of the domain name registration system to register names of famous people or businesses with which they have no connection. Avon, Hertz, and Panasonic all found that their names were already taken by cybersquatters. Because registration of domain names is relatively simple and inexpensive—less than U.S.$100 in most cases—cybersquatters often register hundreds of such names as domain names. Cybersquatters then put the domain names up for auction or offer them for sale directly to the company or person involved, at prices far beyond the cost of registration. With the help of WIPO, an international domain name dispute resolution system has been created to solve the problem of cybersquatting.

INTELLECTUAL PROPERTY RIGHTS

Intellectual property can be divided into two categories: *industrial property*, which includes inventions (patents), trademarks, industrial designs, and geographic indications of source; and *copyright*, which includes literary and artistic works. Rights related to copyright include those of performing artists to their performances, music producers to their recordings, and broadcasters to their radio and television programs.

Industrial Property

A *patent* is an exclusive right granted for an invention. A patent provides protection to the owner of the patent for a limited period, generally twenty years. Once a patent expires, the protection ends and an invention enters the public domain; that is, it becomes available to commercial exploitation by others. The patent owner may give permission to, or license, other parties to use the invention. The owner may also sell the right to the invention to someone else.

LAW AND ECONOMICS IN ACTION 8.2

CHEAP ANTI-AIDS DRUGS

South Africa is gripped by the world's largest AIDS epidemic. Some 11 percent of the population is infected with HIV. Patented anti-AIDS drugs, or rather anti-retroviral drugs, which do not cure the disease but can prolong a patient's life, are expensive—too expensive for a poor country such as South Africa. Recently, after much discussion and international pressure, a deal was made whereby large drug multinationals give "voluntary licenses" to a South African drug company called Aspen to make cheap generic versions of the anti-retrovirals to which the multinational holds patents.

Reference: "Me Too," *The Economist* (May 24, 2004): 67.

A *trademark* is a distinctive sign that identifies certain goods or services as those produced or provided by a specific person or enterprise. Its origin dates back to ancient times, when craftsmen reproduced their signatures, or "marks," on their artistic or utilitarian products. The system helps consumers identify and purchase a product or service because its nature and quality, indicated by its unique trademark, meet their needs. In effect, a trademark lowers transaction costs. When you see "McDonald's" anywhere in the world you know without fur-

Shell 1930
trademark

Shell 1999
trademark

FIGURE 8.1   **Shell Oil Company Trademark Change over Time**

ther investigation what to expect. If you were in a strange city and wanted a hamburger, you would not have to go from restaurant to restaurant searching for what you are looking for.

A trademark ensures the owner of the mark the exclusive right to use or to authorize another to use it in return for payment. Otherwise others will be able to "pass off" what they are selling as something it is not. The period of protection varies, but a trademark can be renewed indefinitely beyond the time limit on payment of additional fees. In the United States, a party can use a trademark until it is "abandoned." Trademark protection also hinders the efforts of counterfeiters. Trademarks can change over time, as can be seen in Figure 8.1.

An *industrial design* is the ornamental or aesthetic aspect of an article. The design may consist of three-dimensional features, such as the shape or surface of an article, or of two-dimensional features, such as patterns, lines, or color. An industrial design must appeal to the eye. Industrial designs are applied to a wide variety of industrial products and handicrafts such watches, jewelry, electrical appliances, vehicles, and textiles. When an industrial design is protected, the owner is assured an exclusive right against unauthorized copying or imitation of the design.

A *geographical indication* is a sign used on goods that have a specific geographical origin and possess qualities or a reputation that are due to that place of origin. Agricultural products typically have qualities that derive from their place of production and are influenced by specific local factors, such as climate and soil. Examples are "Tuscany" for olive oil produced in a specific area of Italy, or "Roquefort" for cheese produced in France.

Copyrights

Copyright is a legal term describing rights given to creators for their literary and artistic works. The kinds of works covered by copyright include literary works such as novels, poems, plays, reference works, newspapers, and computer programs; databases; films, musical compositions, and choreography; artistic works such as paintings, drawings, photographs, and sculpture; architecture; and advertisements, maps, and technical drawings.

The original creators of works protected by copyright and their heirs have certain basic rights. They hold the exclusive right to use or authorize others to use the work on agreed terms. The creator of a work can prohibit or authorize

- reproduction in various forms, such as printed publication or sound recording;
- public performance, as in a play or musical work;
- recordings of it; for example, in the form of compact discs, cassettes, or videotapes;
- broadcasting by radio, cable, or satellite;
- translation into other languages;
- adaptation, such as a novel into a screenplay.

Many creative works protected by copyright require mass distribution, communication, and financial investment for their dissemination (for example, publications, sound recordings, and films); hence, creators often sell the rights to their works to individuals or companies best able to market the works in return for payment. These payments are often made dependent on the actual use of the work and are then referred to as royalties. These economic rights have a time limit, according to the relevant WIPO treaties, of fifty years after the creator's death. National law may establish longer time limits. In the United States, as in Europe, the time limit extends to seventy years after the creator's death (see Law and Economics in Action 8.4). Copyright protection in Europe also includes moral rights, which involve the right to claim authorship of a work and the right to oppose changes to it that could harm the creator's reputation.

ECONOMICS OF INFORMATION GOODS

General Economic Characteristics

Ultimately, the protection of intellectual property involves protecting the right to information. The idea for a new invention, a poem, a mark, or geographical indication can all be seen as pieces of valuable information. These goods and rights all pertain to intangible, almost ethereal, concepts. This elusive nature of information goods corresponds with what in economics is defined as a "public good." As you may recall from Chapter 3, public goods have two characteristics. Public goods are nonexclusive, meaning that one cannot exclude others from using them or benefiting from them. It is easy to exclude others from using your laptop. A laptop is a tangible object and you can forbid others from coming near it. But when you, in an inspired moment, utter a memorable thought such as "beauty is in the eye of the beholder," you cannot stop others from using these words to impress their friends. Ideas, inventions, and designs are like that: Others only have to see or hear them to be able to use them. The other characteristic of a public good is nonrivalry: Using a public good does not diminish it or make it disappear. It can be used over and over again. A private good, such as icing, will be gone once the cake is eaten, or a washing machine will wear down after a decade's use. But an idea or invention goes on forever; it can be used and applied again and again without diminishing its worth. Nonexclusion and nonrivalry make it impossible (or at least very hard) to internalize the benefits of the good. Others can easily run away with it, and the creator cannot claim compensation for her idea or invention.

Designing a workable market for information goods is further complicated by production costs. Very often the cost of producing the original is very expensive. After that copying tends to be inexpensive. Take, for instance, Hollywood Godzilla-type "B" movies. It takes millions to make a first copy. In effect, these are fixed costs. But that first copy can then be easily multiplied in innumerable copies on a DVD for mere cents. In other words, the marginal cost of additional copies of the film is very low. Or think about the development of a new antidepressant, which takes years of costly research and experimentation; but once the chemical formula is established, the actual costs of the chemicals used may be tiny. Thus, copiers can free ride for a fraction of the cost of inventing. This specific cost structure has two implications. First, because information goods are so easy and cheap to copy and transmit, the problem of piracy is endemic; the need to prevent and prosecute is neverending and requires permanent updating of intellectual property rights. The Napster case mentioned in the beginning of this chapter illustrates this. Second, as explained in Chapter 2, efficiency requires that the market price for a good should reflect the marginal cost of producing an additional unit or copy of that good. If the marginal cost of copying a movie or a pharmaceutical formula is very low, then selling the good for this minuscule marginal cost makes it impossible to earn back the initial investment costs of developing the good. Legal protection of intellectual property rights enables the creator to claim her "right" to information goods and benefit from that right by charging for its use, leasing it to others, or selling the right to a third party who can then exploit it. Markets for information goods can be defined in which property rights to those goods can be traded. Intellectual property rights expand the scope and extent of markets in society. And as we have seen, well-functioning markets increase the welfare of society.

An intellectual property right gives the creator an opportunity to charge a higher price than marginal cost and make a return on his investment. It does this by granting the exclusivity (usually for a limited duration) similar to that of a monopolist, as discussed in Chapter 2. It is important to note that creating something original and protected does not necessarily mean that you have the power to raise prices and restrict entry like a conventional monopolist. In order to understand, think of your last doodle on a napkin or the last song you made up. Both of these would be protected by intellectual property law but are not likely to make you a monopolist. Why? Because there are likely to be many good substitute creations that compete with yours. Thus, intellectual property rights are *necessary* to allow you to act like a monopolist but they are not *sufficient*.

As a final complication, information goods are "experience goods." This means that it is usually impossible for the buyer to determine the value of the information good until he has experienced it. We do not know whether we like a book or a movie until we have read or seen it. We do not know whether we need a computer program until we have used it. Experience goods suffer from a Catch-22. People will not buy the good until they have experienced it, but once they have experienced it they do not want it anymore. This characteristic complicates the trade in information goods, but there are plenty of solutions. Movie and book reviews make it possible for consumers to make up their minds before buying a book or going to a movie. Songs are plugged on the radio to seduce music fans into buying the CD. Versioning is a trick that is used for computer programs. A simple version of a computer program can be downloaded free from the Internet to whet the appetite for the same program with more gimmicks.[2]

These specific economic characteristics of information goods point in one direction: Information goods will be undersupplied unless ownership is protected. The public good characteristic of information goods makes it hard to charge every individual user for what he or she is willing to pay for the enjoyment of a creation or invention. For this reason it is difficult for the creator or inventor to appropriate the full value of his creation or invention. The special cost structure of information goods provides plenty of occasions for piracy and hence "stealing" what belongs to the creator or inventor, which diminishes his eagerness to supply. Finally, the experience goods characteristic also makes trade and supply less attractive. Undersupply will be the probable outcome without a legal intellectual property system that assigns tradable rights to creators and inventors and makes it possible for them to earn their value to society.

Intellectual property rights achieve this laudable objective only by granting exclusivity, and possibly a monopoly, to the creator and inventor. This is a threat to welfare because it allows the owner to charge a price higher than the marginal cost price and to supply less of the good than is efficient. The economic effect of intellectual property rights is always between a rock and a hard place. Easing this tension requires that the exclusivity which intellectual property rights grant be limited in scope and in duration. In effect, the benefits from the protection of intellectual property must be the costs of its protection.

Before we examine the optimal level of protection for intellectual property, there is one final remark. What we discussed in this section on the economic characteristics of information goods pertains mostly to artistic and utilitarian creations, which are covered by copyright and industrial design law, and to inventions, which are the subject of patents. The economic analysis pertains only partly to the intellectual

---

2. This and other special characteristics of markets for information goods can be found in Carl Shapiro and Hal Varian, *Information Rules* (Boston: Harvard Business School Press, 1999).

property rights allocated to trademarks and geographical identifications. These are also information goods, but the purpose of intellectual property rights in these cases is not so much to combat undersupply—although it does that as well—but to avoid unfair competition and decrease consumer confusion and search costs. As already discussed, you know what McDonald's, Coke, or Hertz stand for. Suppose someone wants to name his or her restaurant McDonald's or a new soft drink Coke. Three related things happen. First, if you are in the mood for the real Coke, you will have to engage in a search to determine who is selling what you want. Second, because your search costs are now higher you may decide that the benefits of the search are lower than the cost and you just buy the first Coke you see. If it is inferior to the original, you get less utility for the money spent. Finally, if the trademark is not exclusive, you will find sellers attempting to free ride on the efforts of others who have established their name. When they do this they are "passing off."

All of this means the trademarks differ in another way from other forms of intellectual property. In the case of patents and copyright, duration is limited because there is a sense that at some point the creative person has had sufficient opportunity to internalize the benefit of his or her efforts. The need for information and clear signaling does go away with time. The transaction-cost-reducing effect of trademark exclusivity may be as powerful in 2020 as it is now. Consequently, there is no time limit on trademarks (i.e., they can be renewed) and on geographic indications.

"COPY"-RIGHT VERSUS AUTHOR'S RIGHT

The principal philosophical theory applied to the protection of intellectual property rights has been utilitarianism. Inventions and works of arts have social value because they improve our production possibilities or enhance consumer welfare. The U.S. Constitution grants power to Congress to create patent and copyright laws: "to Promote Progress of Science and useful Arts." Economic theory has translated this utilitarian approach into practical economic arguments to stimulate the creation and trade of utilitarian products. The utilitarian framework has been central to the development of copyright law in the United States.

The European and certainly the French approach is to base the protection of intellectual property rights on the personal interest of the creator, on his or her right to a reward and entitlement. In Europe "copyrights" are called "droit d'auteur" in France and "derecho de autor" in Spain, stressing the personal rights of the creator more than the economic rights to sell and license copies. The European approach is based on "personhood theory." A creation is intertwined with the creator's personal identity. Hence the property of a creation is personal as opposed to fungible. For instance, under the French national law an author has the right to withdraw or retract; that is, an author may purchase at wholesale price all the remaining copies of his or her work. The author also has the legal right to reply to criticism.

International law (Berne convention) recognizes the "moral rights" of the author. Moral rights include the *right to integrity*: mutilation or distortion that would prejudice the author's honor or reputation is *not* permitted; and *the right of attribution*: the true author has the right to have his or her name on the work, and nonauthors are prevented from having their names attached to the author's work. Moral rights also stress the personal connection of the author to the work and the importance of an artist's reputation. Copyright is a property right, whereas the author's moral right is an extension of the author's character and personality. Personality is not transferable, which is why the author always retains the moral rights even after he or she sells or transfers the copyright to another person or company.

References: Peter S. Menell, "Intellectual Property: General Theories," in *Encyclopedia of Law and Economics,* ed. Boudewijn Bouckaert and Gerrit de Geest (Cheltenham: Edward Elgar, 2000); Ronald B. Standler, "Moral Rights of Authors in the USA," 1998, retrieved from: http://www.rbs2.com/moral.htm.

Balancing Costs and Benefits

This chapter has already described the important benefits of granting property rights in intellectual creations. The costs of intellectual property fall into two categories. They are the costs of administering the system and of exclusive rights that close off others from beneficial uses. Theoretically, there is an optimal level of protection. This would be the level of protection that would maximize the net social benefits of intellectual property. From an economic perspective, the chief implication of this effort is to create intellectual property rights but to limit them. In practice, intellectual property rights are limited in two ways. One is the "scope" of protection and the other is duration of protection.

The Scope of Protection

Although scope limitations apply to all forms of intellectual property, it is easiest to understand the concept in the context of copyright. Interestingly, here the theory and practice are similar: The rules economic analysis would suggest as being consistent with a rational approach to copyright are similar to the ones courts have adopted. As an illustration, think about a copyrighted book. Suppose very small portions of the book are copied by someone else. In this case, the law may be that the copying is *de minimus* and the author's rights are not violated. In other words, the copying is so insignificant that it is unlikely to reduce the value of the work. In addition, the legal fees and administrative costs of a legal reaction every time there is a tiny infringement would be costly. The benefits of copying small portions may be high: Think about a young researcher who uses quotations from various authors to establish the state of the literature. Having established how far science has gotten until now, the young scientist can then make her own contribution standing "on the shoulders of giants." It makes little economic sense to protect authors from insignificant uses of their work.

CASE 8.1 **Sweat of the Brow:** *Feist Publications, Inc. v. Rural Telephone Service Company,* 499 U.S. 340 (1991)

Intellectual property rights are a response to the fact that creative people may not be able to internalize the benefits of their ideas. The problem of internalization is not, however, confined to instances in which ideas or creative instincts simply pop into the minds of talented people. For example, suppose an "author" works hard on research and publishes a novel based on historical fact. Or, as in *Feist Publications v. Rural Telephone Service Company,* suppose one publisher copies verbatim the factual information (in this case, names, addresses, and phone numbers) compiled by someone else. The problem with respect to both the historical novel and the telephone book is that a great deal of investment and personal effort may go into the final product but ultimately facts are created. The issue is whether copyright law is designed to protect "sweat of the brow" independent of the originality of what is created. In *Feist*, the Supreme Court ruled that the copyright laws do not protect factual information regardless of the amount of effort expended in compiling it. The problem is that effort often results in information, the benefits of which are difficult to protect without legal protection. On the other hand, granting anyone exclusive rights to information that already exists also results in social costs. You should note that any original way of arranging and classifying the facts and any expressive element of even a historical novel are still protected. It is the bare bones facts that are not, regardless of the sweat of the brow.

Two other limitations deal not with the significance of what is taken but with the high costs of reserving exclusive use by the authors. For example, suppose in preparing the book, the author spent considerable time in the library, on the Internet, and traveling in an effort to discover facts that are included in the book. Factual information is not protected at all. If you think about it, this makes some sense. Facts are not created by an author. They are discovered. Perhaps more important, think of the consequences of protecting facts. Suppose someone compiled a list of phone numbers. If copyright protected the list, anyone republishing the phone numbers would be an infringer. In effect, if an author were assigned the rights to facts, this would be like granting true monopoly power and would be very costly to society.

The second limitation of this nature is that copyright does not protect ideas—only their expression. Suppose the book was a love story describing the relationship between two young people from feuding families, making it difficult for the lovers and ultimately leading to a tragic outcome. Could an author copyright this familiar story line? No. To assign exclusive rights to the Romeo and Juliet "concept" or "idea" would foreclose others from a fundamental structure on which many stories are based. In theory and in practice, copyright cannot be extended so far.

Perhaps the most important narrowing of the scope of protection is called "fair use." For some purposes, others may copy the original work and there is no infringement. For example, suppose a critic writes a review of the book and quotes from it extensively to make a point. Or suppose another author writes a parody of the book to illustrate how foolish it is. In the process, much of the original is copied. In effect, the original is used to inform the public and to make an entirely different type of work. The idea here is that the fair use is socially beneficial and unlikely to be the type of use the original author would make of the work. The benefit of narrowing the scope of protection is arguably more beneficial to the public than the loss in incentive to the author.

The Duration of Protection

Although the law concerning the scope of protection can be squared, in at least a general way, with optimizing the level of protection, the same cannot be said of duration. For example, the length of protection should be a function of how much protection is needed to bring forth a work. This would mean various durations or, at the very least, copyright terms that would be relatively certain. In the United States, copyright duration is currently for the life of the author plus seventy years. It does not vary with the value of the work but with the life expectancy of the author. There is very little economic support for the policy.

To understand what would be involved in determining optimal duration, think in terms of marginal social benefits and marginal social costs of intellectual property rights.[3] Marginal social benefits are the extra benefits to society due to the presence of intellectual property rights and the resulting incentive for creators and inventors to produce. Over time, these marginal social benefits decrease. They start at a high level because of the great impact that a new creation or invention can have, but each year the social benefits decrease because the invention or creation is spread more and more throughout society: More people have already seen, heard, or used it. The creators and authors themselves benefit less and less from more returns further away in time. First of all, because most authors and creators—like other people—have a declining marginal utility of money in general, and second, the further away in the future the benefits, the smaller their discounted value will be and, hence, the smaller the influence of a longer stream of income on creative activities now. Figure 8.2

---

3. This duration analysis is based on the work by William Landes and Richard Posner, "An Economic Analysis of Copyright Law," *Journal of Legal Studies* 18 (1989): 325–363.

shows the path of marginal social benefits decreasing over time. Time is shown on the horizontal axis and dollar amounts on the vertical axis (assuming for convenience that benefits—and costs—can be measured in dollars).

Granting intellectual property rights to creators and inventors introduces social costs to society because it allows a monopoly situation to come into existence. Monopoly pricing is a first element of these marginal social costs of copyright, patent, and industrial design laws. Monopoly causes welfare losses, and the longer monopoly rights are prolonged, the more welfare damage is done. The other element is that intellectual property rights restrict the availability and diffusion of creativity and knowledge across society. The development of creativity and of knowledge is a cumulative process in which each sequential step provides knowledge useful and sometimes even essential for the next step. The longer society has to wait before the intellectual property rights fall into the public domain, the longer additional benefits from new creations are withheld from society. Also, it has been

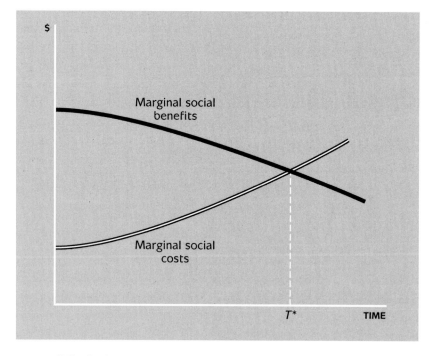

FIGURE 8.2 Optimal Duration of Intellectual Property Rights

argued that the cost of tracing copyrighted work and the transaction costs of maintaining the copyright system increase the longer the copyright duration.

As time goes by, the marginal social benefits of copyright goes down and the marginal social cost goes up. At some point in time, $T^\star$ in Figure 8.2, marginal social costs surpass marginal social benefits. At that point, the presence of intellectual property rights costs society more than the rights benefit society, and the assignment of property rights should stop. $T^\star$ is the optimal duration for intellectual property rights. $T^\star$ is also the point where the net total benefit (i.e., total benefits minus total costs) of intellectual property rights has reached its maximum for society. In each year when marginal social benefits are higher than marginal social costs (i.e., in all the years to the left of $T^\star$), the net benefit for society increases. In the years past $T^\star$, marginal social costs are higher than social benefits; total net benefits to society diminish when intellectual property rights are extended beyond $T^\star$.

This theoretical analysis of the optimal duration applies to all types of intellectual property, and the implication is that we should consider the costs and benefits of assigning intellectual property rights case by case. It would be more efficient to consider case by case what the benefits and costs of each property right amount to and act accordingly. In actuality, in some countries a distinction is made between short and long patents as a result of at least an implicit comparison of the cost and benefits of patenting smaller and major inventions. The principal problem of implementing such a plan across the board is that it would raise the cost of administering a system of intellectual property. Each author or inventor would certainly argue for the longest possible term.

LAW AND ECONOMICS IN ACTION 8.4

THE SONNY BONO COPYRIGHT EXTENSION ACT

In 1998, the U.S. Senate passed what became known as the Sonny Bono Copyright Extension Act. The act was named after the late congressman and singer who, according to his widow, claimed that copyright "should be forever." The act extended copyright from fifty to seventy years after an author's death, and for works produced "for hire" and owned by firms,

from seventy-five to ninety-five years after publication. The act also har-
monized American law with a new European Union directive. Disney, with
other media giants, had lobbied hard for the law, which happily stopped
early images of Mickey Mouse from entering the public domain. Without
the law, Mickey's copyrights would have begun expiring in 2003. This is
not the first time Congress has extended copyright; it has done so eleven
times in the past forty years. The copyright extension also covered hundred of thousands of books, movies, and songs including works by Ernest
Hemingway and George Gershwin.

The most bizarre aspect of the act was that it extended the copyright
term not only for new works but for works already in existence. To the
extent copyright is designed to provide an incentive, the retroactive extension is hard to justify. What is already created can hardly be taken back.
Certainly not by dead authors. In *Eldred v. Ashcroft*,[4] the U.S. Supreme
Court upheld the act and "reasoned" that authors who created before the
extension might have been motivated by the thought that if Congress ever
extended the copyright term, the extension would likely be retroactive.

Reference: "Free Mickey Mouse," *The Economist* (October 10, 2002): 65.

There are two things to remember although they are economically
irrational in many respects. First, the fixed term approach is far less
expensive to administer than a case-by-case approach. Second, even
if copyright term seems illogical, effective use of limitations on scope
can bring some rationality back into the system. For example, the
author who, in 2005, draws a simple little doodle on a napkin while
sipping latte at Starbucks will have the same copyright term as the
composer of a complex symphony. On the other hand, there is far
less to protect and the scope of protection is likely to be far less for
the doodle.

QUESTIONS FOR DISCUSSION

1. Copyright protection extends to any work that contains some originality and has not been copyrighted even if a previous author produced exactly the same thing. Patent protection, on the other hand,
   extends only to inventions that are novel. Reinventing something

   4. 537 U.S. 186 (2003).

that already exists means no patent protection. Is there an economic rationale for this distinction?

2. Copyright and patent both exist for a limited period of time. Trademark protection, on the other hand, generally exists as long as the owner makes use of it. Do you see an economic rationale for this distinction?

3. Do you think greeting card publishers change their designs each year because of copyright protection? Would you favor a law that denies copyright and patent protection to creative works and inventions when they would come into existence without intellectual property laws?

4. Discuss: Copyright protection should always end on the day the original author or artist dies.

5. In this chapter, we showed that information goods have characteristics similar to those of public goods. But arguments can also be made to show that information goods lead to positive externalities. What arguments would that be? We discussed externalities in Chapter 4. We showed that negative externalities could be "internalized" using taxes. Similarly, positive externalities can be "internalized" using subsidies. Discuss: If the government would sufficiently subsidize the production of information goods, we could do away with copyright.

Economics
of Contract Law

CHAPTER NINE

The Economic Functions of Contract Law

I N AN ORGANIZED SOCIETY, PEOPLE HAVE OBLIGATIONS to one another. The general obligation to behave in a careful manner and not harm others gives rise to the area of law called torts. The next unit of this book is devoted to tort law. People create obligations beyond those required by law when they make contracts. Contracts are critical to a smoothly functioning and growing economy. They permit people to rely on each other and to specialize. They permit the independence that distinguishes primitive societies from modern industrial ones. This unit, which consists of four chapters, is devoted to the law and economics of contract law.

The legal definition of a contract is an agreement that is supported by *consideration*. Agreement in this context means that someone has made an offer—proposed an exchange—and another party has accepted—consented to the proposed exchange. Consideration is what one party gives in exchange for the act (performance) or promise of the other party. For example, if you sold your car for $5,000, the car would be consideration for the $5,000 and the $5,000 would be consideration for the car. A topic that usually comes up whenever one discusses contracts is the enforcement of what are called *gratuitous promises*. These are promises such as, "I promise to give you $100 on your birthday," made from one person to another without any exchange or consideration. In some cases, these promises are enforced.

This chapter focuses on contracts generally and Chapter 10 focuses on gratuitous promises. Chapter 11 discusses the possibility that contract law can be used to redistribute income. Chapter 12 is devoted to the consequences when one person breaches a contract. All of these issues have important economic implications.

When contracts are approached from an economic perspective, there are two broad questions. First, is there an economic rationale for having a publicly supported system of law devoted to contracts? Second, why do people make contracts in the first place? These questions are related. It would make little sense to invest in a system of contract law if the underlying purposes for contracts were not socially beneficial.

We can dispense with the question of why people make contracts fairly easily. Going back to the car example, why would you sell your car for $5,000? If you are rational and not being forced, it is because you prefer the things you can buy with the $5,000 over continuing to possess the car. Similarly, why would someone pay $5,000 for your car? It would be because he or she prefers the car to anything else that can be obtained for $5,000. Obviously, unless third parties are negatively affected by the exchange, the making of the contract means reaching a Pareto superior outcome.

Pareto superior outcomes can result when the exchange takes place immediately or when the two parties exchange promises to do something later. For example, I may go into your ice cream shop and pay you $3 at virtually the same time you hand me an ice cream cone. On the other hand, I may make a promise today to perform at your nightclub six months from now, and you may make a promise today to pay me a certain amount at that time. This second example gives you an insight into what most contracts are actually about: allocating risks. When I promise to perform in six months, I am taking the risk that a better opportunity will not come along that I might prefer. And by agreeing to pay me a certain amount, you are accepting the risk that my popularity might decline and you could hire me for less. Or a building contractor may agree to buy wood to be delivered when it is needed in six months. The contractor assumes the risk that the wood will not be less expensive in six months and the seller assumes the risk that the price of wood will not increase and he or she could have sold it for even more. In short, one of the most important functions of contracts is to facilitate agreements through which parties allocate risks.

Given that people can make exchanges at any time without the help of a system of rules and courts that enforce contracts, why do we need such a system? This chapter discusses four economic-based rationales for the existence of a system of contract law. First, you will see that a system of contract law can have a dramatic impact on transaction costs. Following is an explanation of how a system of contract law can be used as a tool to protect third parties from the external effects of contracts. Next, we learn that a system of contract law has a regulatory element as it controls the means that people use to persuade each other. For example, contracts resulting from high-pressure tactics are sometimes not enforced. Last, we see that by having a system of contract law, the public can influence distributive outcomes. This function is discussed briefly here and more fully in Chapter 11.

THE TRANSACTION COSTS–REDUCING FUNCTION OF CONTRACT LAW

As a general matter, the transaction costs–reducing function of contract law involves a balancing process. First, it makes sense from a societal point of view to ensure that mutually beneficial exchanges take place. Society's investment involves the costs associated with searching and shopping, negotiating and drafting the contract, and monitoring and enforcing the execution of contractual obligations. In theory, the amount invested does not exceed what is called the "benefit of the bargain," which is the total gain to the parties. Because we want to maximize the difference between the costs and benefits of contracting, it makes sense to minimize the costs of contract formation and enforcement—just as it makes sense to minimize the cost of any investment. Sometimes these costs will be minimized when they are public costs (borne by society); in other instances, they will be minimized when they are private costs that the parties to the contract must incur themselves. One way to maximize the benefits of contracting is to make sure contracting costs are absorbed either publicly or privately—depending upon which alternative is more efficient at performing the cost-reducing function at issue. As you will see, these determinations can be viewed as taking place at both a macro and micro level.

The Macro Level

To understand how cost minimization works at a macro level, pretend that you are a building contractor. A customer comes to you with the plans for a house she wants you to build. Contractors, as you may know, do not usually do all the work themselves; they hire plumbers, electricians, roofers, and other subcontractors to complete different portions of the job. Each of these subcontractors will work at a different time over the next few weeks. You will be faced with a number of contractual issues. Your customer will not make a contract with you unless you can give her a firm price, which will be based on the charges each subcontractor will charge you for their parts of the job. You cannot do this, though, unless each of the subcontractors gives you a firm price. You may add up all the subcontractor costs and add some profit for yourself and come up with a total of $200,000. Because your customer does not want to pay the $200,000 all at once, you agree that payments will come in four $50,000 installments. This probably all seems simple. You have a contract, enforceable in court, with the customer and each of the subcontractors.

But wait! This all assumes that you have a system of contract law. Suppose you do not, and the customer comes to you and says she will pay $200,000 for the house but only when it is completed. Are you willing to build it and accept the risk that you will be paid when the house is finished? Suppose you start building it and hire a subcontractor to build the foundation. Do you pay first or does the subcontractor do his work first? Unless you hand him dollar bills as each bit of the foundation is built, someone will have to take a pretty big risk. Of course, after the foundation is built, you need another subcontractor. Maybe you could then sell the foundation to your customer and move on to the next step. But then again, your customer wants a completed house, so you engage the next subcontractor, again at the risk of eventually being paid by the customer.

The picture you are getting is that contract law greatly facilitates planning. With enforceable contracts, you know the customer will pay or be held liable. You also know that each subcontractor will be at the job site when his or her part of the job is to be performed or he or she will be liable for damages. Another way to put this is that it facilitates reliance. You can spend whatever you need to spend and plan accordingly because you will be able to *rely* on others.

It is true that houses could be built and contracts enforced without contract law. Private businesses would likely emerge that would administer these private agreements. For example, they might hold your customer's money until you complete the first stage of construction. The customer would get the money back if you did not complete the performance. Of course this too involves making contracts that need to be enforced. A system of contract law might be supplied through private markets, but the cost could be quite high.

LAW AND ECONOMICS IN ACTION 9.1

SOURCES OF CONTRACT LAW

Contract law is nearly all state law rather than federal law. In addition, it is generally "common law," which means it is composed of general judge-made rules as opposed to statutes enacted by state legislatures. This raises the possibility that different states could have different contract rules that could lead to difficulties when contracts are made between people in different states. One reaction to this has been the adoption in every state except Louisiana of the Uniform Commercial Code. The UCC, as it is called, is still state law but consists of a set of statutes that are very similar from state to state. The rules apply to the sale of goods only. Contracts between parties in different countries can also lead to problems if the different countries have different rules and the parties have not specified which set of rules will govern their agreement. Now many countries have agreed to the Convention on the International Sale of Goods. The CISG works in a manner similar to the UCC except that it applies to agreements between contracting parties in different countries. Given the scope of international trade, you can understand why this set of contract rules is potentially of enormous importance.

Without knowing it, you are already familiar with how some contracts are treated in the absence of formal contract law. Think of the last gangster movie you saw. Typically, contracts for illegal purposes are not enforced by the courts. So what happens when a supplier of illegal drugs does not deliver or the buyer does not have the money or a loan is not repaid? The parties have their own private enforcers and those who breach might find their kneecaps broken or find themselves taking a very long swim.

In a world without contract law, individual parties would have to look to self-help for enforcement or support a legitimate private industry devoted to contact management and enforcement. There is no guarantee that the private "law" that would emerge would be uniform. Plus, many beneficial contracts might not be made because the costs of contracting would exceed the benefits from the contract. A public system of contract law replaces a private industry of enforcing legitimate contracts. A nationwide, generally uniform system of contract law is considered less expensive than numerous private agreements. More technically, there are increasing returns to scale with a uniform system of contract law and a central enforcement system. Thus, from an economic perspective, one of the principal purposes of a public system of contract law is to lower the cost of making and enforcing contracts.

The Micro View

The system of contract law consists of individual elements including enforcement mechanisms, rules for how to form a contract, and generalized standards for assessing whether parties have formed a contract. Thus, the parties do not have to address each of these issues every time they form a contract. This has an obvious transaction cost–reducing effect. Contract law provides many *default* terms for contracts when the parties have not specifically addressed those terms. For example, the contract the parties form may leave out things like the method of payment or time of payment. Contract law will provide terms that are appropriate for the parties and the industry in which they operate.

Much of the transaction cost–reducing impact of contract law is a result of what are called *gap-fillers*. Gap-fillers are default contract terms that become part of the contract when the parties either choose not to or forget to include a specific term. For example, if the parties do not specify otherwise, it is assumed that goods are delivered before they are paid for. There are also default positions for the types of warranties that come with a product and contract remedies. In fact, if the parties indicate that they intend to form a contract but purposely leave the price term open, courts will fill in the blank. All of these possibilities take the pressure off the parties to think of every issue that may arise and thus reduce the costs of contracting. They also lower the risk of "opportunistic behavior" by a party who has second thoughts and searches through the contract to find a technical reason to claim it should not be enforced.

Sometimes uniform default terms are not suitable for certain contracts. In these instances, a court will fill in the blank by assessing the context in which the contract was formed. Here the critical terms are *course of performance, course of dealing,* and *trade usage.* The course of performance refers to a practice that has evolved between the parties as a contract is performed. Course of dealing is a practice that has evolved between the parties over the course of more than one contract. Trade usage refers to practices or standards that have evolved in the trade in which the parties are involved. When parties leave out a term, courts will often attempt to determine what they would have specified had they thought of the term. For example, suppose you run a restaurant and have a contract with a company that delivers fresh linens each week on Friday. When they do, you pay them although there is nothing in the contract about when payment is to be made. If a conflict comes up about when payment is due, a court will fill the gap in the contract by reference to the course of performance. Or if there is no course of performance because the issue arises when the first delivery is made, the court will fill the gap with course of dealing or trade usage. You should be getting a picture of contract law as a lubricant that allows the contract machinery to move smoothly.

LAW AND ECONOMICS IN ACTION 9.2

TRADE USAGE AT YOUR LOCAL HOME DEPOT

Suppose you are fixing up your apartment. You do some precise measurement for a bookcase. The first shelf is to be four inches above the floor—that way your fold-away, super-stepper exercise machine will fit under it. You go to Home Depot and ask for a piece of 2 × 4 lumber to serve as your base. You go home and construct your bookcase and then attempt to slide the super-stepper under it. It does not fit. Finally, you measure the space under the bottom shelf. It is only 3½ inches. You go back to Home Depot and complain. You know that you specifically said that you wanted a piece of 2 × 4 which you say should be, well, two inches by four inches. You point out that your 2 × 4 is only 3½ inches wide and, in fact, only 1¾ inches thick. The salesperson informs you that in the retail business the expression "2 × 4" is not to be taken literally. Although sixty years ago a 2 × 4 piece of lumber was actually two inches by four inches, that is no longer the case. For many years 2 × 4 has just been a name for lumber that is actually 1¾ × 3½ inches. This is, you are told, a matter of common knowledge so much so that any contract that says 2 × 4 will be interpreted to mean 1¾ × 3½. In effect, the *trade usage* of the term "2 × 4" is 1¾ by 3½.

Related to gap-filling is interpretation. Sometimes the parties will think they have addressed an issue only to find they actually disagree on what the term means. Courts will engage in interpretation using the standards discussed above. An overriding idea is to apply an objective as opposed to subjective standard. In short, courts adopt the interpretation that seems reasonable given the words and context. Applying a subjective standard to determine for certain what one party or the other party meant would be a futile alternative. This means that a party wishing to apply a narrow or unusual interpretation to a term has the burden of making sure that the desired meaning is evident from the contract.

A good example is a case that is taught in law schools involving the sale of "chicken." When the seller delivered old tough chickens that were edible only after stewing, the buyer protested, claiming that "chicken" means young tender chickens and that the seller knew that. In an opinion authored by famed jurist Learned Hand, the court noted that the party with the narrower definition had the burden of proving that the parties were referring to younger chickens. In other words, the risk of a deviation from the definition of "chicken" as *any* chicken was allocated to the party favoring the narrower definition.[1] As an economic matter, this means that the "cost" of making certain that the contract terms are "accurate" is to be incurred by the party claiming the less typical definition. Is this the efficient way to handle the problem? If you think about it, it probably is. Most of the time the

---

1. *Frigaliment Importing Co. v. B.N.S. International Sales Corp.*, 190 F.Supp.116 (1960).

"obvious" intention will hold and it would be inefficient to require the parties to address the matter each time a contract is formed. When there is a deviation from the norm, the party wanting the specialized definition is the most likely to know of that particular meaning and motivated to account for it. This means that the step of making sure the contract is accurate in atypical instances is undertaken by the party in the best or less expensive position to intervene. More important, the public does not incur the cost of discovering what the party really meant.

As noted in the introduction to this chapter, contracts are basically tools for allocating risks. A great deal of gap-filling and interpretation is related to how a risk was allocated. The question of risk allocation comes up most obviously in the case of two specific questions. The first deals with the extent of a party's liability when a contract is breached. As you will see in Chapter 12 on contract remedies, the parties may agree ahead of time as to the consequences when one party does not perform. If they do not, an array of contract remedies come into play to fill the gap.

The second risk allocation question comes up when performance becomes more difficult or substantially different from what was anticipated. Sometimes when this occurs, one party will ask to have its performance excused. For example, a swimming pool contractor might agree to build a swimming pool for a homeowner for $20,000. The ground in the geographic area has always been sandy, but when the contractor begins excavation of this pool, he runs into solid rock that will cause construction expenses to double. Similarly, a person wishing to operate a wine and cheese shop may rent a business property. Shortly after signing a long-term lease and opening, the city in which the shop is located may pass a law prohibiting the sale of alcoholic beverages from that site. In both these cases, the question arises of just how much risk was allocated to the party wanting to be excused. Did the pool owner assume the risk of running into solid rock? Did the wine and cheese shop owner assume the risk of a new city law prohibiting alcohol sales? Very often these questions are not covered by the contract because it would raise transaction costs enormously for the parties to contemplate every possible contingency. Courts will usually excuse a party if the contingency is unanticipated, it changes the nature of performance substantially, and the party asking to be excused did not assume the risk. We will return to this perplexing issue in Chapter 11.

Although it is clear that courts lower the costs of contracting by gap-filling and interpretation, it is important to note that lowering costs means lowering costs generally, not just private costs. As already noted, if one thinks of contract law as designed to lower transaction costs, then a related goal is to achieve this end efficiently. This means that courts will not get involved when the gaps are too broad, interpretation too difficult, or when it is not clear whether the parties even intended to make a contract. As an economic matter, what goes on in these instances is that the risk of making or not making a binding contract is shifted to the private parties because they can address the problems at a lower cost than public institutions.

THE PERVASIVENESS OF RISK ALLOCATION

You have already seen how contracts allocate risks. For example, suppose you run a house-painting service and are hired to paint a house for $1,000, including the paint, and to be finished within one week. Suppose further that you live in Florida. Clearly, you have the risk that the price of paint will not go up and that no better jobs will come along in that time period. This is the easy part. Now suppose two things occur that are not in the contract. First, although you did not notice, the house is made of special wood that requires that an expensive sealer first be applied. This means twice the work you had planned on and a much lower profit. Second, right after signing the contract, hurricane warnings are posted and it becomes impossible for you to complete the job in one week. Your reaction may be to tell the owner that you will not paint the house. He may claim that you have breached the agreement and you point out that there is nothing in the contract about sealers or hurricanes and that neither you nor the owner thought about these things. You ask a court to excuse you from your obligations. Sometimes a court will do this but only if it decides that the two risks were not assumed by you. Here is where things get a little sticky. In fact, you did not think of these problems and neither did the homeowner. This means that the court is really not deciding who assumed the risk but who it makes sense to regard as having assumed the risk. There is an important educative element to the court's decision. In effect, by ruling one way or the other, the court is saying that "from now on" this type of risk will be assumed by a certain party. In the future, painters and homeowners should consider this risk allocation the default position unless there is express language in the contract stating otherwise.

One approach to risk allocation is for the court to assign it the way the parties would have if they had thought about it. This makes sense because contracting parties tend to allocate risks between them so that the party assuming the risk can do so less expensively than the other party. For example, given that you are an experienced house painter and already familiar with all kinds of surfaces and their specialized characteristics, it is likely that you would have assumed the risk of different types of surfaces. So, a court ruling that you did assume the risk is really saying that from now on if one party holds him or herself out as a house painter, the other party is permitted to assume that the painter knows all about the different needs of different surfaces.

The hurricane example is a closer call. Neither party can keep the hurricane from coming, so the question is who should absorb the loss associated with a delay in having the house painted. Both parties live in Florida and know about the possibility of a hurricane. The question is whether the one week deadline should be read to mean "even if there is a hurricane." What do you think? Hint: Does it make a difference that the home owner has better information about what will happen if the painting is not done in a week?

One way to minimize public costs (and all costs) of contracting is to require the parties to observe certain formalities before beginning the gap-filling and interpretive process. The most important of these—offer, acceptance, and consideration—were introduced at the beginning of this chapter. In short, the party wishing to have a contract enforced must demonstrate that one of the parties actually did make a definite offer to enter into a contact and that the other party responded in a way that reasonable people would regard as signifying an acceptance. The acceptance must not equivocate, deviate from the offer, or mention new terms. In addition, the interaction must involve some kind of exchange or consideration. On these three cornerstone matters, courts tend to be fairly strict. As an economic matter, it would make little sense to devote a great deal of judicial resources to gap-filling and interpretation without clear indications from the parties that they intended to form an exchange with benefits flowing to both parties.

CASE 9.1 Did They Form a Contract? *Harvey v. Facey,*
A.C. 552 (Privy Council of Jamaica 1893)

One of the more interesting cases dealing with the formality of
offer and acceptance is *Harvey v. Facey,* an 1893 British case. The
problem started when one party, who was interested in purchasing
a piece of property known as "Bumper Hall Pen," wrote to another
and asked, "What is the lowest price you will take for Bumper Hall
Pen?" The owner of the property replied with the following:
"Lowest Price of Bumper Hall Pen is 100 pounds." To this, the
original party sent a letter saying "I accept" and claimed that a
contract had been formed. The argument was that the owner of
the property had indicated a willingness to sell (made an offer)
with the statement about the lowest price. The argument of the
landowner was that he had not offered to sell the land but had
indicated the lowest acceptable price at which he would sell. The
court sided with the landowner, ruling that an offer must contain
within it an indication that a party is willing to make a contract.
Stating what amounted to a reservation price was not the same as
indicating a willingness to sell at that price. Do you agree?

THIRD-PARTY EFFECTS AND PUBLIC POLICY

Contracts that harm third parties are often discouraged directly by
criminal law. For example, it is unlawful for individuals to agree (make
a contract) to steal from someone or to harm that person. Contract
law also plays a role here. Just as contract law can lower the transaction costs for transactions that increase the utility of all parties, it can
withhold that assistance from contracts that are likely to decrease utility. It does this by adhering to the rule that courts will not enforce
contracts that are against "public policy." This does not mean that
such contracts will not be made and performed, but when there are
difficulties, the parties will be left to their own devices to sort things
out. If this brings to mind images of Mafia enforcers, you are on the
right track. Contracts that are made in shady contexts are risky and
involve a high-transaction-cost environment. The overall effect is one
in which the contract law system subsidizes beneficial transactions and
withholds that treatment from transactions that are harmful.

This leads to the question of how to distinguish the contracts that
are against public policy from those that are not. This is not always

easy to determine in advance. For example, you might think the law reacts to contracts in which one party takes advantage of another party. The idea is that it is against public policy to drive too hard a bargain. This type of analysis gets sticky very quickly because it requires a court to evaluate agreements that both parties may at one time have viewed as acceptable. How is a court to determine, after the fact, when there is sufficient unfairness to hold the contract unenforceable? Typically, courts do not invoke the rationale of "against public policy" in these cases and, for the most part, courts steer clear of deciding what is "fair" and "not fair" when it comes to contracts. Chapter 11, which is devoted exclusively to distributive matters, discusses this difficult issue.

The concept of public policy usually comes up when third parties are involved. For example, contracts for the sale of unlawful drugs are not enforceable. An argument can be made that the exchanging parties both experience an increase in welfare and that it makes no sense to withhold the assistance of the system of contract law. The reasoning, however, is that the interests of people *other* than the contracting parties are involved, and although the two principal parties may have consented to the contract, the third parties have not. Obviously, in one sense, a contract with negative third-party effects cannot be Pareto superior. More important, once negative third-party effects are considered, it is not even clear that overall welfare is enhanced.

The easiest cases to predict and understand involve contracts that are about or related to illegal activities. As already noted, contracts for the sale of illegal drugs will not be enforced. Similarly, some courts have refused to enforce contracts for goods or services that are complements to the illegal good. For example, some courts have held that contracts for the sale of drug paraphernalia will not be enforced. In these instances, the law has already declared that third parties have a right to be free from the externalities of these activities. If parties could use the contract law system to further the same activities that are illegal, it would amount to using the system to subsidize the illegal conduct. This would, in turn, require increased expenditures on the enforcement of criminal law.

More difficult are instances in which third parties are negatively affected but the activity is not illegal. Here it may be important to understand a subtle distinction. Consider two contracts. Under contract A, an owner of land sells it to someone who is accumulating enough land to build a shopping area. When the shopping area is built, traffic will increase and neighboring land values will fall. Under contract B, two attorneys who are partners in a law firm decide to dissolve the partnership and also agree that they will practice law in two separate towns in order not to compete with each other. Here, third parties are worse off because the market for attorney services is less competitive. In practice, courts would likely enforce the first contract but are less likely to enforce the second one. Yet, as already indicated, in both instances third parties are worse off.

So what is the difference? If you look at these possibilities closely, there is an important difference that, as an economic matter, seems to justify the different treatment by the courts. In the case of the land sale, whatever value the buyer and seller attribute to what they will receive under the contract is independent of the impact on the value of neighboring properties. On the other hand, the agreement between the attorneys not to compete is of value to either party only if third parties are made worse off. In other words, unless the market for legal services really does become less competitive, the agreement itself is of no interest to the parties. The public policy rationale is most apt when third parties are affected in a negative way and the value exchanged by the parties is a result of that impact.

Even in this sense, it would be a mistake to conclude that there is a simple, predictable outcome in every case. Courts sometimes weigh the economic effects of promises not to compete like the one entered into by the attorneys above. Consider three types of instances in which covenants not to compete are used. One involves news broadcasters. Think of your local news programs at 6:00 and 11:00 and, more than likely, the anchor person has a contract that says that if she stops working for that station she may not go to work for a competing station. If you ever use a travel agent, he or she probably works with other agents in the same office. Very often these people also have agreements not to work for another agency if they leave. Finally, a chef may start a restaurant and decide to sell it. Very often, the chef will have to agree not to open a new restaurant in the same area.

In all three cases, competition may be less and public policy called into question. Imagine a world in which it is known ahead of time that these agreements would not be enforced. Most television viewers like a particular newscaster and may not care what station has to be tuned in to see that person. Given this, what would the motivation be for any station to train, develop, and advertise a particular newsperson? Whether you perceive much in the way of ultimate benefit from competition by local television stations, the way those stations convince you that one is "better" than another is by promoting the people who do the news and sportscasting. And since consumers do develop preferences, some newscasters do a "better" job than others. In effect, if covenants not to compete were not enforced in this context, television stations would not offer the quality of service they do now.

The problem that arises in the case of the travel agent is that consumers tend to focus on the individuals who deliver personal services—travel agents, hair stylists, physicians—and not on the company they happen to work for. So if a travel agent leaves one firm for another, all of his or her customers will "travel" to the new agency. This may seem fine, but it undercuts the willingness of the agency owner to hire and train new employees—precisely the type of investment that is necessary to ensure their competence. Unless some agency has the right to enforce such agreements, consumers might actually be worse off.

The example of the chef is a little different, but the outcome is the same. If you were a chef and operated a restaurant and believed that your success depended on consumer satisfaction, your interest would be in building goodwill. You would depend on repeat business and you would invest in the restaurant's image. After working hard, you might decide to retire or move on. The first thing you might be asked when you get ready to sell is, "Do you plan to open a restaurant nearby?" The concerned buyer will want to make sure that you do not take the customers who have enjoyed your good cooking with you. If you cannot make an enforceable contract not to reenter the business in competition with the one you sold, the price for which you can sell will decline. And the less you are able to resell for, the less interest you may have in perfecting your culinary skills, and your customers may be worse off.

In all three examples, the key is to allow the investor to recoup some of the investment so the investment that takes place is one that makes consumers better off. On the other hand, we also know that consumers are made worse off by anticompetitive agreements. One of the jobs of the courts is to balance these two interests. The general approach is to permit covenants not to compete as long as they are no broader than necessary to protect efforts that benefit consumers. "Breadth" is determined by the length of time the agreement not to compete lasts, the geographic area, and the way the prohibited activity is defined. For example, in the restaurant case, it might be acceptable to have a contract that prohibits the seller from opening a new restaurant for three years in the same town. On the other hand, an agreement that the seller could not open any business in the state for ten years would likely not be enforced because it is broader than necessary.

In sum, one of the functions of contract law is to distinguish among contracts on the basis of their value to the public. Contracts that are counter to public policy are not enforced, and the consequence is that the cost of making and enforcing them is high. And in some cases, the function of contract law is to balance the interests of consumers in free competition and short-run benefits with an interest in encouraging investment that may benefit those same consumers in the long run.

REGULATING THE MEANS OF PERSUASION

Suppose you are shopping for a computer on eBay. The seller says it works great. You buy it and it arrives but does not work because its electronics were fried by a lightning strike. Or suppose you go to your grandmother's house and she begins to tell you how she came to buy 1,000 hours of tango lessons. Or you hear about a relative who recently paid $800 for a new refrigerator that you just saw for $400 at another store.

All of these instances represent real-life examples of contracts that courts found were *avoidable* by the buyers. Avoidability means that one party has the option of refusing to go through with the contract. Typically, contracts are avoidable by a party when courts feel the other party has used an unacceptable means to achieve the contract. In effect, by using the avoidability tool, courts are able to discourage the use of some means of persuasion and to encourage the use of other means. For the most part, the various doctrines that make contracts avoidable are consistent with channeling behavior so that it is more

likely that Pareto superior outcomes will be achieved. (A more theoretical explanation of how this works is set out in the chapter appendix.) In fact, most of the rulings by courts about avoidability fall into
one of two categories. Some deal with efforts by sellers or buyers to
mislead their counterparts. Others concern instances in which individuals fall victim to the coercive influence of the other parties.

Misrepresentations and Nondisclosure

Fraud, which is knowingly misleading another, is technically a tort
and people who are victims of fraud can recover damages, including
(sometimes) punitive damages. A person who is induced to make a
contract as a result of a fraudulent statement can also choose to avoid
the contract. The economic rationale for this is easy to understand.
Suppose you visit your local used car lot looking for a low-mileage
car that will be dependable transportation to and from school. You
find a car that looks pretty good and the odometer says 20,000. The
salesperson says the mileage is accurate and, all things considered,
you are willing to pay $5,000 for the car. A deal is struck at $4,500
because you value the car more than anything else you could buy for
$4,500 and the salesperson values your $4,500 more than keeping the
car and having a chance to sell it to someone else.

A week later a trusted mechanic tells you that the odometer has
been tampered with and that the mileage is more like 100,000 miles.
If you had known the car had 100,000 miles on it, the most you
would have paid would have been $1,000. In this case, your per-
ception of having traded your $4,500 for something worth more to
you than $4,500 is wrong from the start. Whatever Paretian gain
there appears to have been is an illusion and traceable to the seller's
fraud. Of course, this could all have been avoided if you had had
everything the seller said checked by professionals. If you were
shopping for a car and going from dealer to dealer and considering a number of cars, this could get expensive. You appear to have
the choice of expending a great deal in search costs or taking the
risk of ending up in a transaction you never intended to be in. Contract law does not force you to choose between taking the risk of
being lied to and expending a great deal on verification. By not
enforcing contracts that are the result of fraudulent representations,
contract law removes the incentive to misrepresent and decreases

search costs as well as the likelihood of exchanges that are Pareto inferior.

Fraud involves knowing misrepresentations. Contract law will also allow buyers to avoid contracts when the sellers have made innocent or even mistaken misrepresentations.[2] Moreover, misrepresentation can be more than just *stating* something that is incorrect. For example, if you are selling a house that has a termite problem, it would be a misrepresentation to paint over the holes the termites have made in order to conceal the damage. This is not to say that you must voluntarily disclose to potential buyers information about all the imperfections in the house. In general, the idea is that that you cannot purposely or artificially raise the search costs of the buyer. When you make it more difficult to find the imperfections, this is what you do.

CASE 9.2 **May I Have This Dance, and That One and That One and . . . :** *Vokes v. Arthur Murray, Inc.,* 212 So.2d 906 (2nd Dist. 1968)

One issue that arises quite often is when a statement is a misrepresentation and when it is an allowable sales pitch that the buyer should have been wary of. A case that has drawn a fair amount of commentary for a variety of reasons is *Vokes v. Arthur Murray, Inc.,* a 1968 Florida case. Mrs. Vokes, a fifty-one-year-old widow, visited the Davenport School of Dance. She initially bought sixteen half-hour lessons for $14.50. Evidently, she spent several hours at the studio chatting with the smooth-talking sales personnel. She seemed to enjoy the company and the constant suggestions that she had the potential to be an excellent dancer. She signed up for 545 more hours of dance lessons. Before they could be used, she signed up for 926 more hours. All the while, she was complimented on her progress and reminded of her potential. She purchased 123 more hours and later 151, 481, and 347 additional hours. In all, she entered into fourteen contracts and bought over 2,300 hours of dance lessons before, evidently, she got the idea that maybe, just maybe, she really was not going to need all these lessons and that her potential might not be as great as the instructors were suggesting. The court held that, under

---

2. Buyers are also permitted to enforce the contract under the mistaken description. For example, in the fraudulent car case, the buyer could ask for contract damages as described in Chapter 25.

these facts, the contract could be avoided. Although the dance studio could encourage Vokes, the court held that it had crossed the line into misrepresentation as to her eventual potential and improvement. What do you think? Aren't buyers supposed to watch out for themselves when obvious appeals to vanity are made?

It is important to note that parties are not able to avoid contracts when their misimpression is their own. For example, compare two cases. In one, a baseball card collector goes into a shop and sees a card he thinks is a Barry Bonds rookie card and buys it. If he turns out to be wrong, the contract is not avoidable. In the other, the collector goes into the same shop and buys the same card after being told that it is a Barry Bonds rookie card. Here the contract would be avoidable. Two matters of economic consequence are happening here. First, the card seller has made no misrepresentation, so it makes little sense to use avoidability as a means of directing his or her behavior. Second, each party assumes the risk of his or her information. This places the incentive to be accurate about assumptions and statements on the person making them. Because they are the only ones able to know the likely validity of the information, the allocation of risk here is economically efficient.

This raises the question of whether one party is required to warn the other party that he or she is acting on inaccurate information. For example, if the card shop owner in the above example knows the card is not a rookie card, does he or she have to alert the buyer? As a general rule, there is no requirement to correct the mistake of the other party. More technically, contracts that involve "unilateral mistakes" usually are not avoidable. An economic rationale that has been offered for this is that people make investments in information. If the law required everyone with superior information to reveal it to the other party, the effect would be to reduce the incentive to become well educated or informed.[3] In addition, greater research and education are often beneficial to society generally. For example, suppose you were an art major in school or have spent a great deal of time reading about art. This is an investment in "human capital." You see a valuable

3. Anthony Kronman, "Mistake, Disclosure, Information, and the Law," *Journal of Legal Studies* 7, no. 1 (1978).

painting at a yard sale and the price is $5. You know it is worth $2,000 and likely headed for a dumpster by afternoon if no one buys it. Your knowledge about the painting reflects the investment you have made in your education. If, as a general matter, you and others are not permitted to profit from these types of investments, opportunities to preserve resources for the public generally may be lost and the incentive to educate yourself may decline.

Coercion

As you might expect, contracts that are entered into under circumstances in which one party is substantially controlled by the other party are not likely to achieve Pareto superior outcomes. The preference that is expressed may not be the true preference of the party who is controlled. Contract law has two broad doctrines that allow those who have been unfairly influenced to avoid their contracts. One doctrine involves *duress* and the other *undue influence*. Under the doctrine of undue influence, there is not a threat but the circumstances are such that the party is unable to express himself or herself freely. Undue influence usually occurs when a party is susceptible to high pressure and the pressure is applied. A classic case would be when several people badger another—perhaps a tired or elderly person—at an inappropriate time and place and eventually are able to overcome the person's actual preference. From an economic perspective, it is as though those applying the pressure are using the other party as a conduit for their own preferences.

In the case of duress, the party must show that the other party made an improper threat to force him or her to enter into the contract. Obviously, what constitutes undue influence or duress is highly subjective. Some basic rules, however, are clear. The first is that courts do not apply these doctrines liberally. To do so would open the door to instances in which individuals seek to escape contractual obligations when they are simply having second thoughts about contracts they have made. A liberal approach would affect the stability of contracts, increase uncertainty, and raise the cost of contracting to parties because they would have to draft contractual provisions to restore the certainty.

Second, the claim of duress is not available to a party unless the improper threat is made by the other party to the contract. This is an important distinction. Often individuals enter into contracts because they are in desperate straits or are under pressure from third parties. For example, a landlord may threaten to evict a tenant unless the rent is paid the next day. The tenant may then sell some valuable jewelry to raise money and feel that the sale of the jewelry was made under duress. There are, however, two problems with applying the doctrine. First, the landlord has not made an improper threat and the threat is not made by the party to the jewelry sale.

The most common type of duress involves instances in which one party performs part of a contract and then stops and demands more money. For example, in a case from the early 1900s, a cannery hired a group of workers in San Francisco to go to Alaska for the summer to catch fish.[4] A wage was agreed to, but when the workers arrived in Alaska they refused to work unless the contract price was "renegotiated." The employer agreed at the time but refused to pay when fishing season was over. This decision was affirmed by the court. As a general matter, when a person refuses to finish performance of an already existing contract unless the other party pays more, the promise to pay the additional amount is not enforced. This makes economic sense from the standpoint of Pareto efficiency. When the parties make the original contract, it is beneficial to both parties. When a change occurs that is beneficial to one party and makes the other party worse off, the impact is distributive only and is also Pareto inferior.[5]

CONTRACTS AND DISTRIBUTIVE GOALS

One of the basic rules of contract law is that courts will not rule on the *adequacy* of consideration. What this means is that contracts have to involve an exchange to be enforceable, but beyond that courts will generally not respond to appeals that the bargain was lopsided or unfair. As an economic matter, this is like courts saying they will not

---

4. *Alaska Packers' Ass'n v. Domemico,* 117 F. 99 (9th Cir. 1902).

5. The rule that is applied here is that a modification of a contract without new consideration is not enforceable. The idea is that a party would not change a contract on one side only unless inappropriate pressure is applied. Although this is the general rule, courts will enforce these one-sided changes if made voluntarily.

get involved in interpersonal comparisons of utility. For example, if you pay $50 for a copy of a classmate's notes in a course, courts generally will not get into whether you got a fair deal. The idea is that if you both legitimately agree to the bargain, then both parties are better off. To then consider who got the better end of the deal involves a distributive matter.

Although this is the general rule of contracts, there can be little doubt that courts do respond to the balance in the exchange and often appear to apply some standards of fairness. For example, if you go back to Case 9.2, you may get the sense that the court really felt the buyer had acted foolishly and made a bad decision. You would not be alone in this interpretation. In fact, there are many instances in which courts appear to be attempting to achieve "just" outcomes while claiming to apply standard contract doctrine. In addition, a limited number of instances show that courts may openly respond to unfairness.

In Chapter 11, the potential for contract as a tool of distributive justice is examined as well as the means available in contract law to achieve these kinds of ends.

QUESTIONS FOR DISCUSSION

1. Suppose courts adopted the view that they would not engage in gap-filling or any other efforts to interpret contracts. In effect, if the parties did not dot every "i" and cross every "t," contracts would be unenforceable. This would force parties to be more careful in drafting contracts. Isn't this more efficient than the current system in which the courts insert missing terms and interpret ambiguous terms? Why or why not?

2. Imagine a society in which courts do not enforce contracts. Can you think of ways individuals wanting to make enforceable agreements might respond? Do you think that ultimately the market would respond with means of enforcement? If so, why should it be a matter for the government?

3. It is often said that a contract that is not supported by consideration is illusory and not enforceable. Do you understand what that means? What is the economic function of the consideration requirement, if any?

4. Suppose you agree to sell your notes from this class to a classmate for $50. On the way to get the notes photocopied in your car, a cigarette butt discarded by a passenger in the car lands on the notes and burns them. You have no copies. Your classmate says you breached the contract. You say that you did not assume the risk of a carelessly discarded cigarette butt. Which is the more efficient way to assume the risk?

5. Jackson is elderly and lonely. Every day he is visited by Joan, a young, attractive and interesting woman. It is his only social contact and he values it a great deal. Lately, Joan says she will have to stop coming because she needs to earn some money. In fact, she has plenty of money. After several days of hearing Joan say that she may not come back, Jackson agrees to pay her to keep coming. As an economic matter, should this contract be enforced?

APPENDIX: INDIFFERENCE ANALYSIS AND CONTRACT ENFORCEMENT

The text suggests that much of contract law can be squared with making it less likely that agreements resulting in Pareto inferior outcomes will be enforced. This analysis requires a digression into the basic economic explanation for why exchanges take place. First it is necessary to review indifference curves and the Edgeworth Box. In Figure 9.A1, the x axis indicates the quantities of good X an individual might have, and the y axis indicates the amounts of good Y. Each curve plots the possible combinations of X and Y that give the individual the same amount of satisfaction. For example, X could be apples and Y bicycles. Each point along a specific curve represents a different combination of bicycles and apples, but each combination would leave this individual feeling equally well off. As the curve suggests, as the individual has fewer apples, she must have more bicycles to maintain the same level of satisfaction. On the graph, each curve represents a different level of satisfaction with the curves farther away from the origin representing higher levels of utility. The indifference map of George might look like Figure 9.A1. If George has eighty apples and two bicycles, he would be located at point A on curve I.

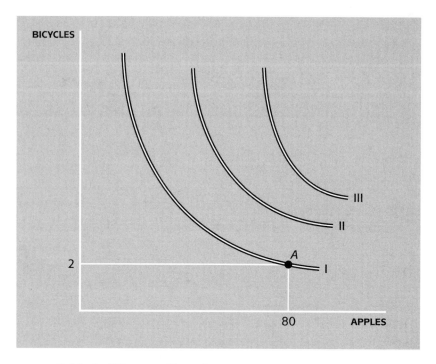

FIGURE 9.A1 Indifference Map: George

Of course, an exchange requires another participant. Thus, Figure 9.A2 depicts the possible indifference curves for Martha. Again, each curve represents a separate level of satisfaction and shows the combinations of bicycles and apples that result in the same level of satisfaction. And, as in Figure 9.A1, as the curves move out from the origin, they represent different and higher levels of satisfaction. If we suppose Martha has twenty apples and eight bicycles, she will be located at point *A* on curve II.

This seemingly lopsided allocation of bicycles and apples obviously creates an opportunity for exchange. The two indifference maps can be combined into what is called an Edgeworth Box. The size of the Edgeworth Box is determined by the total number of bikes and apples that Geroge and Martha have. In Figure 9.A3, the two sets of indifference curves are on the same graph with George's origin located at the bottom left corner and Martha's origin at the upper right corner. Point A in the Edgeworth Box corresponds with point A in Figure 9.A1 on indifference curve I for George and with point B in Figure 9.A2 on indifference curve II for Martha.

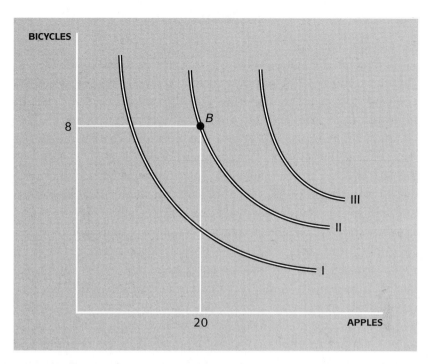

FIGURE 9.A2 Indifference Map: Martha

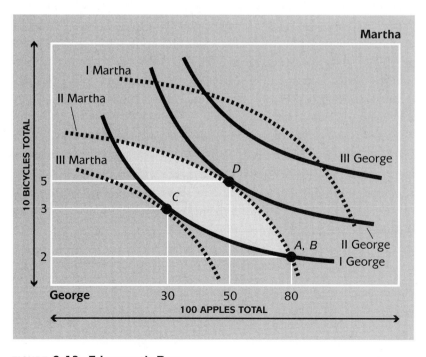

FIGURE 9.A3 Edgeworth Box

As noted in the text, whether by design or accident, a great deal of contract seems to be designed to avoid excessive advantage-taking by one party to a contract of another. Put differently, does the exchange improve the position of both parties? The question for contract purposes and for purposes of Pareto superiority is whether the parties can exchange bicycles for apples in such a way that they are both better off. In other words, can they both move to higher indifference curves while being restricted by the fact that there are a total of one hundred apples and ten bicycles in the entire economy? There are, in fact, a number of possible points at which both parties would be better off.

To visualize this, consider point C where George's indifference curve I is tangent to Martha's indifference curve III.[6] The point represents thirty apples and three bicycles for George and seventy apples and seven bicycles for Martha. At this point, George is still on indifference curve I and he is as happy as he was with eighty apples and two bicycles. Martha has moved up to indifference curve III and, therefore, is better off. In essence, George has paid fifty apples for one bicycle. While this is actually an unlikely exchange because it leaves George no better off, it forms the outside limit of a possible exchange. Similarly, point D, where Martha has five bicycles and fifty apples and George has five bicycles and fifty apples, represents a point at which George is better off and Martha stays on her original indifference curve. This point also represents a limit on their exchange because under no circumstances would Martha enter into an exchange that made her worse off.

Economists refer to the area between indifference curve I for George and curve II for Martha as a lens. Movements from the original allocation to points within the lens leave both parties better off. Movement to points outside the lens leave at least one party worse off. Points on the edge of the lens make one party better off without making the other party worse off.

---

6. The quantities shown in figure 9.A3 are for George. Martha owns the rest. For instance point *A,B* corresponds with 80 apples and 2 bicycles for George and hence with 20 apples and 8 bicycles for Martha. The total is always 100 apples and 10 bikes. Point *C* has 30 apples and 3 bicycles for George and 70 apples and 7 bicycles for Martha. In point *D* they each have 50 apples and 5 bicycles.

Because both parties presumably desire to move to the highest possible indifference curve (i.e., that which is farthest from their respective origins) and because these moves must be consistent with moving
to higher indifference curves of their partners, it is possible to narrow
the focus even more. The critical points are those at which the indifference curves are tangent to each other. For each indifference curve
of George, there is an indifference curve for Martha that is tangent to
George's curve at some point. A line drawn through these points of
tangency is called the contract curve. The contract curve shows a series
of possible exchanges or "prices" of apples in terms of bicycles, or vice
versa, that will improve the positions of both parties. The actual price
the parties establish will be determined by their negotiations.

In a general way, when one examines the rules concerning which
contracts will be enforced and which ones will not, it is possible to
argue that the rules—especially those dealing with fraud, misrepresentation, duress—favor enforcement when the contract puts the parties within the lens.

CHAPTER TEN

Promissory Estoppel

A S YOU SAW IN CHAPTER 9, THE STANDARD DEFINI-
tion of a contract is an agreement supported by consideration. In other words, a contract involves a contemporaneous
exchange or an exchange of promises. One promise is made because
the other party also makes a promise. What happens when consideration or a promise comes from only one party? This is the problem of
gratuitous promises. For example, your great-aunt promises to give you
$1,000 for your birthday, or your employer promises to give you a
$400 monthly payment when you retire. The key here is that your aunt
does not make the promise to induce you to have a birthday and the
employer typically does not make the promise of post-retirement payments to induce you to retire. There may be sound economic reasons
for enforcing these promises even though they are not contracts. Before
we turn to the economics of *promissory estoppel*, the next section provides some context in the form of a short review of how courts have
dealt with the issue. The following section then examines both distributive and efficiency rationales for enforcing gratuitous promises.

PROMISES

As a historical matter, courts routinely announced that gratuitous
promises were not enforceable. In reality, this was true sometimes and
not true other times, and by the late nineteenth and early twentieth
centuries, there was a clear tendency for courts to find a way to enforce

these promises. Two methods were generally used to do this. One was *estoppel en pais* or *equitable estoppel*. These are tools a court could use to prevent a party from using certain defenses in a lawsuit or claiming that he or she did not say something that he or she did say. In *Ricketts v. Scothorn*, an 1898 case, a grandfather discovered, to his dismay, that his granddaughter was working in a department store—evidently a shameful thing at the time. He told her that he found this upsetting and promised to give her $2,000 so that she could quit. He did not require her to stop work, but she did. When she attempted to collect on the promise, the executor of his estate (he had died by this time) argued that there was no obligation to pay because the promise was not enforceable as the granddaughter did not promise to stop work. In legal terms, the grandfather's promise was not supported by consideration. Ordinarily, that defense would have been successful. The court, however, applied the concept of estoppel en pais and held that the equitable (fair) thing to do was to preclude the estate from using the defense that there was no contract. The idea was that the grandfather had made a promise hoping to induce an action by the granddaughter. Once that action took place, it would be unfair to allow him or his estate to assert the defense of *no consideration*. Technically, the promise was not enforced. Instead, the "contract" was enforced because the grandfather was precluded from arguing that there was no consideration.

The second method courts used to enforce gratuitous promises was to find that consideration did exist, no matter how small or improbable. Notions of estoppel were not necessary because a court could find consideration, even though it may have taken some effort. A good example is *Allegheny College v. National Chautauqua County Bank of Jamestown*, which involved the promise of a donation to Allegheny College.[1] The promise was broken before payment was made and the defendant (donor) argued that there was no consideration for the promise. In other words, a promise that was not part of a contract was not enforceable. In the document where the promise was made, the donor wrote that "this gift shall be known as the Mary Yates Johnston Memorial Fund." In what most legal scholars regard as very imaginative reasoning, the judge held that the school's obligation to identify

1. 159 N.E. 173 (1927).

the origin of the gift was consideration given by the school to the donor, making the promise enforceable. No one, however, studies this case and others like it without understanding that the court had merely opted to enforce a gratuitous promise and found a pretense of consideration to do that.

As the twentieth century progressed, courts increasingly enforced gratuitous promises and gradually dropped the fiction that these promises were actually contracts. What has emerged is the following rule: "A promise that the promissor should reasonably expect to induce action or forbearance on the part of the promissee or a third party and that does induce such action or forbearance is binding if injustice can be avoided only by enforcement of the promise."[2] This doctrine is known as *promissory estoppel* and, within the context of American contract law, its development is one of the most important of the twentieth century.

LAW AND ECONOMICS IN ACTION 10.1

PROMISSORY ESTOPPEL AND AT-WILL EMPLOYMENT

Promissory estoppel provides a backstop for people who have believed and acted on the promises of others only to have the rug pulled out from under them. A continuing issue concerns the treatment of what are called "at-will" employees. These are employees who can be dismissed for any reason at any time. Most workers are in fact at-will. Now suppose you have a job and you are offered another one that requires you to quit your existing job. On Friday you quit one job and on Monday you show up for the new one. The new employer tells you that he has changed his mind and does not need you. As an "at-will" employee, you cannot claim that a contract has been breached since the second employer could fire you at any time for any reason. On the other hand, you did "rely" on the promise of a new job. This fact pattern has been repeated and the dismissed employees have attempted to use the doctrine of promissory estoppel. Their argument is that they relied on a promise. The employers make two

---

2. Twice in the twentieth century, judges, legal scholars, and attorneys have compiled the general rules of contract common law. The result is the The Restatement of Contracts and The Restatement (Second) of Contracts. The rule cited here is Section 90(1) of the Second Restatement.

arguments. First, the *reliance* was unreasonable since the employee knew he could be fired for any reason. Second, there is no *harm* because the employer always had the right to fire the employee.

Courts have reacted differently to the promissory estoppel claim. In a 1981 Minnesota case, *Grouse v. Group Health Plan, Inc.,*[3] the court agreed with the employee's promissory estoppel claim, explaining:

> [W]e . . . hold . . . that under the facts of this case the appellant [plaintiff] had a right to assume he would be given a good faith opportunity to perform his duties to the satisfaction of respondent [the defendant] once he was on the job. He was not only denied that opportunity but resigned the position he already held in reliance on the firm offer which respondent tendered him.

On the other hand, in a recent Florida case, *Leonardi v. City of Holly-wood,*[4] the employee quit his job to take a job with the City only to find that he was in effect fired before he could begin work. The court refused to apply promissory estoppel, reasoning:

> [W]e need not look any further than § 90 of the Restatement (Second) of Contracts to conclude that Leonardi's reliance on City's offer was unreasonable. Had City allowed Leonardi to begin working, it could have terminated his employment immediately thereafter, before accrued any wages. Similarly, had he not quit his prior position, his employer also could have terminated him at will. In either scenario, we do not believe the doctrine of promissory estoppel would allow him to recover his lost wages.

As you examine the materials that follow, think about which view makes more economic sense.

Is it possible that the uncertainty of not knowing whether the promise of employment will be kept could lead to expensive contracting and enforcement expenses?

THE ECONOMICS OF GRATUITOUS PROMISES

The important question from an economic perspective is whether a policy of enforcing gratuitous promises is efficient. In the previous chapter, four reasons for having a system of contract law were listed: The system (1) lowers transaction costs, (2) provides a basis for protecting third parties, (3) regulates means of persuasion, and (4) allows

---

3. 306 N.W.2d 114 (1981).
4. 715 So.2d 1007 (1998).

courts to pursue distributive goals. A system of enforcing gratuitous promises is likely to be consistent with only the first and last of these—lowering transaction costs and affecting distributive goals. After all, the simple making of a promise is unlikely to have a negative impact on third parties. In addition, although it is possible to force someone to make a promise, the analysis and treatment would not differ from that found when the promise is part of a contract. Of the two rationales that are important, the second one may be easier to understand as an analytical matter, so we will get it out of the way first.

Distributive Goals

By having a means of enforcing gratuitous promises, courts can opt to enforce promises that have desired distributive effects. As the rule quoted above indicates, courts tend to enforce these promises when promissees have acted on the promises by spending their own money or changing positions in a way that will be detrimental if the promise is not kept. A good example is a case from 1959, *Feinberg v. Pfeiffer Co.*[5] There an employee (Anna Feinberg) of a firm was told that when she retired she would be paid $200 per month. The firm asked nothing in return. She had worked for the firm for thirty-seven years and worked a short time after the promise and then retired. A few years later, after a change in ownership, the firm stopped making the payments, arguing that the promise of payment was gratuitous. Here, the court enforced the promise because Feinberg had relied on it by retiring earlier than required and not seeking alternative employment as she grew older. In short, she had relied to her detriment. To the court, the distributive outcome of enforcing the promise was preferred over not enforcing it because of the hardship that would have been felt by Anna Feinberg.

It is important to distinguish this interest from one based on efficiency. For example, in the *Feinberg* case, once reliance has occurred, a decision to use an efficiency standard would require deciding whether Anna Feinberg or the owners or shareholders of the firm she worked for would derive greater utility from the funds. This would involve an interpersonal comparison of utility, a comparison economists generally do not make. Thus, it is easier to reconcile this type

5. 322 S.W.2d 163 (1959).

of case with a desire to redistribute income. This is not meant to suggest that a distributive goal is unimportant as far as the law is concerned. The emergence of promissory estoppel suggests that distributive and moral concerns are often more important to the courts than possibly more complex economic efficiency concerns.

Efficiency Rationales

More difficult analytically is an efficiency rationale for promissory estoppel. The complexity of the economic analysis can be understood by examining two possible arguments that seem to have economic appeal at the outset but actually fail to provide strong support. First, in the case of contracts, the law plays a role in reducing the transaction costs associated with Pareto superior exchanges. In the case of gifts, one cannot know if the outcome is Pareto superior. It is true that the recipient of the gratuitous promise will be better off.[6] One also has to assume that the maker of the promise is also better off—otherwise why make it? The problem is that the promissor's sense of well-being is a function of the imagined degree to which the recipient is better off. In effect, the promissor engages in an interpersonal comparison of utility, but there is no reason to think promissors are more adept at assessing the utility of someone else than a court or a government agency.

Another approach to this is equally unpersuasive. The reasoning here is that people who make promises and break them harm others. The harm is comparable to a negative externality that they should internalize. The problem is that the damage is due to the reliance and one way, and perhaps the better way, to avoid the harm is for all people who hear promises to just ignore them. In effect, people rely because they mistakenly believe the promises they hear. It would make at least as much sense to require promissees to internalize the costs of their reliance as it would to require promissors to internalize them.

The key to the economic analysis is to focus on a more general question. From an economic perspective, the issue is whether a promise-enforcing *rule* is more efficient than a rule of not enforcing

---

6. Of course this is not always the case. Someone may promise to give you a huge and ugly painting or a bloody nose. In most instances, however, the promissee can turn down the unwanted promise.

promising. One way to approach this question is to imagine a legal system considering two competing rules. Rule 1 is to enforce gratuitous promises. Rule 2 is to not enforce gratuitous promises. These two mutually exclusive rules could be put up for auction at a society-wide auction. The higher-valued rule would be adopted. Value in this hypothetical auction would be determined by the costs saved or benefits derived from a promise-enforcing rule as opposed to a nonenforcement rule. There are two details about this construct you should note. First, your initial reaction may be to think that all promissors would prefer a rule that allows them to change their minds without consequence and all promissees would prefer that promissors be held to their promises. This analysis does not really play out, though, because all people are at one time or another are both promissees and promissors.

The second point is that an economic justification for enforcing promises has to be one that focuses on the specific question of why it would make economic sense not to allow people who make promises to change their minds. This is an even more intriguing question because such a rule is more likely to be efficient if the promissors themselves value a rule that requires them to keep their promises. Although the actual efficiency of promissory estoppel is an empirical matter, are a number of theories address the reasons that promissory estoppel is efficient.

Lowering the Costs of Enforcing Commitments

The economic rationale for a policy of promissory estoppel that is easiest to understand focuses on the costs of making a sincere promise. Suppose you want to make a promise to a friend that you will give her $200 at the end of the month. You really mean it and want her to believe it. On a practical level, unless she regards you as 100 percent trustworthy or knows the law will enforce your promise, it is not possible for you to make a promise that she will regard as indicating a full commitment. In effect, she will discount its value—say to $175. There are some choices available to you. You could just give her the money now. The problem is that you lose the use of the money between now and the date of the gift. You could also give the money to a third party—call this peson a "promise keeper"—and pay him or her a fee in exchange for agreeing to present the $200 at the time specified. This obviously involves transaction costs to you. If courts enforced gratuitous promises, you could avoid both of these alternatives and transaction costs would be lower.

This does not mean that a policy of promissory estoppel is cost free. There is a public cost of operating a system of promise enforcement which, as you will see below, can be quite complex. It seems likely, however, that a public system with generally uniform requirements would be less expensive to operate than a private system with possibly hundreds or thousands of "promise keepers" with different forms and procedures. In effect, having a legal system that forces you to keep your promises may be less expensive than making payments to private firms that "force" you to keep your promises.

Lowering the Cost of the Promise

A rationale for promissory estoppel that is generally attributed to Judge Richard Posner is that enforcement of promises can lower the amount a promissor has to promise to have a desired impact.[7] An example is useful here. Suppose your great-aunt, on learning you are going to college, promises to send you $100 each month for each month you are enrolled. Again, unless you have 100 percent confidence in your aunt or know the courts will enforce her promise, you are likely to discount its value—to, say, $90. The more you distrust your great-aunt and the further in the future a payment is due, the more you would discount the amount. For example, you might value this year's payment at $80 and a payment four years from now at only $30.

Your great-aunt may also understand this. Under a regime in which promises are not enforced, the great-aunt will either have to give you the money ahead of time, make a separate contract with a third party to make the payments on time, or promise you more than $100 per month. For example, the great-aunt could promise you $120 per month so after discounting it is worth $100 to you. One of the effects of promissory estoppel is that promises that are made can be for lower amounts. In other words, $100 means $100 and the discounting will not occur.

7. Richard A. Posner, "Gratuitous Promises in Economics and Law," *Journal of Legal Studies* 6 (1977): 411.

From the point of view of the promissor, enforcement seems advantageous. In effect, a promise to make a gift of a certain amount in the future is less expensive to the promissor if everyone believes the promise will be kept. But does it really matter? Suppose your great-aunt promises you $120 which you discount to $100 and then the great-aunt pays you $100. The $100 would seem to fulfill your expectations, and whether promissory estoppel exists or not, the promissor pays $100. Promissory estoppel in this case seems to carry little advantage over routine overstatements by promissors about what their intentions are.[8]

On the other hand, consider this possibility. You are as smart as your great-aunt and know that a promise of $120 means that she intends to pay only $100. In effect, you know that the statement of $120 actually stands for $100 and you discount from there, meaning that the value of the promise is still only $80. How can the promissor overcome this? One way would be to promise even more than he or she intends to give and to follow through on this. After several instances of this, promissees will come to believe that a $100 promise means that $100 will be delivered. In short, it may take an extended and expensive period for individual promissors to establish a reputation for honesty. A less expensive way to achieve the outcome is to have promises made in the context of a legal regime that both parties believe will enforce gratuitous promises.

BENEFICIAL RELIANCE

A somewhat more complicated efficiency-based argument for enforcing gratuitous promises has been offered by Charles Goetz and Robert Scott.[9] The focus here is not directly on promissors but on promissees. Again, an example will help you understand the underlying logic. This time, your great-aunt decides to give you $1,000 in ten months. She could make the promise now or avoid the promissory estoppel

8. It is important to note that there may be another advantage to having faith that the promise will be kept and planning for that before the gift is actually made. This is discussed below.

9. Charles Goetz and Robert Scott, "Enforcing Promises: An Examination of the Basis of Contract," *Yale Law Journal* 89 (1980): 1261.

issue altogether by saying nothing and just presenting you with the gift in ten months.

Whether your aunt tells you about the gift or not, the fact is that you will be $1,000 richer in ten months. The question is whether there is any economic benefit to knowing ahead of time that the gift is on the way. Goetz and Scott argue that knowing ahead of time gives rise to "beneficial reliance." It works like this. Suppose you are saving $100 a month for ten months so you can go on a ski vacation. You get no utility from that $100 other than a sense of well-being associated with knowing you are prudent. If you knew ahead of time about the gift and could depend on it, the saving would not be necessary. Thus, the comparison is between ten months of saving and ten months without saving with the knowledge that $1,000 will be coming as a gift. Either way, at the end of the ten months you have money for the ski trip. And, if you can save, you have an extra $1,000 on hand.

The difference lies is the way you allocate your resources depending on whether you know about the promise. If you do not know, you save rather than spend on current consumption. If you do know that your aunt is taking care of the "saving problem" and that you can depend on the promise, you can transfer the $100 a month to current consumption. In effect, you rely on the promise by using the money to satisfy current needs. It is almost like you are able to spend the aunt's gift in advance by spending what you would have saved. This ability to spend rather than accumulate wealth is the beneficial reliance. You are able to achieve greater levels of utility during this ten-month period.

SELF-PATERNALISM

An additional efficiency-based argument rests on the idea of self-paternalism. Paternalism, as you know, involves making decisions for others based on what you think is "best" for them. Self-paternalism means we sometimes do things to bind or limit ourselves to help avoid decisions we might make later. If you have ever been on a diet and have removed ice cream from the refrigerator to avoid the temptation to eat it, you have been involved in self-paternalism. Even laws about various vices—such as gambling or drinking—can be traced to self-paternalism.

Self-paternalism can be linked to efficiency fairly simply if you believe people are rational maximizers of self-interest. If so, those who choose rules that bind their future actions are simply maximizing their utility. Suppose they choose to vote against legalizing gambling. The utility derived may simply be the sense of not having to worry that they will succumb to the temptation to gamble. In the case of promise making, we may all realize that we are subject to the temptation to break promises but have a preference that we act honestly and that we are perceived as acting honestly by keeping our promises. By favoring a rule that enforces promises, we are forced to avoid the temptation to deviate from these ideals.

SOME COSTS OF PROMISSORY ESTOPPEL

This analysis suggests there are a fair number of economic rationales for enforcing gratuitous promises. It is for these reasons, in a world in which rules are determined by the value attributed to them, that promissory estoppel might be adopted. There are, as you would expect, costs of a rule of promissory estoppel that must be balanced against the benefits. The most obvious cost is that of administering a system of obligations based on gratuitous promises. Although this is a cost of all law, in this instance the possibility of minimizing even the public costs deserves some scrutiny.

One of the reasons for not enforcing gratuitous promises is the moral hazard such a policy creates. Specifically, it creates the possibility that one party can claim—virtually out of whole cloth—that another party made a promise that may not have been made. You can understand the greater moral hazard by comparing this with the more traditional contract in which consideration and promises or actions by both parties are required. In the latter instance, a court is likely to have much more to go on in determining the validity of competing claims. To some extent the moral hazard is lessened by the general requirement that the gratuitous promise must be relied upon in order to be enforced. It is doubtful that many people would go to the trouble of actually taking an action that would otherwise be detrimental as a means of achieving a promissory estoppel scam.

Aside from the problem of a moral hazard, promissory estoppel also means that courts frequently address questions of what constitutes a promise. It is a promise to say "I will give you $100 tomorrow," and it is probably not a promise to say, "I would like to give you $100 tomorrow." On the other hand, what about, "I am planning to give you $100 tomorrow." A similar ambiguity arises with respect to whether the promisee should have relied and whether the promisee did rely. Does reliance mean taking an action that is wholly dependent on the promise or can it be taking an action that might have been taken anyway? For example, you are already planning a vacation and you hear a promise from that great-aunt that she will pay for the vacation and then you take the vacation. Have you relied?

The point is that promissory estoppel does entail a fairly large public commitment. Some of this cost could be eliminated by a rule like this: "Gratuitous promises will be enforced only when they are in a notarized signed writing." This is not, however, the rule. And, of course, all the costs could be eliminated if the older rule of not enforcing gratuitous promises had been maintained.

LAW AND ECONOMICS IN ACTION 10.2

THE COMPLEXITIES OF PROMISSORY ESTOPPEL

Doubtless, the application of promissory estoppel opens the doors to complicated issues. Take, for example, *Pertz v. The Edward J. DeBartolo Corporation*,[10] in which the plaintiff, Pertz, had a job in Cleveland. His wife got a job in Florida but they did not want to move to Florida unless Pertz's employer would allow him to work part of the year in Cleveland. Pertz asked the employer if he could cut his work schedule back to a few weeks a year. The employer's response was a promise that Pertz could have a job with the firm as long as it was owned by the same corporation. Pertz relocated to Florida, took out a mortgage, and bought a house. Two years later, the original promissor died and new management informed Pertz that the employment arrangement was over. Pertz sued under the theory of promissory estoppel and asked for damages. This is a garden-variety promissory estoppel case and the issues raised are both common and elusive. For example, how much would you say that Pertz was damaged by the broken promise? If Pertz relied on the employer's response to move to Florida, how long does this reliance go on? What if the promise had been broken five or ten years after it was made? Would the reliance still

10. 188 F.3d 508 (1999).

exist? If not, when is the cut-off? Finally, does it make sense to expend judicial and public resources on straightening out problems that more diligence by the parties at the time could have avoided? By the way, Pertz's case was thrown out by the trial court. When he appealed, the appellate court ruled that the lower court should have tried the case. Ultimately the parties settled.

A second cost that is equally obvious is that adoption of promissory estoppel means that a cost is imposed on those who change their minds. There are actually three facets of this cost. First, one impact is to eliminate a great deal of casual promise making. This is probably a good thing. On the other hand, it may curb the promise making of some who are just not sure they will be able to follow through. This may seem beneficial too, but think about it. Would you rather be given a promise that you will receive $1,000 that has a 90 percent chance of performance or hear no promise at all? One impact of promissory estoppel may be to eliminate the former. Finally, even those who fully intend to keep their promises are likely to attribute some value to the "insurance" of knowing they can back out if necessary.

These possibilities suggest that the economic case for promissory estoppel is a close one—particularly when you consider that the issue has nothing to do with whether a person can simply give a gift to someone else. Once given, a gift generally cannot be taken back. The issue is the enforceability of promises to make future gifts. It may be that the most compelling arguments for promissory estoppel are based on distributive concerns and a morality-based belief that it is simply wrong to break a promise.

QUESTIONS FOR DISCUSSION

1. Generally, courts will enforce gratuitous promises if they have been relied on. Can you think of an economic rationale for including the "reliance requirement?"

2. In Chapter 6, you learned about the Coase theorem and the possibility that the market will reverse assignments by courts that are inefficient. The same analysis can be applied to rules generally. Is

it possible that the rule not to enforce was inefficient and that courts have simply moved to a more efficient rule?

3. In the text, the possibility of a rule that says "Gratuitous promises will be enforced only when they are in a notarized signed writing" is discussed. How do you rank this in terms of an efficient approach to the enforcement of promises?

4. A much-discussed work-life incentive scheme in personnel economics consists of a mechanism whereby workers are paid less than they are worth when young and more than they are worth when old.[11] This tilted compensation profile over a worker's career corresponds with what many personnel managers believe is happening in their own organizations. Older workers are paid high salaries, not because they are very productive when old, but high payments at older ages serve to motivate them during the early years of their career. One could see this work-life incentive scheme as a system in which the employer promises to pay higher wages later. Suppose a certain employer fires his workers before they reach age forty, so he never has to pay high wages. Could these workers sue under the theory of promissory estoppel and ask for damages?

11. Edward P. Lazear, *Personnnel Economics*, (Cambridge: MIT Press, 1995), 39–40.

CHAPTER ELEVEN

Contract Law and Distributive Issues

O NE OF THE TENETS OF CONTRACT LAW IS THAT COURTS do not examine what is called *adequacy of consideration.* This means that after a court decides a valid contract has been made, it will not question whether the terms are fair. For example, suppose you see a stereo system advertised in the classified section of the newspaper for $1,000. After examining it, you decide that it is a terrific system and that you would be willing to pay as much as $2,000. You do not know it, but the seller will actually take as little as $500. In effect, you value the stereo by $1,500 more than the seller and that $1,500 is called the *benefit of the bargain.* Suppose you pay $1,999 for the system. Obviously, most of the benefit has been captured by the seller.[1] But, unless that result was due to duress, misrepresentation, fraud, or one of the other factors that make the formation of the contract itself a problem, a court will not look any further.

What courts will take into consideration and what they shy away from looking at is roughly consistent with the distinction between efficiency and distributive goals. For example, if the stereo purchase made you and the seller better off, the outcome is Pareto superior. If you

---

1. In terms of the indifference curve found in the appendix to Chapter 9, this would mean that you have hardly moved at all from your original indifference curve.

are a rational self-maximizer, presumably you would not pay $1,999 for the stereo unless you preferred it to keeping the $1,999. And, obviously, the seller is better off with your $1,999 than with the stereo. It is at that point that contract law officially ends its inquiry. The next step, if it takes place, of questioning whether the benefit of the bargain was divided fairly broaches the distributive issue. Most would say that this is a different issue from whether the exchange has resulted in a Pareto superior or efficient outcome. On the other hand, if third parties derive utility from the perception of fairness, the distinction between efficiency and distributive outcomes is not so simple. This possibility is more easily addressed, however, after the efficiency/equity distinction is understood.

Although courts rarely "officially" get involved in distributive issues, there is little doubt that contract law has been used to achieve distributive goals. For example, Case 9.2 discussed the "dance lessons" case, one that is well known among most people who have attended law school. There, the court allowed a middle-aged woman to avoid a contract in which she bought 2,300 hours of dancing lessons. The court reasoned that the sellers had misrepresented her potential as a dancer. If accepted at face value, this would appear to be a matter of efficiency and that is the "official" interpretation of that case. In effect, the misrepresentation meant that she was not better off by virtue of the transaction. Hardly anyone accepts that interpretation at face value; most believe the court simply found the exchange too disfavorable for the purchaser. Indeed, the wording of the court's opinion paints a picture of a lonely widow who was essentially out of her league when it came to dealing with smooth-talking dance instructors—a little like you if you pay $1,999 for the stereo that the seller would have priced at $500.

The dance lessons case and many others represent instances in which courts interpret (bend?) the rules to achieve an outcome that seems distributively just. For example, courts have used the consideration requirement and doctrines involving duress, undue influence, and promissory estoppel as means of achieving what are seen as more equitable outcomes. Aside from imaginative interpretations, there are also more direct theories under which courts can upset a bargain that seems unfair. In fact, a relatively recently developed doctrine—*unconscionability*—allows a court to directly assess the fairness of the exchange and to refuse to enforce contracts that are deemed excessively lopsided.

In this chapter, we consider the consequences of these efforts by the courts in whatever way they are expressed. You should know a few things to start. First, it is tempting to think that consideration of the fairness of a bargain means courts are involved in interpersonal comparisons of utility. By implication, this would mean that the courts are on the trail of some measure of efficiency by attempting to reallocate the benefit of the bargain in order to maximize utility. It is not at all clear that this is the objective. There is, to be sure, a tendency to favor the poorer, less educated, or otherwise disadvantaged party, but this seems driven by a sense of social norms of equity and not by efficiency concerns. Second, as you will see, most efforts at redistribution come at the cost of social welfare more generally. In more technical terms, redistributive efforts are centered around turning producers' surplus into consumer surplus.

One thing that seems certain is that reliance on common law courts is misplaced if the expectation is that they will deal with contracts issues to achieve any broad-based income redistribution. There are a number of reasons for this. Courts can respond only to cases that are presented to them, and this will be a very small percentage of the instances in which unfairness has actually occurred. In addition, different courts have different approaches to the issue. Moreover, a court that rules on a particular element of a contract typically does not have the power to control subsequent reactions. This is an important point. When one party takes the lion's share of the benefit of the bargain, it is typically because that party has a bargaining advantage. We say that party has *leverage* or *monopoly power*. A decision that the party has taken undue advantage with respect to price or any other term of the contract does not necessarily remove the leverage. That leverage can then be applied in another way. For example, the decision that a price is too high does not mean the seller cannot lower the price *and* quality the next time around. So, although we may be supportive of decisions that achieve desirable goals in individual cases, there does not seem to be much potential for contract law as a vehicle for alleviating society-wide injustices.

In the first section of the chapter you will be introduced to the most famous instance of a court responding to a distributive outcome. In the second section, the intended and unintended consequences of distribution-affecting contracts decisions will be examined, and the last part presents a more general examination of the prospects for contract law as a tool for addressing distributive concerns.

THE CLASSIC CASE OF UNCONSCIONABILITY

Before taking a close look at the impact of judicial responses to distributive issues in contract, you may wonder how the issues arise. A good case as a starter is *Williams v. Walker-Thomas Furniture*.[2] This is a case that practically every law student in the last thirty years has been required to study. In that case, Williams purchased a number of items from Walker-Thomas that she was to pay for in installments. In the contract was the following clause:

> The amount of each periodical installment payment to be made by purchaser to the company under this present lease shall be inclusive of and not in addition to the amount of each installment payment to be made by purchaser under such prior leases, bills or accounts; and *all payments now and hereafter made by purchaser shall be credited pro rata on all outstanding leases bills or accounts due the Company by purchaser at the time each payment is made.*

You may want to reread the provision. Do you understand it? It takes some study and, to understand it, you have to know that Williams and others tended to buy an item on installments and then buy another one before the first was paid off. When this happened, there would be one monthly payment for all items and that payment would be apportioned to each item. Suppose you bought a television for $1,200 in January and you are paying $100 per month for it. In November, when only one more payment is due, you go into the store and buy a stereo for $1,200, also to be paid off over one year. At that point, the $1,200 for the stereo is combined with the $100 left on the television for a total debt of $1,300. Whatever your monthly payment, it will be applied to each item in a 1 to 12 ratio. Now you will not fully pay off the television until the stereo is paid off. If you buy another item before those two are paid off, the same thing happens. No mat-

2. 350 F.2d 445 (D.C. Cir. 1965).

ter how little you owe on an item, it cannot be paid off until all the items are paid off.

This may not seem important, but when you buy something and pay in installments, the seller is essentially making a loan. The item you buy is collateral—meaning that if you miss a payment the seller can take the item back. The clause in *William v. Walker-Thomas* involves "cross-collateralization." The clause is set up so that if the purchaser misses a payment, all the items purchased are collateral. In other words, in the example, if you missed a payment eight months after buying the stereo, the store could take back both the stereo and the television because technically neither had been paid off and the monthly payment you missed was intended to be for both of them. In the case, Williams missed payments in 1962 and Walker-Thomas attempted to repossess items she had bought as far back as 1957.

Shortly, we will get into the issue of whether Walker-Thomas was as much a villain as it may seem. In the case, the court held that the clause may be unenforceable because it is *unconscionable.* In other words, rather than relying only on a standard legal doctrine like misrepresentation or duress, the court cut right to the point and held that a court may refuse to enforce a contract that is simply unfair. The unfairness in the case was linked not simply to the substance of the clause but to the convoluted wording and the characteristics of the parties. Williams was a welfare recipient with seven children to support on a very modest income. She was far less sophisticated in business matters than Walker-Thomas. All of this was known to Walker-Thomas. The suggestion is that the store knew there was a high probability that it was selling to people who were going to be unable to pay and that it would eventually repossess the items sold.

The important point to note is that the decision was not based on a sense that the contract was not efficient. In other words, there was no misrepresentation, duress, or the usual factors that stand in the way of a welfare-increasing exchange. In fact, if we look at the preference of Williams and assume she is rational, then she preferred making the contract to not making it. In addition, the contract is not illegal. The narrow question is whether a court will assist a party it regards as having acted unfairly when that party asks the court's assistance in enforcing the contract. The doctrine of unconscionability permits a court to decline.

Similar direct attention to distributive concerns is expressed when courts refer to *contracts of adhesion*. A contract of adhesion is one that is offered on a take-it-or-leave-it basis to a buyer typically, but not always, for necessary goods or services. Usually the contract is a preprinted form that has been adopted by all sellers. For example, if you search for an apartment in a college town that has a shortage of housing, you might find that every apartment complex uses the same form and they all include terms that are unfavorable to students. Perhaps they require a very high damage deposit or contain a clause saying that the landlord will not be liable for injuries suffered on the property even if caused by the neglect of the landlord. As in unconscionability, there is no objective principle for determining when a court will refuse a term in a contract because it is a contract of adhesion. The outcome is the same, though. The court ends up adjusting the distribution arrived at by the parties at the time of contracting.

LAW AND ECONOMICS IN ACTION 11.1

DOES A FAIR DEAL DIFFER FROM PERSON TO PERSON?

As a general matter, judicial efforts to effect distributive changes probably have little long-run impact. Still, there are tendencies in the way people are treated in negotiations that cannot be ignored. One of the most interesting studies on this point was conducted by legal scholar Ian Ayres.[3] Ayres devised a research plan in which he sent men and women, some white and some black, out to shop for cars. In an effort to hold constant for all factors other than race and gender, he had the shoppers dress alike, adhere to a prepared script, and present the same educational and credit histories. He compared the groups on the basis of the initial offer made by the auto dealer and the final price after a period of negotiation. Ayres' findings were alarming. The average dealer profit on the initial offer ranged from a high of $2,169 for black women to a low of $818 for white men. For white women, the figure was $829 and for black men it was $1,534. After negotiation, the average profit ranged from a high of $1,237 for black women to a low of $362 for white men. For white women, the figure was $504 and for black men, the figure was $783. Interestingly, shoppers did not get their best deals from their racial-gender counterparts. In

3. Ian Ayres, "Fair Driving: Gender and Race Discrimination in Retail Car Negotiations," *Harvard Law Review* 104 (1991): 817.

other words, black male sellers did not necessarily offer the best deals to black male buyers. This suggests that the price differences were not simply a function of racism or sexism. Underneath it all, it may be that sellers took advantage of preconceptions of what the buyers would "settle for." Learning that one must settle for less, however, may very well be a function of race and gender. As an economic matter, will the market eventually overcome these discrepancies or should there be price regulation? More important, do you see any way that an individual court, using the tools available to it, could effectively respond to this type of activity? What is the solution?

THE ECONOMICS OF EFFORTS TO ALTER DISTRIBUTIVE OUTCOMES

In many instances, probably most, the impact of a judicial effort to address a contractual imbalance is likely to be negligible in any sense other than the distributive adjustment between the parties involved. In other words, finding that one party in one contract got a bad deal may not have implications beyond that contract. In some instances, however, the adjustment may have broader consequences. For example, a court may decide that a certain type of clause in a contract is unenforceable. This can have the impact of a broadly applied policy and operate as a price ceiling or a regulation on contract terms. As you saw in Chapter 7, there can be a negative impact on even those the law is intending to protect.

Unconscionability and Cross-collateralization

A good example is the *Walker-Thomas* case, the overall impact of which cannot be fully assessed. The store in that case operated in a poor neighborhood. The most realistic method of payment was an installment arrangement whereby the seller was, in effect, making a loan to the buyer. Suppose a merchant sells a television for $1,200 with no down payment. The payments are supposed to be $100 a month, but after two months the buyer does not pay. The store is forced to repossess the television on which $1,000 is still owed. In most instances, television sets, furniture, and electronics depreciate in value very quickly after purchase. In the television example, the value of the two-month-old television may be $900 or less and the merchant ends up losing money.

The way this is avoided in most contexts is to require a cash sale or a large down payment. This may not be possible in a low-income context. One way to overcome this limitation is to permit cross-collateralization. In effect, if the payment is not made the merchant repossesses not just the television, which is worth less than the amount owed, but other items as well. The argument that has been made is that if poor people are going to make these purchases at all, cross-collateralization is a means to allow them to do so. If cross-collateralization is not permitted, merchants will react to protect their financial interests by requiring cash payment or higher down payments, or by raising prices. All of these may make the customer worse off than cross-collateralization. In effect, a low-income consumer is able to offer security in the form of cross-collateralization more easily than by any other means.

The actual impact of a decision like *Walker-Thomas* or others addressing distributive matters is impossible to determine without knowing the market conditions. For example, suppose Walker-Thomas was just able to make a normal profit by virtue of protecting itself with cross-collateralization requirements. A ruling that the clause cannot be used may mean the store exits that market. On the other hand, if Walker-Thomas is making an economic profit and has found that cross-collateralization is just a method of keeping that profit as high as possible, the impact of the decision may be distributive only—buyers being better off and Walker-Thomas less profitable but still fully operational.

Contracts of Adhesion

A more complicated problem is presented when a court declares that a buyer is not required to abide by a term of a contract because it is a *contract of adhesion*. A common pattern is one suggested above: A person rents an apartment and signs a lease that includes a clause saying the landlord is not liable for injuries on the premises regardless of who is responsible. This is called an *exculpatory clause*. Later that person is injured and the landlord asks the court to enforce the contract in order to preclude recovery. It is at this point that a court may decide the clause is unenforceable because it is part of a contract

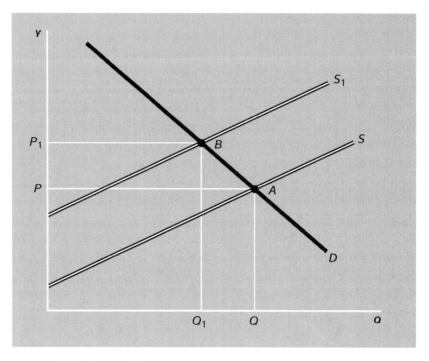

FIGURE 11.1 Cost of Housing

of adhesion.[4] A decision not to enforce the clause is a redistribution in favor of the injured party.

The longer-run impact of this type of decision, again, will depend on a number of factors. In Figure 11.1, assume the exculpatory provision is in effect. D is the demand for apartments and S is the supply. The equilibrium price is P and the equilibrium quantity is Q. Suppose the clause is challenged and declared unenforceable. In effect, landlords will now have to pay for those injured on the property or purchase insurance. In either case, the impact will be for the supply curve to shift upward to S_1. The equilibrium price goes to P_1 and quantity goes to Q_1. Renters will either be safer or they will be compensated for their injuries. At the same time, price will increase and

---

4. Other possibilities include a judicial declaration that a clause is unenforceable if it limits a warranty or the amount of damages that can be collected if there is a breach of contract.

quantity will decrease. The exact amount of the price increase is a function of the elasticity of demand and supply.

Perhaps more important but possibly misleading is the impact on consumer surplus. In the graph, consumer surplus before the change was equal to the area PAY. After the change and the alteration by landlords, it is smaller, at P_1BY. In effect, a policy that was supposed to result in redistribution in favor of consumers has made them, as a whole, worse off. This does not mean that the redistributive effort with respect to the plaintiff in the case was not successful. It is just that a court cannot stop reactions that may make consumers generally worse off.

Still, the overall impact cannot be known with certainty. One thing that happens when a court declares a clause in a contract unenforceable is that it forces the seller to offer what is essentially a different product or service. An apartment that is safer or that includes what amounts to insurance is a different product from one without insurance, and the change may have an impact on the demand side of the market. Figure 11.2 is the same as Figure 11.1 except, in addition to

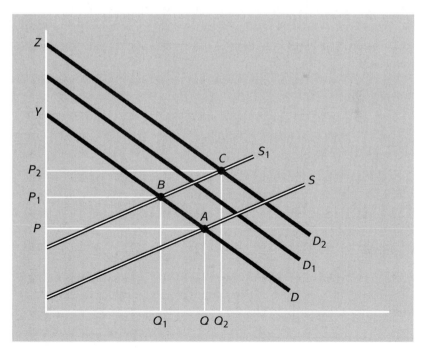

FIGURE 11.2 Cost of Housing after Demand-Side Reaction

D, there are two other demand curves (D_1 and D_2) illustrating possible demand-side responses to the court's ruling. The amount the curve shifts vertically upward is a measure of the value consumers attribute to the product differences. Recall that the shift upward in supply was a measure of the cost of the change to suppliers. If demand shifts upward by more than supply has shifted upward, then consumers are better off since they value the change in quality by more than its cost. The new price is P_2 and the new quantity is Q_2. Even though price is higher, consumer welfare is also increased. In the graph, you can see this by comparing consumer surplus PAY with P_2CZ.

You may want to think about what is going on here. It is only at the first stage that the court is actually able to engage in any redistribution. That first decision refusing to enforce the exculpatory clause actually did result in a gain to one party and a loss to the other. That type of redistribution cannot be sustained if the landlord is able to raise prices as the graphs illustrate. This is not to say that renters will not be better off. If they are, though, it is because the court has reallocated a right in a way that turns out to be efficient. Thus, a possible beneficial outcome results because the court has engaged in a reallocation that would have occurred in the market but for transaction costs.

Price Limits

In some instances, distributive concerns are expressed by controls on prices. This can occur by judicial use of the doctrine of unconscionability or by legislative enactments. An example of the judicial use of the unconscionability doctrine is *Jones v. Star Credit*, in which a freezer with a maximum retail value of $300 was sold for $900.[5] The court refused to enforce the contract. An example of a legislative response to distributive concerns is an Alabama statute with this wording:

> It is . . . evidence of unconscionability if any person, during a state of emergency declared due to natural causes pursuant to the powers of the Governor . . . charges a price that exceeds, by an amount equal to or in excess of twenty-five percent of the average price of

5. 298 N.Y.S.2d 264 (1969).

which the same or similar commodity or rental facility was obtainable in the affected emergency area during the last 30 days prior to the declared state of emergency; and the increase in price charged is not attributed to reasonable costs incurred in connection with the rental or sale of the commodity.

These types of measures are obviously like traditional price ceilings that you studied in Chapter 7. The ultimate economic impact can vary depending on market conditions. The most basic analysis is depicted in Figure 11.3. With supply and demand as illustrated, the market-clearing price is P. A price ceiling set any lower than P results in a shortage because, at that price, the quantity demanded exceeds the quantity supplied. There are three aspects of the outcome to note. Obviously, price is lower than it would otherwise be. In addition, price is not relied upon as the rationing mechanism. Finally, the quantity exchanged (Q_1) is less than it would be if price were the rationing mechanism (Q).

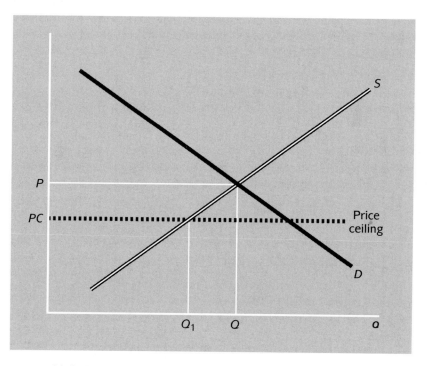

FIGURE 11.3 Impact of Price Ceiling

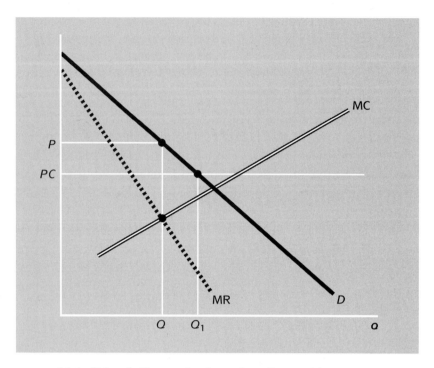

FIGURE 11.4 Price Ceiling under Imperfect Competition

This analysis assumes that the market is competitive. Suppose instead that the market is imperfectly competitive. As you know, price and quantity will not be determined by supply and demand but will be set at a profit-maximizing level. In Figure 11.4, marginal revenue (MR) and marginal cost (MC) intersect at quantity Q, and the profit-maximizing price is P. Suppose the price ceiling is set at PC, which is below the profit-maximizing price. Note the difference between this outcome and the outcome when the price ceiling was imposed on a competitive market. This time, price goes down and remains the rationing mechanism. In addition, as long as the ceiling price exceeds marginal cost, the quantity sold will not decline.[6] If fact, in the market depicted here, the quantity will increase to Q_1. The point is that,

6. In effect, the price ceiling causes the marginal revenue curve to change its shape. It is equal to the price ceiling until it intersects with the demand curve. At that point, it drops down to the usual marginal revenue curve.

at least in the short run, the price ceiling may achieve the type of distributive goal it is intended to achieve.

One final possibility deserves note. In Alabama, as the quoted statute indicates, and in other states, there are laws that limit the amounts by which prices can be increased in times of emergency. For example, suppose the price of an electric generator at the local home improvement store is $500. Then a hurricane roars through a community causing an extended electricity outage. The outcome is a sudden and significant increase in the demand for generators. As you know, if the market is permitted to set the price, an increase in demand with no increase in supply will mean higher prices. If you have followed the news in recent years in the aftermath of hurricanes, you know that this is not merely a theoretical point. In the short run and especially in times of emergency, supply is likely to be relatively inelastic. Local merchants may raise prices. What seems distasteful to many, however, are sellers who buy needed items in areas that are not affected by the storm and transport them to the storm-affected areas and offer them for sale at prices greatly in excess of the pre-emergency price. Newspapers refer to the practice as "price gouging."

Before getting into the detailed analysis of price gouging, it is important to understand that in every market and in every sector there is a difference between a short- and a long-run supply curve. (This is one of the many contributions Alfred Marshall made to economics.) A short-run supply curve is more inelastic; a long-run supply curve is more elastic. The difference is that in the long run, there is more flexibility and adaptability on the supply side. Suppose a sector is in a long-run equilibrium with an efficient number of suppliers of efficient size responding to what is normal demand. Then, all of a sudden, demand increases structurally. In the beginning, the price will increase along the existing supply curve. The price increases substantially, but this will signal to existing and potential suppliers that there is a profit to be made in this market. New suppliers will enter this sector and incumbent suppliers will expand their production plants. In the long run, more supply will be forthcoming and in the longer run, the long-run, elastic supply curve will be valid. In the long run, the equilibrium quantity traded on the market will be greater than it is now and the long-run equilibrium price will be lower. The important point is that today's "price gougers" may serve the function of drawing forth increased supply in the future.

Figure 11.5 will assist readers in understanding the impact of the price limitations in times of emergency. The pre-emergency equilibrium price is P. After the hurricane, the emergency price equals P_1 and the emergency quantity traded is Q_1. When supply is inelastic, the limitation on price increases has little impact on the quantity sold. In fact, if the pre-emergency price is $500, it may be more accurate to view the supply curve as vertical at that point, meaning that, if warranted by demand, local stores would deplete their entire inventory at that time. Without the price control, the market clears at the equilibrium price P_1. With the price limit E, because supply is inelastic, the number of units sold does not substantially decrease. Sales slightly diminish from Q_1 to Q_e. In fact, as illustrated here, the redistributive effort is successful in a sense because consumer surplus under the price limitations (Area $ENM'L$) exceeds what consumer surplus would have been if price had moved to competitive levels (P_1ML). In effect, P_1RNE has been shifted from producer-sellers to consumers. The cost (deadweight loss) of this shift, welfare-wise, is triangle $NM'M$. To see this, compare total welfare arrived at when the mar-

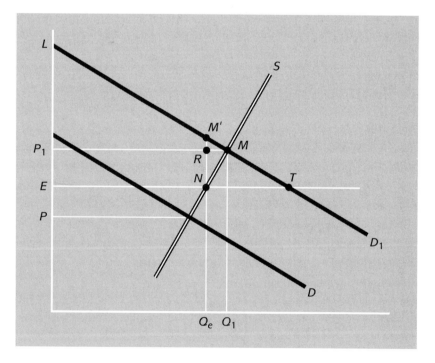

FIGURE 11.5 Price Controls in Times of Emergency

ket clears at emergency price P_1 and quantity Q_1 with total welfare when the government sets the price at E and Q_e is transacted on the market. On the other hand, at price E, there is a shortage—the quantity demanded at that price exceeds the quantity supplied. This shortage is measured by the distance NT. Correspondingly, there is foregone consumer surplus of $NM'T$. This shortage will cause upward price pressure and might create a black market for generators.

At this point the issue of "price gougers" comes in. Their entry could be illustrated in two ways. One would be to view the supply curve from a longer-run perspective, in which case the curve would be less inelastic. Or, their entry could be reflected as a shift to the right of the supply curve. The new suppliers, however, cannot "produce" at the same prices as the incumbent home improvement retailers. In the typical instance, it will mean renting trucks, buying inventory (at retail prices), and venturing into a geographic area in which there may be dangers and even difficulties obtaining fuel. Now, however, the comparison for the gouger to make is between his or her marginal cost—which will include many costs that in other contexts may be viewed as fixed—and price E. If marginal cost accounting for all risks and including an acceptable profit is greater than E, the gougers will stay away and many willing and able buyers will not be able to purchase generators. Suppose, however, that the government did not put in a price limit E but let the price rise to P_1. This post-emergency equilibrium price could very well be higher than the marginal cost of the gouger. In that case and with sufficient competition among them, gougers would supply the emergency area with generators at a price equal to their marginal costs.

CASE 11.1 **The Unconscionability Standard:** *Weaver v. American Oil Co.*, 276 N.E.2d 144 (1972) and *Furgason v. McKenzie Check Advance of Indiana*, 2001 WL 238129 (2001)

You should not infer from these materials that the doctrine of unconscionability is used frequently by courts. It is not. In addition, the doctrine can vary from state to state and from time to time. As noted in the text, however, courts can react to unfair bargains in a number of ways other than ruling that they are unconscionable. Two cases from Indiana will give you a feel for how the doctrine of unconscionability is used. In the first case,

Weaver v. American Oil Co., a gas station operator signed a contract with American Oil, the company that supplied the gasoline. In that contract was a "hold harmless" provision. This means that the gas station operator will not sue the oil company even if the oil company does something negligent on the operator's property. In addition, the gas station operator was required to pay for any damage even if caused by the oil company. At it turns out, an oil company employee sprayed gas on the station owner causing serious injury. The gas station owner claimed that he should be able to sue and that the exculpatory provision was unconscionable. The court agreed, offering the following reasoning:

> The facts reveal that Weaver had left high school after one and a half years and spent his time, prior to leasing the service station, working at various skilled and unskilled labor oriented jobs. He was not one who should be expected to know the law or understand the meaning of technical terms. The ceremonious activity of signing the lease consisted of nothing more than the agent of American Oil placing the lease in front of Mr. Weaver and saying 'sign', which Mr. Weaver did. There is nothing in the record to indicate that Weaver read the lease; that the agent asked Weaver to read it; or that the agent, in any manner, attempted to call Weaver's attention to the 'hold harmless' clause in the lease. Each year following, the procedure was the same. A salesman, from American Oil, would bring the lease to Weaver, at the station, and Weaver would sign it. The evidence showed that Weaver had never read the lease prior to signing and that the clauses in the lease were never explained to him in a manner from which he could grasp their legal significance. The leases were prepared by the attorneys of American Oil Company, for the American Oil Company, and the agents of the American Oil Company never attempted to explain the conditions of the lease nor did they advise Weaver that he should consult legal counsel, before signing the lease. The superior bargaining power of American Oil is patently obvious and the significance of Weaver's signature upon the legal document amounted to nothing more than a mere formality to Weaver for the substantial protection of American Oil. "An 'unconscionable contract' has been defined to be such as no sensible man not under delusion, duress or in distress would make, and such as no honest and fair man would accept. There exists here an 'inequality so strong, gross and manifest that it is impossible to state it to a man of common sense without producing an exclamation at the inequality of it.' 'Where the inadequacy of the price is so great

that the mind revolts at it the court will lay hold on the slightest circumstances of oppression or advantage to rescind the contract.'"[7]

The facts of this case reveal that in exchange for a contract which, if the clause in question is enforceable, may cost Mr. Weaver potentially thousands of dollars in damages for negligence of which he was not the cause, Weaver must operate the service station seven days a week for long hours, at a total yearly income of $5,000–$6,000. The evidence also reveals that the clause was in fine print and contained no title heading which would have identified it as an indemnity clause. It seems a deplorable abuse of justice to hold a man of poor education, to a contract prepared by the attorneys of American Oil, for the benefit of American Oil which was presented to Weaver on a 'take it or leave it basis'.

More recently in 2001, an Indiana court was faced with an issue in the context of a series of "payday" loans. You have probably seen these businesses that offer short-term loans at high interest rates that the borrower is expected to pay off when he or she gets paid. In this case, *Furgason v. McKenzie Check Advance of Indiana,* Furgason borrowed money eleven times. Most of the time, the agreements signed included arbitration clauses. Under these clauses, the parties agree that if there is a dispute they will not go to court but will hire an independent third party to resolve the issue. Furgason felt this was a great disadvantage to her and claimed the clause was unconscionable and that she had entered in a *contract of adhesion.* The court responded to both claims:

UNCONSCIONABILITY

Ms. Furgason contends that the arbitration agreements are not enforceable under Indiana law because they are unconscionable. This attack rests primarily on *Weaver v. American Oil Co.,* 276 N.E.2d 144 (Ind.1971). Ms. Furgason contends that there was a great disparity in bargaining power because she was unaware of the terms contained in the arbitration agreements and was even unaware that she had ever signed any arbitration agreements; that the arbitration agreements create an extreme inequality such that National Cash Advance has taken advantage of her financial situation; and that National Cash Advance has failed to meet its burden of showing that the arbitration agreements were explained to her and that there was in fact a real and voluntary meeting of the minds.

---

7. Official Comment, Uniform Commercial Code § 2-302.

In *Weaver,* the Indiana Supreme Court held that a filling station operator did not have to indemnify a petroleum company under the terms of a lease that included a one-sided "hold harmless" clause. The court held the clause was unconscionable as written and was unknown to the filling station operator. The court noted that the operator "was not one who should be expected to know the law or understand the meaning of technical terms." "There [was] nothing in the record to indicate that Weaver read the lease; that the agent asked Weaver to read it; or that the agent, in any manner, attempted to call Weaver's attention to the 'hold harmless' clause in the lease." In addition to noting that the "hold harmless" provision was typed in fine print and included in a preprinted form contract, the Indiana Supreme Court held that the operator did not have equal bargaining. Ms. Furgason contends that she did not understand that the arbitration agreements meant she was giving up her right to go to court and agreeing to arbitrate her claims. Nevertheless, on ten separate occasions she voluntarily agreed to arbitrate her claim with National Cash Advance. Ms. Furgason separately signed and dated each of the ten arbitration agreements. National Cash Advance plainly brought the arbitration agreements to Ms. Furgason's attention. . . . Unlike the oil company in *Weaver,* National Cash Advance did not require Ms. Furgason to sign an unknown, one-sided "hold harmless" clause. National Cash Advance specifically required Ms. Furgason to sign and date each arbitration agreement separately. The arbitration agreements were not typed in fine print. Although Ms. Furgason contends that she did not understand the terms of the arbitration agreement or that she was giving up her right to go to court, and denied that she had ever even entered into an arbitration agreement, the language of the contract clearly and explicitly provides for arbitration of disputes arising out of the contractual relationship. Even as a consumer, Ms. Furgason cannot "use [her] failure to inquire about the ramifications of that clause to avoid the consequences of agreed-to arbitration."

CONTRACTS OF ADHESION

In general, a contract of adhesion is a "standardized contract form offered to consumers of goods and services on essentially [a] 'take it or leave it' basis without affording consumer realistic opportunity to bargain and under such conditions that consumer cannot obtain desired product or services except by acquiescing in form contract." . . . Before such a contract can be deemed unenforceable, there must be not only superior bargaining power, but also additional factors such as, "a lack of meaning choice as in the case of an industry wide form contract heavily weighted in favor of one party and offered on a take it or leave it basis." . . . Although the arbitration agreements were offered to Ms. Furgason as a standard contract, she has not shown that there was a lack of meaningful choice in the market. The fact that one party to the contract is unwilling to do business with a customer who insists on altering the terms of a standard contract does not mean the contract is not enforceable. Ms. Furgason has not proven, or even offered to prove, that she could not have transacted business with another payday loan establishment without the same or similar arbitration agreement.

The cases obviously deal with different types of clauses, but they may also indicate a slight change in philosophy. The 1972 court seems more willing to examine the personal characteristics of the disadvantaged party. Can you find any significant economic distinction between the cases? The court in *Furgason* seems to suggest that she could have known what she was giving up with a small amount of effort. On the other hand, the cost to Weaver of understanding what he was getting into may have been significantly higher. As an economic matter, should this make a difference?

CAN CONTRACT LAW WORK AS A TOOL TO ACHIEVE DESIRED DISTRIBUTIVE OUTCOMES?

You may notice a trend in cases that deal with distributive problems. In the dance lessons case, the disadvantaged party was unsophisticated and probably unwise to smooth sales tactics. In *Walker-Thomas*, the disadvantaged party was also relatively ignorant and probably had little choice but to deal with the neighborhood merchant. Even the Alabama statute imposing price controls during emergencies seems designed to protect people with little bargaining power. In all of those instances and others like it, the decisions by the courts address particular transactions that to many will seem unfair. It is equally true, however, that what the courts actually address is the manifestation of what many may regard as systemic inequities. Addressing individualized inequities may have little connection with correcting problems on a larger scale and can actually make the class of people a court attempts to protect worse off.

If you are a firm believer in allowing markets to work, you may add something else to the mix. Merchants who take advantage of consumers by charging exorbitant prices and earn an economic profit in doing so should set off a market adjustment. For example, if the owners of Walker-Thomas are getting rich through cross-collateralization, the theory is that firms will enter the market and offer consumers better deals. Even in the case of emergency prices that the Alabama statute is designed to treat, the same thing should happen. If merchants realize there are huge profits to be made by selling for high prices during times of emergency, it would make sense that they would react by carrying larger inventories. Carrying large inventories makes sense if demand is always volatile or if the periods of volatility are somewhat predictable. For example, it would make sense to carry more inventory of some items during hurricane season.[8] This increase in supply will pull prices back down. The theory would mean that even the ignorant, downtrodden, and powerless will, assuming low entry barriers, be delivered from advantage-takers by market adjustments. Of course, the market may be slow to react, and waiting for it to react may be politically unaccceptable. During this period, unfair outcomes are the cost of broader social benefits later on.

If markets are slow to react and if one senses that the basic reaction of contract law to the scattered array of instances of advantage taking is less than satisfactory, the questions are whether contract law has any potential for addressing the systemic realities that make some people prey on others. It is possible that contract law can sometimes be used as a way to reflect and strengthen social norms. In contracts, the more general signal could be that it is socially unacceptable to take maximum advantage of the ignorance and misfortune of others. It also may suggest to those who are habitually disadvantaged that they have the "right" to assert themselves.

These possibilities do not seem promising in a system like the one in the United States in which contract law is largely a common law

---

8. Of course, if the emergencies are not predictable at all, then carrying extra inventory may be too expensive to justify.

matter and different jurisdictions have different philosophies. Systemic change at the contract *formation* process is more likely to offset some of the market imbalance. An example would be a requirement that loan terms be spelled out in plain English so they cannot be easily misunderstood. Similarly, a period of time after signing a contract before one becomes fully committed to it would permit some reflection and additional time for information gathering out of reach of a smooth-talking salesperson. Obviously, more pie-in-the-sky systemic changes like better educational opportunities could play a role here as well. After-the-fact reactions seem ultimately to hold little promise.

QUESTIONS FOR DISCUSSION

1. Compare these possibilities: After a hurricane and electrical outage, sellers descend on the stricken area and offer ice for ten times the usual price. After a hurricane, physicians flow into the sticken area and offer to treat the injured at ten times their usual fees. Is there a meaningful economic distinction?

2. Many times people enter into "unfavorable" contracts, the terms of which they do not understand. Plus, they do not bother to read all the small print. Is there any economic reason to use public resources to rescue these people from the deals they have made? Is it possible that small print, with convoluted language spread throughout multiple pages is actually a way one party raises the costs to the other party of understanding the terms of a contract? Does this make a difference in how you think about the issue? What if the government compiles a "blacklist" of unfavorable terms which, if used in a contract make that contract unenforceable? Some private law countries, such as The Netherlands, include a blacklist like this in their Civil Code.

3. Suppose you found that minorities and women consistently paid higher prices than white men for virtually everything. Would you favor a law that says "one price for all?" What if it were shown that white men are just better negotiators?

4. Going back to the example of the landlords and the exculpatory provision, suppose the clause is declared unenforceable. As dis-

cussed, this implies that the landlords then offer both a rental contract and an insurance contract. They are then bundling two products into one. Bundling was one of the problems Microsoft ran into as it was selling Windows and Internet Explorer in one package. Why would the bundling of a rental contract and an insurance contract not be problematic?

CHAPTER TWELVE

The Economics of Contract Remedies

M ICHAEL JACKSON. WHAT DOES HE HAVE TO DO with a book about law and economics? Like many people, he has an occasional legal problem. One of these problems arose when Mr. Jackson agreed to perform a series of concerts to commemorate the millennium. He was supposed to perform a total of four concerts. Two were charity concerts in Seoul, South Korea, and Munich, Germany; two others, in Sydney, Australia, and Honolulu, Hawaii, were for profit and were scheduled for December 31, 1999, with a quick jet trip between venues. In October 1999, Jackson announced that he would not perform. The result was a breach of contract action by the concert promoter asking for over $21 million. The promoter claimed that he had spent $10 million promoting the concerts and would have made $10 million in profits. Plus he was required to pay off over $1 million in debts Jackson had incurred.[1]

Except for the celebrity involved and the national attention the lawsuit attracted, this was a pretty standard breach of contract case. Moreover, the damages the promoter claimed are the types usually found in a breach of contract case. Although there are numerous contract

---

1. In late 2003, after a two-week trial, a jury awarded the plaintiff $5.3 million, which was roughly equal to the expenses incurred for the two benefit concerts only.

remedies, the most fundamental one is designed to put the plaintiff in the position he or she would have been in after performance of the contract. Here the key word is "after." In legal terms, we try to give the plaintiff his or her *expectancy*. You could view this as allowing the plaintiff to achieve the same level of welfare that he or she would have experienced had the contract been performed.

The first section of the chapter examines various measures of damages. You will find that contract damages can be reconciled with economic goals. The next section is devoted to specific performance. When the remedy is specific performance, a court orders the breaching party to do what he or she had promised to do. The third section considers restitution, a remedy that allows the plaintiff to recover whatever he or she has contributed to the breaching party and recoveries in the case of promissory estoppel. The last part discusses the remedial consequences of *excuse*, which occurs when a court rules that one of the parties does not have to perform his or her side of the bargain.

CONTRACT DAMAGES

Expectancy

Getting Started

The central remedy in a contracts case is expectancy. This is the amount necessary to put the nonbreaching party in the same position financially that he or she would have been in had performance occurred. Here is an example. You see a BMW Mini for sale in the newspaper for $22,000. You drive it and like it and make a contract with the owner to buy it for $22,000. You give him $2,000 as a deposit. You are supposed to show up with the money in five days and he will give you the title. The day before the exchange is to take place he sells the car to someone else. The next day you start searching for the same car and the best price you can find is $24,000. How much do you need to recover to be in the position you would have been in had there been performance? The answer is $4,000. Think about the position you would have been in: $24,000 less money, but you would have the car. To be in that same position the seller needs to return your $2,000 plus give you $2,000. Since you have $20,000 left that you were going to pay for the car, you can combine that with the $4,000 and buy the substitute car. What is the outcome in terms of the impact on you?

$24,000 for the car. There may be different ways to calculate expectancy damages depending on whether you have made a down payment, but when the dust settles, the plaintiff should be in the position he or she would have been in, at least as far as wealth goes. This last point is important. In this case, you would not have to actually buy the second car to collect damages. In fact, more abstractly, the position you would have been in is that you would have paid $22,000 for a car or any asset that turns out to be worth $24,000 because it cannot be replaced for less.

You may wonder what this has to do with the Michael Jackson millennium case discussed in the introduction. Arguably, if Jackson had performed, he would have generated enough ticket sales to allow the promoter to pay for all his promotional expenses and to make a healthy profit. In that case, unlike our simple example here, expectancy includes making additional income. This is the case in a great number of commercial contracts. For example, if you are renting a space for a store and it is not ready when you expect it to be, part of your loss would be the profit you would have made had the store space been ready in time.

The Efficient Breach

One of the more interesting questions posed when examining contract law from the perspective of economic analysis is whether expectancy is consistent with efficiency. At first, the answer seems to be yes. Go back to the car you almost bought. Let's suppose that the reason the seller breached is because he got an offer for $30,000. When damages are paid, he makes a $6,000 profit by breaching. You receive your expectancy, the seller is made better off by breaching, and the party actually buying the car values it in excess of $30,000. Two parties are better off and one is no worse off; this looks like a Pareto superior outcome. The key in all of this is to set damages at expectancy. If they are lower than expectancy, resulting in undercompensation, you would be worse off. If they are higher than expectancy, resulting in overcompensation, the *efficient breach* may not occur. For example, in this example, if there were a rule that all contract breachers are required to pay $10,000, the efficient breach would not occur.[2]

---

2. But the parties may be able to bargain around this problem, as you will see when you read about liquidated damages and specific performance.

In effect, the efficient breach occurs when the remedy is set to protect your expectancy and to allow the other party's performance to be purchased by someone who values it more.

This even works out in a case like that involving Michael Jackson. Suppose Jackson did breach the contract to perform the millennium concerts but only because he was offered a huge sum to perform for Bill Gates at the annual Microsoft gala. As long as Bill Gates offers Jackson enough to allow Jackson to give the promoter his expectancy and still make a profit by performing at the Microsoft affair, his breach will be efficient. In effect, the loss of expectancy is the externality associated with the contract breach and as long as the car seller or Michael Jackson, or whoever, internalizes that externality by paying expectancy, he or she is free to breach and resell the goods or services and the outcome is efficient.

There is, however, a problem here that you may have already spotted. Expectancy as a measure of damages is a liability rule. (You will recall that liability rules are those that allow parties to commit a *wrong* and then compensate the injured party.) This means that we substitute fair market valuations for the actual amount by which performance was subjectively valued. For example, on the car you received $4,000, which put you in a position to buy a similar car. Suppose the car had something special about it that would not show up in a fair market determination. Maybe it is the actual one that once was driven by your Aunt Sally (aka Mustang Sally) and it holds special memories for you. In fact, if really pushed, you might have paid $34,000 for it. Simply giving you damages as though it is worth $24,000 does not put you in as good a position utility-wise as you would have been. The other two parties may be better off but you are worse off, and the breach cannot be said to be efficient. In effect, the breach may or may not be efficient depending on how close your subjective valuation matches up with objective market values.

Beyond this, there are some practical problems that make the determination of expectancy a bit sticky.

The Employment Contract

Suppose you are to be paid $200 a week for the next ten weeks to work at a shoe store. After five weeks, the employers say you are no longer needed. In a sense, you "expected" $1,000 more dollars. On the other hand, you expected to be working. To give you $1,000 seems to give you more than your expectancy. After all, you did not expect a paid vacation. In theory, the $1,000 would have provided some utility and the work some disutility. If possible, you should be paid the monetary equivalent of that difference—the lost net utility. Obviously, that is impossible to do.

To solve this problem, courts have generally arrived at the rule that you are entitled to the $1,000 minus what you could earn in a similar job. The idea is that if you take a similar job you will incur the expected amount of disutility, and if that job pays less, you are entitled to the difference in salaries in order to return you to the expected level of utility. This seems to work out fine in theory, but two problems arise. First, what if you do not accept the other job and therefore do not incur the disutility or earn the income? Does the employer have to pay you the $1,000? The answer here is no. If you choose not to work, the breaching employer is still permitted to subtract what you could have earned at a similar job. This makes sense. Otherwise, you would end up in a better position than if the employer had not breached. Second, what happens if there are no comparable jobs? Here the rule is that you receive the full salary. This results in an obvious overcompensation, but there appears to be no easy way to resolve the problem.

CASE 12.1 *The Bloomer Girl*: *Parker v. Twentieth Century Fox Film Corp.*, 474 P.2d 689 (1970)

The difficulty of determining expectancy is illustrated by *Parker v. Twentieth Century Fox Film Corp.* Shirley MacLaine (Parker) sued Twentieth Century Fox for $750,000 after it decided not to make a film she was slated to star in. The film was a musical, *The Bloomer Girl*. Twentieth Century Fox defended itself by showing that it had offered Parker a comparable role in a western titled *Big Country, Big Man,* which she declined. More fundamentally, Parker claimed that her expectancy was $750,000. Twentieth Century Fox argued that the expectancy was $750,000 for a movie performance and awarding Parker $750,000 without subtracting what she could have made in *Big Country* would result in overcompensation. The court ruled in Parker's favor. This may seem a little extreme in an employment contract where the expectancy is net utility. This is the utility from the income (and possibly some aspects of the work) minus the disutility from the work. *The Bloomer Girl* was a musical set in the United States. *Big Country* was a western to be made in

Australia. A requirement that Parker appear in *Big Country* or have the income subtracted from the $750,000 almost certainly would have left her with less net utility than the contract. Of course, receiving $750,000 while not working probably left her in a higher net utility position. That, however, is the dilemma of employment contract remedies.

When Expectancy Includes Lost Profits

In the Michael Jackson case, the plaintiff claimed that Jackson's cancellation meant he lost the profit he would have made on the concerts. Literally, this is a part of his expectancy; if the contracts had been performed, he would have earned a profit. The problem is that unlike many other instances of determining expectancy, lost profits are always somewhat speculative. One cannot be sure what they would have been. This leaves courts that adhere to an expectancy measure in something of a bind. The rule that has been fashioned is that plaintiffs may recover lost profits as long as they can be shown with reasonable certainty.

Reasonable certainty has no solid definition. As a practical matter it means that when lost profits are at stake, the plaintiff bears the risk of demonstrating to the jury a figure based upon dependable projections of what might have been. This could be done by showing past profitability. In the Jackson case, the promoter might have shown a history of high ticket sales for past concerts and that tickets were selling fast for the millennium concerts. The allocation of the risk in this way has an economic justification in that the plaintiff—the one standing to lose the profit—is typically in a better position to know what is at stake and can either bring this to the attention of the other party or take some measures to make sure the loss does not occur. In fact, it is an ideal place for agreeing on a term to be placed in the contract indicating the amount of damages that will be paid if the defendant does not perform. This is called a *liquidated damages clause* and will be covered below.

The Cost of Performance/Value of Performance Problem

Sometimes when a party fails to perform, there can be two measures of expectancy. Suppose you hire a landscaper and provide him with the plans to plant flowers and shrubs on your property. You go away for a few days and, when you return, you discover that the landscaper took "liberties" with your plan and made many changes. The shrubs are where the flowers were supposed to be and vice versa. To make it easy, there is no question that there has been a breach. Knowing all about expectancy, you have three landscapers visit your property and ask them what it will cost to redo the landscaping so you will get what you expected. The average of the estimates is $2,000.

The landscaper also knows a thing or two about expectancy and asks three real estate appraisers to visit your property. He shows them all the plans you had provided and asks them to tell him the difference between what the property would be worth if he had followed the plan to a tee and what it is worth as it is now. The answer is $200. His argument is that for $200 you can be in the position you would have been in as far as your wealth. In addition, he says that giving you $2,000 would be foolish. If you tear up the lawn and replant, it would be wasteful and if you just keep the money it would be a windfall.

This is one of those places when both law and economics are unable to provide a clear guiding principle. Officially, the law says the measure of recovery is the cost to actually have the contract performed, which would be the $2,000, but the law also says that when the cost is disproportionately high, the remedy is the difference in value—the $200. For some time, courts accepted the reasoning that $2,000 in damages for a $200 loss in value was wasteful. Now that reasoning has been discarded, as it should have been. If the recovery is for $2,000, there is nothing forcing the prevailing party to replace the plants. But, if he does replace the plants, what does that mean? As an economic matter, it means he or she valued replacing the plants more than anything else that could be done with the $2,000. From an economic perspective that is efficient, not wasteful. In fact, an argument can be made that the higher amount is appropriate only if the landowner does plan to tear up the property and replant. When that occurs, we know the damage to the landowner was associated with the actual performance as required and not simply the loss in the value of the land. One solution to this is to rely on a remedy called *specific performance*. You will see why when we discuss this remedy below.

CASE 12.2   Cost of Performance or Value of Performance?
Peevyhouse v. Garland Coal Mining Co., 382 P.2d 109
(1962)

In 1954, Lucille and Willie Peevyhouse leased their farm to
Garland Coal, which operated a strip mine on the property. In
addition to paying for the coal, Garland promised to restore the
land to its pre-mining condition. It did not, and that is where the
trouble began. The cost to restore the land would have been
$29,000. Restoration of the land would have increased its value by
$300, which Garland appeared more than happy to pay. In this
case, the court awarded the Peevyhouses $300. According to
Garland and the court, anything more than that would be a
windfall. How do you feel about this? Suppose the Peevyhouses
accepted less in payment for the coal because they thought they
were getting $29,000 in repair? Suppose you visited the property in
the late 1990s (as a student of one of your authors did) and
discovered a piece of property that nature had restored so that it
was beautiful and natural? Does that mean the Peevyhouses
actually were treated fairly?

Reliance Measures of Damages

In some contracts cases, the measure of damages is called
reliance rather than expectancy. Under reliance, the objective is to
return the contracting party to the position he or she was in before
making the contract. For example, in the Michael Jackson case, the
promoter asked for the funds already spent in promoting the concerts plus the lost profit. Reliance would include only the first of
these. It is the expense incurred because you are relying on the other
party to perform.

As you would expect, reliance is not the first choice as a measure
of damages for most plaintiffs because it is typically lower than
expectancy. Sometimes, however, a court will permit a plaintiff to
recover reliance only when it is not satisfied that the plaintiff can accurately predict what expectancy would have been. This would occur
in a case like the Michael Jackson case if the judge thinks the estimate
of lost profit is just an educated guess. What is really going on is that
there is a loss but neither party is sure how much it is. Courts tend
to allocate to plaintiffs the risk of losses that are hard to predict, reasoning that plaintiffs are in a better position to know just how much

harm would be suffered if there is a breach and would know how much they should insure against to avoid the loss.[3]

In terms of the *efficient breach,* the reliance measure of damages probably falls short of expectancy. It really is as though one party can buy his or her way out of a contact by just paying the other party his or her expenses up to the point of the breach. Still, there is some economic rationality to the reliance measure. People make contracts in hopes of getting more out of the deal than they put into it. Rational people then would not spend more in reliance on the performance of someone else than they hope to get back from that person in the exchange. Unless they make a bad deal, expectancy will always exceed reliance. Thus, reliance is something of a surrogate for expectancy that at least ensures that the error of overcompensation does not occur. The possibility of under-compensation does, however, remain.

Liquidated Damages

As already noted, the parties can agree in advance to what the damages will be if there is a breach of contract. This is called a *liquidated damages clause.* You may be familiar with these provisions. A university may contract to have a new football stadium built and the contract may stipulate that the stadium must be completed by August 15 to be ready for the fall football season. If a breach occurs and the stadium is not ready, calculating the damages will be very difficult. Would it be the cost of canceling the game, the cost of transferring to the visiting team's field, or the cost of locating another venue? Since courts will not allow a plaintiff to more or less speculate about the damages, the parties may plan for the problem in advance and stipulate what the damages will be. For example, the damages might be $1,000 a day for each day the stadium is not completed after the deadline.

A type of liquidated damages you may know about is a deposit. Suppose you agreed to buy a new bicycle at a local bike shop for $1,000 and you are going to pick it up in five days. In order to make sure the shop owner understands you are serious, you leave $200 as

---

3. One very useful way of dealing with this risk is to rely on a liquidated damages clause. Basically it allows the parties to put in the contract what the damages will be if there is a breach.

a deposit. In many instances, but not all, you are implicitly agreeing that if you do not come back, the shop owner may keep the $200.

Courts tend to have mixed feelings about liquidated damages clauses and often refuse to enforce them. A distinction is made between clauses that are reasonable estimates of the likely damages if a breach should occur and *penalty clauses*. An example of the latter in the stadium example would be a clause that says "contractor will pay $100,000 if the stadium is not completed by the deadline." This is viewed as a penalty because it seems designed to force the contractor to finish no matter what. The tip-off in this case is that the amount is the same whether the builder is one day or three weeks late. Yet we know the damages must be different depending on how long the delay is. Consequently, the flat $100,000 does not appear to be an effort to set the liquidated damages amount at the estimated amount of actual damages.

It is not completely clear why courts traditionally were not keen on enforcing these clauses. One theory is that early common law courts resisted allowing private parties to move into an area reserved for the courts by establishing damages ahead of time. Another theory, now pretty much discarded and probably never accurate, is that liquidated damages could stand in the way of the efficient breach. That reasoning would go like this: Think again about the car you almost bought. Suppose you agreed to buy the car for $22,000 and there is a $10,000 liquidated damages clause. There is no prepayment. The fair market value of the car, again, is $24,000 and the purchaser who would like your seller to breach is willing to pay $30,000. If the seller must pay you $10,000 if he breaches the contract, there would be no breach even though you may place a value on the car of only $24,000. The efficient breach does not occur.

If you think about it, unless there are high transaction costs, this may not at all be how this would play out. Knowing that there is a $30,000 buyer, the seller would approach you and ask to be excused from the contract. You might say no, counting on the $10,000 in liquidated damages. Do you think you would really get that? Probably not. If you are too stubborn, the seller is much better off just delivering the car that is only worth $24,000 to you. The fact that the seller can simply deliver the car is the leverage he or she has to determine whether you would be willing to sell your right to the car for something less that $10,000. In this case, it is likely that you will agree to relinquish your contractual right to the car for a payment. The least you would take is $2,000 (the amount by which the value of the car exceeds what you were paying), and the most the seller would be willing to pay is $8,000. Most likely you will find a price that both of you find acceptable. You will recognize this as the Coase theorem at work. The $10,000 clause technically gives you the right to the car, but it is likely that you will sell that right to someone who values it more. Technically, there is no breach, but the car does end up in the hands of the buyer who values it more.

One possible stumbling block here is *bilateral monopoly*. Bilateral monopoly occurs when there is only one buyer and one seller. Here, the seller of the car is the only one interested in buying your contract right to it. And the seller is the only possible purchaser of that right. It is possible that an impasse could occur long enough for the new buyer to lose interest and move on. But for the most part, the idea that it is economically wise to refuse to enforce liquidated damages clauses because they stand in the way of efficient breaches is based on a misunderstanding of the parties' ability to bargain around the problem.

In general, in the absence of coercion, duress, or any of the factors that may taint the contract formation process, there is little economic basis for not enforcing a liquidated damages clause. First, the process of not enforcing a portion of a contract while leaving the rest intact changes the bargain the parties struck and replaces it with one they did not agree to and may never have agreed to. For example, suppose you own a home and want to have a swimming pool built in your backyard. You get bids from two contractors. One bid is a little higher, but you prefer that contractor because he guarantees to finish construction on time or pay you $5,000. You like that level of reassurance and are willing to pay extra to get it. This would, in most instances, be viewed as a penalty and not be enforced by the court. The rest of the contract stays intact but now it has become, in effect, a contract you had not agreed to. Second, liquidated damages can perform a valuable function even if not a reasonable estimate of actual damages. They permit a party who is new in a trade or who has had some difficulties in the past to become reestablished by, in effect, offering a promise that has more behind it than the amount a court would award.

SPECIFIC PERFORMANCE

When the contract remedy is specific performance, a court orders the breaching party to the contract to do what was promised. Specific performance is, therefore, literal expectancy. Unlike damage remedies, which are liability rules, specific performance protects a party's right to performance with a property rule. There are two big limitations on granting specific performance. First, when it comes to a personal service that was supposed to be performed, a court will not order a party to perform. A court, therefore, would not order Michael Jackson to perform a concert. When the government forces someone to perform a service, it is a form of slavery and violates the U.S. Constitution.[4] The second big limitation is that courts will not award specific performance if there is an *adequate remedy at law,* that is, there will be no specific performance if the plaintiff can be adequately compensated with money.[5] This is both a historical and a practical limitation. Courts do not have huge sophisticated staffs and it would be impossible for a court to supervise and make sure every performance it ordered was carried out. In effect, the administrative costs of this remedy can be quite high. For example, it would be very difficult for a court to determine whether a house was built exactly to specification. Consequently, the basic specific performance case is one in which the defendant is ordered to deliver something that is unique or that might be very difficult for the plaintiff to replace. In these cases, market value may be difficult to determine or there may be great subjective or sentimental value attached to the specific item that was to be exchanged. The remedy when the seller of land breaches is routinely specific performance. This is because the courts view every parcel of land as unique.

4. Interestingly, a court may order a person not to do something that may have the effect of doing what he or she was contractually obligated to do in the first place. For example, in the Michael Jackson cases, a court might have ordered Jackson not to perform anywhere else on New Year's Eve, thereby making the performances he had contracted to do look more inviting.

5. The idea *at law* refers to a division in the court system between courts of law and courts of equity. The award of specific performance was made only by courts of equity, and those courts did not have jurisdiction when a court of law could adequately consider and address a matter.

If it were not for administrative and legal impediments, routine granting of specific performance would make a great deal of economic sense. To understand why, think again about the example involving the landscaping. The cost to redo the landscaping as required under the contract was $2,000 and the lost value was only $200. The problem was determining your subjective expectancy and awarding damages that would put you in the position you expected to be in. Now imagine that specific performance is ordered and the landscaper is required by the court to make the $2,000 repair. This means that as a legal matter, you own a right to have the landscaping done over. But you might be willing to sell that right back to the landscaper and allow him not to redo the lawn.

Suppose the landscaper drives his pickup truck and workers to the property one day and begins to work but just before starting says, "I sure hope this is worth $2,000 to you." Maybe it is. If so, you allow the work to continue and the outcome is efficient. Remember, it is not efficient just because you value the work more than $2,000. It is efficient because the efficient breach requires the breaching party to internalize the full cost of your loss. If you allow the repair to take place, this internalization also takes place.

You might, however, doubt whether replanting the yard really is worth $2,000 to you. In reality, maybe you will only feel $1,200 better off with the new landscaping. As the cost of redoing the job is $2,000, the landscaper would be willing to pay any amount up to $2,000 not to redo planting. You might end up selling your right to have the job redone for something between $1,200 and $2,000, and the Coase theorem would be at work again. In effect, specific performance works like any other property rule in that if a bargain is struck, both parties are better off. The expectancy of the nonbreaching party is protected and internalized by the breaching party, and whether redoing the landscape is efficient will be determined by the market.

Given the potential for specific performance, you may be surprised to learn that it is reserved for special cases. Again, there is a cost of administering the remedy because a court may have to continuously supervise the performance of the breaching party with the possibility of constant bickering about whether the performance is as expected. It is far less costly for a court to simply order a one-time payment.

TWO LESS-IMPORTANT REMEDIAL ISSUES

Two remedies that are technically not contract remedies are often awarded in settings that are sufficiently contract-like in nature as to deserve some mention here.

Restitution

Restitution, although typically measured in dollars and rewarded in the context of a contract, is not a measure of damages at all. It is the measure of the benefits one party has conferred on another or that one person illegally took from another. In other words, it is not measured by the *loss* to one party but by the *gain* to another. As a technical matter, when one party breaches a contract, the plaintiff may opt to ask for restitution instead of damages. Here is how it could come up. You make a $1,000 down payment on a car you agree to pay $10,000 for. The rest of the payment and the car are to be exchanged in a week. In the meantime, you find that the car is worth only $8,000 and realize you have made a big mistake. Somehow you get lucky and the seller breaches the contract. Obviously, here you do not want expectancy because your expectancy is to actually lose money. Most courts will allow you to ask for restitution which means that you would get your money back.

Restitution can also be used to make sure expectancy is set at the right figure. Suppose you have a contract to work for one month taking tickets at a local movie theater. At the end of the month—and only at the end of the month—you will receive $400. After three weeks, you quit and there is no question that you breached the contract. The employer finds someone for the rest of the month to do your job for $150. This is $50 more for that week than you would have been paid, and the employer may ask for $50 in damages. If she gets it, her outcome will far exceed expectancy because she will have received one month of labor for only $100. Even though the employer did not breach the contract, the guiding principle is that she is entitled to no more than expectancy. The problem is that you cannot both breach a contract, as you did, and then claim that you are entitled to damages. After all, you missed out on the best way to avoid being damaged: Do not breach. Still, the employer should get no more than expectancy. Here is where restitution plays an important role. Restitution allows you to recover for the benefits conferred on the employer even though you breached your contract. So the employer recovers for damages of $50, and you recover the unpaid salary of $300 under a theory of restitution. Now the employer has received a month of labor for $400.

Reliance Damages in Promissory Estoppel Cases

In Chapter 11, you learned about one of the most significant changes in contract law in the twentieth century: the near-uniform adoption of promissory estoppel as a theory of recovery. One facet of this theory that is not yet settled is what the recovery should be when a promise is broken. In some jurisdictions, the remedy is to enforce the promise just as it was made. In others, the answer is to enforce the promise only to the level it was relied upon. An example may be useful. Suppose you promise a friend that you are going to give her $100 tomorrow. That evening she buys a new radio for $50 in reliance on your promise. You then change your mind. Does she recover $100 or $50?

Two economic interests come into play here. On one hand, many of the rationales for enforcing gratuitous promises are promoted if the full promise is enforced. For example, beneficial reliance is likely to be greater if one knows the entire promise will be enforced. Enforcing the entire promise is also much easier to administer than a policy of attempting to determine what level of reliance has taken place. On the other hand, it may be that the externality of a broken promise is measured by the extent to which the promisee has relied. If so, this is the amount that should be internalized by the one breaking the promise.

Is there an economic rationale for setting damages at expectancy for contracts and at the level of reliance for gratuitous promises? As already noted, there is not a completely clear answer but a distinction can be made. In the case of a contract, there is an exchange of promises that makes both parties better off. If you promise to buy a friend's CD collection for $200, we know that that collection was necessary to induce you to give up $200. In effect, your choice has signaled to the market that the CDs are worth more than $200 to you, and to set the remedy any lower than the value of those CDs means running the risk of inviting an inefficient breach.

In the case of a promise to make a gift to you of $200, information about what would be efficient is more limited. It is impossible to say that you value the gift more than the person to whom it might be transferred if the promise is broken. In fact, maybe overall welfare is increased if the promissor breaks the promise and gives it to someone else or even breaks the promise and keeps what was promised. Forcing the promissor to pay the full amount prohibits these transfers. In effect, enforcing the promise at expectancy may mean that efficient promise-breaking does not occur.

Limiting recovery to reliance is a bit of a compromise. It does promote the interests discussed in Chapter 11. At the same time, after returning you to the position you were in before the promise, it allows the promissor to reassess. Again, there is nothing economically compelling about this compromise, but in the absence of a market signal with respect to the value of the promise to the promissee, there really is no compelling reason to force the delivery of what was, after all, a gift.

WHEN PERFORMANCE IS EXCUSED

Sometimes when one party breaches a contract there is no recovery. Defendants can invoke a number of defenses with the premise that performance became so much more difficult or different from what was anticipated that it should be excused. The analysis goes back to the discussion of gap-filling in Chapter 9. One of the gaps discussed related to just how air-tight the obligation to perform is. For example, I may make a contract to rent my house to you. What if lightning strikes it and it burns down? Do I have to pay damages? Or I rent a vacation cabin in the Bahamas, but a hurricane prevents me from getting there and I refuse to pay. Again, am I liable for damages?

One of these gaps concerns conditions under which a party may decline or be unable to perform and not be liable for damages. This is called *excused performance*. It may occur to you that excusing performance does a great deal of damage to the idea of expectancy and the idea of an efficient breach. For example, if my house does burn down or if I am not required to pay for the vacation cabin, the "why's" of nonperformance do not affect the fact that you do not receive expectancy. Nothing about the increased difficulty or impossibility of performance also makes it impossible to pay damages.

The answer begins with reconsidering what the parties actually exchanged. A typical example might be one in which a food processing company agrees to buy all the carrots produced from a farmer on his land for $3 per bushel. The carrots are to be harvested in three months. Here, the farmer is assuming the risk that there will not be a carrot shortage driving up the price of carrots to more than $3 per bushel. He is also assuming the risk that a profit can be made at that price. The food processor is assuming the risk that there will not be a glut of carrots during the growing season that results in carrots selling for $1 per bushel.

CASE 12.3 Long Live the King: *Krell v. Henry,* L.R. 2K.B.
(Ct. App. 1903)

> Changed circumstance cases and the issue of excuse typically arise when costs of raw materials skyrocket or something that was supposed to be sold or rented is destroyed. One of the more celebrated cases took a different form altogether. In late June 1902, Edward VII was to be crowned King of England. C. S. Henry wanted to see the parade and rented an apartment along the planned parade route for the two days the parade was to take place. The windows of the apartment overlooked the street the king was to come down. The rental fee was adjusted upward for the special event. Just before the coronation was to take place the king became ill and the coronation was postponed until August 9. C. S. Henry did not pay and was sued by Krell, the owner of the apartment. Henry asked to be "excused." The problem was that Henry's performance was not impossible—all he had to do was pay money. Moreover, the apartment was ready and waiting. The problem was that it was no longer useful for what the parties intended. The English court held that the excuse was appropriate when the purpose of the contract was "frustrated."

Suppose that for the first time ever there is locust attack in the region of the farmer's land. The crop is destroyed and the farmer cannot deliver. It is a breach if the farmer assumed the risk of locusts. If the farmer did not assume the risk, then performance is excused. The answer is not found in the contract and thus calls for a gap-filling exercise that examines the fundamental assumptions of the contract. If both parties assumed the *absence* of a locust attack, then one of the underlying premises has changed and the contract itself is not enforced. Failure to perform is not a breach and expectancy does not apply. Instead, the contract is essentially canceled. Excuse means that the disappointed party never bought a guarantee of performance under all circumstances.

The issue of excusing performance is ultimately one of risk allocation in a context in which the parties did not actually consciously allocate the risk at all. Still, the court has to choose whether the party unable or unwilling to perform actually did assume the risk of the unexpected event. The best outcome from an economic standpoint is to find that the party did assume the risk if he or she was in a better position to anticipate the event, assess the consequences, and insure against it. That party was most likely in a position to avoid the losses of the unexpected event at a lower cost than the other party. Obviously, for the two parties actually in litigation, the event did happen and the risk was not minimized by the party who could do it more efficiently. Still, a decision reflecting that philosophy is more likely to encourage efficient risk allocation by future parties.

When a party is not excused, the plaintiff is entitled to damages. Does that mean there is no remedy if a party is excused? No. In fact, when performance becomes impossible, one party or the other may have partially performed at a great deal of expense. In these situations, courts tend to look to restitution and attempt to determine how much each party has benefited the other party and allow them to recover those amounts.

QUESTIONS FOR DISCUSSION

1. The most basic contract remedy is expectancy. In theory, it puts the plaintiff in the position, utility-wise, that he or she would have been in had there been performance. Is this superior to a remedy that returns the plaintiff to the position he or she was in before the contract was formed? Why?

2. You agree with a friend that he will sell you his rookie Barry Bonds baseball card for $100. The market value of the card is $130. Before you make any payment, your friend threatens to breach. What remedy would be in order to make sure the breach is efficient?

3. If expectancy is the measure of damages that encourages only efficient breaching, why not routinely award plaintiffs specific performance since it is "literal expectancy?"

4. Under which of the following instances is a court most likely to award specific performance? A seller refuses to deliver a new Ford automobile. A seller refuses to deliver the contract under which the Red Sox sold Babe Ruth to the Yankees. A seller refuses to deliver soy beans.

5. Explain why liquidated damages clauses will not discourage efficient breaches.

6. Jim buys Jill's restaurant. About one-half of Jill's income is from the sale of beer and wine. Just before payment is due, the city passes a law prohibiting restaurants in Jill's neighborhood from selling beer and wine. Jim asks to be excused from performance. Should he be?

7. Suppose you buy a sweater at a department store. After a couple of days you discover that the sweater always charges itself with static electricity and you get shocked whenever you touch something. You are not happy and want to return the sweater. Compare in terms of efficiency the following policies that the department store might have for returns:
   a. The department store has a "not satisfied, money back" rule if you bring the sales receipt in within ten days.
   b. The department store has a "not satisfied, money back" rule, but gives store credit only.
   c. The department store has no policy whatsoever and you have to go to court if you want to collect damages.

UNIT FOUR

Economics
of Tort Law

CHAPTER THIRTEEN

Torts: The Economics of Liability Rules

T HIS CHAPTER BEGINS THE UNIT ON TORT LAW. IN law, a tort is simply a "wrong" committed by one person against another. From an economic perspective, these wrongs are externalities—the cost of a person's action that is not internalized and not, therefore, accounted for in his or her decision making. Tort law is fundamental to society because it, along with contract law, defines our responsibilities or "duties" to each other. More specifically, tort law determines when one person will be compensated for having suffered the externality of another's action. Torts can take a variety of forms: someone throws a rock at you and hits you, someone's dog bites you, a driver runs into the side of your car at an intersection, the dentist's drill slips and bores through your gum, a surgeon leaves his Pez dispenser in your abdominal cavity, the cup of coffee you buy is so hot that when you spill it you are scalded, a part on a new toy breaks and cuts your 3-year-old child, someone writes and publishes an article about you that is inaccurate and damaging to your reputation. As you can see, many different things, including some very strange things you read about in the newspaper, are torts.

Before looking closely at tort law, two pieces of information will help you get the topic into perspective. First, torts are usually divided between intentional torts—instances in which someone deliberately injures you—and unintentional torts or accidents. In both cases, the principal focus is to set rules of liability that will minimize the costs to society of these "wrongs." The case of an intentional tort is not very interesting from an economic perspective because the person who intentionally causes the harm is obviously the best person to pay for it. That way the person can consider the benefits of his or her action and compare all the costs. Thus, most of the economic analysis of torts rules of liability, including the one presented here, is devoted to unintentional torts.[1]

Second, many things that are torts are also crimes. For example, suppose someone drives carelessly and harms you or your property. There are criminal laws against reckless driving and the person may go to jail. The reasoning is that, as a society, we have made a decision that reckless driving should be deterred. Driving in a way that endangers others is seen as a "public wrong," and the finding that a crime has been committed does not result in compensation for the victim. Victim compensation is the domain of private law in the form of torts. Thus, the person who injured you may go to jail as a matter of criminal law and may be required to compensate you as a matter of tort law. Conversely, a person may be found not guilty of committing a crime but still be liable for damages in a civil action. This is because the standard for determining guilt in a criminal case— "beyond a reasonable doubt"—exceeds the standard for finding liability in a civil case—"by a preponderance of the evidence." This was exactly what happened in the cases involving O.J. Simpson in the mid 1990s. The former football star was first tried in criminal court for the murder of his ex-wife and another person and found not guilty. Later, he was sued for damages in a civil court by the families of the victims and found to be liable for their deaths.

This chapter begins our examination of tort law by addressing four topics. The first is the categories of costs that result from accidents. The second is the economic objectives of tort law. Third is the relationship between tort law and transaction costs. The fourth is what specific rules of liability are consistent with the economic objectives. The answer to this question can get complicated, but it is easier if you remember that the goal is to create incentives for effi-

---

1. Another area of analysis, found in Chapter 14, is damages and is important from the standpoint of intentional and unintentional torts.

cient behavior—behavior that minimizes the costs of accidents. The last part of the chapter focuses on *strict liability*. Under strict liability, the party who pays for the harm may not be negligent. Succeeding chapters will examine issues related to damages, the very important topic of products liability, and the physician's favorite, malpractice.

WHAT ARE THE COSTS OF ACCIDENTS?

From an economic standpoint, there are three types of accident costs.[2] First are the ones you are most familiar with. These are the actual losses suffered by victims; personal injuries, damaged property, and lost income would all fall into this category. If you have ever been in an automobile accident or know someone who has, you can probably list most of the costs. There is the damage to the car. You lose the use of the car too. You may be injured and receive treatment. You may miss work and the income you would have earned. Perhaps you are unable to ski or bowl or enjoy those activities as much as you did before the accident. Someone you know may have experienced a great deal of pain and suffering. And, tragically, there can be loss of life. All of these are *primary costs*. Secondary costs refer to the way in which society absorbs these losses. Take, for example, an accident that results in $10,000 damage to your car. You may have to pay to have the car repaired or the loss might be distributed over 10,000 people at $1 each. The question is whether society "feels" the loss less severely when it is spread in the form of small losses over many people as opposed to being absorbed by one person. If people generally experience diminishing utility for money, the social cost will be lower if the loss is broadly distributed. Secondary costs will play an important role in products liability, which we discuss in Chapter 15. Tertiary costs are the costs of administering a tort system. This includes resources spent on attorneys, judges, expert witnesses, court reporters, and the opportunity costs of jurors and other participants. Without

---

2. The seminal work identifying the costs of accidents and discussing them is by Guido Calabresi, currently a federal judge and also a law professor at Yale University. Guido Calabresi, *The Costs of Accidents: A Legal and Economic Analysis* (New Haven: Yale University Press, 1970).

accidents, these costs would not exist, but as long as there are accidents, there must be a system in place to sort things out.

A complicating factor is that these three types of costs—primary, secondary, and tertiary—do not necessarily move in the same direction. As you will see in the discussion of products liability, measures that minimize secondary costs do not necessarily minimize primary costs. For instance, a manufacturer who is expected to pay for all the injuries caused by defective products will calculate the expected costs of this and include them in the price of his products. This minimizes secondary costs by spreading them over all users of his products. However, if the manufacturer pays for all injuries, this might make it less likely that purchasers will exercise adequate care, leading to more accidents and higher primary costs. Similarly, a set of rules that, in theory, encourages the minimization of primary and secondary costs may be very expensive to administer, thereby leading to high tertiary costs.

THE ECONOMIC OBJECTIVES OF TORT LAW

Internalization

As suggested at the outset, tort law is about internalization and to some extent, therefore, about allocative efficiency. Take a straightforward example. You own a pizza delivery service near a college campus and your drivers make use of your fleet of automobiles to deliver the pizzas. In Figure 13.1, the x-axis is the number of pizzas you deliver each week and the y-axis is the cost of production and the price. D is the demand for pizzas and S is your supply. Remember that supply is a reflection of your costs of production. The equilibrium price is P and the equilibrium quantity is Q.

Suppose every once in a while one of your drivers has an accident and knocks over a mailbox. Actually, not once in a while but more like fifty times a year, and it costs $10 for the mailboxes to be replaced. These are primary accident costs—externalities that your drivers impose on others. In effect, they are costs of production that you may escape paying if the owners of the mailboxes are not compensated. The question is whether you internalize them or not. On the graph, supply curve S assumes that you do not. In other words, S understates the actual costs of production. You know from Chapter 2 that

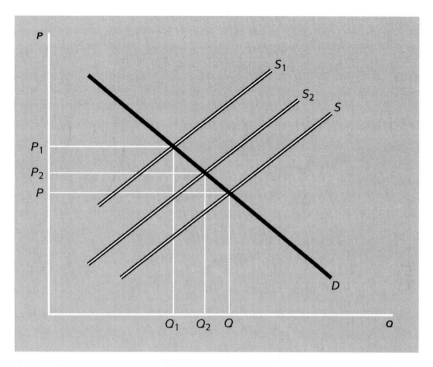

FIGURE 13.1 The Impact of Internalization

this means you are producing at allocatively inefficient levels. In this case, you are selling and producing too much: Your pizza price is too low as it does not reflect the cost of runover mailboxes. A smoothly functioning system of tort law will force you to internalize these costs and your supply curve will shift to S_1. Your level of production will fall to Q_1 and your price will increase to P_1. In effect, from an economic perspective, tort law assists in achieving allocative efficiency.

As you will see, the internalization objective is approached from two different perspectives. Sometimes individuals are required to internalize the costs of their actions when they are determined to be *negligent*. In very general terms, a person is negligent when the cost of avoiding an accident is lower than the expected harm. Other torts cases are governed by a rule called *strict liability*. A person is strictly liable when the law requires him or her to internalize the costs of an action whether or not he or she is negligent. Both of these internalization theories will be explored in some detail below.

Cost Minimization

There is another equally important goal of tort law and that is to minimize the costs of accidents and the costs of prevention. The first part of this "minimize the cost of accidents" is obvious. But some accidents may be less costly to avoid than to pay for once they occur. Go back to the example of $500 per year for uprooted mailboxes. Ideally, you would internalize $500. On the other hand, suppose all the mailboxes could be spared for a one-time investment of $200 if extra-wide rearview mirrors were installed on the cars in your fleet. Internalizing a one-time cost of $200 is certainly preferable to internalizing $500 annually. This is true from your point of view because it means a lower cost of production. On the graph, this would mean the shift that occurs is to supply curve S_2 rather than S_1. The quantity will not decrease as much and the price will not increase as much as it would if you were paying $500 per year. It is also beneficial from the point of view of society because fewer resources would be used to achieve the same end.

On the other hand, if the cost of the new mirrors exceeds $500 per year, your choice may be simply to pay for the mailboxes each time one is knocked over. The point is that sometimes it will make economic sense to avoid an accident and sometimes it will make economic sense to allow it to happen. One goal of tort law is to make sure the lower-cost option is chosen.

There is another variation of the cost minimization objective that you should note. Suppose, as the pizza business owner, your lowest cost to avoid damage to the mailboxes is a one-shot $200 investment. Alternatively, no mailboxes would be damaged if all of your customers, numbering 2,000, would put a five-cent reflector on their mailboxes. In effect, for $100 all the mailboxes could be saved. This would be the best outcome if the goal were to minimize the costs of accidents and their prevention. The rule that would achieve this would be to find you not liable for the mailbox damage.

The objectives of tort law are therefore twofold: (1) We would like the costs of accidents and their prevention to be internalized by those responsible; (2) the amount to be internalized should be the lower of the accident cost or the cost to avoid the accident. When the accident is to be avoided, we want the lowest-cost-accident-avoider to take the steps necessary. From an economic perspective, rules of liability—that is, assigning responsibility—should be designed to achieve these outcomes.

You should be aware of some practical problems that complicate matters. In the mailbox example, you can envision the process as having two steps. First, is it more efficient to avoid the accident or allow it to happen? In this case, it is clearly more efficient to avoid the accident. Second, which party is the lower-cost-accident avoider? That is the party we would like to internalize the harm in order to give that party an incentive to take the lowest-cost prevention measure. In the example, that means you would not be liable for any mailboxes that were knocked over if they did not have reflectors. Mailbox owners would have the choice of spending five cents on a reflector or paying for a new mailbox if it is knocked over.[3]

The examples discussed so far assume that one party or the other, acting alone, can avoid the accident. This is called *alternate care*. This may not always be the case. Sometimes neither party may be able to avoid the harm at a lower cost than the harm itself. Or sometimes one or both will be able to avoid the harm, but the lowest-cost avoidance requires action by both parties. In other words, *joint care* is the most efficient strategy. You will see the complication this introduces as we work through the analysis.

A Graphical Representation

One more way to think about tort law is to view it as a method of allocating resources in order to minimize the costs of accidents. In other words, the objective is to direct resources into accident prevention as long as the benefits—in terms of accident costs avoided—exceed the cost of prevention. You can visualize this by comparing the total cost of prevention with the total cost of harm or by engaging in the type of marginal analysis that is commonplace in econom-

3. In the economic analysis of tort law, one generally describes accident costs in terms of expected costs. This is the probability of an accident happening times the cost if it does. In the mailbox example, owners would compare the five cents with the probability of a mailbox collision times the replacement cost. (As a rough calculation, we assumed above that fifty mailboxes are run over every year and there are 2,000 customers/mailboxes; that is, the probability is 0.025. As soon as mailboxes are more expensive than $2, it pays to install a five-cent reflector (0.025 times $2 is five cents).

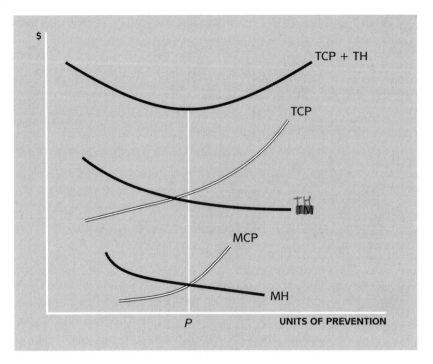

FIGURE 13.2 The Costs of Prevention and Harm

ics. In fact, you could view the issue as determining the benefit-maximizing level of care. The approaches are illustrated in Figure 13.2.

In Figure 13.2, the x-axis is units of prevention and the y-axis is dollars. The curve labeled TCP is the total cost of prevention. As the number of units of prevention increases, that curve rises.[4] The curve labeled TH is total harm. As you would expect, the total harm declines as the number of units of prevention increases. These are both components of primary accident costs and the objective is to minimize their sum. The curve labeled TCP+TH is the sum of total prevention costs and total harm. Its lowest point is at level P and this would be the optimal level of care.

---

4. We are assuming that society is using the lowest possible cost of prevention. To turn back to the pizza example, if reflectors on the mailboxes are a cheaper means of prevention than extra-wide rearview windows in cars, then the curve TCP reflects the cost of the reflectors.

Below these curves, there are two others that illustrate the marginal analysis. The curve MCP is the marginal cost of prevention. In other words, it shows the additional cost to society of each additional unit of "prevention." The curve MH is the marginal value of the harm avoided. It shows the *decrease* in accident costs associated with each unit of care. Obviously, as long as a unit of care costs society less than the accident costs avoided as a result of that unit of care, it is efficient to exercise that unit of care. This is the case on the graph out to *P*. Beyond that point, units of care are more expensive than the resulting decrease in accident costs.

The graph illustrates two points. First, an economically ideal system of tort law would be one that assists society in reaching point *P*. Second, from an economic standpoint, many accidents, including many that are tragic, may be inefficient to avoid. This may seem unacceptable to you as it does to many people who do not believe that cost-benefit analysis is the humane way to go about determining how much damage and, in particular, human suffering should be avoided. There is an understandable aversion to applying business decision rules to matters of human suffering but the reality is that we do it every day.

Think about an easy example. Highway fatalities number 50,000 per year. That number could be cut if there were a nationwide forty-mile-an-hour speed limit and automobile manufacturers were required to add even more safety equipment. Do you think Americans would ever dream of doing that?—probably not, because the costs in terms of out-of-pocket expenditures and inconvenience from extended travel times would be too high. Much the same analysis can be applied when the decision is made not to include seat belts in school buses. The costs would be high and the benefits in terms of injuries avoided would be relatively few. Consequently, most states do not require school buses to be equipped with seat belts. In effect, we consistently engage in the sort of cost-benefit analysis that we may feel is immoral.

The reality is that the decision to allow accidents to occur is a constant one and may not be that difficult to accept when the perspective of limited resources is adopted. Suppose society does decide to use resources worth $10,000 to avoid harm of $8,000. One possibility to consider is that those same resources might have been used to avoid $15,000 of harm elsewhere or to create $15,000 of pleasure. In a world of scarce resources, the choices to be made are sometimes not for the squeamish. But they do occur.

TORTS AND TRANSACTION COSTS

The efficiency of tort rules that require the lowest-cost accident-avoider to internalize the cost of an accident, or the cost of preventing it, can be illustrated from another perspective and connected to the terminology used by courts. When a court finds that one party is at fault or liable for an accident, the issue is expressed as whether one party had a "duty" to the other. For example, if your employees are running over mailboxes, a court might find you liable by saying that you have a "duty" to take care not to damage the property of others. This also means that mailbox owners have a "right" not to have their property destroyed by pizza deliverers.

The assignment of duties and rights is the mechanism through which courts may establish efficient tort rules. Interestingly, courts are more likely to get it right when they attempt to allocate duties and rights the way the market would. In order to understand this, go back to our example. In the original version of the example, the cost of the accidents was $500 and homeowners, through the use of reflectors, could avoid these costs for $100. You, as the owner of the pizza business, could avoid the damage for $200. Now suppose there is an auction for rights and duties expressed as the "right to be free of the cost of mailbox damage." If homeowners are the high bidders, it will impose on your pizza delivery company the duty to pay for damaged mailboxes or to avoid damaging them. In this auction, the most homeowners would pay would be $100. This is because they could protect their mailboxes for $100 and would pay no more than that to have someone else be responsible. You would pay up to $200 because this is the least it will cost you if you are assigned the duty. Your $200 bid will win the auction and you will be free of liability. The auction result is the efficient one and the cost of the accidents or their prevention is minimized at $100.

Another way to illustrate the point is to consider the possibility that a court chooses the inefficient assignment and holds you liable for mailbox damage. Homeowners possess the right to be free of the damage and you are assigned the duty. You would like to buy the right from homeowners and would pay up to $200 because that is the cost to you of avoiding the accidents. Homeowners would be willing to sell the right for anything in excess of $100 because possessing the right means they save only $100. Obviously, what has been set up here is a Coasian exchange. In a transaction-cost-free environment, you will buy the right from customers who then will install reflectors at a total cost of $100.

You can probably see the problem you will encounter as a pizza delivery entrepreneur. For this exchange to take place, you will have to contact all your regular, irregular, and potential customers, somehow get them together, and propose the purchase. And they will have to decide what price is acceptable and how to divide up the amount received for giving up their right to safe mailboxes. In other words, if the starting point is that homeowners possess the right, transaction costs associated with coordinating their sale may be too high to permit the exchange to take place. This is an instance in which an inefficient assignment by a court may not be corrected by a market transaction and it is particularly important that a court, if efficiency is the goal, make the right initial assignment. In fact, in the case of most accidents—events that are not expected to happen—transaction costs tend to be high because transaction costs include being able to anticipate future events and negotiate about liability.

THE NEGLIGENCE STANDARD

A great deal of tort law is built around the idea of negligence. When courts consider whether a person should be compensated for losses due to the actions of someone else, they follow a fairly complicated process of determining (1) whether the injuring party (the defendant) had a *duty* to the injured party (the plaintiff); (2) whether the injuring party acted like the *reasonable man;* and (3) whether the injury was actually caused by the actions of the injuring party. When there is a duty and the unreasonable actions of the defendant cause the harm, the defendant is negligent and liable. For legal purposes, causation simply means that the damage would not have occurred "but for" the defendant's conduct.

The ideas of *reasonable man* and *duty* can be given economic definitions. For example, a person is said to own a *duty* if he or she could avoid the accident at a lower cost than the expected harm. A *reasonable man* is one who makes the lower-cost choice between preventing and not preventing the accident. Even though we can break apart each concept and find an economic equivalent, in truth the economic approach to accidents is somewhat more streamlined. The basic negligence question is whether the defendant could have avoided the harm to the plaintiff at a cost that was below the expected cost of the harm. In fact, this test of negligence is not strictly the invention of economists. In 1947 Judge Learned Hand, in a famous case, *United States v. Carroll Towing Co.*, developed what is now called the Hand formula for assessing negligence. Under the formula, the burden of avoiding the accident (B) is compared with the product of its costs (L) and the probability (P) it will occur. When B is greater than PL the defendant is not negligent, and when B is less than PL the defendant is negligent. In the more technical economic terms introduced earlier, B would be the marginal cost of prevention (MCP) and PL would be the marginal harm (MH).

As an example, consider the possibility that I own a dachshund—those little wiener dogs that often bite. At a cost of $200 I can build a fence that will prevent the dog from racing into the street and biting passers-by. Without the fence, the probability of that happening is .1 and the cost of a bite in terms of pain and medical treatment is $5,000. Here B is $200 and PL is $500. The burden exceeds the expected harm; therefore, I would be said to owe a duty to passers-by to keep the dog under control.

Most courts do not articulate the analysis as a formula, but much judicial analysis can be reconciled with the Hand formula. Many cases, though, involve more than a straightforward application of the formula to the defendant. In fact, nearly every state now employs an analysis that compares the actions of both parties. The progression in complexity is illustrated through this series of examples.

HOW DO YOU REALLY FEEL ABOUT
COST-BENEFIT ANALYSIS?

Cost-benefit analysis in the context of human suffering and human lives is very controversial. Maybe the most publicized case involved the Ford Pinto. In the late 1960s, Ford needed a car to compete with subcompacts from Volkswagen and Japanese car companies, so they rushed the Pinto

into production. The major problem was that the machines for making the Pinto were set up before the Pinto had been fully tested and designed. Engineers were fully aware of a faulty bumper and gas tank that would easily leak fuel and explode from fairly weak rear-end impacts and often stick the doors of the car shut, but they were given strict weight and cost requirements for the car and could not add safety features, even inexpensive ones. The best method for protecting the gas tanks—using a patent Ford owned and used on other cars in its line—was estimated by Ford to cost $11 per car. (Later estimates ran as low as $5.08 or even $1 for a simple plastic barrier that would have prevented thousands of deaths.) In a memo, Ford explicitly compared the $11 per car cost to the costs it expected from deaths and injuries relating to the defect ($200,000 per death) and put the car into production without fixing the defective fuel tank. Later on, it became clear that Ford had seriously miscalculated the number of injuries the car would cause, and burn victims began to win large settlements from the company. However, it was still more profitable to manufacture the car instead of recalling it, and Ford manufactured the Pinto until it was finally ordered to recall in 1978.

Picture yourself on a jury in a case and the defendant's attorney says her client knew its product would lead to injuries and death but that it had calculated it all out and discovered that it was less costly to allow the harm to occur than to avoid it. Would you be receptive to that defense? Judges generally report that when tort defendants are found to have engaged in exactly the calculations the Hand formula suggests, juries are extremely unreceptive. A detailed empirical study confirms this. In an article published in 2000, W. Kip Viscusi found that jurors tended to punish businesses that engaged in the type of analysis an efficient approach to torts seems to require.[5] What do you suppose the reasoning is? Do jurors want businesses to waste money? Are juries just short-sighted and unsophisticated? Is it possible that *reasonable people* actually do not apply a cost-benefit analysis? The implication is that it is in the private interest of potential defendants to take higher than socially efficient levels of care.

Illustration 1: One Party Negligent

To understand the simplest negligence case and the one in which the Hand formula performs well from an economic standpoint, suppose you are sitting in your car waiting for a red light to change when someone crashes into you. The damage to your car is $8,000 and you

5. "Corporate Risk Analysis: A Reckless Act," *Stanford Law Review* 52 (2000): 547.

require medical care adding up to another $22,000. As it turns out, the accident was the result of worn-out brakes on the other car, which could have been repaired for $50. Further suppose the probability of crashing into someone when driving with faulty brakes is .01. In terms of the Hand formula, *B* is $50 and the *PL* is .01 × $30,000 or $300. As $300 is larger than $50 for replacing the brakes, from an economic perspective, the driver who ran into you made the wrong decision as far as minimizing the cost of accidents and he would be negligent and liable. According to the theory, if drivers are held liable for these mishaps, they will be encouraged to maintain their brakes in good working order.

It might have been possible for you to avoid the accident or the damage. For example, you could have installed a high-tech warning device that detected cars that were approaching too fast to stop. Or perhaps a crash-resistant car would minimize the harm to the car and to you. However, it is almost certain that these measures would cost more than $300 and, from an economic standpoint, should be discouraged. A basic negligence rule patterned after the Hand formula encourages the efficient outcome here.

CASE 13.1 A "Simple" Tort Case: *McCarty v. Pheasant Run, Inc.,* 826 F.2d 1554 (7th Cir. 1987)

As discussed earlier, Richard Posner is one of the most economically oriented of all federal judges. This opinion reveals his application of economics to tort law. The case involved a fifty-eight-year-old woman who was attacked while a guest at a hotel. She sued the hotel, claiming negligence due to the fact that the sliding door in her room was not locked. A jury found against her. She then appealed to have the judgment reversed. Here is some of Judge Posner's reasoning for denying her request:

> There are various ways in which courts formulate the negligence standard. The analytically (not necessarily the operationally) most precise is that it involves determining whether the burden of precaution is less than the magnitude of the accident, if it occurs, multiplied by the probability of occurrence. . . . If the burden is less, the precaution should be taken. This is the famous "Hand Formula" announced in *United States v. Carroll Towing Co.,* 159 F.2d 169, 173 (2d Cir.1947) (L. Hand, J.), an admiralty case, and since applied in a variety of cases not limited to admiralty. . . .

. . . The formula translates into economic terms the conventional legal test for negligence. This can be seen by considering the factors that the Illinois courts take into account in negligence cases: the same factors, and in the same relation, as in the Hand Formula. Unreasonable conduct is merely the failure to take precautions that would generate greater benefits in avoiding accidents than the precautions would cost.

Ordinarily, and here, the parties do not give the jury the information required to quantify the variables that the Hand Formula picks out as relevant. That is why the formula has greater analytic than operational significance. Conceptual as well as practical difficulties in monetizing personal injuries may continue to frustrate efforts to measure expected accident costs with the precision that is possible, in principle at least, in measuring the other side of the equation—the cost or burden of precaution. . . .

Having failed to make much effort to show that the mishap could have been prevented by precautions of reasonable cost and efficacy, Mrs. McCarty is in a weak position to complain about the jury verdict. No effort was made to inform the jury what it would have cost to equip every room in the Pheasant Run Lodge with a new lock, and whether the lock would have been jimmy-proof. The excluded exhibits (of which more later) were advertisements for locks, and Mrs. McCarty's lawyer expressed no interest in testing the claims made in them, or in calculating the expense of installing new locks in every room in the resort. And since the door to Mrs. McCarty's room was unlocked, what good would a better lock have done? No effort was made, either, to specify an optimal security force for a resort the size of Pheasant Run. No one considered the fire or other hazards that a second-floor walkway not accessible from ground level would create. A notice in every room telling guests to lock all doors would be cheap, but since most people know better than to leave the door to a hotel room unlocked when they leave the room— and the sliding glass door gave on a walkway, not a balcony—the jury might have thought that the incremental benefits from the notice would be slight. Mrs. McCarty testified that she didn't know there was a door behind the closed drapes, but the jury wasn't required to believe this. Most people on checking into a hotel room, especially at a resort, are curious about the view; and it was still light when Mrs. McCarty checked in at 6:00 P.M. on an October evening.

It is a bedrock principle of negligence law that due care is that care which is optimal given that the potential victim is himself reasonably careful; a careless person cannot by his carelessness raise the standard of care of those he encounters. The jury may have thought it was the hotel's responsibility to provide a working lock but the guest's responsibility to use it. We do not want to press too hard on this point. A possible explanation for the condition of the door as revealed by the police investigation is that Mrs. McCarty on leaving the room for the evening left the door unlocked but with the safety chain fastened, and she might have been reasonable in thinking this a sufficient precaution. But it would not follow that the hotel was negligent, unless it is negligence to have sliding doors accessible to the public, a suggestion the jury was not required to buy. We doubt whether a boilerplate notice about the dangers of unlocked doors would have altered the behavior of the average guest; in any event this too was an issue for the jury.

LAW AND ECONOMICS IN ACTION 13.2

THE ECONOMICS OF RESCUE

One element of American law that concerns many is that people do not have a duty to come to the rescue of others. As long as I did not put you in peril, I have no obligation to help you out. So if you are in trouble swimming or stuck on your roof without a ladder, I am not liable if I ignore you. From an economic perspective, what is worrisome about this can be visualized through the Hand formula. If I see you stranded on the roof, the expected cost of your ladder-less efforts to get down may be $1,000. The burden to me of helping out may be $1. It certainly seems that it would be efficient for the law to provide me with an incentive to come to your aid. The reasons for the lack of a duty probably have little to do with economic considerations, but at least three arguments have been offered for why the *no duty* rule may be efficient. One, offered by judge and author Richard Posner is that it would discourage those who are capable of rescue from going to areas where rescues might be necessary. In effect, good swimmers might avoid swimming pools. Second, the duty to rescue would eliminate the psychic income received by those who engage in rescues. Both of these possibilities mean fewer rescues. Another possibility is that it would encourage excessive risk taking. Typically, efficient levels of any activity occur when those who engage in those activities internalize the costs. One of the costs of many activities is the risk of harm. If this risk/cost can be shifted to others by a duty to rescue, people might take an inefficiently high level of risks.

Illustration 2: Both Parties Negligent

We can expand the negligence model to consider what is called contributory negligence. As a legal matter, *contributory negligence* is the term used for instances in which the victim of an accident is also negligent. The word "also" is important here because as a matter of legal procedure, the victim (plaintiff) would prove that the injuring party (defendant) was, in fact, negligent. The defendant could then escape liability altogether by showing that the plaintiff was *also* negligent.

An actual case provides a good example. *Haeg v. Sprague, Warner & Co., Inc.*[6] involved what, for want of a better term, involved "spite" driving. Two parties were approaching the same intersection at a right angle. The plaintiff, Haeg, could see the defendant, Thompson, and also tell that the defendant was speeding.[7] As the plaintiff went through the intersection, the defendant collided with him. It was revealed, however, that upon reaching the intersection, Haeg had actually taken his foot off the gas and more or less coasted through. (Hence the phrase "spite driving"—something that may seem foreign to you unless you have ever lightly touched your brakes when being tailgated.) Haeg did not want to be hit by Thompson, but he wanted him to have to react. Haeg made the all-too-familiar claim "I had the right of way!" Clearly, the defendant was negligent by virtue of his speeding and could have avoided the accident at a lower cost than the expected harm. This too was the case for Haeg. The outcome of the case was that the defendant escaped liability due to the contributory negligence of the plaintiff.

The problem that this type of case creates can be illustrated by thinking in terms of what the costs of avoidance might be for Haeg and Thompson. Before continuing, however, you may note one way that the application of economics to law is a bit artificial. To apply economics, we must attempt to quantify the costs of accidents and the costs of avoiding them. In many instances, as in the case of *Haeg v. Sprague, Warner & Co., Inc.*, a court does not present its reasoning in terms of "costs" as traditionally understood. Thus, an economic analysis of law may require more precision than is found in many, if not most, judicial opinions.

6. 281 N.W. 261 (Minn. 1938).
7. The actual defendant was Thompson's insurance company, but for simplicity Thompson will be identified as the defendant.

Along those lines, assume that the burden for Thompson of slow-ing down is $5 and the burden for Haeg not to coast through the intersection is $10 and that both figures are below the expected acci-dent cost.[8] The good news here is that if either party avoided the acci-dent, it would be preferable to allowing it to happen. The problem is that Thompson is the lower-cost accident-avoider at $5, but the con-tributory negligence rule would seem to give Haeg the incentive to avoid the accident at $10.

This problem could be solved if the contributory negligence rule were something like this: "you are liable if you are the lower-cost accident-avoider *and* you do not take the avoidance measure." In our example, that means Thompson would still be negligent even though Haeg also fails the Hand formula test. Unfortunately, at least from the standpoint of economics, it is not clear that courts apply a consistently efficient rule. Indeed, even in the law and economics literature, there is controversy not about which party we would like to shoulder the burden of avoiding the crash but whether judicial analysis is refined enough to fashion the efficient rule.[9]

To some extent, the question is whether a party, in order to be regarded as acting reasonably, must allow for the other party's care-lessness. For example, if Haeg is permitted to assume—despite what he sees—that Thompson is driving nonnegligently, then the decision to coast through the intersection is not negligent. After all, if Thomp-son were not speeding, slowing down would not increase the likeli-hood of an accident. Under this interpretation of the law and with the relative burdens as given, the outcome is that Thompson is negligent and the outcome is the optimal one. Thompson will spend $5 and Haeg will spend nothing.

While the "you may ignore the negligence of the other party" rule solves the problem when the numbers are as described above, suppose

8. The costs could reflect costs of equipment but in many instances they sim-ply reflect the value the parties attribute to their preferences.

9. Those wishing to pursue the controversy may want to compare Richard Posner, *Economic Analysis of Law*, 6th ed. (New York: Aspen Publishers, 2003), pp. 172–177 and Steven Shavell, *Economic Analysis of Accident Law* (Cambridge: Harvard University Press, 1987), p. 18, with David Barnes and Rosemary McCool, "Reasonable Care in Tort Law: The Duty to Take Corrective Precau-tions," *Arizona Law Review* 36 (1994): 357.

the numbers are reversed: Thompson's burden is $10 and Haeg's is $5. The rule is that one does not need to allow for the negligence of the other party. Again, as plaintiff, Haeg can escape a contributory negligence claim by showing that if Thompson had acted reasonably, the collision would not have occurred. Again, slowing down would not have made a difference had Thompson not been speeding. Thompson, the higher-cost accident-avoider will now spend $10 to avoid the accident and Haeg will spend nothing. Here the outcome is not optimal.

The outcome is better in those cases in which the lowest cost of avoiding the accident is through joint action. In the example, suppose the expected cost of the accident were $10 and it could be avoided if Haeg invested $11 *or* Thompson invested $12. In this case, the efficient outcome would be for the accident to happen, and that would be the outcome under a traditional application of negligence. On the other hand, suppose the accident could be avoided if both parties spend $4 for a total of $8. If either party fails to make the $4 investment, the accident will occur. It may be possible to reach the efficient outcome here depending on how the court defines contributory negligence. For example, if neither party takes action and Haeg is determined to be contributorily negligent even though he could not avoid the accident for $4, "future Haegs" will be motivated to invest their share. Conversely, if he does contribute his share and Thompson does not invest her $4, the accident will occur but Thompson will be liable for the full amount. Obviously, Thompson will have the incentive to invest the $4 in order to avoid paying damages. Since both invest $4 the accident is avoided. In effect, the efficient outcome can be achieved if negligence and contributory negligence, in the joint care case, are defined as not taking the optimal level of care *given the interdependency between the parties.*

In fairness, this analysis may be beyond many courts. What is clear is that under a negligence/contributory negligence system in both alternative care and joint care cases, the accident-cost-minimizing outcome is theoretically possible if the concepts of negligence and contributory negligence are defined in exactly the right way. It is also clear that this level of economic sophistication is not typically found in judicial opinions.

There are other objections to a negligence/contributory negligence regime beyond the difficulty of ensuring that the efficient outcome is achieved. The problem is that the entire loss, once the dust settles,

falls entirely on one party or the other. To many courts and state legislatures, this outcome is seen as unfair, especially in instances in which
either party could have acted to avoid the cost. As a consequence, virtually every state now employs a version of what is called comparative negligence.

Illustration 3: Comparative Negligence

The general goal of comparative negligence is to escape the all-or-
nothing outcome of negligence/contributory negligence. A sense of
how it works can be understood by relying again on our spite-driving
example. Haeg, the spiteful driver and plaintiff, could have avoided
the accident for $10 and Thompson for $5.[10] Also suppose the
expected accident cost is $100 and the actual cost of the accident is
$1,000. On a comparative basis, Thompson is more negligent because
he could have avoided the accident less expensively. The typical
calculation is that Thompson is two-thirds responsible and Haeg is
one-third responsible.[11] Of course, this example simplifies things substantially. In reality, the cost of avoiding an accident is not so easily
calculated. In the typical case, the jury is simply asked the percentage
contribution of each party to the accident.

The actual form of comparative negligence can vary. In its pure
form, the percentage of the plaintiff's responsibility is subtracted from
the recovery regardless of how high it is. For example, a plaintiff who
was 75 percent responsible for a $1,000 accident would still recover
$250. In another form, however, the plaintiff recovers nothing if he or
she was more than 50 percent responsible. Below the 50 percent level,
the plaintiff recovers after deducting his or her level of responsibility.
Finally, some states have applied what is called a *slight-gross* system.
Under this system, the plaintiff recovers nothing if he or she was more
than "slightly" responsible. Each version of comparative negligence has

10. Again, in an ideal case, at least from the standpoint of applying economics, these figures would reflect the actual costs of better brakes or a louder horn.
In reality, the costs often reflect an effort to place a dollar value on preferences.

11. The reasoning is that Thompson is twice as responsible as Haeg because
he could have avoided the accident at half his cost. The ratio of responsibility is
2:1. To represent his responsibility as twice that of Haeg's in the context of a
total of 100 percent of responsibility, his portion must be set at two-thirds and
Haeg's at one-third.

different implications for minimizing the cost of accidents. Here we stick to some basic points but, once you grasp those points, it is a relatively simple matter to work through the permutations.

Either Party Can Avoid the Accident

One issue that arises in comparative negligence is whether too much or too little will be invested in accident avoidance. In our spite-driving example, either party could avoid the accident at a lower cost than the expected harm. The optimal outcome would be for Thompson to avoid it at $5. On the other hand, if the accident occurs as it did in the actual case—Thompson speeding and Haeg acting spitefully and with the two-thirds versus one-third division—Haeg will collect $667.67 from Thompson and absorb $333.33 of the loss. Thompson will be motivated to invest the $5 to avoid his share of the loss and Haeg will be motivated to invest $10 to avoid his share. This is not the optimal outcome as $15 is spent to avoid an accident that could have been avoided for $5.

A suboptimal outcome of the opposite variety can also occur. If either party takes the necessary care, the accident does not occur at all. Depending on this, both parties may expect the other party to do the rational thing. The outcome is that no care is taken even though an accident with an expected cost of $100 could have been avoided for $5, $10, or, at worst, $15. You have seen this occurrence before in the context of the prisoner's dilemma (in Chapter 3).

One other possibility is important. Suppose the expected cost of an accident is $100. Thompson could avoid it for $80 and Haeg for $90. Although the costs are close, it is still efficient to avoid the accident. On the other hand, if the accident occurs, Haeg will be 47 percent responsible; the expected recovery is $53 and he will absorb $47 of the expected loss. (You have to write this in expectation terms. The actual cost is $1,000, but the probability that it will happen is 0.10.) Thompson would be liable for 53 percent. Due to the loss-dividing element of comparative negligence, neither individual will be motivated to invest in avoidance because the portion of the harm he or she is responsible for will be lower than the cost of avoidance.

This result may vary depending on the form of comparative negligence applied. For example, in a *slight-gross* system, the plaintiff's claim for damages is not reduced as long as his or her contribution to the accident is slight relative to the defendant's. In these instances, there is a lower hazard of inefficiently low levels of care resulting from loss-splitting.

There is a solution to the problems that arise under comparative negligence. A rule could be applied that negligence means not taking the *least* expensive method of avoiding an accident when you are the party who can avoid the accident at the lowest cost. In all of these examples, Haeg would not be negligent, contributorily negligent, or even comparatively negligence and Thompson would have an incentive to take the optimal course of action. In effect, the parties are compared, but then the liability falls entirely on the party who is comparatively more negligent. In reality, judicial opinions in accident cases are not consistent with this rule, in large measure because the goal of comparative negligence is to avoid the all-or-nothing outcome.

Joint Care Minimizes the Cost of the Accident

A final possibility occurs when neither party alone can avoid the accident at a lower cost than the expected loss but together they could. For example, in the spiteful driving example, suppose the expected harm is $20. It can be avoided if Haeg invests $10 *and* Thompson invests $5 and this is the best possible outcome. If either party fails to make the necessary investment, the accident will occur and Haeg will be 33 percent responsible and Thompson 66 percent responsible. Should this happen, Haeg will recover 66 percent of $20 or $13.33 and he will absorb $6.66 of the loss. On first impression, he seems unlikely to spend $10 to avoid a $6.66 expected loss and the accident will be permitted to happen no matter what Thompson does.

There is, however, an interdependency here that changes the analysis. If Haeg does take the risk and does not invest the $10, he has a problem. Thompson can avoid all liability, even though the accident will still occur, by investing $5. Is he likely to do this? Yes, because it means he escapes expected damages of $13.33 even if the accident occurs—because he is not negligent. Consequently, if Haeg does not invest and Thompson does—as he clearly will be inclined to do—Haeg's actual damages would be the full $20. The parties, acting in their self-interest, are likely to achieve an efficient outcome. Again, though, it is important to keep in mind that you would be hard-pressed to find a judicial analysis that considers all these possibilities.

HAVE A McCOFFEE ON YOUR AUTHORS

There is tort law in theory, as you have it here, and the reality of law. One of the most interesting recent cases illustrating the difference and the importance of playing your cards right when there is a dispute involves McDonald's (very) hot coffee case. Stella Leibeck, an eighty-one-year-old woman, was scalded while trying to open a coffee cup, she suffered third-degree burns and spent seven days in the hospital receiving skin grafts. McDonald's was aware of the hot coffee problem and had generously settled many other cases related to burns, but they offered Stella a whopping $800. She took them to court. During the case, it became clear that McDonald's served its coffee at 180 degrees, about twenty degrees hotter than most other restaurants, and that the extra twenty degrees added quite a bit of risk of third-degree burns. According to McDonald's, consumer surveys, and a number of coffee experts, coffee should be served at very hot temperatures to taste its best. McDonald's was unable to use this fact to its advantage. They refused to settle at any point before the trial began, even for the $225,000 the judge-appointed mediator recommended. During the trial, a McDonald's executive and a human-factors engineer appeared callous and uncaring to some jury members, pointing out that the coffee needed to be hot to taste good and that the numbers of people burned were "statistically insignificant." In the end, Mrs. Liebeck was awarded $160,000—a sum reduced by $40,000 due to her comparative negligence. McDonald's was then assessed with $2.7 million in punitive damages for engaging in malicious and wanton conduct with regard to their defective coffee product.

STRICT LIABILITY

All forms of liability relying on a negligence standard can be distinguished from strict liability. Under strict liability, a party is liable for damage regardless of whether negligence is involved. This may seem inefficient if other parties are lower-cost accident-avoiders, but for the most part, strict liability is applied to those who are already engaged in activities regarded as inherently dangerous. The typical example would be a construction company engaged in the use of explosives or someone keeping wild animals on his or her property. Plus, strict liability is probably less expensive to administer than negligence, meaning that it is advantageous with respect to tertiary accident costs even if it falls short on minimizing primary accident costs. It minimizes tertiary costs because the rule is simple and straightforward and no intricate or elaborate proof of negligence of either party needs to be constructed.

One of the important characteristics of strict liability is that it forces the actor to account for the amount of dangerous activity.[12] An example is useful here. Suppose you are mining in an area a few miles from several homes. Each time you set off an explosion, some windows are broken in those homes. As it turns out, your blasting is not negligent because the expected cost of the window damage is consistently below what it would cost you to prevent it. Under a negligence system, you would not be liable although the blasting obviously results in an externality that is absorbed by the homeowners. Under strict liability, you will still be liable to the homeowners.

The economic importance of this can be illustrated with a demand and supply curve. In Figure 13.3, D is the demand for whatever you are mining—say, copper; S is your supply under a negligence system. Remember that the determinant of the supply curve is the cost of the resources consumed. In the graph, the equilibrium price is P and the equilibrium quantity is Q. The problem is that the cost of broken windows is as much of a cost of production as any other input and it is not accounted for in your supply curve or your decision making. Under strict liability, though, you will be liable for the window damage (or the cost of avoiding the damage if that is less expensive). This means S will shift to S_1. The equilibrium price will go up to P_1 and quantity will decline to Q_1. This is the allocatively efficient level of output as now all the costs of production are internalized.

At the simplest level, you would think that the level of care and the party exercising it would be the same under strict liability as they would under a negligence standard. For example, suppose the expected cost of a particular mishap is $1,000. Under a negligence standard, a potential defendant will spend up to $1,000 to avoid being found negligent. Similarly, the defendant who is potentially strictly liable will also spend up to $1,000 to avoid the accident. Still, for a number of reasons the level of care may differ. The possibility of a

---

12. See Steven Shavell, "Strict Liability v. Negligence," *Journal of Legal Studies* 9 (1980): 1.

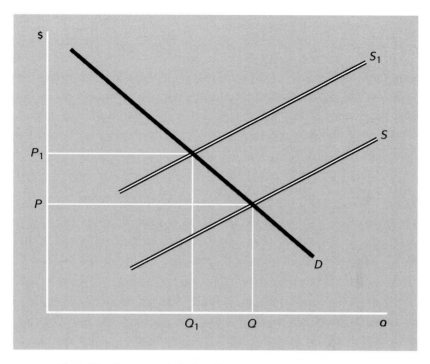

FIGURE 13.3 The Impact of Strict Liability

difference can be traced to three sources. First, as just illustrated, the potentially strictly liable defendant will compare the cost of prevention with the harm caused by a practice or a series of events that are preventable and, thus, may take greater care than would be taken under negligence.

Second, under strict liability, liability is determined *before* a comparison of harms and costs of accident avoidance is made. This means the following could occur. Suppose blasting costs $10,000 a year in broken windows. Special windows could be installed by homeowners for $9,000. The company doing the blasting could use special blast suppression measure that cost $11,000. If the company is strictly liable, it will not install the suppression equipment, but would pay homeowners $10,000. If a negligence standard were applied, the company would not be liable and homeowners would install the special windows. (You may note here that even if the company is strictly liable, there may be a way to avoid the harm for $9,000. Do you see how?) The point is that the comparison of damage and avoidance cost is strictly an internal cost-minimizing decision taken on by the party who knows that it will be liable should the damage occur.

A third possibility stems from the impact of findings of liability on reputation and goodwill. Under a negligence standard, a finding that a person has acted negligently means a person is *at fault*. Spending what is necessary not to be found negligent removes that stigma. Under strict liability, however, even if one is not at fault one is still liable. If this information is public, it is unlikely that a distinction will be made between what it means to be liable under negligence and strict liability. The outcome is that actors under a strict liability standard may invest more than is socially optimal to avoid accidents.

Another factor to think about when it comes to strict liability has to do with tertiary accident costs. Under a system of strict liability, some of the costs of administering the tort system may reduced. This is because the plaintiffs are not required to prove negligence, and therefore litigation costs on a case-by-case basis should decline. In effect, average cost per plaintiff is less. On the other hand, the relatively low cost of prevailing under strict liability may attract plaintiffs who do not have compelling cases. This threatens to drive up tertiary costs, and when those cases are decided incorrectly, primary costs are increased as well.

There is an important caveat to the strict liability case. Suppose there is an activity that is inherently dangerous but a plaintiff seems to go out of his or her way to subject himself or herself to it. One example of this that appears in the case law involved a defendant who had caged tigers on his property. One evening a guest decided to visit the tigers, put his fingers in the cage, and the tigers did what tigers sometimes do. On an economic basis, it makes little sense to hold the tiger owner liable when the accident could have been avoided so easily by his guest. In fact, when you think about it, the cost that has occurred here seems to be generated by the visit to the cage rather than the tiger owner. If so, it makes economic sense for the victim to internalize the cost. This is, in effect, what the law does by creating a contributory negligence defense for the party who would otherwise be strictly liable.

You have seen the basic rules now as they pertain to tort liability. In a sense, this is the beginning of the analysis. A very big issue is how to determine the proper damages to achieve the correct economic incentives. Even the best rule of liability fails to achieve efficiency if the damages paid are under or over actual losses.

QUESTIONS FOR DISCUSSION

1. In this chapter, we make the point that from an economic efficiency point of view, the objective of tort law and tort liability should be to minimize the cost of accidents to society. Does this rule imply that
   a. we are not interested in the number of accidents that occur?
   b. we are not interested in small accidents that cause only minor costs, but only in major accidents?

2. In this chapter, we state that tort law is about the internalization of the cost of accidents. Suppose that in a given country the government has set up a system of universal health care to which all citizens have free access ("free" in the sense that the cost of health care is paid out of general tax revenue). Whenever an accident occurs that results in any bodily harm, large or small, the health care system takes care of it. Does this mean the tort system will be inefficient as far as liability for bodily harm is concerned?

3. Throughout this chapter, the cost of avoiding an accident is expressed in dollars. If you think about it, however, sometimes negligence is the result of speeding, spite, or just doing something because it is convenient. How does this affect your view of the application of economics to negligence?

4. Go back to Case 13.1 on *McCarty v. Pheasant Run, Inc.* If you were to apply a precise economic analysis to that case, describe how you might go about it.

5. Compare strict liability with negligence. Why not make everyone strictly liable for any damage he or she causes? In what circumstances would this be more or less efficient than a system based on negligence?

6. This chapter notes that comparative negligence may not result in an efficient tort system. On the other hand, it is often viewed as more equitable than a strict negligence or contributory negligence system. Do you understand why?

APPENDIX: A GAME THEORETIC APPROACH

This appendix is designed to demonstrate how rational, strategic behavior of plaintiffs and defendants leads to different social outcomes (which are not always desirable) in terms of costs of accidents under different legal tort regimes. A game theoretic approach is used.[13]

Take the example of a cyclist (the plaintiff) who might be run over by a car driven by the defendant. We assume, to keep the setting dry and simple, that the car runs over the cyclist on his bike, but there is only material damage to the bike, which can be repaired for $100. We also assume that the cyclist and the car can either take due care or no care at all. Due care for the cyclist means that she makes sure the bike has good functioning brakes and that there are lights in the front and the back of the bike that make her clearly visible when biking at night and in the fog. It also means that she is careful when driving on a busy road. Taking due care comes at a cost, which for simplicity is assumed to be $1. Due care for the driver of the car means keeping up the brakes and the lights in good order and making sure to drive extra carefully in an area where people are riding bikes. We assume that the cost of due care is also $1 for the driver. If the cyclist or the car driver take no care, there is no cost. If the cyclist and motorist use due care, they will not be considered negligent. Due care is at or above the negligence standard.

The probability of an accident happening—whereby the car runs over the bike—depends on the level of care of both the driver and the cyclist. If neither of them exercises any care, the accident will happen with a high probability of 0.10 (one out of ten). In that case, the expected damage will be $10 (0.10 × $100). If either the driver or the cyclist exercises due care, the probability of the accident happening goes down by half to 0.05 (one out of 20). In that case, the expected damage to the bike goes down to $5 (0.05 × $100). Finally, if both take due care, the probability of the accident happening becomes even smaller and is only 0.01 (one out of 100). Expected damage is now only $1. This example illustrates what is meant by a situation in which "joint care" helps to reduce the probability of an accident occurring, and thereby the expected cost of the accident. The information is summarized in Table 13.A1.

13. An introduction to game theory applications in law is the book by Douglas G. Bird, Robert H. Gertner, and Randal C. Picker, *Game Theory and the Law* (Cambridge: Harvard University Press, 1994).

TABLE 13.A1 Costs of Care

CYCLIST: LEVEL OF CARE	DRIVER: LEVEL OF CARE	CYCLIST: COST OF CARE (A)	DRIVER: COST OF CARE (B)	EXPECTED COST OF DAMAGE (C)	TOTAL ACCIDENT COST (A + B + C)
No care	No care	0	0	10	10
Due care	No care	1	0	5	6
No care	Due care	0	1	5	6
Due care	Due care	1	1	1	3

This chapter has made the point that the objective of tort law should be to minimize the cost of accidents. As can be seen from the last row, the total cost of an accident is lowest when both the driver and the cyclist take due care. In this simple example this is the optimal social outcome. If you compare the situation in which both parties take due care with the situation in which only one of them takes due care, it is clear why the double due care case is optimal. The cost when both take due care is $2 compared to $1 when only one of them takes due care, but the expected cost of damage goes down by $4 (from $5 to $1). The reduction in expected accident cost more than compensates the increase in care cost. This is even more so if you compare the situation when both take due care with that of neither taking due care. In that case, total cost decreases from $10 to $3.

If the optimal outcome requires them both to take due care, we can use game theoretical reasoning to figure out what version of tort law leads to this optimal situation, assuming both the cyclist and the driver act rationally and strategically. To do this, we need to explain some rudiments of game theory.[14] A game theoretical problem has three main ingredients:

1. The players of the game
2. The strategies available to the players
3. The payoff each player receives for each strategy

14. The theory of games was invented in 1944 by John von Neumann and Oskar Morgenstern when they published the first edition of their book *The Theory of Games and Economic Behavior* (Princeton, N.J.: Princeton University Press). Game theory is used nowadays in many scientific fields and to model many diverse subjects going from strategic behavior of competitors in a market to the brinkmanship of superpowers in a nuclear arms race.

Game theory is called so because the problems that are dealt with are comparable to those encountered in parlor games. Think about what happened in New York on May 11, 1997, when IBM's Deep Blue chess computer defeated the then reigning world champion Garry Kasparov in a classic chess match. The *players* on that day were Deep Blue and Garry Kasparov. The available *strategies* were all the possible sequences of moves allowed by the rules of chess. The *payoff* for the winning IBM research team who built Deep Blue was the prestigious Fredkin Prize for Computer Chess and $100,000. The payoff for Kasparov was the recognition in history books as being the first ever human world champion chess player beaten by a machine.

In the "game" we are considering in this tort law example, the players are the motorist and the cyclist. The strategies are much simpler than in a game of chess and consist only of the binary decision either to take due care or no care. The payoffs are expressed in expected costs. All in all this is a very simple version of a game model. Much more complicated game models can be and are developed, with more players, more complicated strategies, and more intricate payoff systems. But this simple model suffices to show how game models work and to illustrate their intellectual power.

No Liability

Start with a situation in which there is no tort law whatsoever, which implies that the motorist is not liable for the accident. The game problem is normally presented in a bimatrix such as the one shown below. This bimatrix summarizes in a very concise way all we need to know about the "game." There are the two players (cyclist and motorist) with two possible strategies (no care or due care). The payoffs are in the matrix. By convention, the first payoff in the bimatrix is for the row player (in this case the cyclist); the second payoff is for the column player (the motorist). The four possible combinations are shown in Figure 13.A1.

The upper left corner is the situation when neither the cyclist nor the motorist takes any care. The accident will happen with probability 0.10 and the expected damage is $10 (in the bimatrix we use negative amounts for costs). Because there is no liability rule whatsoever, the cyclist suffers this damage. The motorist pays nothing. Neither has any cost of care. Now move to the upper right corner. This is the

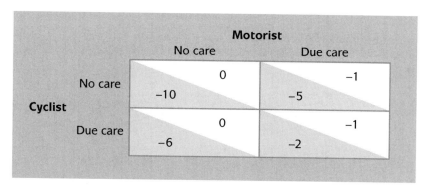

FIGURE 13.A1 Game Outcomes: 1

case when the cyclist takes no care and the motorist takes due care. Expected damage for the cyclist is now $5. The motorist has $1 cost of care. In the bottom left corner the combination presents the case with the cyclist taking due care at a cost of $1 but also suffering damage of $5. The motorist has no costs. Finally, in the bottom right corner, both parties take due care, each at a cost of $1. The expected damage goes down to $1. This damage has to be paid by the cyclist.

Now let's "solve" the game. Solving means that we will look at the possible strategies the players can follow and reason through the game and see which ones they will probably choose. The players have what is called complete but imperfect information. They know what the rules of the game are (they know there is no liability for the motorist) and they know what their own payoff and the other player's payoff is in each of the four possible cases. What they do not know is what strategy the other will choose. But this is something they will try to reason through.

They reason this through in a way that is similar to what a chess master or a chess computer program does. They think about what move the other player will choose for every possible move they can make. In the game of chess, the chess master or computer program thinks about many possible consecutive moves into the game; they go very deep into the possible future development of the game. The chess master does this using his brain power and his intuition and creativity; the computer program does it by brute force by calculating through millions of possible game sequences. In this game of the cyclist and the motorist, we do not need to go that deep. We also assume that the players are rational, which in this simple setting means that they will go for the highest possible profits or, for this case, the lowest possible losses.

Start by thinking through the possible strategies of the cyclist. There is a reason for beginning with her as you will discover in a minute. She will have to decide whether to take due care or no care. But the payoffs from her actions depend very much on what the motorist will do. The essential characteristic of a game is precisely this strategic interaction. If she puts herself mentally in the position of the motorist she will quickly discover that he has what is called a dominant strategy. A dominant strategy is a strategy that the motorist will choose if he is rational and no matter what the cyclist decides. It is obvious from the bimatrix that the motorist has costs of $1 if he takes due care (see right-hand column) and no costs ($0, see left-hand column) if he takes no care, *independent* of what the cyclist does. The cyclist must conclude from this consideration that the motorist will always choose no care. This narrows her consideration to the first column. If she chooses no care, then her loss will be $10 (top left corner); if she chooses due care, her loss will be only $6 (bottom right corner). That is what she will pick. She chooses the strategy of due care. In the end, this "game" between the motorist and the cyclist will logically end up with the motorist taking no care and the cyclist taking due care (the bottom left corner of the bimatrix).

From the point of view of society, this is not the optimal choice. The optimal choice is the one that minimizes the total cost of accidents. That happens when both take due care (the bottom right-hand corner of the bimatrix). Hence, a no-liability regime does not lead to the most socially desirable outcome.

Before going on to the next legal tort regime, let us note a couple of things about this simple model. First, it is very important for the solution of the game that the motorist act "rational" in the sense that he will always pick the least-cost solution, which in this example means taking no care. When the cyclist makes her choice, she can rely on the motorist being rational and following his dominant strategy. This type of behavior might be counterfactual. Motorists in real life might care enough about people and about cyclists to take due care apart from whether they will be held liable. Second, note that the cyclist does not have a dominant strategy. Her payoffs in each case depend on the choice made by the motorist.

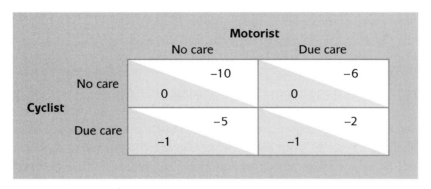

Strict Liability

Now examine whether strict liability leads to the optimal minimum cost situation. Under strict liability, the motorist is liable for damage whether or not negligence is involved. In this case, the bimatrix is the one shown in Figure 13.A2.

The cyclist has a dominant strategy and is in a situation similar to the situation the motorist was in under no liability. She will opt for the no-care strategy. The motorist assumes that this is the way she will behave and concentrates on the first row only. He will decide to follow the due care strategy, minimizing his expected costs. The solution to this game problem is that the cyclist takes no care and the motorist takes due care (top right-hand cell of the bimatrix). Again the solution is not socially optimal as it does not minimize the total cost of accidents. It is clear that the strict liability case in some sense mirrors the no-liability case. In the no-liability case, the motorist has no incentive to exercise care. In the strict liability case, the cyclist has no incentive. That is why neither of these cases leads to a socially optimal solution. As we know, joint care reduces the probability of an accident happening sufficiently to make up for the extra costs of care. Thus, in this instance we need a tort liability system with built-in incentives to exercise care. Let us turn to the legal system of contributory negligence.

Contributory Negligence

Contributory negligence was for a long time the prevailing principle in Anglo-American tort law. In this case the cyclist can recover damages only if the motorist is negligent and she is not. Or to formulate it as we did in this chapter, the defendant (motorist) can escape liability altogether by showing that the plaintiff was *also* negligent. In the example here, being negligent means exercising no care. In the contributory negligence case, the bimatrix is the one in Figure 13.A3.

The top left cell is where neither the motorist nor the cyclist takes any care. They are both negligent. Because the cyclist is *also* negligent, the motorist is not liable for the damage of $10. In the top right cell, the motorist is not negligent and the cyclist is. The cyclist will have to pay for the expected $5 damage. In the bottom left cell, the motorist is negligent but the cyclist is not. The cyclist has a due care cost of $1. The motorist is liable for the damage of $5. Finally, in the bottom right corner, both take due care. The cyclist can recover damages, however, only if the motorist is negligent and she is not. In this case the cyclist has to pay for the expected damage (and for the cost of due care). The cyclist has only cost of due care.

Again, the cyclist has a dominant strategy. If she takes due care, her cost will always be lower, independent of what the motorist decides. Knowing that, the motorist will concentrate on the bottom row and choose due care. The solution of this "game" of contributory negligence leads to the bottom right-hand case with both "players" choosing the strategy of due care. This is the socially optimal solution with minimum total cost.

To put a fine point on this, compare the bimatrix for contributory negligence with the first matrix for no liability. The only difference between the two matrixes is in the bottom left-hand corner. In the

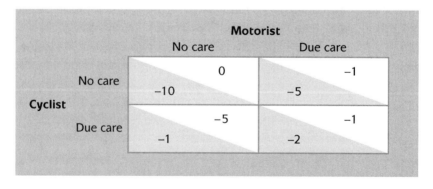

FIGURE 13.A3 Game Outcomes: 3

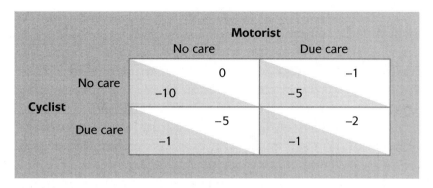

FIGURE 13.A4 Game Outcomes: 4

case of no liability, the cyclist does not recover damages. In the case
of contributory negligence, she does because she takes due care and
he does not. This difference leads to a totally different social outcome. In the no-liability regime, the parties ended up in the bottom
left-hand corner; in the contributory negligence case, they end up in
the bottom right-hand corner. Only the latter minimizes total accident costs.

A slight variation of the previous tort regime of *negligence with contributory negligence* is that of *strict liability subject to a defense of contributory negligence*. In the latter regime, the motorist is liable unless the
cyclist is negligent. The difference between these two regimes is in
the situation in which both plaintiff and defendant exercise due care.
In the *negligence with contributory negligence case,* the cyclist cannot
recover, whereas the motorist is liable for the damages in the *strict liability with contributory negligence case.* If you compare the bimatrix in
Figure 13.A4 with the previous one, you will see that only the bottom right cell is different. Now the motorist pays for the damages.

As you can see, the cyclist still has a dominant strategy (due care)
and, given this dominance, the motorist will also choose due care.
Again the solution minimizes the social cost of accidents. In this sense,
these two regimes are similar.

Comparative Negligence

As we point out in this chapter, the general goal of comparative
negligence is to escape the all-or-nothing outcome of the negligence
and strict liability regimes. The essence of *pure* comparative negli-

gence is that liability is split according to how much the parties contributed to the damage. We assume that to establish how much parties contributed depends on how much care they took. To enrich the model, we add a third level of care. We call that level "some care." Taking some care entails cost of $0.5. To keep things simple, we assume that if either of the parties or the two of them take "some care," the probability of the accident occurring is 0.05 (the same as when one of them but not the other exercises due care). We address the regime of comparative negligence with some rather extreme rules. If both take no care or both take some care, the damage is split down the middle. If both take due care, the motorist is not liable for the damage.[15] This information can be found in the diagonal cells of the matrix in Figure 13.A5. In the "no care, no care" cell, the total damage is $10 and is split equally between the two parties. In the "some care, some care" cell, the total damage is $5. Again this is split equally ($2.5 each) and added to that comes $0.5 cost of some care, for a total of $3 each. Finally in the "due care, due care" cell, damage is $1 (which the cyclist cannot recover) and each carries $1 cost of due care. In the off-diagonal cells, we assume that the player who exercises, comparatively speaking, the lower level of care has to pay for the damages. In each of these off-diagonal cases, the damage is $5. No care does not cost anything, some care is half a dollar, and due care is a dollar.

There are two ways to solve this somewhat more complicated game. The first begins by noting that due care always dominates no care. To establish this for the cyclist, compare the first numbers in the top row with the first numbers in the bottom row. And for the motorist, compare the second numbers in the first column with the second numbers in the last column. Neither of them will ever choose no care under this regime. Having established this reduces the problem of a comparison between some care and due care. This means we have to concentrate on the bimatrix at the intersection of the some care and due care columns and rows. In the bimatrix in Figure 13.A5, the motorist has due care as a dominant strategy. This implies that the cyclist can only compare the bottom right-hand cell (cost of −$2 for due care)

15. You will be asked in one of the questions for discussion to show that the solution of this game is unchanged if the motorist is liable for the damage in this case rather than the cyclist.

		Motorist	
Cyclist		No care	Some care	Due care
No care	-5 / -5	-0.5 / -5	-1 / -5
Some care	-5 / -0.5	-3 / -3	-1 / -5.5
Due care	-5 / -1	-5.5 / -1	-1 / -2

FIGURE 13.A5 Game Outcomes: 5

and the one above that (cost of −$5.5 for some care). The cyclist will choose the bottom cell and exercise due care. As can easily be seen, the bottom right-hand cell is the socially optimal solution with the lowest cost (to check this add up the numbers in each cell).

The other way to solve this game is to search for the Nash equilibrium. The Nash equilibrium is the central solution concept of game theory.[16] It is a combination of strategies in which no player could do better by choosing a different strategy given the strategy the other has chosen. Or to put it more directly, each player has chosen the best strategy in response to the other. To show that the bottom right-hand cell is the Nash equilibrium of this game, let us pick another cell at random and see whether it is a Nash equilibrium. Take for instance the cell in which the cyclist takes some care and the motorist takes no care (−0.5, −5). Given that the motorist has decided to take no care, taking some care is the best possible choice for the cyclist (it is the smallest loss for the cyclist in the first column). But given that the cyclist has decided to take some care (look at the second row now), no care is not the best possible strategy for the motorist. The motorist

16. John Nash received the Nobel Prize for Economics in 1994 for his discovery of this equilibrium concept in the early 1950s. For those interested in reading more about this remarkable scientist, see Sylvia Nasar, *A Beautiful Mind: A Biography of John Forbes Nash Jr.* (New York: Simon and Schuster, 1998). Or watch the movie.

would be better off to exercise due care if the cyclist opts for some care. That is where the motorist will want to go. And that is why the combination "some care, no care" is not a Nash equilibrium. Look at the bottom right-hand corner cell now: the combination of due care for both. As the motorist has decided for due care (look at the third column), choosing due care is the best strategy for the cyclist. And given that the cyclist has chosen due care (look at the third row now), choosing due care is the best option for the motorist. In this sense, the bottom right-hand cell is a Nash equilibrium to the game.[17] This Nash equilibrium is also the optimal lowest-accident-cost solution.

QUESTIONS FOR DISCUSSION

1. Starting from the numbers in Table 13.A2, derive the game theoretic solutions for a tort regime of no liability, strict liability, and contributory negligence and discuss whether the tort regime leads to minimum accident costs.

TABLE 13.A2 Cost of Care Problem

CYCLIST: LEVEL OF CARE	DRIVER: LEVEL OF CARE	CYCLIST: COST OF CARE (A)	DRIVER: COST OF CARE (B)	EXPECTED COST OF DAMAGE (C)	TOTAL ACCIDENT COST (A + B + C)
No care	No care	0	0	10	10
Due care	No care	3	0	6	9
No care	Due care	0	3	6	9
Due care	Due care	3	3	2	8

2. a. Again in Table 13.A2, in the example for comparative negligence, assume that if both the cyclist and the driver take due care, the driver is liable for the damage (i.e., change the numbers in the bottom right-hand cell from $-2; -1$ to $-1; -2$). Show that this will lead to the same solution (same Nash equilibrium).

   b. What happens when cyclist and motorist both exercise "some care," and they have to split the damage down the middle; that is, the numbers are now $-1.5; -1.5$? Is there an even better solution in this case?

---

17. This game has only one Nash solution, but some games can have many Nash solutions.

CHAPTER FOURTEEN

Compensatory Damages

T HE MOST REFINED PROCESS OF DETERMINING WHO
should be liable when an accident occurs will not be very
useful as far as minimizing the costs of accidents if the damages awarded are not determined correctly. The problem is very similar to making sure a business accounts for all its costs of production. In day-to-day activities, unless we account for the externalities imposed on others, we may engage in too much of the activity or too little, or not invest in avoiding an accident that could be avoided at less than its cost.

This chapter is about the process of determining damages. The basic rules apply for all tortious damages—intentional or unintentional—although the presentation will generally be in terms of compensation when an accident occurs. In some instances, the process will seem to be fairly easy. For example, if the left front fender of your 1999 Toyota is crumpled, it is easy to determine the cost of replacing it. In many other instances, however, the damage resists measurement. For example, how much do you compensate someone for the loss of an arm or for the inability to participate in a hobby from which he or she derived a great deal of pleasure? When everything is considered, the process is by necessity an imprecise one. Still, some standard methodologies have emerged.

In the pages that follow, we first examine how damage calculations are integrated into the economics of tort law. The following five sections deal with specific types of damages: property damage, lost income and the lost value of services, personal injuries, hedonic losses, and the impact on indirect parties.

From an economic perspective, the focus is largely on the defendant and determining the costs of the defendant's tortious conduct. This is what the defendant should internalize. Courts very often adopt a different perspective. In general, courts focus more on plaintiffs. The issue is not one of making sure the defendant and potential defendants are guided by the right incentives. Instead, it is on making sure that the plaintiff is compensated. In many instances this difference in focus will not matter. When it does matter, more likely than not it is when courts are dealing with nonpecuniary losses. These are losses that do not represent out-of-pocket costs or lost income to victims. To an economist, the disutility caused by pain from an injury or the anguish one feels when someone close is harmed is as valid an externality as any other. On the other hand, as a historical matter courts have been slow to recognize these losses and to this day do not embrace them as fully as economists do. Part of the reason for this reluctance is that courts like to deal with facts and hard evidence and confine jurors to a limited scope of discretion. Nonpecuniary losses are typically not susceptible to this preferred level of control.

DAMAGES AND EFFICIENCY

The Theory of Damages

Before examining some of the details about damages, it is useful to think about how damages fit within some of the basic notions of efficiency. First, note that compensation means an amount which, if paid, would put the victim in a position that would be equally attractive utilitywise as not suffering the loss in the first place. In slightly more technical terms, the victim should be indifferent between the injury and the monetary compensation. This is difficult to determine in a great many instances, but it is the baseline definition of what it means to be compensatory.

The objective can be illustrated by using indifference curves. You may recall from prior courses and from Chapter 9 that an indifference curve shows the combination of two goods or services that result in the same level of utility. Or it can show, as it does here, the combination of one good and a mix of all other goods. Thus, the curve in Figure 14.1, labeled *A*, shows all the combinations of ski vacations and all other goods that would result in the same level of utility. Ski vacations are along the *x*-axis and all other goods are along the *y*-axis. On the graph, utility increases as the curves move away from the origin. There is a third axis rising out of your book that measures utility; curves farther out are higher up on this axis. This can be seen by using the pop-up version of the graph.

The exact point you occupy on any indifference curve will be determined by your income. The straight line, I, represents all the combinations of ski vacations and all other goods and services you could buy with your current income. The idea is to use that income to reach the highest indifference curve. The highest indifference curve will be the one that I is just tangent to. So, let's suppose you are at point A_1 on curve *A* and this is four ski vacations a year plus the "all other goods" as indicated. Now you are in an accident. There are generally two things that can happen. First, you may miss work or even have your ability to earn income permanently affected. The consequence

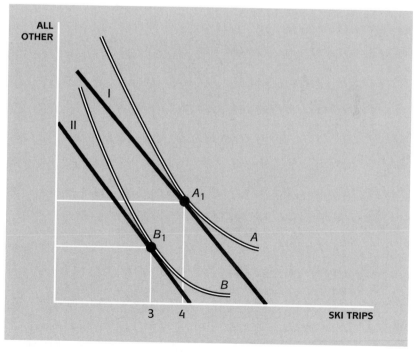

FIGURE 14.1 Compensatory Damages: Income Impact Only

is that your income-earning capacity is reduced to II. You are on a lower indifference curve (B) because you can afford less. In the graph, you are down to three ski trips and less of everything else as indicated by point B_1. If you are compensated, the damages will have to be the difference between your earnings at I and II. If you are restored to I, you can return to the original indifference curve.

The second possibility is a bit more complicated and is depicted in Figure 14.2. You begin with indifference curve A and income line 1. Here the accident has no impact on your income but has left you with a disability that limits your skiing. In more general terms, it has limited your ability to allocate your income efficiently. At best, you can manage only one trip a year instead of four. A vertical line has been drawn at one ski trip. In effect, every point along any indifference curve that involves more than one ski trip is unobtainable. With your original income, it would be impossible to achieve your original indifference curve (A). It would be fine for you to take one ski trip and increase your purchases of all other goods, but your budget does not permit you to purchase enough additional goods to bring you back to

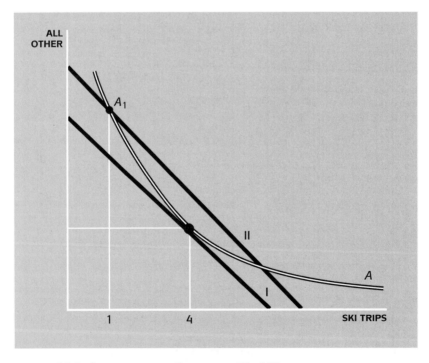

FIGURE 14.2 Compensatory Damages: Disability

your original indifference curve. For the loss from skiing to be offset by purchasing other goods, your income will have to be increased. In the graph, the necessary increase is measured by the difference between budget line I and budget line II.[1] Budget line II allows you to achieve point A_1 on your original indifference curve.

Of course, this is theory and you may wonder if it always works in real life. Suppose rather than an injury that meant you could not ski, the injury meant you could not see or smell or live a pain-free existence. Can you imagine an increase in your budget line that would return you to your prior level of utility?

Compensation or Not?

As noted earlier, courts tend to focus on victims. And so far, the assumption has been that the victim actually receives the damages assessed against the defendant. From an economic standpoint, this may not be necessary. A distinction can be made between a requirement that the liable party internalize the damages and the requirement that the damages actually be paid to the victim. To the extent tort law is designed to minimize accident costs, it is arguably enough to make sure that the injuring party internalizes the correct cost of his or her actions. Whether actual compensation is paid is, at least in part, a distributive issue involving an interpersonal comparison of utility.

LAW AND ECONOMICS IN ACTION 14.1

THE COLLATERAL SOURCE RULE

The issue of whether the focus should be on accurately compensating victims or making sure that the amount internalized by injurers is correct is a critical one in the context of a legal doctrine called the *collateral source*

---

1. It is important to note that the new higher income does not enable you to reach a higher indifference curve. To reach higher levels of utility with income II, you would have to be able to use more than one ski trip and this is not possible. Actually income II is calculated in such a way that you can exactly reach the original level of utility. If you get more than the difference between income I and II you are overcompensated. In that case, you could reach a higher level of utility (even with only one ski trip). But you will never again be able to choose freely the number of ski trips you really want. It will always be a restricted choice. The higher income is meant to compensate for the loss of freedom.

rule. Here is the problem. You are driving along and a careless driver crashes into you. Under your insurance policy, your insurance company is required to pay for the damage to your car. In addition, you have a valid claim against the driver who caused the damage. The driver who caused the damage (or his insurance company) says he should pay you nothing because you would then recover twice. If the collateral source rule applies—the law in many states—you may recover from both sources. As an economic matter, you can see the dilemma. If the collateral source rule does not apply, you are accurately compensated, but the person who injured you will incur no costs and will not be given an incentive to minimize accident costs. If the rule does apply, you receive a double recovery, but the injuring party is forced to internalize the cost of the harm to you. Your feelings about this will depend on whether tort law is more about accurate compensation or accurate internalization. From the standpoint of economic efficiency, accurate internalization is the principal concern.

The claim that compensation is not required stems from the Kaldor-Hicks standard of efficiency. If damages fully reflect all the externalities of the injuring party's actions, then the victim *could* have been fully compensated for his or her loss. What this means in a context of an accident as opposed to simply taking something from someone is this: The injurer is viewed as the party who "takes" from the victim. If he or she knowingly creates a risk of harm to another, the conclusion is that he or she values the careless conduct by more than those who are injured value avoiding the conduct. In effect, an involuntary but Kaldor-Hicks exchange takes place.

The Kaldor-Hicks argument has two weaknesses. Although compensation may simply be a distributive matter, it is hugely important to victims. In fact, potential victims often pay to buy insurance—that is, uninsured motorist coverage—to avoid the possibility of not receiving compensation. In short, a policy of no compensation may itself create a cost—the cost of Kaldor-Hicks—that would increase the damages that must be paid above the amount that would be necessary if paid to the injured party. Kaldor-Hicks damages—those not actually paid—would have to be calculated at a higher rate than damages that are paid.

Perhaps the biggest hole in the Kaldor-Hicks argument is one that is common to liability rules generally and applies whether compensation occurs or not. A theory of minimizing the costs of accidents requires that the costs (and the price paid by the injurer) be accurate. The problem can be expressed in terms most people can relate to. Suppose you have had your Honda Civic for seven years and it has never been in a wreck, has been well taken care of, and then it is totaled. The market value of a seven-year-old Civic with the mileage yours had is $3,000. The other party or his insurance company writes a check to you for $3,000 and you begin combing the used car lots looking for a replacement. Perhaps you attached sentimental value to the car. Are you likely to feel indifferent between the situation you find yourself in and not having been in the wreck at all? Probably not. The same analysis holds for bodily injuries including the use of a limb. We attempt to place a dollar value on that loss, but this is not likely to be the same as the least someone would have taken in a voluntary transaction. If it is not, then even the amount not paid is of questionable accuracy. In fact, the amount one would take in a voluntary transaction could be infinite.

There is yet another argument that applies even if compensation occurs. It stems from the question of whether people value the conscious act of consent. Take two possibilities. A person can negotiate with you and buy your car at your reservation price (the lowest you find acceptable) or the person can collide with your car and pay the same amount after a court orders him or her to do so. If you value the act of controlling your transactions, then there will be a difference between a price that makes you whole in the voluntary exchange and a price that makes you whole in the involuntary exchange. If damage awards are based on voluntary exchanges, as they must be, there may be a bias toward underestimating damages. It is important to note that the comparison is between the reservation price and the market price and not between the price you might receive in a negotiated hypothetical exchange and the market price. In the case of the negotiated exchange, part of the price received may exceed the amount necessary to be fully compensatory.[2]

2. This raises the question of why in involuntary exchanges the "buyer" is able to pay only costs as opposed to cost plus some portion of the gain from the exchange, assuming one exists in an involuntary context.

Implicit in these theories is an assumption that people understand the risks they take and compare costs of care with expected harm and so on. In all likelihood, the "choice" to act carelessly or not, at least when made by individuals,[3] is probably rarely done with an understanding of the financial consequences. It is clear that the parties causing accidents rarely feel that they made the right choice. Nor are victims typically indifferent between collecting damages and not suffering an injury in the first place. No economists actually claim that people are as rational or as analytical as the theories seem to suggest. Still, there are tendencies in behavior that are consistent with these general ideas. People do take risks based on a rough assessment of the consequences. Requiring them to pay damages means they will take fewer risks because the "price" of risky behavior is higher. And the better the measurement of damages, the stronger the likelihood that something like efficient behavior will take place. It may not be important to worry too much about whether tort law can ever be shaped to minimize accident costs or to achieve Pareto efficient or Kaldor-Hicks efficient outcomes in a literal sense. But as general goals and justifications for certain rules, these standards are good starting points.

PROPERTY DAMAGE

Obviously, compensatory damages, whether paid or not, must include any damage to property. In law it is customary to distinguish between real property and personal property. Real property, or *realty* refers to land and buildings. Personal property consists of all tangible possessions. For the most part, determining the proper compensation for damages to either kind of property can be a straightforward matter. For example, suppose someone drives his or her car over the wheel of your bicycle, bending the rim. The rim needs to be replaced and the bike will be in the shop for a week. The damages are not simply the amount necessary to replace the rim but the loss of use of the bicycle too. This is usually put at the fair rental value. This one is easy but, as you well know, nothing is as ever as simple as it may seem at first and compensation for property damage is no exception.

3. As you will see in Chapter 16 on products liability, manufacturers may be different in the sense that they may take the "rational" level of care in designing a product.

In the context of property, the most difficult problem is deciding exactly what is "compensatory" when the cost of repairing damage is different from the diminution in the value of the property resulting from the damage. In the bicycle example, the cost of a new rim might be $50 and the market value of the bike may have decreased by $50 because anyone buying it in its damaged condition would realize that for $50 it could be fixed. In other instances, the cost of repair may be less than the diminution in value. Suppose a careless driver swerves, jumps the curve, and mows down a section of a hedge at someone's house. A property appraiser might tell the owner that the market value of the property has declined by $500 and the landscaper might tell him that the hedge can be replaced for $100. In this instance, the proper measure for the driver is to internalize the cost of repair. There is, after all, no economic reason to ask the driver to internalize a cost that reflects a relatively inefficient way of compensating you. What this suggests is that the proper outcome of the cost of repair versus diminution in value is to choose the lesser of the two. You may have seen this at work in the context of automobile wrecks in which the question is often asked, "Was it totaled?" The meaning of the question is whether the cost of repair exceeds the market value, in which case the damages are set at replacement cost.

The "lesser of the two" is not clearly the best answer when cost of repair exceeds the diminution in value. In the hedge example, suppose the cost to have the plants delivered to the property and planted and maintained until they are like their predecessors is $1,000. The hedge, however, is a small part of the property and largely hidden from view so the diminution in value is $100. Here a diminution in value recovery will not permit the owner to restore the property to its original state.

In this circumstance, what is the proper measure of the externality? Is it the $100 or is it $1,000? Note that this does not raise the issue of market value as compared to reservation price. Both of the figures here are actually based on market values. Although it is dangerous to generalize, there may be some tendency in these cases to award the diminution in value rather than the cost of repair.[4] This outcome has a great deal of appeal from an economic standpoint. The

---

4. Dan B. Dobbs, *Law of Remedies: Damages, Equity, Restitution* (St. Paul: West, 1993), 711.

idea is that if the diminution in value measure is accurate, one could sell the damaged property for its new market value, add the damages, and then buy a parcel comparable to the original one. On the other hand, diminution in value is not enough to permit literal restoration of the property.

You should not infer that courts arrived at this solution through any kind of acceptable economic reasoning. In fact, the opposite is true. The general reasoning has been that the cost of repair measure was unsatisfactory because it meant one of two things. If the plaintiff received an amount that was higher than the diminution in value and did not make the repairs, the view was that there would be a windfall for the plaintiff. This missed the point that, from an economic perspective, the focus is on internalization by the defendant. How the plaintiff profits is a distributive question. On the other hand, if the plaintiff made the repairs, courts tended to regard this as wasteful because the repairs would not be reflected in the market value. This too misses the point; if the plaintiff chooses to make the repairs, he or she evidently regards that as resulting in greater utility than anything else the money could be spent on. The idea of waste here is a more general expression of what people "should" do rather than a meaningful economic concept.

This reasoning does not address the economic problem of choosing diminution in value over cost of repair when diminution in value is lower. Put simply, in many of these cases, diminution in value is not the measure of damages because the victim would not have willingly sustained the damage (or sold his right not to suffer the damage) for the diminution in value. Perhaps the property in the example has been in the victim's family for generations and is not interchangeable with other property, and the only accurate measure of damage is the repair cost. Or suppose the hedge was planted by the owner and his children as some kind of family celebration. Here, even repair cost may understate the value of the damage done. In both cases, a $100 recovery means that the careless driver does not fully internalize the cost of the harm.

As it turns out, the law is somewhat sensitive to these instances in which individual valuations differ from market values. First, remember the issue does not arise when the repair cost is below the decrease in market value. In instances in which is it higher, courts will still permit repair cost as long as it does not exceed the diminution in value by a substantial amount. It is ultimately hit or miss on whether the cost of repair measure is the correct one. It is impossible to know since the damage suffered is unique to the victim (but not less valid as an economic matter). There is some legal and economic sense in limiting cost of repair recoveries, when they are in excess of diminution in value, to instances in which the difference is not excessive. When cost of repair exceeds diminution in value, a moral risk comes into the picture. The plaintiff can argue that the cost of repair is the only proper recovery, but there is no way to check the validity of the claim that diminution in value is inadequate. As the difference between the two possible measures of damages becomes greater, so too does the incentive for the opportunistic plaintiff to overstate the harm.

CASE 14.1 **Compensation in Atypical Cases:** *Douglass v. Hustler Magazine*, 769 F.2d 1128 (7th Cir. 1985)

The area of torts covers far more than car crashes and other accidents. For example, defamation is a tort. It can be a tort to invade the privacy of another or to portray him or her in a false light. The remedies in these cases are difficult to determine, especially when the victim is a celebrity who is actually publicity hungry. Some of these difficulties are illustrated in *Douglass v. Hustler* in which an actress sued *Hustler* magazine for publishing nude photographs without her consent. She won on a theory of "false light invasion of privacy," and *Hustler* appealed both liability and damages. The appellate court's response to the damages issue follows:

> Finally, the award of compensatory damages was so excessive that the jury must have been carried away by "passion and prejudice" (perhaps as a partial consequence of the slide show). The jury must have accepted all or most of the expert's estimate that Douglass had lost almost $717,000 (present value) in earnings as a result of the invasion of her right of privacy, and must then have added on almost $300,000 in damages for emotional suffering; for it thought it was awarding a total of $1,000,000 in compensatory damages, half against each defendant, for a single tort committed jointly by the two defendants. . . . *Hustler*'s argument is that the amount of compensatory damages that the jury thought it was awarding— $1 million—was so excessive as to show that the jury must have

been swept away by passion and prejudice, in which event there must be a new trial; a jury whose judgment on damages was so impaired cannot be trusted to have determined liability accurately, either.

The more than $700,000 in lost earnings to which Robyn Douglass's economic expert testified was his estimate of the present value of the earnings she would have had from making commercials for advertising agencies in Chicago, had not the publication of "Robyn Douglass Nude" in *Hustler* cut off that stream of earnings by scaring away the agencies. There are two problems with the estimate. One, subtler and less important, is that in discounting to present value the economist failed to correct for the extreme riskiness of the earnings stream for which he was trying to find a present value. An award of damages is a sum certain. If it is intended to replace a stream of earnings that is highly uncertain—surely an understatement in discussing earnings in the field of entertainment—then risk aversion should be taken into account in computing the discount (interest) rate. The riskless rate of interest might be as low as two percent, if inflation is ignored, and this would be the proper rate if the earnings stream that the damages award was intended to replace was one that would have been obtained with certainty. But earnings are not certain; particularly are they not certain in the entertainment industry. The appropriate interest rate is therefore higher than two percent, implying a lower award of damages. This adjustment is needed to reflect the preference of a risk-averse individual for a smaller amount, received with certainty, to a larger expected amount that is subject to great uncertainty. (Most people are risk averse in relation to substantial financial matters, though many people drawn to economically risky occupations such as entertainment must be less so.) The expert and the jury ignored this point.

The more serious problem is that the expert's computation ignored Douglass's opportunities in other markets. She may be *persona non grata* to advertising agencies in Chicago because of *Hustler,* but Chicago is not the world; and not only is she continuing to appear in movies but there is not a shred of evidence that she could not have made commercials in other cities, less staid than Chicago, such as New York and San Francisco. The economic expert (a professor of finance) testified rather guilelessly that it was as if one division of a multi-division corporation had been driven out of business; Douglass's "Chicago acting career" had been shut down. But having limited time, she cannot have an indefinite number of separate "divisions"; if she is shut out of one market, it frees up time to devote to others. Maybe there are no others to which she could devote all the time she once spent working for Chicago's advertising agencies, but there is no evidence that her resources are completely immobile. *Hustler*'s violation of her right of privacy created earnings opportunities for her, by freeing up time previously devoted to making commercials for Chicago advertising agencies. And while these opportunities may have been less lucrative than those that *Hustler* destroyed, any income they would have yielded her had to be deducted in estimating her damages from the tort, under the doctrine of avoidable consequences, which is the counterpart to the duty in contract law to mitigate damages.

The $300,000 for emotional distress is an absurd figure. Though distressed by the *Hustler* incident, Douglass suffered no severe or permanent psychiatric harm—nothing more than transitory emotional distress (some of it from obscene phone calls stimulated by the publication). The figure is ridiculous in relation to the highest judgment yet upheld on appeal in a series of cases arising from the Chicago Police Department's former practice of "strip searching" women arrested for minor crimes (mainly traffic offenses): $60,000. . . .

We do not want to be understood as suggesting that because the plaintiff posed nude for *Playboy* magazine, with its audience of millions, she has no vulnerability to emotional distress from seeing herself nude—perhaps represented as a lesbian—in the pages of *Hustler*. But it would be extremely naive to regard her as a blushing violet who can be presumed to have suffered an emotional injury so serious that $300,000 is a reasonable estimate of its pecuniary equivalent.

What do you think? Does the opinion reflect an effort to quantify the externality of the publication of the photos?

LOST INCOME AND VALUE OF SERVICES

A routine part of many torts cases is the calculation of lost income. There is no debate in law or economics that harms resulting in lost income represent an externality that should be internalized by the party causing the harm. This can be the income of an individual or even a business that suffers losses caused by the intentional or unintentional actions of another. Closely related is the question of imputed income. For example, suppose the injured person works in the home and does not receive a weekly or monthly check. Yet, these services do have value and would have to be bought on the market if not provided by a family member. These possibilities raise different issues initially and then a common one. The common one and the one for which there is a standard methodology is the determination of the present value of the losses. The distinction arises with respect to the data that go into the present value formula.

Lost Income

The typical case is one in which an individual is injured in an accident and unable to continue in his or her job. This could be for a set number of years or for life. The damages are equal to the income lost. Note that there is no offset for the "disutility saved" as a result of not having to go to work. Although the methodology is pretty standard, all sorts of issues arise in these estimates. How long will the disability continue? Is the disability full or partial? How fast would the victim's income have increased year to year, if at all, if the injury had not occurred? This last question can result in a fair amount of controversy because it means examining the probability that the injured might have become unemployed or disabled at some time in the future. It may require looking into the prospects for the industry in which he or she was employed. For example, suppose the plaintiff is a twenty-six-year-old professional football player. He is not a big star and tends to move from team to team. His age means he may be nearing the end of his career in any case. In the past, he has been suspended from playing football due to drug use. On the other hand, in the past he has had some lucrative endorsements and there is some probability that an outstanding season would mean the endorsements will return. Moreover, by playing another five years the player would qualify for certain fringe benefits, and statistics show that the longer a player stays in the game the more likely it is that he will find a high-paying position at the end of his career. Now, that player is injured by a careless driver while walking from his car to the practice field to begin workouts with a team with which he has a two-year contract. This case probably lies on the extreme end of the difficulty continuum but contained within it are examples of the questions a court must answer and for which economists—as expert witnesses—are often called on.

Lost Services

At least as sticky an issue arises when the injured person does not receive a salary but works nonetheless. The typical example is a stay-at-home spouse who cooks, takes care of the children, cleans the house, walks the dog, pays the bills, makes arrangements for music lessons, and drives the children to and from their "appointments." It could also apply to a spouse who works outside the home but on week-ends helps care for the children, changes the oil in the cars, and does minor repairs. In theory, an injury means having to go outside the home for these services at an out-of-pocket price.

There are two ways to value these services. First, the person providing them could in all likelihood earn an income outside the home. This is the opportunity cost of the services. The other is to determine the cost of the services if they were provided by others who do require payment.[5] This could involve adding up the costs of taxis, yard care services, cooks, house cleaners, and others. The question, though, is which amount the injuring party should internalize. A good case can be made for applying the second approach. Not just in theory but in reality, if a person who works in the home is injured, the family does not stop cooking, cleaning, and mowing its yard. The damage has made it necessary for the family to pay to have those services performed.

This approach avoids one of the pitfalls of applying the opportunity cost approach. For example, suppose a talented musician mows her yard rather than playing a gig that would have resulted in a $500 payday. The problem with awarding the $500 is that the plaintiff has already signaled a preference for mowing her own yard and avoiding the payment of $30 over performing and earning $500. Awarding the $500 amounts to compensation for the victim's less preferred choice.

Present Value

Assuming damages—of whatever variety, including those discussed elsewhere in this book—extend into the future, there remains the task of determining the present value. This is necessary because, when damages are awarded, they are typically awarded as one lump sum.

---

5. See generally, Michael L. Brookshire, *Economic Damages* (Cincinnati: Anderson Publishing, 1987), 63–74.

You are almost certainly familiar with the process of determining present value using the following formula:

$$PV = \sum_n \frac{Y(n)}{(1 + r)^n}$$

PV = sum over all future years n of lost income in year n divided by $(1 + r)^n$

where PV is present value, n is the year of the future income, and r is the discount rate. In the usual case, the present value of all lost future income is determined by making the calculation for each year and summing.

Interestingly, it is in the application of this formula that courts have disagreed. The disagreement centers on the relationship between inflation and the discount rate. In the usual calculation of future income, an adjustment is made for inflation. That adjustment is then offset by using the proper discount rate. The discount rate most frequently used is the interest rate the injured party could have earned on a safe investment. The interest rate itself has two components. You can understand this by thinking about why interest is paid when you put money in a savings account. To some extent, the bank must pay you interest because inflation means the money you deposit may not be worth as much when you withdraw it. Thus, you must be compensated for this risk. In addition, even if there is no inflation, you are agreeing to give up the use of your money. You must be compensated for this too. If there were no threat of future inflation, the only loss to you is that you do not have your money available. The portion of the interest rate that compensates you for this is called the real interest rate. The remainder of the interest rate reflects the fact that the money you do receive in the future may be worth less due to inflation. Together they are the nominal interest rate.

In theory, if you did not adjust for inflation in determining future income, you could use a discount rate that also did not account for inflation. One thing to note: Adjusting or not adjusting for inflation means literally accounting for the fact that dollars in the future may be worth less. This is a separate matter from the question of whether your salary would go up as you became more productive. In all likelihood both and adjustment for inflation and productivity increases will be necessary.

Perhaps surprisingly, courts have been all over the map on how to account for the relationship between the discount rate and the inflation adjustment for future income. Some courts allow for an inflation adjustment in future income and discounting by the nominal interest rate. Some do not allow inflation adjustments for future income but then allow discounting by the real interest rate only. These two approaches should achieve the same outcome. Some do not permit inflation adjustments in future income or any discounting at all. This favors plaintiffs. Some do not permit an inflation adjustment for expected income but do permit discounting. This, of course, is more favorable to defendants.

The most important issue from an economic standpoint is that the damages the defendant pays accurately reflect the harm caused. In this sense, the defendant-favoring and the plaintiff-favoring approaches are not satisfactory. On the other hand, remember that one of the costs of accidents is the cost of sorting things out, including having a trial and expert witnesses and so on. The method that allows for no inflation adjustment and no discounting—sometimes called the *total offset approach*—may actually reduce tertiary costs by streamlining the damage assessment process. That method is not the best in terms of minimizing primary accidents costs because it may mean the cost shifted to the defendant is not an accurate measure of the damage caused. This loss, however, may be offset by decreases in tertiary costs.

LAW AND ECONOMICS IN ACTION 14.2

THE VALUE OF BODY PARTS

As you have seen, when a person's earning capacity is diminished through an accident, an effort is made to place a value on that loss. Sometimes the loss can be tracked directly to the loss of a limb or one's sight or hearing. When these losses occur on the job, the victim is often covered by worker's compensation. These are state-administered programs that amount to insurance coverage. Although it seems distasteful, worker's compensation laws do place values on limbs and organs. Here are the most recent "values" from two states that vary substantially. The loss of a hand was "worth" $37,000 in Alabama but $228,000 in Pennsylvania. An arm in Alabama was worth a bit more at $48,000 while the compensation rate in Pennsylvania was $264,000. The loss of one eye in Alabama was $27,000 and in Pennsylvania it was $177,000. These variations are extreme, but it's useful to remember that worker's compensation is not a way of actually compensating for the loss of an arm or an eye but is supposed to track, in a very general way, the loss of earning capacity resulting from that loss. Thus, it would make sense for a low-wage state like Alabama to be consistently lower than a relatively high-wage state like Pennsylvania. In addition, a great deal of the variation occurs because states differ in the methods used to calculate these amounts.

PERSONAL INJURY AND PAIN AND SUFFERING

The idea of placing a value on the personal injuries and pain and suffering of victims of torts is one of the most controversial elements of damage calculations. How do you value the loss of a limb or the loss of eyesight? Is there any amount of money that compensates for years of pain? The difficulty of addressing these questions can be captured by thinking in terms of what you would sell a limb for or what you would take in exchange for your hearing or to be in pain for a period of time. Obviously, there is no satisfactory method of placing a monetary value on these things, but that is not a reason to shy away from the issue. The truth of the matter is that however poor a substitute money may be for these harms, it is ultimately the only one we have.

One place to start that is relatively easy is the out-of-pocket expenses incurred by someone who has been injured. Doctor's fees, hospital bills, medicines, therapy, and other costs all fit into the measure of damages. Some of these expenses may be absorbed before trial and others after. To the extent they are incurred before trial, the plaintiff is entitled to interest on the funds used. And to the extent the care may extend into the future, a present value calculation is necessary.

Recoveries for pain and suffering are clearly required to ensure that defendants fully internalize the costs of their damage to others. There is no generally accepted economic approach for establishing these costs. There are two theoretical possibilities. First, one could ask people what they would accept to undergo pain and suffering. Without some objective measure of pain and a standard for levels of pain tolerance, there may be no connection between the answers given and the actual loss to the one injured. Second, one could study the expenditures on pain relief by those who suffer certain categories of pain. In effect, one could establish "market value" for certain types of pain. But again, pain is probably far too subjective to quantify, and in all likelihood, income limits expenditures on pain relief. In effect, individuals may be unable to demonstrate the value of being pain-free because of limited income. On the other hand, if asked what they would take to be subjected to the pain, the amount may be much higher than they are willing and able to pay.

You may read in the newspaper from time to time about proposals to cap awards for pain and suffering. These efforts are typically sponsored by insurance companies who claim that overzealous juries award excessive damages for pain and suffering that then cause insurance rates to increase. It may seem like a good idea to cap pain and suffering damages if it is true that juries sometimes award pain and suffering out of a sense of sympathy or to punish defendants and not as the result of an effort to match the pain with the amount of money that would permit the victim to purchase sufficient pleasures in life to offset the pain. In addition, caps can make the system more predictable and less risky. Still, the economic goal of damages is to make sure that those who cause harm actually internalize the costs and make decisions on the basis of those costs. The fact that pain and suffering damages may be high means that any effort to cap them would result in an extreme level of under-internalization.

HEDONIC LOSSES

There is a general tendency to think of losses in terms of suffering of victims. Beyond pain in the usual sense, some injuries mean that people, even if they do not experience pain, find that they to do not enjoy life as much as they once did. This could include instances in which certain activities become impossible as well as instances in which death means the victim loses all enjoyment of life. For example, perhaps the injured party enjoyed skiing but has been told that skiing means risking a permanent injury. An impact on a victim's sight could mean less enjoyment of everything from watching television to visiting art galleries. In reality, this sort of loss is probably best combined with pain and suffering and treated along with pain and suffering as part of a decreased quality of life measure. This is not the way the law has developed, and although courts may allow juries to award damages that almost certainly include hedonic losses, the idea of accounting for loss of enjoyment of life is not one that is readily accepted. Still, a proper measure of damages should include some amount for this type of loss since it represents a loss in utility.

As with many damages courts are slow to accept, hedonic losses are difficult if not impossible to quantify. An easy example demonstrates this. Suppose an avid skier spends $30,000 per year on ski vacations. After an accident, skiing is either too painful or creates a risk of further damage. One thing we know is that the loss is worth at least $30,000. We know that because the skier had demonstrated that skiing was worth at least that much. But even here the analysis begins to crumble. First, even in the ski example, we do not know the loss; all we seem to know is the lowest value of the loss. Second, some extremely enjoyable activities are free or very inexpensive. Third, suppose skiing is impossible but the plaintiff now has time for something that is almost as enjoyable. As with pain and suffering, the value of hedonic losses is probably impossible to know.

There have been efforts to quantify hedonic losses in cases when the injured party dies. The idea of compensating someone who is killed in an accident may seem bizarre to you, but remember the goal from an economic perspective is not compensation but quantifying the external effects of tortious conduct. The issue here is determining the value of a life. This is different from the value of a person's productive capacity. That question goes to the earnings that are lost. Instead, here, "value of a life" means, literally—how much do you value being alive?

BEWARE OF DAUBERT!

A word that can strike fear in the hearts of expert witnesses is "Daubert." This is the name of one of the parties in a 1993 Supreme Court opinion, *Daubert v. Merrell Dow Pharmaceuticals, Inc.*,[6] in which the Court

6. 509 U.S. 579 (1993).

announced rules under which expert testimony would be allowed in a trial. The way this usually works is that one side of a dispute asks the judge not to allow an expert to testify. A "Daubert hearing" is then held and the judge either agrees or disagrees. According to the Supreme Court, the judge must make sure the testimony is useful, reliable, and the product of a methodology that is generally accepted in the relevant discipline. Now think of the valuation of hedonic losses and the idea that you can extrapolate from whether someone did or did not buy a smoke detector to a determination of the value to that person of his or her life. If a plaintiff hired an economist as an expert and that expert was going to use that methodology, would you, as the attorney on the other side, ask for a Daubert hearing? And if you were the judge at that hearing, would you permit the exclusion of the expert's testimony? In one relatively recent case, *Hein v. Merck & Co. Inc.,*[7] a judge refused to allow the testimony reasoning that it would be "more probably not true than true." Do you agree? If you believe that hedonic losses exist, how would you go about quantifying them?

The methodology employed here takes the value one attributes to a small portion of life and extrapolates it to a full life. The logic goes like this. Suppose the probability of being killed in a house fire is 2 in 1,000,000. If you buy a smoke detector, the likelihood of being killed in a house fire is 1 in 1,000,000. The smoke detector costs $10.00. In effect, the market transaction could be said to "reveal" that you consider one-millionth of your life to be worth $10.00. If so, your entire life must be worth $10,000,000. Conversely, if you did not buy the smoke detector, the argument would be that your life was worth something less than $10,000,000. You can understand how the same kinds of inferences could be drawn from whether the plaintiff smoked or wore a helmet when riding a bicycle. For a variety of reasons, these studies almost certainly do not reveal what a person would accept as payment for his or her life, but that may be too high an expectation. The objective from an economic perspective is to quantify externalities. Taking the life of another is clearly a very serious externality. Studies like these and others that may develop as economists examine the matter further may be the best hope of bringing something predictable into the internalization process.

7. 868 F.Supp. 230 (1994).

One final note is important. You may ask where all these damages go if the victim dies. For example, why should a dead victim be entitled to lost wages if he or she is not around to enjoy them? Similarly, how can there be a hedonic loss if there is no one to enjoy life? More generally, what is the point of compensating someone who is not there to be compensated? Again, remember that the objective from the standpoint of economics is not compensation. In fact, earlier in this chapter we discussed whether compensation matters at all. The key is to make sure the individual or business considering an action compares its benefits with all the harm. This harm includes all costs including the losses in utility, happiness, or anything else that would have existed but for the conduct. Put simply, defendants cannot lower the costs of their conduct by making sure the person they are imposed on is dead. The actual recovery becomes part of the victim's estate.

INDIRECT VICTIMS

Sometimes those who suffer most when damage occurs are the relatives of the victim. For example, parents may lose a child or one spouse may lose the other. To some extent, the indirect damage to these victims is accounted for by the damages collected by the direct victim. For example, if a spouse who is killed or injured was the principal wage earner, the surviving spouse will end up receiving the lost income. This same idea was once even applied to children. More specifically, if a person's child was killed that parent could receive the money the child would have brought into the family at least until the child would have left the home. Parents of a child who did not and was unlikely to contribute to the family's income would receive nothing. They would and do, however, receive compensation for medical care and so on because those expenses, at least until the child is an adult, are technically the responsibility of the parents.

This notion that spouses and children are simply income-earning assets and the only loss is the income that their "owners" could have claimed falls well short of accounting for the full cost to the spouses and parents of victims. It is true to the goal of full internalization to recognize that distress and sense of loss suffered by family members exists quite apart from anything experienced by the victim himself or herself. The law is somewhat responsive to this problem but not fully so.

As already noted, for years the only award for the loss of a child was the lost income. So extreme was this "income-earning asset" view that parents were also seen as having escaped the responsibility of feeding and clothing the child and these savings were deducted from the award of the earnings. That position has now softened and some states—but not all—allow recovery simply for the anguish or, in economic terms, the disutility of losing a loved one.

To some extent, the issues raised by compensation for pain and suffering, hedonic losses, and anguish lead to the question of just how far the internalization process should go. Suppose an auto accident resulting from careless driving ties up traffic, delaying your drive to the beach by an hour. Should you be compensated for the hour loss? Or when you drive by the accident, you catch sight of someone with a bloody arm who is crying and this upsets you. All these effects are externalities caused by the careless driving. When you think of these examples, though, you get a sense that the search for damage precision may eventually go too far. One reason is that there simply is no precision there. On a more practical level, efforts to increase precision are expensive not just in terms of basic research but, more important, in terms of tertiary expenses. Trials become longer, attorneys' fees increase, jurors are in court longer, and more expert witnesses are hired. At some point, the social gains from compensatory precision are outweighed by the costs of attempting to achieve that precision.

QUESTIONS FOR DISCUSSION

1. The emphasis of the law is fair compensation of victims. The emphasis of economics is internalization of external costs. Are these the same? Why or why not? From the perspective of economics, does it matter whether the victim is actually compensated?

2. Defamation is a tort. It involves making false and damaging statements about someone else. How would you determine the damages for defamation?

3. As noted in the text, the value of a life is a controversial matter. One way of getting to a value is the "willingness to pay" method whereby the cost incurred to improve safety is used to determine

the value one must attribute for the full life. The method is obviously imperfect; can you think of another one?

4. This chapter is largely based on a view that people are capable of internalizing the cost of the harm they cause. On the other hand, most people buy insurance to pay for their liability when they are careless. Does this upset the whole system?

5. How does an "exact" calculation of the monetary equivalent of pain and suffering help in internalizing the cost of the accident? Suppose people differ in how they experience pain. Those who experience less pain will get less compensation than those who experience lots of pain. But is it not enough for adequate internalization by the defendant to gear damages toward pain and suffering by the average person? Could this be used as an argument to cap damages for pain and suffering?

6. When parents file a "wrongful life" lawsuit, they claim that they were denied the opportunity to decide to abort a pregnancy. Had they known the child would be born with a disabling defect that is likely to result in paralysis and profound learning disabilities, they might have chosen abortion. How would you calculate damages in a wrongful life case?

CHAPTER FIFTEEN

Punitive Damages

I N SOME INSTANCES IN WHICH A DEFENDANT IS LIABLE for a tort, he or she will be required to pay punitive damages. In other words, the defendant must do more than simply compensate victims; he or she must pay some amount above and beyond—frequently way above and beyond—what would return the plaintiff to his or her original indifference curve. The existence of punitive damages means that as far as policy objectives go, there is an overlap between tort law and criminal law.

From an economic perspective, the rationale for permitting punitive damages connects directly to the ideas of internalization and allocative efficiency. In fact, the goal is not necessarily to "punish" in the conventional sense but to ensure that the defendant pays a socially compensable amount—an amount equal to the full harm caused. Courts making decisions about punitive damages seem to have a generalized understanding of their economic function but are concerned with other policies as well.

In the first section of this chapter we examine why a compensatory damage may not generate the level of internalization needed to minimize the costs of accidents. The next part takes a close look at the standards applied by the U.S. Supreme Court to assess punitive damages. These are the standards that all courts must follow. In the third section we look at some empirical evidence about the impact of punitive damages, and in the last part examine a final question about how to measure punitive damages if the goal is to extinguish harmful behavior.

WHEN DO TORT REMEDIES FAIL TO ACHIEVE EFFICIENT OUTCOMES?

For tort damages to result in the correct pricing information to be transmitted to those who may cause accidents, all externalities must be accounted for. The reality is probably very far from the ideal. Sometimes the reasons are obvious. Damages may be calculated incorrectly or courts may restrict the types of damages that can be recovered, such as hedonic losses and pain and suffering—but from an economic point of view these are actual costs. Other possibilities may be less obvious.

A basic example is one in which damages are low per person but widespread in society. Suppose a short segment on the rim of a can of food is not sanded smoothly and you get a small scratch on your finger when you open the can. This may seem like a small matter, but suppose that five million cans of the food are produced and that one person in ten is scratched by the rough edge. Now 500,000 suffer some minor harm but not one of them regards it as serious enough to file an action. In sum, an externality associated with the production of the food is not internalized by the manufacturer.

To make matters worse, suppose each cut causes $2 worth of discomfort for a total of $1 million and for $100,000 the manufacturer could install a buffing device that would solve the problem. Unless the manufacturer is found liable for something in excess of $100,000, no corrections will be made. Put simply, it is just not worthwhile for any one customer to complain. Something called a "class action," to which we will return, is one way to respond to this problem, but allowing a single plaintiff to recover punitive damages may also achieve the desired outcome.

A similar situation can arise even when people do sue. For example, assume that a producer of canned sardines is not careful about certain packing safeguards and several thousand cans of sardines that are tainted with bacteria are distributed and eventually eaten. The victims are scattered throughout the country. Some people are unaffected by the sardines, some get a little queasy, and others get very sick missing as much as six months of work. For the sake of the discussion, assume the total damage is $5 million. As you might expect, some people—whether queasy or very sick—may not see the connection between their illness and the sardines. Some may make the connection but just shrug it off. Some people may make the connection and be highly motivated to sue. Some of these, however, may retain inept attorneys or run into judges or juries who are not receptive to their claims. Others may settle for substantially less than what would have been recovered at a trial. After all the dust settles, the defendant, the sardine producer, pays out a total of $3 million—$2 million short of the full internalization. As you can see, in this instance, as a "pricing" system the tort system is imperfect.

Punitive damages are necessary to adjust the price of what is produced so the costs of production are accurately accounted for. In terms of the sardine example, it is possible that only one victim sues and recovers $1,000 in compensation for his or her sickness. Somehow that award must be adjusted so the manufacturer actually behaves as though the carelessness cost $5 million. The idea is not necessarily to completely extinguish a certain type of behavior but to make sure it is undertaken at efficient levels. Thus, in the sardine example, punitive damages of $4,999,000 might be awarded.[1] If it is less expensive than $5 million to avoid the harm in the future, the firm will take the necessary measures. On the other hand, if the cost of avoiding tainted sardines exceeds $5 million, it might choose not to take corrective measures.

Before taking a close look at how courts actually treat punitive damages, three qualifying comments are important. In the sardine example, we assumed one person recovered. Suppose instead three people sued and recovered. If they all recovered $1,000 each in compensatory damages, there remains the $4,997,000 in additional damages. This amount cannot be awarded to all three plaintiffs or we would have payments of $15 million for $5 million in social cost.

While it may be possible for a court to know what recoveries have taken place, it cannot know what recoveries will take place in the future. Thus, the general rule is that punitive damages should be adjusted for the probability that the wrongdoer will be held liable again

---

1. This assumes compensatory damages are $1,000.

some time in the future. For example, suppose harm is caused ten times and costs $1,000 each time for a total of $10,000. It is also anticipated that the wrongdoer will only be caught twice. Here, the punitive damages for each plaintiff would be $4,000. It would not be $5,000 because $1,000 will be recovered as compensatory damages.[2]

Second, you may be thinking that it seems unfair for someone receiving, say, $5,000 in damages to collect that plus $100,000 in punitive damages. Fair or not fair, it is important to note that it does not matter from the standpoint of allocative efficiency who gets the punitive damages. The point is to create the correct incentives for the careless firm; directing punitive damages to the poor or for higher education would serve this end as well. There is a limit, however, to the idea of taxing away punitive damages awards. People with very small claims must be able to recover some or all of the punitive damages in order to have an incentive to bring their cases. In addition, potential plaintiffs with legitimate claims have a less than 100 percent chance of prevailing and will incur unreimbursed expenses. For example, a person with a legitimate $1 million claim may have an expected net recovery of $600,000. Similarly, the careless party's expected loss may be substantially lower than $1 million. Punitive damages can raise the expected recovery and increase the incentive to bring an action when the realities of the court system may make the effort less attractive.

The third point is that there may be motivations for punitive damages other than traditional economic ones. For example, think again about the tainted sardines. Suppose we want more than a rule that allows the sardine producer to decide whether it is efficient to take the care necessary not to make people sick—maybe because we feel shocked about the mere possibility that what you can buy every day in a grocery store might poison you. Here we might want to use punitive damages in a literal sense to make it so costly to the manufacturer that it stops the practice (the lack of care) even though it is technically efficient.

This last point leads to some interesting tension in the way people feel about punishment and efficiency. Suppose a giant oil tanker runs

---

2. For an excellent discussion, see A. Mitchell Polinsky and Steven Shavell, "Punitive Damages: An Economic Analysis," *Harvard Law Review* 111 (1998): 869–949.

aground in the Florida Keys because of the carelessness of its inebriated captain. A massive oil spill occurs resulting in extensive economic and ecological damage valued at $1 billion dollars.[3] The event is reported on CNN every hour for two weeks, and there is no way the operators of the tanker will escape liability. Should there also be punitive damages? The answer may depend on what you think punitive damages should do. If they are strictly for internalization purposes, as long as the social cost is accurately internalized by the operators of the ship, they are of no use. On the other hand, suppose the whole event results in a great deal of anger and people want to somehow vent that anger. Awarding punitive damages is a way to do that. In fact, one of the generally accepted rationales for punishment is "retribution." Retribution refers to the idea of inflicting punishment simply because it seems just to do so. Thus, we may want punitive damages to include both an amount equal to all the harm caused and then a "kicker" to exhibit that the activity is morally unacceptable.[4]

LAW AND ECONOMICS IN ACTION 15.1

THE MINIVAN

In the mid-1990s, a lawsuit was filed after a young child was ejected from a 1985 Dodge Caravan when the latch on the rear hatch failed. The child died. In the course of the trial it was determined that the latch was designed and introduced in the 1960s and was generally no longer in use. In mid-1988, Dodge changed the latches in the new model to a safer one but did not tell the people with the old vans. The hatch latch did not meet the safety standard for ordinary passenger doors. It appears that Dodge delayed changes to the latch for fear that a change would lead to an inference that the original latches must be faulty. Finally, Dodge had destroyed films it had made examining the performance of its minivan in crashes. These are the types of factors that anger jurors and lead to huge punitive damage awards. This was, in fact, what happened in the case. Some of the factors here, however, do not seem to have that much to do with the

---

3. See Polinsky and Shavell, "Punitive Damages," 903.

4. For an excellent discussion of these issues in the context of a judicial opinion, see Judge Calabresi's concurring opinion in *Ciraolo v. City of New York*, 216 F.3d 236 (2000).

full internalization or economic rationale for punitive damages. What do you think? If you were the judge in a case in which these factors were presented, would you instruct the jury to ignore them?

Reference: Milo Geyelin, "Why One Jury Dealt a Big Blow to Chrysler in Minivan-Latch Case," *Wall Street Journal*, November 11, 1997, A1.

PUNITIVE DAMAGES IN THE COURTS

The best-known and most discussed effort by the U.S. Supreme Court to announce a coherent approach to punitive damages is *BMW of North America v. Gore*, a 1996 case.[5] It was followed more recently by *State Farm Mutual Insurance Co. v. Campbell* and *Phillip Morris USA v. Williams*.[6] Some attention to the details is useful here because, whether the decision is consistent with the economic ideal, it is the guideline all courts must observe because it comes from the Supreme Court. Although these cases are the last word on what courts may do with respect to punitive damages, the analysis applies only to the question of whether the assessed punitive damages are too high.

The *Gore* (not Al) case started out in Alabama when the eventual plaintiff bought a BMW for over $40,000. It was sold as a new car but had been damaged and repaired for $600 before being sold. This was not disclosed. At the time, BMW had a policy with respect to cars damaged while being manufactured or transported. If the damage was less than 3 percent of the car's value, it was repaired and sold as a new car without notice to the dealership or the buyer. If the damage exceeded 3 percent, the car was repaired and eventually sold as used. ($600 was under the 3 percent threshold, so BMW was following its policy.)

Gore eventually discovered the repair and sued BMW in Alabama state court. He claimed compensatory damages of $4,000 and was able to convince the jury of that amount through the testimony of a BMW dealer who said that a repaired car of that nature was worth $4,000 less than an undamaged car would have been. Gore also asked for punitive damages. He discovered that BMW had done virtually

---

5. 517 U.S. 559 (1996).
6. 538 U.S. 408 (2003) and 127 S.Ct. 1057 (2007).

the same thing—repairing without disclosure—nearly 1,000 times. Thus, one could argue that the total social cost of BMW's practice was $4 million. The jury agreed and awarded Gore the $4 million. BMW appealed to the Alabama Supreme Court which reduced the punitive award to $2 million in part because it would not allow Gore to recover for cars sold outside of Alabama. Part of the problem on this point was that the activity that resulted in BMW's liability in Alabama was not necessarily illegal in other states. BMW then appealed to the U.S. Supreme Court, which held the award excessive and referred the case back to the lower court.

The Court applied its standard a few years later in *State Farm Mutual Insurance Co. v. Campbell*. In that case an insurance company that was obligated to defend its clients in a lawsuit and to pay the damages lost by the clients essentially misled the clients about what it was doing and did not act in their best interests. At a jury trial in Utah, the plaintiffs were awarded $1 million in compensatory damages and $145 million in punitive damages. Economically, this award would make sense if it approximated the total damage to those whom the insurance company had similarly misled and none of those victims had recovered. Again, the Supreme Court found the award excessive.

Finally, these themes played out again in 2007. In *Phillip Morris USA v. Williams*, the plaintiff was awarded $79.5 million in punitive damages by a jury as a result of damages to her husband and others as a consequence of illnesses after smoking cigarettes. Their claim was that Phillip Morris led smokers to believe that the product was safe. The Court struck down the punitive damage award because the jury had been permitted to consider the harms to others resulting from smoking.

In all cases, the Court listed three factors to be weighed in determining whether punitive damages are excessive: (1) how reprehensible the conduct was, (2) the disparity between the actual harm and the amount of punitive damage, and (3) the sanctions for comparable conduct. Perhaps most important, damage to others may not be part of the award.

Central to the Court's concern was that potential defendants should have notice of the consequences of tortious conduct. This overall objective of the Court makes sense—an element of behaving as though costs have been internalized is knowing what those costs are likely to be. In fact, the Court goes so far in this direction as to suggest that punitive damages might be capped at some fixed multiple of compensatory damages. Caps of some kind may be economically beneficial by reducing uncertainty, but it is at the expense of achieving allocatively efficient outcomes.

Beyond the view that potential defendants should have some inkling of what their liability will be if they injure others, the Court's approach to punitive damages is a classic example of the difference between a strictly economic treatment of an issue and the outcome when a variety of factors are involved. Take, for instance, the Supreme Court's reliance on the reprehensibility of the conduct. This might make sense if reprehensibility related to the probability that the wrongdoer will be caught. In other words, a lower probability of being found out cuts in favor of higher punitive damages. And, to some extent, the Court does make it clear that punitive damages can be higher when people try to deceive others.

Similarly, the Court's linkage of reprehensibility to intent and repeat offenders makes economic sense. In other words, when the damage is done purposefully, greater freedom is permitted to award punitive damages. The purposeful actor understands what is happening and can anticipate the expected cost and is willing to disregard that cost. One possibility is that the person actually gets greater pleasure from the activity than the expected recovery. Or the person may get some utility out of gambling on not being caught. In these instances, punitive damages may be, even in excess of total social harm, warranted for moral reasons or because we prefer to channel the "transaction" into a market of willing buyers and sellers.

On the other hand, in the context of reprehensibility, the Court seems to distinguish between instances of violence and physical harm and those in which the losses are economic only. The idea is that we find physical and violent harm more morally repugnant than a simple financial con job. In fact, in *Gore*, the Supreme Court found none of the signs of reprehensibility. This type of analysis can lead in the wrong direction as an economic matter. Supposedly, this means that if two defendants caused the same level of harm, punitive damages could be lower for one defendant if the harm he or she caused were economic rather than physical. There is no doubt that it is difficult to monetize physical harm, but the idea that the same level of harm could be treated differently is inconsistent with the overall goal of internalization.

Similarly, the Court's view that the punitive damages must not be disproportionate with respect to the actual harm can miss the point by a long shot. You may recall the example above of the can with the sharp edge. Suppose 500,000 people are injured by the can at an expense of about $2 each. When we discussed the example earlier, it was used to indicate why all those injured would not sue. Now, however, suppose someone does sue and collects compensatory damages of $2. Suppose further that some kind of proportionality standard is imposed. In fact, the Supreme Court has mentioned ratios of three or four to one, but suppose the multiple is actually 100 to one. That means punitive damages of $200 and a gross level of under-internalization by the producer of the faulty cans.

The point is that a punitive damages cap based on the relationship between compensatory damages and punitive damages makes far less economic sense than a cap based on the likelihood of recovery by other plaintiffs. In fact, the guidance by the Court could actually be interpreted to send things in the wrong direction economically speaking. When the harm is slight, there may be a tendency to say that the multiple should be low and when it is higher, a higher multiple is permitted. Given that slight harm cases are exactly the ones in which there may be few plaintiffs, the logic would be that in these cases large multiples would be appropriate.

The Court's view that acceptable punitive damages are dependent on the sanctions for comparable conduct is similarly slanted. In effect, conduct that is equally harmful should be "punished" by comparable amounts of punitive damages. This is certainly an idea that appeals to society's sense of fairness. And there may be some economic justification in the sense that one type of harmful conduct should not be over- or underpriced relative to another. Still, the idea that a court should determine the proper level of punitive damages by reference to the damages available in other instances may simply mean that both damage levels are inconsistent with allocative efficiency.

CASE 15.1 The Theory and Reality of Punitive Damages: *Davis v. The Upjohn Company*, 682 N.E.2d 1203 (Ill. 1997)

This chapter describes the economics of punitive damages, and in this area, as much as any other, there is a distinction between the economic rationale approach and what the courts do. The discussion of the Supreme Court standards is indicative of this. The excerpts from a more garden-variety case, involving damage resulting from an eye medication that caused severe damage to a patient to whom it was administered will prove instructive. Here a jury awarded $3 million in compensatory damages and $125 million in punitive damages. The judge in the case ordered the punitive damage award reduced to $35 million. The drug company (Upjohn) appealed and the punitive damages were reduced even further to $6 million. This portion of the opinion deals with the punitive damages.

Upjohn next contests the punitive damages judgment, asserting: (1) there was insufficient evidence to support liability for punitive damages; (2) a new trial must be awarded with respect to punitive damages; and (3) the punitive damages award is grossly excessive.

Illinois courts have long been concerned that punitive damages not be awarded improperly or unwisely. The purpose of punitive damages is not compensation of plaintiff, but punishment of defendant and deterrence; therefore, these damages can be awarded only for conduct that is outrageous either because defendant's acts are done with an evil motive or a reckless indifference to others' rights.

Punitive damages are similar to criminal penalties and are permissible only in cases in which torts "are committed with fraud, actual malice, deliberate violence or oppression, or when the defendant acts willfully, or with such gross negligence as to indicate a wanton disregard of the rights of others."

There was evidence presented here that Upjohn not only knew of the adverse effects of [the medication], but promoted and developed this off-label use through financial and technical assistance to doctors. After those doctors wrote up their case reports with Upjohn's assistance, Upjohn distributed them, thereby helping to create the literature touting the periocular use of [the medication]. There was sufficient evidence of willful and wanton conduct to justify the imposition of punitive damages.

Upjohn's contention that the jury instructions on punitive damages were inadequate is not persuasive. The jury was instructed that "willful and wanton conduct" means "a course of action which shows an utter indifference to or conscious disregard for the safety of others." Given the status of Illinois law on punitive damages discussed above, we cannot say that the instructions do not state the law accurately. The circuit court did not abuse its discretion in giving these punitive damages instructions to the jury.

Upjohn also maintains the court erred in permitting argument concerning Upjohn's net worth. Upjohn, however, cannot show the court abused its discretion in admitting evidence of its net worth. Upjohn has failed to demonstrate that the evidence was irrelevant and prejudicial with respect to either compensatory or punitive damages.

Upjohn's most persuasive argument is that the punitive damages awarded are excessive and should be reduced.

In reviewing punitive damage awards, the question of excessiveness turns on whether the amount is so large that it outruns the justification for exacting punitive damages, namely retribution and deterrence of future outrageous conduct. A reviewing court considers the degree of reprehensibility of defendant's conduct, the relationship between the punitive damage award and the harm caused by the conduct, defendant's gain from the misconduct, and the financial condition of defendant. This court's inquiry is thus one of degree: When arrayed along the spectrum of wrongful acts, was the conduct at issue here so extraordinarily outrageous as to justify extraordinary punitive damages? The circuit court, in its review of the punitive damages awarded, answered that question in the affirmative, although it remitted the jury's award by almost 75%. The original award of more than $124 million amounted to precisely 7% of Upjohn's net worth; the remitted amount is still more than 2% of the company's net worth and more than eleven times the amount of compensatory damages awarded.

When we consider the factors set out by the United States Supreme Court and Illinois courts, we find that the amount of punitive damages awarded in this case far outruns the justification for imposing punitive damages. We agree with the circuit court that Upjohn's conduct was sufficiently reprehensible to support an award of punitive damages, however, there is no reasonable relationship between the amount of the punitive damages and the harm caused by the conduct. Further, although Upjohn is a large corporation with a net worth of approximately $1.7 billion, punishment in the amount of 2% of its net worth is excessive in the extreme.

Illinois courts have recognized that the level of compensatory damages may be an appropriate measure of punitive damages. It is important, however, not to belittle the meaning of the jury's decision and the determination of the circuit court that a $35 million dollar award was proper given Upjohn's willful and wanton conduct. We believe that a punitive damage award twice that of the compensatory damage award will send a strong message to pharmaceutical manufacturers of the necessity to warn of the known potential adverse effects of their drugs. The twin goals of retribution and deterrence would both be met by such an award. [W]e enter a remittitur of the punitive damages to $6,095,639.52.

If this were an essay on the economics, what grade would you give it?

EMPIRICAL QUESTIONS

There is, as you know, a debate about the use of punitive damages. Insurance companies and large corporations tend to be on one side of the debate and claim that huge awards are causing insurance rates to increase and profits to decline. On the other hand, attorneys who represent plaintiffs are typically on the other side. The issue has taken on a huge political dimension under the title "tort reform." On the more scholarly side of things, the debate also takes place and seems to do so on two levels. The issue is not what the economically sound level of punitive damages should be. Instead, scholars look at the institution of punitive damages and ask whether it makes much of a difference. In other words, given the disconnect between theory and what courts and juries actually do, do the benefits of having a regime of punitive damages outweigh the costs? At another level, the debate is more specific and focuses on whether the image of courts and juries run amok and administering punitive damages in a way that would make an economist want to hide is the correct one.

One of the more interesting studies taking the more "macro" view is by W. Kip Viscusi.[7] There are in fact four states that do not permit punitive damages. So, in effect, Viscusi was able to conduct a survey that was not unlike a controlled experiment. The question was whether residents of those four states were, in fact, any less safe as a result of the lack of punitive damages. Viscusi's evidence suggests quite strongly that the lack of punitive damages does not make those states less safe. There are interesting implications of this outcome. The results suggest that the cost of administering a system of punitive damages is unjustified. On the other hand, it is sometimes hard

---

7. W. Kip Viscusi, "The Social Costs of Punitive Damage Awards against Corporations in Environmental and Safety Torts," *Georgetown Law Journal* 87 (1998): 285–342.

to alter company policies by state, and the nonpunitive-damage states may be involved in a bit of free riding on the states that do have punitive damages. Perhaps a better test would be to compare a large group of contiguous states without punitive damages with a large group with punitive damages.

The more detailed empirical work is aimed at determining whether there are any consistent patterns in the awarding of punitive damages that would support arguments that they are often unpredictable and grossly disproportionate to the harm caused. Here, it appears that reports in the popular press may lead to an unrealistic view of punitive damages. Studies show that punitive damages awards are available in less than 10 percent of cases. And, in one study, the ratio of punitive awards to compensatory awards is in the range of 1.6 to 1.[8] Depending on a variety of factors, this rate may actually be too low to force complete internalization. And it is possible that the reason people are no safer in punitive damage states than in other states is because the states with punitive damages are also "underpricing" tortious conduct.

A FINAL COMPLICATION

The relationship between punitive damages and allocative efficiency is quite evident. Equally clear, it is not certain that courts are capable of applying a sufficiently refined analysis to achieve allocatively efficient outcomes. An additional complication arises when one considers the broader theory of punitive damages. To an economist, the purpose of punitive damages is to insure full internalization and, if the activity giving rise to the damage to others continues, so be it. If you think about it, the economic approach is more closely related to Kaldor-Hicks efficiency except that some parties are compensated. This is because those who commit torts are permitted to "take" from others and, even with a fully adjusted award for punitive damages, simply pay the cost of the harm done. In effect, punitive damages may or may not stop the conduct.

---

8. See Michael Rusted, "In Defense of Punitive Damages in Products Liability: Testing Tort Anecdotes with Empirical Evidence," *Iowa Law Review* 78 (1992): 1; Stephen Daniels and Joanne Martin, "Myth and Reality in Punitive Damages," *Minnesota Law Review*, 75 (1992): 1–64.

On the other hand, sometimes punitive damages seem to be predicated on the idea that if wrongdoers fully internalize the costs of their actions, they will stop. This view of punitive damages assumes that the benefits to the wrongdoer are equal to the harm that is externalized. This is, however, not always the case. When it is not the case *and* the goal is to extinguish the behavior, then punitive damages must be set at or above the benefits to the defendant rather than at the level of harm to the plaintiff. Extinguishing behavior might or might not be efficient in this case.

The benefits may exceed social cost in a number of ways. For example, the defendant may just be rolling the dice by not taking an expensive measure that costs $200,000 and produces an expected harm of $250,000 if a projected twenty-five people are injured. Let's say that only one person is injured at a cost of $10,000. The other expected twenty-four injuries just do not occur. Should punitive damages be $240,000 in order to remove the incentive to take the gamble? The economist's answer is yes. Moreover, this is an unlikely scenario. If the firm makes its decision on the basis of expected damages, it would not have "rolled the dice" in the first place—it would have taken the $200,000 measure.[9] In an instance in which the firm made a lousy decision but got lucky—experienced a windfall—when few people are injured, it is hard to see a good efficiency-based argument for what would amount to a redistribution from owners to the single victim.

Second, suppose an insurance agent cons customers into thinking that he is acquiring insurance coverage for them. He actually makes a bundle investing the money and is able to pay all the damages in a lawsuit by those he conned and earn a profit. Here there are good arguments for punitive damages equal to the gain in order to stop the con man altogether. First, the "service" provided by the agent/investor is one that is available in the market at a low transaction cost and the clients could purchase there. In other words, each individual could express his or her preference at prices in the market with a greater assurance that their resources would be allocated efficiently. Second, a skilled agent/investor would not have to con people out of money in order to generate investment funds. Thus, we want there to be no incentive for one with inferior skills to enter the market.

9. See Polinsky and Shavell, "Punitive Damages," 918.

Another possibility is that someone may simply derive pleasure from harming others. In fact, the benefit felt by this person exceeds any possible measure of the harm. This is an instance in which basic moral considerations and limitations on what can be bought and sold in the market—voluntarily or involuntarily—will require equating punitive damages with the gain to the wrongdoer.

Finally, think again of the tainted sardine case. Suppose the distributor could institute a new bacteria-reducing program for $1 million, and the total cost of illness from the bacteria is $800,000. It distributes the sardines and has expected damages of $800,000, based on a fair market value of the losses suffered by victims. Transaction costs are high, so there is no realistic possibility of buying each individual's right not to be sick. On the other hand, if sardine buyers were asked what it would cost to allow the manufacturer to make them sick, they would have reported at least $1 million. This, of course, brings us back to the classic problem associated with liability rules generally. When those who violate the rights of others are permitted to do so "at cost," there is a legitimate question of whether the outcome is efficient at all. This may be a matter of reconsidering how we define social cost. If "social cost" is set at less than the least amount for which victims would be willing to sell their right not to be harmed—that is, the reservation price—then it is set too low to achieve any form of efficiency. In these instances, it may not be necessary to raise punitive damages to the full gain of the wrongdoer, but leaving them at "social cost" is also an inadequate measure. Of course, one may argue that the problem is not so severe since reservation prices may be roughly the same as objectively determined "social costs" as reflected in market transactions. The problem with this is that many of the costs incurred in the context of torts—illness, injury, mental distress—have no marketplace counterpart.

QUESTIONS FOR DISCUSSION

1. Do you think punitive damages should be set to require firms to internalize the cost of harmful conduct or to encourage them to stop the harmful conduct? Is there a difference between these two objectives? If so, how does it affect the calculation of punitive damages?

2. You have now studied both torts and contracts. In torts cases, punitive damages are available in appropriate cases. In contracts cases, punitive damages are not available. What is the economic justification for this distinction?

3. An individual plaintiff who collects punitive damages presumably also receives compensatory damages as well. Given this, why allow the plaintiff to keep the punitive damages? Why not take most of any punitive damage award and put it to use for something socially beneficial? Would this reduce the likelihood that punitive damages would advance the interests of allocative efficiency?

4. What do you think of the Supreme Court standards? Those standards appear to be inconsistent with efficiency. Can you articulate what goal they may be consistent with?

5. As a pricing system, torts is imperfect. Even with a combination of compensatory and punitive damages, torts does not adequately cover private and social costs in practice. Would it not be better to replace the tort system with a government agency empowered to force producers to internalize the social costs of their products and services?

CHAPTER SIXTEEN

Products Liability

O NE OFFSHOOT OF TORT LAW THAT HAS BECOME increasingly important deals with products liability. As the title implies, the issue is determining when manufacturers are liable for injuries to customers that occur as a result of using their product. In this context, the emphasis shifts from individualized mishaps between two parties to whether a manufacturer who puts products into commercial channels should be liable for harms to those using the products. Put in terms you are now familiar with, when should a manufacturer internalize the costs of the harms? What makes this area of study intriguing is that an internalization requirement is often more like a requirement that manufacturers insure their customers. In effect, a decision that a manufacturer internalize the cost of products liability into the product price can be seen as a requirement that customers pay for an insurance premium on each unit bought. Consequently, this is an area in which tort law and consumer preferences are intertwined.

Two additional factors make a separate examination of products liability useful to undertake. First, you will recall from Chapter 13 that one of the costs of accidents is *secondary*. The idea is that there are monetary costs and then there is the overall impact on utility once the monetary costs are distributed. Finding manufacturers liable is arguably a way to spread the cost of injuries in order to minimize secondary costs. Second, how much should manufacturers anticipate the possibilities that buyers of their products may be careless or even stupid? For example, should a manufacturer of a food processor with a sharp spinning blade be required to construct it so that it is impossible for a person to put his hand into the blade while it is spinning? Should auto manufacturers be required to construct trunk latches so that if someone crawls in the trunk and closes the door he or she will be able to get out? Or it is sufficient for there to be signs that say, "Please do not put your hand in the spinning blade," or "Please do not place yourself in the trunk of this car," or (and this is not a joke) on a Batman costume, "Parent: Please exercise caution—FOR PLAY ONLY: Mask and Chest Plate are Not Protective: cape does not enable user to fly."[1]

This chapter discusses the economic rationale for products liability as well as some of the limitations on just how much responsibility should be assigned to manufacturers. The first section examines whether manufacturers should be held to a negligence or strict liability standard. A closer look at secondary accident costs is found in the next part. The third section deals with the impact of products liability on choice, followed by a discussion of the limits on products liability. The last section analyzes the economics of warning labels.

First, however, some preliminary information will provide context. As you might expect, the types of things manufacturers can do that courts view as tortious can vary. For example, perhaps a mechanical product is well designed but one of the screws was not tightened all the way when it was assembled so that a piece may fly off and hit someone. This is a defect in manufacture. On the other hand, it may be that the item is put together exactly as designed but the design is such that users are endangered. For example, maybe a kitchen appliance is designed so that it heats up enough to melt materials that might be near it. This would be a design defect. There are also instances in which manufacturers are liable for not providing adequate warnings about possible hazards.

PRODUCTS LIABILITY: NEGLIGENCE OR STRICT LIABILITY?

You will recall from Chapter 13 that a party is negligent when the marginal cost of prevention is less than the marginal cost of the acci-

---

1. John M. Brooder, "Warning: A Batman Cape Won't Help You Fly," *New York Times,* March 5, 1997, A1.

dent. Strict liability does not include the same kind of analysis. A party is strictly liable and must pay damages whenever it causes harm to another *even if the cost of preventing the harm exceeds the damage caused.* Thus, the term "strictly" liable. The main economic rationale for strict liability is that it requires a party who injures others to think in terms of the *level* of the activity. A typical example is the construction firm engaged in blasting near a residential area. Each blast causes some harm but the harm is always less than the cost of not blasting. Thus, there is no negligence and the cost to the residents is not internalized by the construction company. Strict liability, however, forces the construction company to recognize the harm it causes and internalize the cost. These costs will increase with the amount of blasting it does.

One question that arises is whether manufacturers of products should be liable under a theory of negligence or strict liability. In other words, should plaintiffs be required to show that the manufacturer of a product that injures them could have avoided an injury at a cost that is less than the expected cost of the harm? Or should manufacturers be required to pay for any harm that befalls users of the product?

As it turns out, this distinction may not be as important in the mass production context as it would be in an example like blasting. In other words, the outcomes under strict liability and negligence may not be that different. To understand why, remember that the questions are whether it makes economic sense to avoid the accident at all and who is the most efficient avoider of the accident. Compare manufacturers and consumers with respect to both of these questions, taking the second question first. Suppose the issue is whether a lever should be installed on a lawnmower that means the mower automatically shuts down when an operator's hands are not on the handle. Without the lever, the engine would keep running, but the mower would go nowhere unless parked on an incline. If 200,000 mowers are produced and the cost of each manufacturer-installed safety lever is $0.50, the cost of prevention is $100,000. Or, each buyer would individually have to understand the risk (a cost in itself) and either buy the lever or take it somewhere to have it installed. This is very likely to exceed $.50 per mower.

Take one more example. You are shopping for a motor scooter. Do you know enough about each part to know which ones could fail and lead to an accident? You and every other consumer would have to take an engineer along to check the scooter from top to bottom. And if there were a problem, you would have to have it repaired or shop for another scooter without the same defects. Thus, in answer to the second question—who is the lower cost accident-avoider?— very often, especially when the cause of the harm is related to product design or construction, it is less expensive for manufacturers rather than consumers to avoid the harm because consumers would have to incur higher transaction and production costs than manufacturers.

This also helps answer the first question about whether it is efficient to avoid the harm at all. In our example, given the manufacturer's cost of avoiding the harm, the manufacturer should be held liable if expected accident costs exceed $100,000. This figure would have to be much higher if the comparison were between consumers' costs and expected accident costs. In fact, as a general matter, it will more likely make sense to avoid harm by way of mass and relatively low-cost production. Thus, even under an efficient negligence system, the manufacturer is more likely than consumers to internalize the cost of producing products that harm others.

Another reason the difference might not be very large has to do with when courts apply strict liability to products. As a legal matter, strict liability does not apply in the manufacturing context unless the product is already labeled *unreasonably dangerous*. This means that a manufacturer is not liable—even under strict liability—every time someone is injured while using a product. Instead, courts make an assessment of whether the product was dangerous. For example, the person hit by a stone that is propelled by a spinning lawnmower blade is likely to recover damages because a mower that is not constructed to stop flying stones is likely to be viewed as dangerous. On the other hand, someone who disassembles the guard that keeps stones from flying and is then hit by a stone is not likely to recover damages as the lawnmower itself will not be viewed as dangerous. In effect, before the label *strict liability* is applied to manufacturers, courts apply something like a negligence analysis to determine whether the *unreasonably dangerous* standard is met.

Still, this does not mean that strict liability and negligence are the same. It is possible that a producer of a dangerous product will be strictly liable but at the same time will not be negligent. This would occur if the dangerousness of the product were more expensive to eliminate than the cost of the harm caused. Thus, under negligence, the producer would not be liable to those injured, but the strictly liable party would be. Interestingly, this does not mean that the level of care will change depending on whether manufacturers are subject to a negligence or strict liability standard. The potentially negligent party will compare the cost of harm with the cost of avoiding it and choose the lower-cost strategy. The strictly liable party makes the same analysis and will simply pay damages if the cost of avoiding the harm is in excess of the harm itself. This would suggest that the level of care would be the same. But there is another factor to consider here: The manufacturer may have a higher potential to avoid the harm at a lower cost and strict liability provides an incentive to do so.[2]

CASE 16.1 **Why Strict Liability?** *Indiana Harbor Belt Railroad Company v. American Cyanamid Company,* 916 F.2d 1174 (7th Cir. 1990)

You have seen that strict liability may not be as efficient as negligence, especially when harmful incidents are viewed as single occurrences as opposed to the reflection of a repeated practice. And you have seen that strict liability may be superior to negligence as far as secondary and tertiary costs are concerned. There are additional justifications for strict liability as explained in this case involving a chemical spill at a rail yard in Chicago.

> *Guille* [a case the judge is comparing to the one on appeal] is a paradigmatic case for strict liability. (a) The risk (probability) of harm was great, and (b) the harm that would ensue if the risk materialized could be, although luckily was not, great (the balloonist could have crashed into the crowd rather than into the vegetables). The confluence of these two factors established the urgency of seeking to prevent such accidents. (c) Yet such accidents could not be prevented by the exercise of due care; the technology of care in ballooning was insufficiently developed. (d) The activity was not a matter of common usage, so there was

---

2. Note that this more or less finesses the causation issue because one could ask whether the harm was due to the absence of the lever or because the operator left the mower running or because it was left parked on a hill.

no presumption that it was a highly valuable activity despite its unavoidable riskiness. (e) The activity was inappropriate to the place in which it took place—densely populated New York City. The risk of serious harm to others (other than the balloonist himself, that is) could have been reduced by shifting the activity to the sparsely inhabited areas that surrounded the city in those days. (f) Reinforcing (d), the value to the community of the activity of recreational ballooning did not appear to be great enough to offset its unavoidable risks.

[These six factors] are related to each other in that each is a different facet of a common quest for a proper legal regime to govern accidents that negligence liability cannot adequately control. The interrelations might be more perspicuous if the six factors were reordered. One might for example start with (c), inability to eliminate the risk of accident by the exercise of due care. The baseline common law regime of tort liability is negligence. When it is a workable regime, because the hazards of an activity can be avoided by being careful (which is to say, nonnegligent), there is no need to switch to strict liability. Sometimes, however, a particular type of accident cannot be prevented by taking care but can be avoided, or its consequences minimized, by shifting the activity in which the accident occurs to another locale, where the risk or harm of an accident will be less ((e)), or by reducing the scale of the activity in order to minimize the number of accidents caused by it ((f)). Shavell, *Strict Liability versus Negligence,* 9 J. Legal Stud. 1 (1980). By making the actor strictly liable—by denying him in other words, an excuse based on his inability to avoid accidents by being more careful—we give him an incentive, missing in a negligence regime, to experiment with methods of preventing accidents that involve not greater exertions of care, assumed to be futile, but instead relocating, changing, or reducing (perhaps to the vanishing point) the activity giving rise to the accident. The greater the risk of an accident ((a)) and the costs of an accident if one occurs ((b)), the more we want the actor to consider the possibility of making accident-reducing activity changes; the stronger, therefore, is the case for strict liability. Finally, if an activity is extremely common ((d)), like driving an automobile, it is unlikely either that its hazards are perceived as great or that there is no technology of care available to minimize them; so the case for strict liability is weakened.

The court then went on to rule that strict liability was inappropriate in the case at hand:

The relevant activity is transportation, not manufacturing and shipping. This essential distinction the plaintiff ignores. But even if the defendant is treated as a transporter and not merely a shipper, the plaintiff has not shown that the transportation of acrylonitrile in bulk by rail through populated areas is so hazardous an activity, even when due care is exercised, that the law should seek to create—perhaps quixotically—incentives to relocate the activity to nonpopulated areas, or to reduce the scale of the activity, or to switch to transporting acrylonitrile by road rather than by rail. . . . It is no more realistic to propose to reroute the shipment of all hazardous materials around Chicago than it is to propose the relocation of homes adjacent to the Blue Island switching yard to more distant suburbs. It may be less realistic. Brutal though it may seem to say it, the inappropriate use to which land is being put in the Blue Island yard and neighborhood may be, not the transportation of hazardous chemicals, but residential living. The analogy is to building your home between the runways at O'Hare.

One further element of the court's reasoning is of interest. The plaintiff's attorneys argued that the cost of the spill should be shifted to American Cyanamid because it was a larger corporation than Indian Harbor Belt Railroad. Here is the court's reply.

The briefs hew closely to the Restatement, [the Restatement is a summary of the law] whose approach to the issue of strict liability is mainly *allocative* rather than *distributive*. By this we mean that the emphasis is on picking a liability regime (negligence or strict liability) that will control the particular class of accidents in question most effectively, rather than on finding the deepest pocket and placing liability there. At argument, however, the plaintiff's lawyer invoked distributive considerations by pointing out that Cyanamid is a huge firm and the Indiana Harbor Belt Railroad a fifty-mile-long switching line that almost went broke in the winter of 1979, when the accident occurred. Well, so what? A corporation is not a living person but a set of contracts the terms of which determine who will bear the brunt of liability. Tracing the incidence of a cost is a complex undertaking which the plaintiff sensibly has made no effort to assume, since its legal relevance would be dubious. We add only that however small the plaintiff may be, it has mighty parents: it is a jointly owned subsidiary of Conrail and the Soo line.

Do you think the court was dismissing the possibility of decreasing secondary accident costs or simply ruling that the plaintiff's attorney had done a lousy job?

SECONDARY AND TERTIARY ACCIDENT COSTS

In application, strict products liability is likely to be very similar to negligence when it comes to primary accident costs. In addition, strict liability probably has advantages over negligence with respect to tertiary and secondary accident costs. The advantage may be so great that we would prefer to find manufacturers strictly liable even if the primary cost of the accident is more than the expected harm.

This latter idea—that even if primary accident costs are higher, strict liability may be preferable—may seem nonsensical. Why require people or businesses to waste money? Suppose we have a case in which the comparison between the expected cost of an accident and the costs of prevention is a close call. In the lawnmower example, it might be that the prevention costs are $100,000 and the expected accident cost is $90,000. First, note that no one knows this in advance and—to the extent a court has to work through the process with expert witnesses, attorneys, judges, jurors, court reporters and the like—it may be that we save substantial amounts in tertiary costs by applying strict liability. In fact, just accounting for tertiary costs, it may be less expensive to apply strict liability. As soon as tertiary costs are greater than $10,000, then prevention costs ($100,000) are lower than expected accident costs ($90,000) plus tertiary costs.

There is also the possibility that consumers prefer the strict liability standard even if the (expected) accident costs are relatively small compared to higher prices charged because of strict liability. Suppose somebody has wealth equal to $120,000. He can either buy an unsafe lawnmower for $20,000 and run a risk of 0.05 that he forgets to shut off the lawnmower, which causes damage equal to $40,000. Or he can buy a very safe lawnmower with a lever installed that shuts off the mower if left alone with no risk of damage. The price of a safe lawnmower is $23,000. Assume that the utility he derives from the two lawnmowers (in terms of the ease and comfort they give in mowing the lawn) is the same. We will concentrate on his wealth. In the first case, after buying the lawnmower, he has $100,000 with a 0.05 probability that the lawnmower might cause damage that will reduce his financial wealth by $40,000 to $60,000. So his expected wealth when he has bought the unsafe lawnmower is

$$(0.95 \times \$100,000) + (0.05 \times \$60,000) = \$98,000$$

After buying the safe lawnmower, his wealth is $97,000. That is also his expected wealth because the lawnmower is totally safe and will not cause any damage. If this person is risk-averse, he will always prefer the safe lawnmower in terms of utility even though it is more expensive.

This is illustrated in Figure 16.1. The utility curve of a risk-averse person is concave because his marginal utility is decreasing. If he buys the safe lawnmower, his wealth will be $97,000, unchanged all the time. This corresponds with a utility level equal to D in the figure. If he buys the unsafe lawnmower, his wealth will be $100,000 for 95 percent of the time and $60,000 for 5 percent of the time. His expected wealth will be $98,000. The utility level corresponding with wealth $100,000 equals A. The utility level corresponding with wealth $60,000 equals B. His expected utility is a linear combination of 95 percent A and 5 percent B. A linear combination would be the straight, dotted line connecting points A and B. In our example, the expected utility level on that dotted line is C, corresponding to expected wealth $98,000. Because of the concave utility function, point C lies below

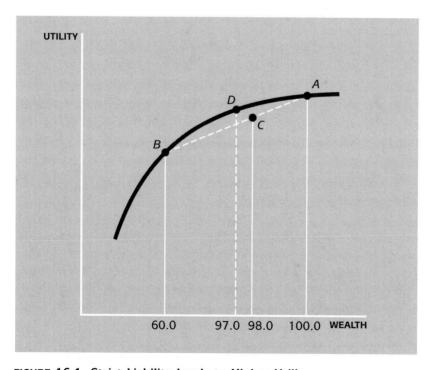

FIGURE 16.1 Strict Liability Leads to Higher Utility

point D. The utility of the unsafe mower is lower than the utility of the safe mower even though the safe lawnmower is more expensive. But paying the extra $3,000 for the safe lawnmower implies that there is no risk whatsoever and that gives the risk-averse consumer more utility. In this case the "insurance premium" paid by the consumer is worth the risk avoidance and so his utility is higher. This is true even though the risk premium is $3,000 and the expected loss is only $2,000 (0.05 × $40,000). But that does not always need to be the case. Suppose the probability of something happening is very, very small. In terms of the figure, point C will move very close to point A. If point C is very close to A, the utility of that C can be higher than point D. In that case, the consumer would prefer the unsafe mower to the safe mower, because the "insurance premium" in the safe mower ($3,000) is then too high compared with the risk the consumer is running.

The argument is that strict products liability may minimize the costs of accidents even if primary costs are not minimized. From this perspective, strict liability would seem to be the better of the two standards. A question that remains is whether it is appropriate for products liability law to be applied so that it essentially forces people to buy insurance. We will return to this question later.

LAW AND ECONOMICS IN ACTION 16.1

LAWYERS, GUNS, AND MONEY

Hardly a week goes by that you do not read in the newspaper a tragic story about someone being accidentally shot by a gun. Sometimes it is a child playing alone. Sometimes teenagers are playing around. It might occur to you to ask, What could be more dangerous than a gun and aren't gun manufacturers constantly paying damages to those who are hurt by the products? Recently, those injured accidentally by guns and their relatives have filed actions against gun manufacturers. You can see the problems they have: Products liability is about products that are in one way or another defective and therefore unreasonably dangerous. Guns, knives, spears, swords, and all kinds of other weapons are in fact dangerous, but they may not be defective. In fact, they may just be really good at doing exactly what they are designed to do. To avoid this obvious problem with invoking products liability law, the claim has been made that guns that do not include child-proof locks—analogous to medicine bottles—are unreasonably dangerous. This effort has not been successful (although some state laws do require child-proof locks) as a matter of products liability law—again, because a gun without a lock is not viewed as defective.[3] This may lead you to think about cigarettes, another obviously dangerous product. Here the efforts of plaintiffs have been more successful. The issue here, however, has often been about the adequacy of the warning that appears on cigarette packages. Even though the warnings indicate that cigarettes may make you sick, they did not tell smokers that cigarettes could be addictive, and advertising suggested that smoking was safe. Interestingly, one of the biggest hurdles faced by smokers was government regulation. The warnings on cigarettes were required by the federal government. The tobacco manufacturers argued that because they complied with the federal government requirements, they should not be liable to smokers who became sick. The U.S. Supreme Court ruled that complying with federal labeling requirements did not mean manufacturers were not liable for misleading the public.

CHOICE, MARKET FAILURE, AND SAFETY

In the torts you have seen up to this point, the typical scenario is someone injuring someone accidentally or even intentionally, but nothing is bought or sold and typically the parties do not have a relationship. In the case of products liability, this is different. The parties do have a contractual relationship and, at least ideally, just as they bargain about price and quantity, they could bargain about different qualities of the item being purchased. In fact, they could even bargain about the risks for which the manufacturer will be liable and the maximum amount of damages that could be paid. It may surprise you to learn that many courts say that contract terms about these last two matters *cannot* be enforced.

The idea of tort law becoming involved when the risk could be allocated via private agreements between parties may concern you further if you believe that products liability may lead to higher prices and

---

3. See *Halliday v. Sturm, Ruger & Co.*, 770 A.2d 1072 (Md. 2001).

fewer choices in the market. Figure 16.2 shows the supply (S) and demand (D) for lawnmowers before products liability has come into play. This is a lawnmower like your grandfather probably owned. The price is P_1 and the quantity is Q_1. Now suppose a couple of cases are decided against manufacturers because stones shoot out from the mower, injuring people. The manufacturers then correct the design of their mowers, which increases the cost of production. The supply curve shifts to S_2 to illustrate the higher cost of production. Next, there are a few successful lawsuits by people who were injured when mowers that were left standing happened to roll away. Now, manufacturers are all compelled to install the automatic-off switch and the supply curve shifts to S_3. And, of course, there are some parts on a mower that tend to get hot and can singe your skin if you touch them. You know the rest. After a few suits by people who touched the hot parts, mower producers use high-tech heat-resistant parts where all the hot parts used to be and we go to S_4. The new price is P_4 and

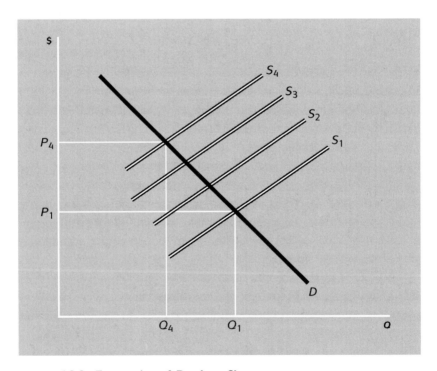

FIGURE 16.2 Economics of Product Change

you either buy a "fully equipped" mower or no mower at all. More-over, because output is lower—now Q_4—the level of employment, perhaps in a small community, may decrease. The same kind of analysis might be applied to cars. Even these days, some people might want to buy a car without airbags and other required safety features.

It seems likely that strict products liability results in higher prices and less variety. It is less clear what the ultimate impact on quantity will be. This is because as the lawnmower "improves," we are actually describing a different product. This may mean that demand increases or decreases. For example, as the lawnmower becomes safer, some people who did not mow their own yards may elect to buy mowers and do their own lawn work. The result would be that the impact on the quantity sold would be somewhat—or even totally—offset. In addition, even with strict products liability, there are ways for consumers to express different preferences for safety. For example, a person buying a full-size Mercedes Benz is probably more interested in safety than someone buying a 50 cc motor scooter.

Still, as a general matter, strict products liability probably does mean less product variety and, consequently, fewer levels of insurance. Consumers may pay more for a product due to the insurance element when they would prefer to self-insure or buy insurance elsewhere. If consumers have preferences about the different elements of products, why not abolish products liability and allow the parties involved to bargain about these matters on an individualized basis?[4] In other words, why not allow a market for safety to "work?"

You may want to consider this question in light of a trip you might take to a store to buy a new bicycle. Would you be willing to read all the small print in the written contract, if there is one, and to go through the owner's manual? Do you think you would understand the passages in the manual about "warranties" and "disclaimers"—not just about one option but about five different models? Just how much do you know about the strength of various metals? How about the density of the rubber in the tires necessary to withstand hitting a small pothole? The point is that transaction costs facing you—particularly of the information-gathering variety—would be enormous, leaving you

4. See generally, Alan Schwartz, "Proposals for Products Liability Reform: A Theoretical Synthesis," *Yale Law Journal* 97 (1988): 353.

with the choice of taking many risks—some of which you would be happy to pay to avoid—or incurring huge costs in order to shape the bargain to reflect your preferences.

CONSUMER SAFETY AND LAWN DARTS

This chapter is principally devoted to the ways rules of liability affect the allocation of externalities. Sometimes the risk of externalities is viewed as so great that the government will step in. This possibility raises the fundamental question of when safety issues should be dealt with by the courts and when the federal government should be involved. The Consumer Product Safety Commission can prohibit the sale of certain products or require manufacturers to include warning labels. A good example of how the process works is the commission's 1988 ban on lawn darts. Lawn darts were like oversized darts that one tossed in the air in hopes that they could descend—with a satisfying thud—on a target. The darts had a nasty tendency from time to time to land on someone's head. The commission's comparison of costs and benefits follows:

BENEFITS

The benefits of the rule will accrue through a decrease in the deaths and injuries associated with lawn darts. While the rule was originally intended to address the risk of skull puncture injuries to children, all lawn darts are found to present this risk, and their elimination will also eliminate the punctures of other parts of the body, as well as the lacerations, fractures, and other injuries, that have been associated with lawn darts in the past. . . . An analysis by the Commission's Directorate for Epidemiology indicates that about 670 lawn-dart-related injuries have occurred annually over the last ten years. Economic studies indicate that the average cost of these injuries was about $7,500 per occurrence. The estimated total yearly cost of injuries associated with lawn darts is about $5 million.

The Commission is aware of 3 deaths associated with lawn darts over the period 1970–1987. If it is assumed that other variables, such as exposure and use characteristics, have remained constant and that the Commission is aware of all such deaths, the darts may present a 17 percent risk of one death in a given year. If a statistical valuation of $2 million for loss of life were assigned, lawn darts would have additional expected losses of about $300,000 per year.

Therefore, the estimated total yearly costs of death and injury associated with lawn darts are about $5.4 million. A reduction of these injuries and of the risk of death will make up the benefits accruing from the rule. Since the average useful life of a lawn dart is estimated to be ten years, and since it should take about 20 years to phase out the lawn darts that are currently in consumers' hands, a portion of the benefits of the rule will phase in each year, until, after about 20 years, the full benefit of the rule will accrue each year and will continue as long as the rule is in effect.

The benefits derived will be further affected by the choice of substitute activities. For example, if consumers chose a risk-free lawn game as a substitute, the reduction in injury would be completely realized after the existing stocks of elongated-tipped lawn darts in consumers' hands have become worn out, been misplaced, or otherwise passed from use. However, if consumers choose a substitute with a similar or higher risk of death or injury, the expected benefits of this action will be offset.

COSTS

The costs of the rule to marketers of elongated-tipped lawn darts are the loss of future sales of a product with a demonstrated steady demand. Annual sales of these lawn darts are estimated at 1–1.5 million units, holding relatively stable in recent years. The typical retail price of a set of four lawn darts is about $5; thus, the total loss of sales will be about $5–7.5 million annually at the retail level. The intermediate and final markups of these products have been estimated at more than 50 percent of the retail price; thus, industry revenues from the sale of elongated-tipped lawn darts likely exceed $2.5 million annually. These revenues will be eliminated. However, the loss of these revenues could be largely recouped by sales of substitute products that will occupy the display and storage space previously allotted to lawn darts.

The impact of lost sales of lawn darts will be the loss of net profit associated with production and marketing of these products, less any profit derived from other products marketed in their stead.

Costs borne by consumers will take two forms. Consumers will be unable to purchase a game which has a proven popularity and will be induced to purchase alternate games to fill that demand. There are ready substitutes available, at approximately the same price; however, it is not clear whether these substitutes provide a similar level of utility (enjoyment) as the products they would replace. If consumers are compelled to purchase more costly games in order to receive the same utility as that provided by prohibited lawn darts, the rule may result in increased costs to consumers. Further, there may be a loss in consumer surplus associated with the unavailability of lawn darts if consumers were willing to pay more than they now pay at retail for the game in order to acquire it, thus indicating that they value the product in excess of the retail price. The extent of any lost consumer surplus is unknown, but is expected to be small.

The Commission also does not expect that the cost to retailers due to foregone profits from the sale of lawn darts will be substantial, since other products could be promoted in the retail space vacated by the prohibited products.

COMPARISON OF COSTS AND BENEFITS

As explained above, the quantifiable benefits of the rule are based on an estimated saving of the $5.4 million annual cost of deaths and injuries once lawn darts are no longer in use. This figure could be offset to the extent that consumers choose to engage in activities that involve risk during the time they would otherwise be playing lawn darts.

So, what do you think? Is it possible that the commission has prohibited something completely when the efficient outcome would be simply to make sure any externalities are internalized?

To be sure, in a world of no products liability, it is likely that private companies and ratings services would evolve—as they have in some industries already—and there would be reports about failure rates of different products. Presumably, the prices of competing products would reflect their relative safety ratings. For example, some lawnmower manufacturers might install the safety lever automatically and sell their mower for $5 more and advertise their product as "the safety mower." Still, these services would come at a cost. In effect, it is not clear how effectively a market for various levels of safety could work.

In addition, not only would transaction costs go up but so too—because of a loss in economies of scale—would manufacturing costs for each particular level of safety. When applied properly, products liability lowers transaction costs by, in effect, treating the manufacturer and you as though you have agreed on certain levels of product safety.

So, on the one hand, with more choices there will be higher transaction costs, higher secondary and tertiary costs, and probably higher costs for any given level of safety. On the other hand, the impact of fewer choices should not be understated. People who pay more for items that include features that they value less than their costs lose consumer surplus. You can understand this by thinking about being required to buy a car that comes "fully equipped" with accessories you have little interest in. As with so many things, the overall economic impact of strict products liability is an empirical question.

CASE 16.2 Drug Safety: The Laetrile Case: *United States v. Rutherford*, 442 U.S. 544 (1979)

Another area in which the government has replaced the tort system with direct regulation is in the approval of medications. The Food and Drug Administration is charged with ensuring that drugs are safe and effective. Do you think drug safety could be handled through contract and tort law? To help focus your thoughts, here is the language from one of the more interesting opinions by the Supreme Court on the issue of drug regulation. The drug Laetrile was taken primarily by terminally ill patients who thought there was at least some chance it would prolong their lives. The Food and Drug Administration had refused to approve the drug. On appeal, a court held that its sale and distribution was legal because the concept of "safe and effective" was not really relevant in the context of the terminally ill. The issue then went to the Supreme Court, which reasoned as follows:

> In the Court of Appeals' view, an implied exemption from the Act was justified because the safety and effectiveness standards set forth in § 201(p)(1) could have "no reasonable application" to terminally ill patients. 582 F.2d, at 1236. We disagree. . . .
>
> A drug is effective . . . if there is general recognition among experts, founded on substantial evidence, that the drug in fact produces the results claimed for it under prescribed conditions. Contrary to the Court of Appeals' apparent assumption, effectiveness does not necessarily denote capacity to cure. In the treatment of any illness, terminal or otherwise, a drug is effective if it fulfills, by objective indices, its sponsor's claims of prolonged life, improved physical condition, or reduced pain.
>
> So too, the concept of safety . . . is not without meaning for terminal patients. Few if any drugs are completely safe in the sense that they may be taken by all persons in all circumstances without risk. Thus, the Commissioner generally considers a drug safe when the expected therapeutic gain justifies the risk entailed by its use. For the terminally ill, as for anyone else, a drug is unsafe if its potential for inflicting death or physical injury is not offset by the possibility of therapeutic benefit. Indeed, the Court of Appeals implicitly acknowledged that safety considerations have relevance for terminal cancer patients by restricting authorized use of Laetrile to intravenous injections for persons under a doctor's supervision.
>
> Moreover, there is a special sense in which the relationship between drug effectiveness and safety has meaning in the context of incurable illnesses. An otherwise harmless drug can be dangerous to any patient if it does not produce its purported therapeutic effect. But if an individual suffering from a potentially fatal disease rejects conventional therapy in favor of a drug with no demonstrable curative properties, the consequences can be irreversible. For this reason, even before the 1962

Amendments incorporated an efficacy standard into new drug application procedures, the FDA considered effectiveness when reviewing the safety of drugs used to treat terminal illness. The FDA's practice also reflects the recognition, amply supported by expert medical testimony in this case, that with diseases such as cancer it is often impossible to identify a patient as terminally ill except in retrospect. Cancers vary considerably in behavior and in responsiveness to different forms of therapy. Even critically ill individuals may have unexpected remissions and may respond to conventional treatment.

The Court thus held that the FDA had acted appropriately by prohibiting the sale of Laetrile. Contract law requires sellers of products to make good on their claims or pay damages. Tort law protects individuals from the harm caused by unsafe products. Why not leave the question of drug safety and efficacy to these areas of law?

HOW FAR DOES IT GO?

When we started this examination of torts a few chapters ago, the basic model centered around making sure that those who harm others internalize the full costs of those activities in hopes of minimizing the costs of accidents. It is sometimes hard to see products liability in exactly that light. A manufacturer places an item in the market and consumers can take it or leave it, but they assume that it's safe. The way to square products liability with the general economic theory is to "view" the manufacturer as creating an externality by producing a dangerous product. Although this may strain the notion of externality, it does typically allocate the risk to the party best able to respond to and lower that cost. On the other hand, it does not take an examination of too many cases to lead one to question whether the idea that the manufacturer is at fault has gone too far because the consumer may be better able to avoid the loss.

To take it to one extreme, we do not want all manufacturers to feel compelled to produce automobiles that are essentially like tanks. Many of the features on those cars would turn out to be useless in all but the most extreme circumstances and the costs of the cars and their operation would be out of the reach of most people. To some extent, the idea of whether the product was defective in manufacture or design takes care of this problem. Similarly, we do not want manufacturers to be liable when someone uses the product in a way it was not designed to be used or when the manufacturer could not anticipate its misuse. In these instances, it is difficult to see the harm as resulting from activity by the manufacturer as much as it is from the use by the buyer. In fact, some years ago, it was estimated that two-thirds of injuries resulting from product use were actually the result of misuse by consumers.[5] And unless some line is drawn, manufacturers will be faced with a choice of whether to anticipate and react to every possible misuse or to require all customers to pay more in order to provide insurance for misusers. If you regard yourself as a relatively cautious and intelligent person, this is likely to be unattractive.

You do not have to have a vivid imagination to come up with your own strange and tragic examples involving misuse. A car owner ignores repeated instructions found in the manual and on the car jack not to crawl under the car while it is jacked up. Someone else gets drunk and falls asleep in a car with the engine running. His foot lands on the accelerator, the car revs for hours and eventually catches fire. A person uses a lightweight chain saw designed for limbs no bigger than three inches in diameter on a ten-inch tree trunk. The saw jumps backward and he or she is cut badly. The stories go on and on.

Obviously, at some point, the burden on the manufacturer of avoiding these incidents far exceeds the benefits. Under a strict liability standard without exceptions, the accidents would occur and the customers and shareholders would end up compensating the "victims." In fact, in these instances, there is little incentive to minimize the costs of the accidents. For manufacturers, it is too expensive and victims are compensated even though they might have avoided the loss at little or no cost.

Obviously, in order to be efficient, the risk of some of the harm resulting from the use of products must be shifted back to users. In terms of the Hand formula (see Chapter 13), the burden to the misusers is likely to be lower than the expected harm. Courts have, in fact, developed a number of defenses that manufacturers may use to avoid liability.[6] These doctrines are slightly different but all come down to a decision that the "victim" was in a position to avoid the

5. Mary Fisk, "An Interview with John Belington," *Trial* 14 (February 1978): 25.

6. David G. Owen, "Products Liability: User Misconduct Defenses," *South Carolina Law Review* 52 (2000): 1.

harm relatively inexpensively. An example is *Daniell v. Ford Motor Co.*[7] The plaintiff, intending to commit suicide, crawled into the trunk of a Ford and then changed her mind. She was trapped for nine days and attempted to recover from Ford since there was no latch inside the trunk. The court rejected the claim after listing a variety of uses for a trunk and concluded "the plaintiff's use of the trunk compartment as a means to commit suicide was an unforeseeable use."

You should not conclude that manufacturers are not liable whenever there is a misuse of the product. The key is the foreseeability of the misuse. For example, although it is a misuse of an automobile to crash it into a tree or another automobile, this is the type of misuse that manufacturers are expected to anticipate. Thus, a defense by the manufacturer of an uncrashworthy car that cars are not intended to be in collisions is unlikely to succeed. Obviously, this is a gray area with respect to how risks should be allocated to minimize accident costs. The problem is that misuse has a joint care–like quality. Potential misusers are obviously in the best position to avoid the misuse in the first place. On the other hand, if misuse is to occur a certain percentage of the time, manufacturers are in a better position to make product modifications that will minimize the consequences. The idea of holding manufacturers liable for foreseeable misuse only is an effort to recognize this relationship.

WARNING LABELS

One way products can be defective is by not including adequate warnings about possible hazards. In fact, it will probably surprise you to learn that most products liability actions are based on a failure to provide an adequate warning. The inadequate warning element of products liability looks, by necessity, more like negligence than strict liability. To understand how, think about what it would mean to be strictly liable for not labeling a product. For example, would the maker of a car be liable if someone drives his or her car into the side of a building and the manufacturer had neglected to put a big warning label on the visor that said "DRIVING THIS VEHICLE INTO THE SIDE OF A BUILDING MAY DAMAGE THE CAR, THE BUILDING, AND YOU."

7. 581 F. Supp. 728 (New Mexico 1984).

Obviously not, and the law reflects this by finding manufacturers liable when four conditions are met. First, the manufacturer knows or should know of the possible harm. Second, those who would receive the warning must be identifiable and are likely to be unaware of the risk. Third, a warning can be effectively communicated. Fourth, the risk of harm justifies issuing a warning. In short, the warning label analysis is one that tends to place the responsibility on the party who can most inexpensively avoid a harm by taking action—in this case, warning those who are otherwise unlikely to know.

In reality, the issue of the economically efficient level of warnings is made especially difficult because it depends on the cognitive abilities of customers, and this can vary considerably from person to person. This issue has also been extended to the question of when warnings should be in two or more languages. You may think there is an easy answer here—the more warnings the better. After all, the cost of an additional warning would seem quite low. It's just a small amount of additional ink on the product or packing. Thus, any plaintiff would seem to be able to win a case by simply illustrating that the manufacturer could have made sure the accident did not occur for no more than a pittance. While it may be true that additional warnings do reduce manufacturers' liability, it is not clear that this is an efficient outcome if the additional print actually makes things more confusing or discourages people from reading any of the warnings.

A legal policy that encourages warnings like the one for the Batman cape quoted at the outset of this chapter ("Cape will not help you fly") may lead to ineffficient levels of warning. For example, consider the following that might be found on the packaging of a Halloween Dracula costume:

1. Caution: This plastic mask will not deflect sharp objects.
2. Child should not ingest parts of costume.
3. Dark colors may make child more difficult to see by passing motorists.
4. This cape will not assist child in flying.
5. Do not use while riding a bicycle as cape can become entangled in spokes.
6. The materials in this costume contain plastics that will melt and could injure the child without igniting if exposed to high temperatures.

7. The wearing of a Dracula costume does not mean child needs blood as a food source.

Research has shown that as the amount of information and warnings goes up, the attention of the reader declines. Thus, as an economic matter, the warnings that make the most sense are about hazards a parent is unlikely to anticipate. In the above example, warnings about dark colors and not flying—obvious matters to any parent—can have the effect of crowding out warnings about hazards a parent might not anticipate. Courts generally do not penalize a manufacturer for excessive warnings that may decrease the effectiveness of more legitimate warnings. After all, plaintiffs complain about failure to warn but not about too many warnings. There is a way, however, that courts have begun to address the excess warning problem. As one court put it, "requiring too many warnings trivializes and undermines the entire purpose of the rule, drowning out cautions against latent dangers of which a user might not otherwise be aware. Such a requirement would neutralize the effectiveness of warnings as an inexpensive way to allow consumers to adjust their behavior based on knowledge of a product's inherent dangers."[8] Excessive warnings about trivial matters may have the effect of rendering more important warnings less than adequate and, therefore, lead to liability for excessive warning.

QUESTIONS FOR DISCUSSION

1. Do you understand why strict liability seems to work better than negligence when the issue is an ongoing practice that causes harm to others? Explain.

2. In a car crash, do you think auto manufacturers should be liable if someone is injured by an armrest on the inside of a door? What if he or she hits her head on the rearview mirror? Explain your thinking. How about the cap on aspirin? Should the manufacturer be liable if a child pops off the cap—even though allegedly "childproof"—and becomes sick from ingesting aspirin?

8. *Loraine v. Hobart Corp.*, 700 N.E.2d 303, 308 (N.Y. 1998).

3. Should the manufacturers of alcoholic beverages be strictly liable when someone drinks too much and winds up in a car wreck? Why not? How would you distinguish that from a lawnmower with a safety guard that prevents spraying rocks?

4. Suppose a manufacturer of automobiles produced an inexpensive model that had no seat belts, air bags, or other safety features. It sells the car only to those willing to sign an agreement under which they agree not to sue the manufacturer if they are injured in the car. Would you enforce these agreements?

5. Go back to the "insurance example" about the safe and unsafe lawnmower. Assume that the damage caused by the unsafe mower is still $40,000, but the probability of the accident happening is only 0.01. What happens to point C in Figure 16.1? Will the consumer still be better off buying the safe mower?

6. In this chapter, you have seen a variety of methods for reducing harms. Products liability law requires manufacturers to choose between avoiding the harm to others or paying damages. The Consumer Product Safety Commission can ban products completely or require the use of warning labels. The Food and Drug Administration will not allow the sale of a drug unless it is proven safe and effective. Does it strike you that there may be considerable overlap here? Can you articulate an economic justification for so many different methods of controlling the harm products may cause?

CHAPTER SEVENTEEN

Malpractice

I N CHAPTER 16, YOU SAW WHAT CAN HAPPEN WHEN A product you buy in the market injures you. Generally, in those instances, manufacturers are said to be strictly liable. That is, they must internalize the cost of the harm done even if it could not have been avoided at a lower cost. Now think about what else you buy in the market: services. Just as faulty screw on a lawnmower can cause injury, you can be injured if a physician makes the wrong diagnosis or the dentist's drill slips and cuts you while he or she is performing a root canal or an attorney neglects to bring up an important point in a case in which he or she represents you. Rather than *products liability* the focus is on *service liability*. In this area the standard applied is one of negligence as opposed to strict liability.

When the service is provided by a member of the professions, the word that is often used is *malpractice*. You should note that malpractice is just a term of art and it does not indicate that the standard applied to physicians, accountants, or architects is any different from that applied to anyone else. The issue in all negligence cases is whether the person acted reasonably given the circumstances. Or in the words of one court, "when a person involved possesses superior knowledge in a given subject, he or she will be required to exercise the prudence of a reasonable person who possesses such knowledge."[1] You also

---

1. *Jewell v. Beckstine*, 386 A.2d 597 (Penn., 1978). See generally, W. Page Keeton, Dan B. Dobbs, Robert E. Keeton, and David G. Owen, *The Law of Torts*, 5th ed. (St. Paul: West Group, 1994), 183–193.

know that the economist's version of the test is whether the marginal cost of prevention is above or below the expected marginal cost of the harm.

To illustrate that this standard is broadly applied, think about this case. In *Jewell v. Beckstine,* a milk truck driver walked into a dairy and slipped and fell on manure. The driver sued the dairy owner on the basis of negligence but failed to recover when the court found that he was contributorily negligent. The driver's own negligence was based on his knowledge about the hazards anyone might encounter walking through a dairy. In other words, given his knowledge, walking without being careful about the manure was not reasonable. On the other hand, a person with no knowledge about dairies who slipped on the floor might be regarded as having acted reasonably.

This is not to say that a case involving a dairy farmer and a physician would look the same. In the case of a physician or an engineer or a comparable professional, it would almost certainly be necessary to call in specialists to testify as expert witnesses. In other words, while the *reasonable care under the circumstances* standard remains, it may be difficult for jurors to know what is reasonable without the guidance of experts. In a malpractice case against a physician, it is likely to be necessary to have other physicians or medical specialists testify about what action would be reasonable under the circumstances. For example, suppose someone came to a doctor with a pain in his leg and the doctor did not have an X-ray made and it was later discovered that had an X-ray been taken a prolonged period of pain and disability could have been avoided with treatment. In a subsequent suit, experts may be necessary to testify that reasonableness under those circumstances means that a person with the knowledge of a physician would have ordered an X-ray.

When it comes to malpractice, note a possible distinction between what an efficiency standard would be and the standard that is actually applied. The efficiency standard, as you know, involves a comparison of marginal costs and benefits. In practice, courts often ask whether the defendant's conduct was consistent with *custom.* In other words, did the physician do what is ordinarily done under the circumstances? Thus, unless the profession's customs are also accident-cost-minimizing practices, there is no guarantee that judicial outcomes will be consistent with efficiency standards.

If the matter of malpractice can all be boiled down to the usual marginal analysis or even a possibly less exacting standard of custom, you may wonder what all the hubbub is about. After all, what negligence seems to say is that if you pass up an opportunity to act efficiently by avoiding an injury at a lower cost than the injury itself, you must internalize the cost. Still, hardly a day goes by without a story appearing in the newspaper about high malpractice insurance rates. Sometimes the word "crisis" is added to give you the impression that something akin to the polar ice caps melting is afoot. The crisis, it is argued by physicians, can be treated if the risk of liability were lowered by disallowing or capping damages for pain and suffering or punitive damages. From an economic perspective, this solves the problem only if pain and suffering have been systematically overvalued and if the policy justifications for punitive damages do not hold.

When all the hyperbole and "spin" is put aside, there is no doubt that physicians, in particular, are now facing tort liability more than ever and that insurance rates have gone up. The question from an economic standpoint is whether this is a move toward more or less efficiency. For example, while the current view among physicians is that something must be "wrong," there is empirical evidence to suggest that what was wrong was underinternalization in the past and that the change toward greater physician liability is actually a correction in favor of greater efficiency. In fact, one study done in the early 1980s found that only one person in ten who is a victim of medical negligence filed an action and only some of them actually prevailed. This would mean that there was underinternalization on a massive scale and, if there was a "crisis," it had more to do with the externalities caused by poor medical care than with malpractice insurance rates that are too high.

Although it is hardly in the realm of polar ice caps melting or rain forests disappearing and the underlying theory and goals of requiring internalization are no different with professionals than with anyone else, there are some elements of the malpractice question that deserve special attention. It is to those matters that the rest of this chapter is devoted. The first issue is relevant in most potential malpractice contexts but is discussed most frequently in the context of medical care. The issue is whether potential liability encourages over-testing or the

practice of defensive medicine. Defensive medicine involves procedures that lower the possibility of physician liability but are not cost-
justified from the point of view of social costs. This is addressed in
the next section. The following one examines the question of whether
increased physician liability can lead to a physician "shortage." This
analysis applies to any professional, but hardly anyone these days
seems to be worried about a shortage of lawyers or architects. Finally,
in the last section, the impact of varying some of the policies affecting physician liability is considered.

MALPRACTICE AND DEFENSIVE MEDICINE

The issue of inefficiently high levels of care or the practice of defensive medicine is best viewed from the perspective of the usual negligence analysis and its relationship to supply and demand. Figure 17.1
is a graph you have seen before. S is the supply and, as you know,
reflects the marginal cost of production. The graph represents the

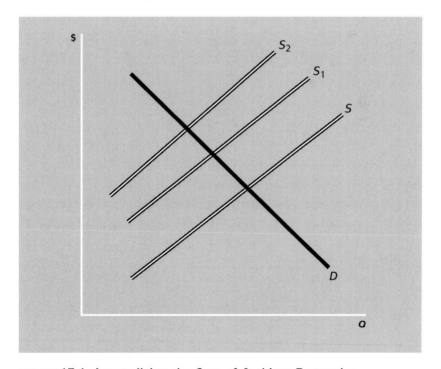

FIGURE **17.1** **Internalizing the Cost of Accident Prevention**

position of a potential defendant. Let's say it is our pizza delivery business from way back in Chapter 13. It is the one whose drivers tend to back over mailboxes. If he can avoid paying for those mailboxes his supply curve would be S. Suppose the expected mailbox damages cost is $200 and the damage could be avoided by installing wide screen mirrors for a total of $100. The choice for the defendant is to internalize the cost of prevention, causing supply to shift to S_1, or the cost of the damage, causing S to shift to S_2. The choice is an easy one and the accident will be avoided.

Now let's add a complication by opening another option to the pizza business owner. He can pay for the accidents or he can buy the mirrors or he could somehow get homeowners to put their mailboxes in safer locations.[2] Suppose the cost to customers of mailbox relocation is $150. Obviously, the efficient outcome is to install the mirrors, but this is a cost the business must internalize. It is in the business owner's *private* interest to encourage the less efficient outcome of having homeowners relocate their mailboxes.

The idea that there is a third and less efficient choice and that the cost of that choice is shifted to others can now be carried over to physicians. Remember, this is a market in which patient/customers are at a serious disadvantage information-wise and must rely on physicians for information about what actions to take. The temptation for a physician may be to avoid internalization of efficient levels of treatment in favor of more expensive treatment that you pay for. Here is a simple illustration. Suppose you go to see your physician with a stomachache. The physician could spend thirty minutes with you and almost every factor that could explain your problem could be covered. In thirty minutes, however, the physician might see three patients and generate more revenue than only seeing you. Another possibility is to see you for ten minutes and then order you to take a number of diagnostic tests. The thirty-minute office visit and the ten-minute visit plus tests may be equally effective in terms of diagnosing the source of your problem but one is obviously better for the physician. The physician, however, may also be motivated by avoiding liability at the lowest personal cost. The physician in this example has two motiva-

2. To accomplish this, the pizza business owner might attend a weekly city commission meeting and urge the commission to require that mailboxes be placed away from driveways.

tions to see you for only ten minutes: (1) He can earn more by seeing three clients instead of one in half an hour; (2) he reduces his risk of liability. In fact, ordering more and more tests reduces the probability of *liability* if there is a misdiagnosis, but it does not reduce the probability of the misdiagnosis itself. Thus, off you go for a battery of tests that are more expensive than the physician would have been but no more likely to determine what treatment you need.

You can see how this problem plays out whenever there is unevenness in the level of understanding. An attorney may spend extra time researching a case knowing that you will pay the bill. An engineer may devote extra time to the design of a factory or order more than an efficient amount of structural support because, again, he will not internalize the cost of the precautions, and you do not know enough to question the treatment. You may ask whether physicians actually do practice defensive medicine. This is not an easy question to answer. To some extent, the answer depends on how accepting you are of efforts to quantify the cost of sickness and suffering. If you do not think human suffering can be reduced to monetary values, you may think defensive medicine is a great idea. On the other hand, we obviously all feel there is some point at which a test is not worth its cost or we would all constantly be visiting doctors and being tested for improbable conditions.

The empirical results on defensive medicine are not conclusive. One study attempted to get at the issue by examining whether decreases in physician liability resulted in decreases in the cost of care, which in turn had an impact on mortality or medical complications. The study found that legal reforms that make physicians less vulnerable to lawsuits did lower the cost of care from 5 percent to 9 percent but had no substantial impact on actual medical outcomes.[3] In effect, lower exposure of liability may have led to less testing. On the other hand, another study indicates physicians may not respond to the risk of liability by over-testing. Instead, they may avoid those areas of practice that are associated with higher risks of liability.[4] This too can be seen as practicing "defensive medicine."

3. Daniel Kessler and Mark McClellen, "Do Doctors Practice Defensive Medicine?" *Quarterly Journal of Economics* (May 1996): 353.

4. Robert Quinn, "Medical Malpractice Insurance: The Reputational Effect and Defensive Medicine," *Journal of Risk and Insurance* 65 (1998): 467.

Given the theory, it may surprise you that physicians are not practicing defensive medicine at very high levels. There are probably three reasons it is not more prevalent. First, physicians typically buy liability insurance that pays when they are negligent. You might expect more defensive medicine in order to lower liability rates. The complication is that most liability insurance rates do not depend on an individual physician's experience but on the overall experience of physicians in a particular specialty in the same geographic area. In effect, a physician is not able to lower insurance rates by over-testing.

Second, in our model, the physician was able to pass the cost of accident avoidance to you because you were relatively ignorant. In reality, it is likely that some other entity pays for most of your medical care and that entity is relatively sophisticated. That entity plays a role in determining what diagnostic tests it will pay for when its members have particular symptoms. Physicians are less likely to require tests that your insurer will not cover. Of course, the physician can still ask you to have the test performed and you will have to pay for it. However, physicians are likely to find it awkward to order tests that your insurer has deemed unnecessary.

In our cynical age this may seem odd, but keep in mind the possibility that physicians do not take maximum advantage of your ignorance in order to avoid liability. Physicians are, after all, subject to standards of professionalism and also must be conscious of their reputations. Over-testing beyond some level would certainly draw the wrong kind of attention. Still, as a general matter, when you consider the part of tort law that deals with the liability of those with superior knowledge, you must be aware that the difference in information can become a factor that results is less than optimal outcomes.

CASE 17.1 Malpractice in the Courts: *Judd v. Drezga*, 105 P.3d 135 (Utah 2004)

Courts deal with malpractice claims on a regular basis. Perhaps more interesting from the standpoint of an economic analysis of law is the reaction of courts to caps on various types of damages. From an economic perspective, actors should internalize the costs of their activities and a cap that prevents that means that the full costs will not be internalized, leading to allocative inefficiency.

When courts consider caps, they consider economic matters only by implication because the question is whether a cap is lawful under the state's constitution.

In *Judd v. Drezga*, the Utah Supreme Court considered the legality of a state law placing a $250,000 cap on noneconomic damages. The cap was challenged in a suit brought on behalf of a child who was brain-damaged as a consequence of a physician's malpractice. One of the tests the court was required to apply was "whether the damage cap represents a reasonable, nonarbitrary method of reducing increasing health care costs and other dangers that the legislature views as clear social or economic evils."

> We cannot conclude that the cap on quality of life damages is arbitrary or unreasonable. The legislature's determination that it needed to respond to the perceived medical malpractice crisis was logically followed by action designed to control costs. Although malpractice insurance rates may not be entirely controlled by such matters, they are undoubtedly subject to some measure of fluctuation based on paid claims. Thus, one nonarbitrary manner of controlling such costs is to limit amounts paid out. Intuitively, the greater the amount paid on claims, the greater the increase in premiums. Limiting recovery of quality of life damages to a certain amount gives insurers some idea of their potential liability. While we recognize that such a cap heavily punishes those most severely injured, it is not unconstitutionally arbitrary merely because it does so. Rather, it is targeted to control costs in one area where costs might be controllable. Despite this court's concerns about the wisdom of depriving a few badly injured plaintiffs of full recovery, the cap is also constitutionally reasonable. Rather than cap all damages, . . . the limitation on recoverable damages in this case is narrowly tailored, by limiting quality of life damages alone. While Judd notes that Utah has not seen large damage awards in significant numbers, this position ignores at least one important factor. Although quality of life damages are very real, they are also less susceptible to quantification than purely economic damages. As amici [non parties to the case who are given permission to participate] point out, "[t]he estimated value of future costs forms the basis of the [insurance] rate-setting process." The difficulty of predicting quality of life damages must be considered by insurers when setting rates and planning reserves. At least in some measure, then, predicting and controlling future costs can result in lower insurance rates. Taken as one of a number of measures enacted to help control

health care costs, the cap on quality of life damages is thus a reasonable approach. Having determined that the damage cap is designed to eliminate a social or economic evil, and that it is a reasonable, nonarbitrary means for doing so, we conclude that [the limitation does not violate the Utah Constitution.]

The court was also asked to determine whether a limitation linked to medical malpractice was discriminatory.

While the damage cap does indeed discriminate against medical malpractice victims with the most severe noneconomic injuries, it does so reasonably, given the statute's purpose. In order to control costs and provide for the continuing availability of health care resources, the legislature was faced with a number of choices. By deciding which reforms to enact, it necessarily discriminated. However, the classifications established by the statute meet the heightened scrutiny test.

Although the classifications deny some victims a full recovery while allowing such a recovery to others, the classifications are not unconstitutional. While medical malpractice victims are deprived of a measure of their remedy where other tort victims are not, enacting damage caps on all tort victims would be imprudent and overbroad given that the legislature's goal was to control *health care* costs. Additionally, although medical malpractice victims, those with primarily noneconomic, or quality of life, damages, are punished by the limitation when compared with those whose injuries are largely economic, this discrimination is permissible given the cap's purpose of controlling costs. As noted above, "caps on noneconomic damages tend to be particularly effective in reducing costs because of the extreme variability of damage award[s] attributable to pain and suffering." Thus, it appears there is support for the proposition that a large measure of the problem identified by the legislature results from fluctuation in cases with high noneconomic damages, and a cap which targets just those problems is therefore not unconstitutional. Because the crisis identified by the legislature is primarily precipitated by the potential for large, unpredictable judgments, establishing a cap that prevents only those types of judgments is reasonably necessary to achieve the legislative purpose, despite punishing the most severely injured victims.

When attempting to resolve problems of policy, the legislature is inevitably forced to draw lines. In this instance the legislature has chosen to enact a cap, limiting the right to recover quality of life damages to $250,000. This cap severely injures young Athan, who will live a life greatly diminished by Dr. Drezga's negligence. But that is a policy choice made by the legislative branch, and we cannot say that it is unconstitutional. The legislature's purpose in enacting the damage cap is a valid and legitimate one. The cap is a reasonably necessary means of achieving that purpose, and it actually and substantially furthers it.

So, what do you think? Is there any economic reason for capping damages as long as they accurately reflect the external impact of an activity? What would be the rationale for capping only one type of damages? Do you have the sense that the insurance and physicians' lobby in Utah is fairly influential?

MALPRACTICE AND THE PHYSICIAN "SHORTAGE"

Because professionals with superior knowledge are held to different standards of what is reasonable behavior, you might ask whether the result is to discourage investments in human capital. For example, if elementary school teachers were liable for doing a sloppy job in the classroom, the number of people majoring in elementary education would probably decline. Here, we are talking about the impact of liability on the supply side of the professional labor market with the supply being of a particular type of knowledge (or a particular occupation). Of course, the more general fear is usually expressed in terms of physicians and whether increased liability will make medical education a less attractive investment leading to a possible shortage of physicians.

The theoretical explanation comes in two steps. First, consider the supply and demand for physicians in Figure 17.2. The supply curve is defined as the number of physicians that offer professional medical services, Q, for a given wage rate, W. If the wage rate for physicians is higher, more physicians will be forthcoming. The demand curve is defined as the number of physicians and their services that society wants given the wage rate it has to pay. The higher the wage rate, the smaller the demand. In reality, there would be different curves for each specialty (general practitioners, pediatricians, etc.) and possibly location (Florida, Alaska, etc.), but the simpler model will suffice. The graph shows an equilibrium at wage W and quantity Q. Whether the market for physicians is actually in equilibrium is a good question.

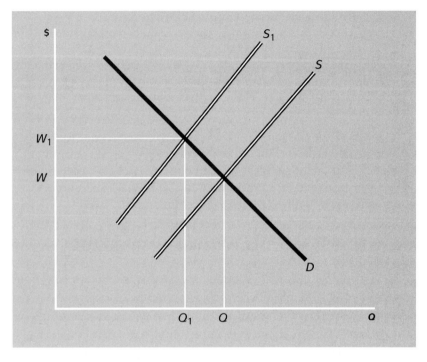

FIGURE 17.2 Physician Services and Increased Liability

Long delays in the waiting room and the need to make appointments weeks in advance suggest that rather than being in equilibrium, there is a shortage. But for now assume there is an equilibrium.

The impact of increased liability costs due to paying damages, increasing the quality of care, or buying malpractice insurance would be reflected in a shift to the left in the supply curve from S to S_1. As they face greater liability and higher malpractice insurance premiums, prospective physicians will demand a higher wage rate to compensate them for the extra professional costs. There is no question that physicians training today face a much greater level of liability risk than those in practice in the 1950s or 1960s. In fact, the number of malpractice claims rose 100 percent from 1975 to 1985.[5] As you can see, the wage that is paid for physicians' services goes up, but unless the demand the curve is perfectly inelastic, the wage increase will be less than the

5. See Patricia M. Danzon, "Liability for Medical Malpractice," *Journal of Economic Perspectives* 5 (Summer 1991): 51.

increase in cost (the vertical difference between S and S_1). This would seem to mean lower incomes and profits for physicians.

The second step in understanding the shortage argument requires you to look at a different market as depicted in Figure 17.3. Supply in this market denotes the availability of physician training, and demand is the demand for physician training. Lower incomes for physicians, or perhaps a less interesting career given a great increase in paperwork, means a shift to the left in the demand curve. A lower demand for medical education (from D to D_1) means a lower equilibrium quantity of medical education and fewer physicians as indicated by the change from Q to Q_1.

Before examining how reality stacks up with the theory, there is a technical matter that should be clear from this. Although people write and talk about physician "shortages," if the two markets work as illustrated here, there is no shortage in a technical sense. There may be fewer physicians, but as long as price is used as the market-clearing mechanism, quantity demanded and quantity supplied will be equal.

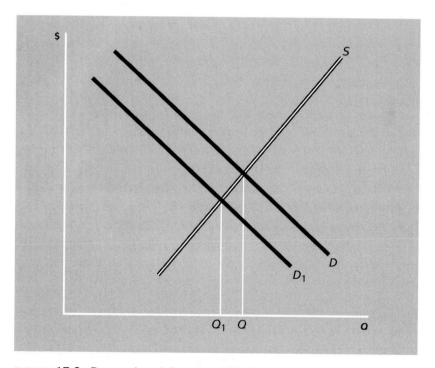

FIGURE 17.3 **Demand and Supply of Medical Training: 1**

This, however, is a different question from whether every person who could benefit from treatment by a physician has access to one.

As it turns out, both steps of the theory are probably inaccurate in terms of how things actually work. First, as an empirical matter, there is evidence that physicians quickly pass on their increased costs in the form of higher fees. Interestingly, one study indicates that whatever the cost increase is, the fee increase is even greater.[6] You might ask how this is possible. Why aren't physicians suffering more as a result of malpractice? First, as you would expect, the demand for most medical care is quite inelastic. If in Figure 17.2 above, the demand curve is completely inelastic—that is, a straight vertical line—physicians would pass on all the increased malpractice costs to their clients. There is even more. In reality, demand for medical services is also shifting to the right. As our population ages and there are more important medical breakthroughs, the shift in demand may mean higher prices and even higher equilibrium quantities. Finally, for those of you who run to the cynical side, you should remember that demand for medical care is often determined by the suppliers. It's a little like McDonald's having a direct link to your stomach that sends you to the drive-in window whenever McDonald's wants you there.

The second step in the model also misses an important factor. In 2002 in the United States, there were about 17,000 spots for those seeking medical education. This supply is relatively inelastic. At the same time, there were about 33,000 applicants. Interestingly, the number of applicants has declined from a 1996 peak of 46,000, but if one assumes all or nearly all of the applicants are qualified, the controlling factor in determining the number of physicians is still the supply of medical training. The impact of this is reflected in Figure 17.4. Even though the demand was substantially higher in 1996 and may have decreased because of liability concerns, those factors do not play a role in determining the number of physicians in training. The demand for medical education by qualified applicants might eventually shift far enough to the left (such as demand curve D_2) to result in lower numbers of physicians, and genuine economic shortages

6. Patricia M. Danzon, Mark V. Pauly, and Raynard S. Kington, "The Effects of Malpractice Litigation on Physicians' Fees and Incomes," *AEA Papers and Proceedings* 80 (May 1990): 122.

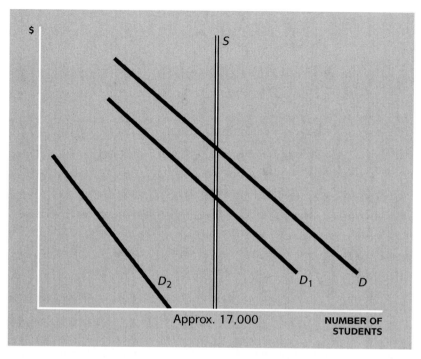

FIGURE 17.4 Demand and Supply of Medical Training: 2

could result. This is far more likely to be the result of the state in which physicians now find themselves—bargaining with insurance companies and other large buyers of their services that, in effect, buy your care for you and have substantial bargaining power.

This analysis of investments in medical education and liability may be unique to this market. After all, the medical profession has substantial say about what goes on with respect to demand and supply. In instances in which professionals or other people investing in education do not have similar power, the simple theory may hold and increased liability may mean decreases in supply. Technically, however, it is still not accurate to identify these changes as ones that create shortages.

SOME INCENTIVE-AFFECTING VARIATIONS

Negligence and Strict Liability

In Chapter 16 we discussed products liability, which is usually identified as *strict liability*. In other words, manufacturers were liable even if the cost of the accident was in excess of the cost of avoidance. Yet, in the context of malpractice, the discussion has centered on negligence. Why not treat suppliers of products and professional services alike? In the case of physicians, the difference would be like this. Under the negligence standard, the physician would be liable for any harm under circumstances in which the expected cost of the harm was in excess of the additional cost of prevention. Under strict liability, the physician would be liable for any bad result caused by a treatment that was not a result of the patient's illness or condition. The term for these outcomes is *iatrogenic*. In other words, physicians would be liable even when they are not negligent.

In theory, as in the case of strict liability, the different standards should not affect the level of care. Under negligence, the physician is motivated to take the efficient level of care in order to avoid paying damages, and the same is true of strict liability. What changes under strict liability is that the physician's reasonable effort does not mean he or she will necessarily avoid paying for the losses following even reasonable care. Still, harm will be avoided when the expected cost is greater than the cost of avoidance and, in general, the economic comparison *should* be the same and the level of care the same. Under strict liability, when the efficient level of care does not eliminate losses the actual outcome may turn on, to whom will the loss be distributed? In the negligence case, the patient has to cover the losses if the level of care is efficient; in the strict liability case the physician pays for the losses. The fact that in the strict liability case the distribution may disfavor physicians may alter behavior.

First, the risk of being on the losing end of a particular distribution can itself be a source of disutility.[7] This alone is a form of social cost, and an effort to avoid it could result in additional care beyond allocatively efficient levels. Care taken to avoid that disutility may be money well spent from the point of view of the physician but not necessarily from the point of view of resource allocation more generally. Both the disutility and costs associated with efforts to escape it can

7. See generally, Marilyn J. Simon, "Diagnosis and Medical Malpractice: A Comparison of Negligence and Strict Liability Systems," *The Bell Journal of Economics* 13 (Spring 1982): 170.

be avoided by staying with the negligence standard. In effect, the system of strict liability may be viewed as *imperfect* compared to the negligence standard. That is, the theory is that both systems will produce the same level of care. The reality may be that strict liability would result in greater care as physicians attempt to avoid internalizing the greater cost imposed on them by strict liability. Another factor that may play a role is the physician's sensitivity to reputation and the failure of the public to understand that liability under a negligence standard is based on fault while liability under strict liability may not be evidence of *fault* in the traditional sense. Again, the result could be a bias toward defensive medicine.

Insurance

Obviously, the way most professionals feel the possibility of an increase in liability is through increased insurance rates. An important issue is how the ability to insure against these losses may affect behavior. More specifically, what happens when the usual comparison of cost of avoidance and expected accident cost is changed to cost of avoidance and expected increases in insurance premiums. Ultimately, because the total cost of insurance over one's lifetime would be linked to the expected harm one is likely to cause, it seems that people would tend to exercise the same level of care whether insured or not. In reality, it is too costly to sell insurance that is completely individualized. Thus, as a general matter, the comparison between cost of avoidance and cost of harm (as reflected in premiums as opposed to actual payments to victims) will be far less precise. The net effect is that greater care may not mean lower insurance costs.

In the case of professional malpractice insurance, this lack of connection is even more pronounced. For example, when physicians buy insurance, the premiums are not linked to individualized experiences. Instead, they are based on the type of practice and the location. For example, rates may be calculated for obstetricians practicing in New York City rather than for obstetricians who graduated from high-level medical schools, have ten years of experience, have 1,000 patients, and have not been found guilty of malpractice in the last ten years. Insurance offered on this basis makes the costs of individual actions less clear to those who could avoid losses and may encourage carelessness.

A final insurance/behavior issue comes up with what is called *no-fault* insurance. No-fault systems are designed to lower the costs of making sure that victims are compensated. More specifically, the victim need not establish who is at fault in order to collect. Recently it has been suggested that a no-fault system can be used in the context of medical malpractice to make sure victims are quickly compensated without the high cost of an extended period of litigation. As you may recall, however, from the standpoint of efficient levels of care, compensation is less important than internalization. It is more important that actors respond to the full costs of their activities including harm to others even if the compensation does not find its way to the victim. So, the question is whether no-fault systems somehow dilute the "message" received by those responsible for choosing levels of care. Or, in the context of medical malpractice, would a no-fault system[8] increase or decrease the likelihood of efficient levels of care? Before discounting the prospects of no-fault insurance, remember that whether the efficient level of care is chosen is only one element of the total analysis of minimizing the costs of accidents. Another category of costs is associated with administering the system. A no-fault approach is consistent with lowering administrative costs.

Still, how does no-fault affect levels of care? To some extent, it depends on how the system is administered. In particular, do those paying claims have control over physicians? To the extent the payment agencies can affect physician behavior, the proper incentives for efficient levels of care may still be in place. In addition, physicians may tend to practice less defensive medicine. On the other hand, the empirical results from other contexts suggest there is cause for some concern. A recent study focused on states that have adopted no-fault policy in the context of automobile insurance. Researchers found that those states have higher rates of fatal automobile accidents than those still relying on a tort system. The same results were found in Canada, Australia, and New Zealand, which also use no-fault systems. The key is to balance the decreased cost of administering the system against a possible drop in the quality of care.

---

8. J. David Cummins, Richard D. Phillips, and Mary A. Weiss, "The Incentive Effects of No-Fault Automobile Insurance," *Journal of Law and Economics* 44 (October 2001): 427.

QUESTIONS FOR DISCUSSION

1. Can caps on damages that actually reflect the harm caused be defended on the basis of economic efficiency? How about this argument: No amount of money can make a person indifferent between losing a child or having the money. Thus, a determination of "actual" damages is no less speculative than a cap on damages.

2. Physicians tend to complain about malpractice insurance prices but do not seem interested in having rates based on the individualized records of each physician. Why do you think this is the case?

3. As the chapter suggests, malpractice is not limited to physicians. In fact, in theory it can be extended to teachers and even economics professors. What would be an externality of teaching malpractice? How would that externality be internalized by the professor?

4. In this chapter, we discussed two possible reasons that a reduced supply of physicians might develop. First, because of the probability of malpractice suits, the occupation of physician becomes less attractive to young people. Second, the number of training slots is restricted so not enough young people can train to be physicians. Explain the difference using demand and supply curves on the market for physicians' training slots. How could the supply of physicians in society be increased in each of these situations?

Economics
of Crime
&
Punishment

CHAPTER EIGHTEEN

Why Criminalize?

E ARLY IN THE FIRST CHAPTER OF *THE WANING OF THE Middle Ages,* Johan Huizinga writes that the unending stream of public executions was an important element in the "moral education of the people."[1] Far into the nineteenth century, executions of criminals were public rituals attended by hundreds, even thousands, beginning with a trip through the streets from the jailhouse to the gallows or guillotine. At the place of execution, a minister would deliver a sermon and administer the last services. The condemned—if so inclined—would make a dying statement expressing sorrow or anger. In modern times, executions proceed in a secluded environment, but they have never lost their public character, which is one of the defining elements of crime and punishment. The public nature of the punishment of crime is important. It embodies both revenge and deterrence. From an economic point of view, deterrence is a major element in the role that criminal law plays in society.

Traditional criminal law theory identifies two major characteristics that distinguish it from civil law. First, the criminal act to do wrong is *intentional*—in contrast with civil cases in which the wrong is usu-

---

1. Johan Huizinga, *Herfstij der middeleeuwen,* 1919. In English translation: *The Waning of the Middle Ages* (Harmondsworth: Penguin, 1924). This remains one of the best books written on life in the Middle Ages.

ally *accidental*. *Mens rea* ("a guilty mind") is the legal term that captures the intentional aspect of a crime. Second, the harm done by the criminal is *public* as well as *private*. Legal theory of criminal law builds on this characteristic of the criminal act and the intentional behavior of the criminal. Moral views on retribution and punishment and what is "right" in this respect have been developed.

The economic approach to crime and punishment focuses on the maximization of social welfare; it looks at ways government can minimize the harm caused by criminal acts to society. As we will see here and in the following chapters on crime, this is chiefly done by deterring crime to efficient levels and doing that as efficiently as possible. In Chapter 19, we will look at the behavior of a rational criminal and discuss what makes him or her decide to commit criminal acts. Building on what we know about rational criminal behavior, we discuss how society can achieve efficient levels of deterrence in Chapter 20. In Chapter 21, the final chapter on crime, we will discuss the empirical evidence on criminals behaving rationally and on the effectiveness of deterring crime.

Although the economic approach to crime provides new insights in how to deal with crime in society, it complements legal theory. The economic view of crime may make you feel a bit squeamish at times. For example, while it may make sense to think in terms of varying the levels of punishment according to the harm caused by a crime, it may seem unreal to think in terms of applying a cost-benefit analysis to crimes like assault or rape. Balancing costs and benefits is, after all, a very different approach from treating criminal acts with notions of morality and principles of right and wrong. What should be kept in mind is that the economic view does not diminish or neglect the importance of a moral view of crime; it is focused on how society can, in an optimal way, deter criminal acts of whatever nature.

The answer to "why criminalize?" may seem obvious; when people harm others, they should be punished. In fact, this is not always the approach society takes. Very often, when one person harms another, the issue is left to private lawsuits. In other words, if someone injures you or damages your property, you can sue them for damages under tort law. Most crimes are also torts. As we have seen in previous chapters tort law aims to internalize the costs caused by faulty actions. We will explain in the first section of this chapter that tort law and the internalization that follows are inadequate instruments when deterrence is the goal. There are two reasons for the inadequacy of tort law: incomplete compensation and negative external effects.

One of the characteristics stressed by legal theory is that crime causes not only private but also public harm. We will come back to the public nature of crime in the second section of the chapter. If we view crime as harm caused to other people and to society, we need to consider why we criminalize when there appear to be no victims. The question of *victimless crimes* is discussed in the final section of this chapter.

THE INADEQUACY OF TORT LAW

To understand the role of criminal law in greater detail, consider this question. What is the difference between somebody who rear-ends your legally parked car and causes it to be a total loss and a thief who steals your car? In both cases you end up having no car. The first case is an accident; the second is a crime. According to legal theory, the dividing line between tort law and criminal law is that the first is concerned with accidental harm, and in the latter case, the harm is intentional. On a scale of culpability, the person doing the harm is *at fault* for having caused the damage if the harm is accidental and *guilty* of a crime if the harm is intentional.

In the case of the wrecked car, the person causing the accident (or the insurance company) will compensate the owner of the car completely, and he or she will be able to buy a new car. Because of the compensation requirement, the person causing the car accident will internalize the cost of the accident and drive more carefully or at least less recklessly.[2] Through internalization, an efficient tort system will effectively avoid the occurrence of inefficient accidents in society. In this sense, tort law is adequate to deal with accidents in society.

On the other hand, some harmful activities just do not fit neatly into the tort/compensation framework. When your house is burglarized, you suffer material damage. The thief steals valuables and might have forced a lock or broken a window. But you also suffer nonmaterial damage: Your privacy has been invaded, which makes you feel

---

2. Of course, as you know, it is not essential that the payment actually go to the victim in order for the cost to be internalized.

uneasy and unsafe. The thief might have taken something that has sentimental value, like a present from somebody who loves you or an heirloom that goes far back in your family. Some activities might also cause bodily harm and in addition leave you traumatized.[3] Vicious robbery and rape are examples. If the criminal gets caught, the victim might receive compensation for the material harm that was done, but what about the physical and psychic harm, particularly those stemming from your loss of a sense of security?

It is this generalized sense of loss to which tort law cannot effectively respond. Both material and nonmaterial harm extend beyond those directly involved in the crime—the criminal and the victim—to the rest of society. If there is a robbery or a string of robberies in the neighborhood, inhabitants feel unsafe, and this affects their way of living. They will not go out as much, they will feel less free to live their lives, and they may spend money investing in home safety measures (such as extra locks and an alarm system). The indirect effects of crime to society go much further than the immediate neighborhood where the crime took place. Increasing crime rates are seen by society as a permanent erosion of the norms and rules that we feel are necessary for a civil society. In this context, it is very difficult to determine who is damaged and how to value that harm. Without that information, the tort/compensation system cannot function.

The inadequacy of the tort system to address these generalized harms is exacerbated by two factors. First, people who take things without paying tend to try to hide their activities. Thus, not all are caught. So even if every criminal who is caught must pay full compensation, there will be many instances in which there is no compensation. Consequently, as will be discussed more fully in Chapter 20, it is important to add an element of punishment to those who are caught in order to have a deterrent effect. Second, the tort system depends on the ability of the party causing harm to internalize the cost of that harm. But suppose that person has no money. If he or she cannot pay the bill, the idea of internalization loses some of its force. At this point, society must resort to other means—such as incarceration—to make the criminal "pay" or to deter the behavior in the first place.

---

3. Note that similar problems of incomplete compensation also occur in accidents and tort law.

Aside from reacting to the amorphous and generalized harm caused by some activity, criminal law is required for another purpose that is more obviously related to efficiency issues. This can be understood by reference to the concepts of liability rules and property rules that you studied in Chapter 5. Tort law rests primarily on liability rules— if a person harms or takes your property, he must pay fair market value. Under a property rule, he may not use or take your property without your consent. This often means a negotiation and settling on a price that may or may not be at fair market value.

Picture yourself in your garage polishing your 1966 original Mini (this was before BMW took over and began making the new Mini). Someone drops by and asks what you will take for it. You think it over and say $7,000, and you mean it. He walks away. The next day, you find that your Mini is missing. In its place is a paper bag with $6,000 in it. There is a note that says, "I checked all possible sources and the fair market value of your Mini is $6,000. Thanks, it's been good doing business with you!!" Technically, what has happened here is that your visitor has attempted to change a property rule to a liability rule. Instead of negotiating for your consent, he has just taken the car and paid fair market value. As you may also recall from Chapter 5, property rules are consistent with efficient exchanges when transaction costs are low—as they would be in the context of the "sale" of your Mini. In the example, the "take and pay" solution is not efficient from a Pareto standpoint because you are worse off than you would have been had you kept the car. And there is no way to assure it is even efficient from the viewpoint of the more permissive Kaldor-Hicks standard since we do not know if the "buyer" actually valued the car enough to compensate you and still be better off. Efficiency is more likely to be assured when, in low transaction-cost settings, the parties make exchanges. From an economic perspective, criminal law can be used to make sure that property rules are not routinely made into liability rules.

In conclusion, in many instances, compensation for harm is unsatisfactory for at least two reasons. First, the costs caused by crime diminish the material welfare and the psychological well-being of the victims and of society at large and hence diminish our wealth or the enjoyment of our wealth. The loss of wealth and welfare is not only immediate but has long-term effects, such as discouraging people from accumulating wealth and investing. Compensation is also unsatisfactory because, in the end, it makes crime more profitable than it should be. Because criminals are not confronted with all the costs of their actions, they will in some sense be encouraged to engage in more criminal activities. Second, the knowledge that society reacts to all harms with liability rules would undercut property rules. Yet, when transactions costs are low, property rules are more likely than liability rules to result in efficient exchanges.

CASE 18.1 The Contours of Criminal Law: *Smith v. Doe,* 538 U.S. 84 (2003)

In these chapters on criminal law, the economic perspective will be one that compares the benefits of deterring certain types of conduct with the costs of deterring the conduct. At an abstract level, it is a simple comparison of costs and benefits. This perspective greatly understates the complexities and limitations of criminal law. Criminal law often involves "rights" that are afforded people without regard for the costs and benefits. When criminal law is applied, as you know from television, defendants are afforded certain rights. For example, the police cannot conduct a search without *probable cause* to believe a crime has been committed. Any evidence found through an improper search, even if incriminating, cannot be used at trial. There is no doubt that guilty people sometimes go free in order for this right to be protected. In addition, the government cannot wait for someone to do something that is reprehensible and then pass a law and punish that person or increase the existing level of punishment. Similarly, people cannot be tried for the same alleged violation more than once. The U.S. Constitution also prohibits the application of cruel and unusual punishment. What this means is that some very effective ways of reducing criminal activity are off limits.

An example will give you a feel for the complexity of the legal issues and the importance of judicial interpretation. You may be familiar with "Megan's Law," the name for state laws that require those guilty of sexual offenses to register with a local law enforcement agency. The law was passed after many of those required to register had already been convicted, served their time, and returned to society. As an economic matter, Megan's Law may be a fairly inexpensive way to reduce criminal activity—because sexual offenders tend to be repeat offenders. On the other hand, it does seem to be tacking on additional punishment for offenders who have served their sentences. After all, few people would like to register as sexual predators. In *Smith v. Doe,* the U.S. Court was asked to rule that Megan's Law violated the prohibition against changing punishment after the fact. The Court reasoned that the registration requirement was not punishment at all and thus did not violate this prohibition. In its opinion it distinguished Megan's Law from early laws that tended to shame or humiliate people:

> Any initial resemblance to early punishments is, however, misleading. Punishments such as whipping, pillory, and branding inflicted physical pain and staged a direct confrontation between the offender and the public. Even punishments that lacked the corporal component, such as public shaming, humiliation, and banishment, involved more than the dissemination of information. They either held the person up before his fellow citizens for face-to-face shaming or expelled him from the community. . . . By contrast, the stigma of Alaska's Megan's Law results not from public display for ridicule and shaming but from the dissemination of accurate information about a criminal record, most of which is already public. Our system does not treat dissemination of truthful information in furtherance of a legitimate governmental objective as punishment.

What do you think? Is a registration requirement punishment? Justices Souter, Ginsberg, and Breyer said yes and would have ruled the registration requirement unconstitutional to the extent it applied retroactively. Was the Court subordinating some rights to advance efficiency?

PUBLIC HARM

Externalities occur when the utility of individuals and the production possibilities of firms are favorably or unfavorably affected by another individual or firm (Chapter 4), and the latter is not penalized for the damage or rewarded for the benefit. Crime, obviously, is in this sense an activity that causes negative external effects. Increasing crime rates lead to feelings of insecurity and diminish the utility of individuals. A society that is ridden with crime will be unable to maintain a prosperous economic system. Think of a mafia-controlled area in which payments are extorted from shopkeepers, and businesspeople are forced to buy or sell at prices that are favorable to the mafia members. Such an area is economically doomed. Business and wealth generation will be lower than it would have been, and the fear and mistrust diminishes the quality of life and welfare of the citizens.

Suppose that through agreements and hired "enforcers" it were possible to respond to the incomplete compensation and externalities problems. Would an economic rationale still exist for having a public system of criminal law? The answer is almost certainly "yes." If a society agreed to minimize incomplete compensation and external effects, it would have to decide how to do that in the least expensive way. The costs of individual private agreements could be added up and compared to the cost of operating a government system designed to achieve the same outcome. Apprehending and judging criminals collectively would undoubtedly be more efficient—as a result of economies of scale—than a series of individual transactions. The larger scale allows for investment in modern investigation techniques (for instance, an enormous database of fingerprints or genetic codes), building different sizes of prisons and other institutions, and developing a hierarchical judicial system. The average cost of apprehending, trying, and punishing a criminal goes down with the scale of the judicial system. This property of decreasing average cost is known as positive returns to scale. Organizing crime-fighting on a collective scale reduces the cost of crime for society.

Another consideration is the hazard of allowing private citizens to enforce the law. Obviously, we do want individuals to protect themselves against crime. They have the right to self-defense and, within reason, we would like them to come to the defense of other citizens when they are threatened. But there are limits to taking the law into one's own hands. These limits differ among societies. Some societies are more lenient, for instance, in allowing families to revenge crimes committed on other family members. These differences in attitude sometimes create conflicts. For example, many western European countries have recently experienced an influx of immigrants who have brought with them their own customs of family revenge. But allowing different groups within a country to have different standards as to what is considered a crime and what is the appropriate procedure and penalty in response to that crime would result in a great deal of uncertainty. This uncertainty increases the cost of the system itself.

To function properly, a society needs norms and rules. Norms are usually based on ethical values emanating from religious and philosophical principles. "Thou shall not kill" and "thou shall not steal" are universal norms held by most societies that have been codified into laws. Activities whereby essential norms of society are broken are usually captured in criminal law.

Norms change over time and differ between societies. Hence, what is forbidden will differ and penal law will change over time. At one time in most European countries, it was indecent to appear topless on a beach. Beginning in northern Europe and gradually moving to southern Europe, this has changed. In most western European countries today, the police will not arrest you even if you are sunbathing naked on a public beach. In addition, at one point the possession of marijuana was a serious crime in most states. After years of relatively widespread use and demystification of marijuana, possession of small amounts is now a misdemeanor in many states. Finally, as discussed below, laws affecting homosexuals have changed markedly in the last twenty years. This also reflects changes in attitudes toward diverse lifestyles.

LAW AND ECONOMICS IN ACTION 18.1

DIFFERENT AND CHANGING NORMS

Not so long ago in the Netherlands, a medical doctor helping a patient with euthanasia would have been committing a crime that was punishable by law. Recently, the Dutch penal code was changed to allow for euthanasia under strict conditions. A patient who suffers unbearable pain and has no prospect whatsoever of surviving can ask his or her doctor to perform euthanasia. The doctor whose conscience does not allow for it can of course refuse. When a doctor consents to help, he has to ascertain that suffering is indeed unbearable and incurable on medical grounds. A second opinion by another doctor is required as well. Each occurrence of euthanasia has to be reported to the public prosecutor's office. The wording of the penal code is such that euthanasia is still considered to be a criminal act unless the doctor and the patient follow the specified requirements. Since this law is fairly new, the boundaries of what is allowed and what is not allowed are not always clear. Recent court cases make a sharp distinction between physical suffering (such as the terminal phase of incurable cancer) and psychological suffering (such as incurable depression). The euthanasia law is still being discussed in Dutch society. Putting the law on the books and finalizing it through court cases illustrates the process of changing a fundamental norm in society.

Rules are not based on deeper ethical and philosophical consider-ations but are there because they are practical. There is no principle underlying the rule that cars drive on the right rather than on the left side of the road. What is important is that there is a clear rule that everybody is required to follow. There are similar rules on how to draw up a contract in business. For instance, whether a contract is binding once a consensus has been established by merely agreeing (saying yes, nodding your head) or whether a contract is legally bind-ing only when it has been put into writing is a convention that soci-ety has to decide. There are pros and cons to each version of the contract rule and different societies weigh the advantages and disad-vantages differently and hence have different rules. What is essential is that there is a clear rule, known to all and binding for all parties.

Obviously, not all citizens are law abiding all the time. Citizens who break the law will be confronted with a legal system of prosecution and punishment to bring them back in line—otherwise they will profit from their illegal acts. A good penal system confronts the criminal with the costs incurred by the victim and society so that, in the end only efficient crime pays.

PURPOSES OF PUNISHMENT

Earlier, you saw that the economic approach to criminal law is compli-cated because rights are assigned to people with no evaluation of their costs and benefits. A further complication is that there are several justi-fications for punishment itself. The one that rings true in the context of economic analysis is that punishment is designed to deter criminal activ-ity. In effect, by raising the cost of these undesired activities, we decrease them. Historically, however, punishment has also been said to exist for rehabilitation, protection, and retribution. Rehabilitation is an interesting one. If successful, the impact would be to actually change the tastes of criminals so they did not find illegal activities as desirable. In a sense, it can be seen as decreasing the demand for unlawful conduct. Protection means isolating those who are criminally inclined from the general popu-lation. In the case of rehabilitation and protection, there are obvious con-nections to an economic perspective. At least in theory, we could compare the costs of rehabilitation and isolation with the benefits. As a historical matter, in modern times, people are less confident that rehabilitation is a worthwhile investment. Perhaps the most intriguing purpose of punishment is retribution. Retribution means that it is somehow appropriate or "right" that those committing crimes be made to suffer. Remember, this is independent of just deterring future crime. In some sense, punishing those who wrong others vindicates those who are law abiding. Although it would be hard to quantify, one might attempt to apply an economic approach and say that retribution is efficient as long as its cost is less than the benefits (psychological) derived by those who demand that the suffering take place.

VICTIMLESS CRIMES

You have seen two principal justifications for criminal law. It prevents people from changing property rules into liability rules, and it is a response to externalities. What about so-called victimless crimes? From the perspective of economics, *victimless crimes*—such as buying drugs, prostitution, gambling, or joining a dogfighting club—would not appear to be subject to punishment. These transactions actually increase the welfare of the individuals involved in the deal. Why is that? The answer goes back to our discussion in Chapter 2 about Pareto efficiency.

Buying drugs, procuring the services of a prostitute, and paying the entry price to a dogfight involves a buyer and a seller. The buyer is willing to pay the price for the good or the service. From an economic point of view, this means that he or she prefers the product or the service to the amount of money he or she has to part with. The buyer must be better off after the sale than before and hence paying for the drug, a prostitute, or to watch a dogfight increases his or her individual welfare.[4] The seller is willing to part with the product or to deliver the service for the price the buyer is paying. The deal makes

---

4. In theory, he does not necessarily have to be better off—just as well off. This happens when he values the product he buys exactly as much as the money he parts with. What is important for the argument is that he is not worse off after the transaction—which he will not be if he enters voluntarily into the deal. A similar reasoning applies to the seller.

both the seller and the buyer better off and increases their welfare. If this were the end of the story, this transaction would lead to a Pareto improvement. If this were indeed the case, buying drugs or joining a dogfighting club would in economic terms not differ from buying a loaf of bread or going to see *The Sound of Music*.

The problem is that many, if not most, "victimless" crimes are not victimless at all. Consider the sale of drugs and dogfighting. The story does not end with the buyer and the seller. There is more going on: These transactions are seen as having a harmful effect on the rest of society. They diminish the utility of the other members of society or, in language from an earlier chapter, create a negative externality.

Let's work out the comparison between victimless crimes and negative externalities for the rest of society. Those citizens who see their welfare diminished because they feel shocked or scandalized or see these transactions as undermining the strength of society are not compensated and hence incur a loss as a consequence of the transactions related to the victimless crime.

As explained in Chapter 4, governments often attempt to reduce the externality, such as greenhouse gas emissions, with the correct *intensity of regulation* or *price* in order to balance the cost to the rest of society with the benefits of the parties that cause the externality. In this sense, the regulation and pricing policies correspond with a liability rule. For some externalities, however, these instruments are unlikely to properly achieve the desired result—as when zero is the optimal amount of the externality or when the externality is that the activity offends generalized moral values. Thus, some transactions—such as dealing in hard drugs in the United States—and certain kinds of behavior—such as adultery in some Muslim countries—are forbidden. Liability rules are not sufficient and society criminalizes these activities.

Typically, we criminalize when the number of participants in the activity is relatively low and the harm caused by each act relatively great. This is different, for example, from driving a car (and thereby creating harmful emissions), as tickets would have to be issued to millions of people to combat small levels of externalities per person. We also criminalize when the externalities are diffuse, after-the-fact compensation of victims is difficult, and third parties are affected both economically and psychologically. Drug-dealing is a good example of this last condition.

Criminalizing activities generally means that we resort to property rules or rules of inalienability. In the case of property rules, the activity may not take place unless those affected by the externality consent in advance. In most instances, the transaction costs will be so high that the law amounts to a prohibition. In the case of a rule of inalienability, the conduct is not permitted at all. Rules of inalienability are most often used when the externality is diffuse and primarily psychological. In effect, it would be virtually impossible to compensate individually all those adversely affected. A good example of this would be when thousands of people are affected only a little bit. Or when lots of people are made "worse off" because they feel offended or consider the transaction morally repugnant to some degree.

Take organizing dogfights as an example. Society does not want people to organize dogfights because a majority of its citizens consider it cruel to the animals. We do not want organizers to make money or spectators to enjoy watching the suffering of animals. For the same reasons, many countries forbid cockfights, bullfights, and other cruel animal "sports." People organizing and watching a dogfight are trespassing a societal norm concerning decent treatment of animals. The majority of citizens consider it their right to have decent norms toward animals adhered to by everybody. Many people in society would "suffer" if these fights were organized. These are the negative external effects caused by the fights. As discussed in the previous section, it is not possible to use a liability rule in this case. It is impossible for organizers and spectators to compensate those members of society who are pained by dogfights for their "suffering." Hence a rule of inalienability is applied.

The moral suffering caused by cruelty to animals in these fights is the most important externality in this case, but there are additional negative effects. For instance, breeding fighting dogs and preparing them for the fights creates fierce and dangerous animals that might cause severe injury to children and innocent people. Also, animal fights usually provide opportunities for betting, which is not always considered a desirable activity in society.

As with most victimless crimes, the definition of what is and is not a crime changes over time and differs among societies. In earlier times, dogfights were not considered a crime, nor are they a crime in some countries today. It is currently illegal to sell organs even though a great deal of economic evidence suggests that it would be efficient to permit organ sales. Ultimately, the only way to attempt to justify this prohibition is by reference to the moral squeamishness of society.

When moral values are involved, the fluid nature of what externalities the law responds to and what it ignores can be quite controversial. In an important decision, *Bowers. v. Hardwick*, which was decided in 1986, the U.S. Supreme Court was asked to evaluate a law passed in Georgia prohibiting and criminalizing sodomy between consenting men.[5] The issue was whether the law violated the U.S. Constitution. The Court was faced with an argument that sodomy between consenting men was a victimless crime. In finding the law acceptable, the Court reasoned that it was supported by the "presumed belief of a majority of the electorate in Georgia that homosexual sodomy is immoral and unacceptable." This raises a very difficult issue in law, which seems to recognize and react to some externalities and not to others depending upon political climate and religious values.

In 2003, the Supreme Court changed its mind. The conduct that was prohibited because of the impact it could have on others was evidently not as reprehensible as initially thought, and the Court overturned its earlier decision.[6] The Court noted that the number of States prohibiting homosexual sodomy had fallen since *Bowers* was decided. In addition, Bowers was inconsistent with law outside the United States. In other words, what was an externality had ceased to be so pressing.

Clearly, the victimless crime rationale deserves careful scrutiny before anything definitive can be said. Specifically, although we tend to criminalize activities that are costly to society, the act of criminalizing itself is costly to society. Thus, a balancing must take place. One must be careful before labeling a "crime" victimless. Most victimless crimes are, in fact, associated with negative externalities. On the other hand, it is also important to consider to what extent the externality is the result of the activity itself or the criminalization of that activity. For example, among the reasons cited for criminalizing the sale of drugs is that drug dealers are unsavory characters and that drug sales

---

5. *Bowers v. Hardwick*, 478 U.S. 186 (1986).
6. *Lawrence v. Texas*, 123 S.Ct. 2472 (2003).

are often associated with violence. Violence affects the safety of others and may lead to the decline in property values. But suppose drug transactions were not illegal and that "drug stores" could sell marijuana and cocaine much like sellers of other drugs like caffeine, nicotine, and alcohol. Is it possible that the number of unsavory drug dealers and violence would decline? After all, caffeine sellers like the corner coffee shop, nicotine sellers like convenience stores, and alcohol sellers like the neighborhood liquor store are not generally associated with a great deal of crime. What this suggests is that some of the harm caused by *victimless crimes* is not the result of the activity but the result of its criminalization.

A Case Study: Ticket Scalping

A fine example of criminalizing what appears to be a victimless crime is the law, found in some places, against ticket scalping. First let's have a look at what is really going on when ticket scalping takes place.

Suppose the Rolling Stones are giving a concert at the local concert hall that has a limited number of seats. Older generations want to see them perform again and relive cherished memories; younger generations are curious to see what exactly they were all about. Many people assume that this might be the last chance to see the Rolling Stones perform before music history delivers its final judgment on them. It is quite possible that there are many more potential spectators than the concert hall provides seats for. In economic terms, there is excess demand. There is a shortage of seats and these have to be allocated in some way. There are basically two ways to allocate these scarce seats: using the market and the price mechanism and using a waiting list or a queue.

Let's first look at how a market would work. Figure 18.1 shows a supply curve and a demand curve for Rolling Stones concert tickets. On the vertical axis, we can read off the ticket price and on the horizontal axis the number of tickets—or the number of seats sold. The supply curve for Rolling Stones tickets is the vertical line, which indicates there is a maximum number of seats available N_{max}. If the concert hall has 3,000 seats at full capacity, N_{max} equals 3,000. The concert organizer wants to sell all those seats at whatever the market price turns out be.

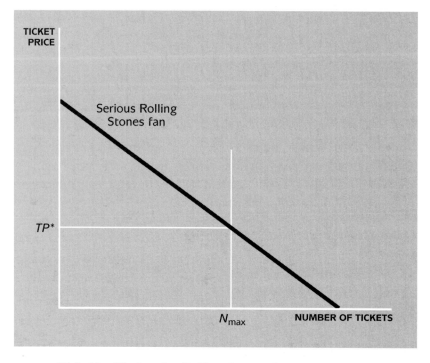

FIGURE 18.1   The Market for Rolling Stones Concert Tickets

The downward-sloping curve in Figure 18.1 is the demand curve. The demand curve shows how many tickets the public wants to buy at any given ticket price. At high prices, the demand for tickets is small. Only a few people (call them serious Rolling Stone fans) want to buy them. As the price decreases, more and more people are interested in buying a ticket. At ticket price $TP^\star$, the number of people willing to buy a ticket equals the maximum number of seats available in the concert hall.

For prices higher than $TP^\star$, fewer people are willing to buy tickets than there are seats available and hence there is excess supply. Excess supply will make the ticket price go down. At prices lower than $TP^\star$, more people are willing to buy a ticket than there are seats available. This is a situation of excess demand and that will make the ticket price go up. Only at price $TP^\star$ does demand equal supply, the concert hall will be sold out, and there is no downward or upward pressure on the ticket price.

In this way, the market uses the price mechanism to allocate scarcity. From an economic point of view, the market does a good job in this respect. It ends up with the ticket price $TP\star$ at which all the available seats are sold. Suppose the capacity of the concert hall is smaller—say 2,000 instead of 3,000 seats. This would make the supply curve shift to the left. In this case, the market price would be higher; the intersection of supply and demand curves would occur at a higher price level.

At first sight, the market mechanism would seem to be an ideal instrument to allocate the scarce number of seats. Yet it is not the mechanism that is used to sell concert tickets. An important reason that organizers do not want to rely on the market is probably that they consider the market price $TP\star$ too high for most Rolling Stone fans. Often the market price will be too high in a situation that starts from excess demand—there are three times as many potential spectators as there are seats in the concert hall. In terms of Figure 18.1, we start from a situation very much below $TP\star$. Large excess demand puts a high upward pressure on the ticket price. When the market has done its job, the ticket price $TP\star$ will in the end be very high—so high that only rich people or those willing to sacrifice can afford to go to see the Rolling Stones. This is a market outcome that concert organizers and performers do not always like. They might want to give all the Rolling Stones' fans a chance to come to the concert as a means of promoting CD sales and to introduce a new generation of fans to the band. In addition, there may be a sense in society that ticket scalpers, rather than being entrepreneurs, are actually comparable to loan sharks and take advantage of people.

What often happens, then, is that the concert organizer fixes a ticket price beforehand and then sells the tickets on a first come, first served basis. The allocation mechanism is that of the waiting line or queue. Because the price is lower than $TP\star$, the situation is one of excess demand. At a price lower than $TP\star$, more people will want to see the Rolling Stones than there are seats available. In such a situation, people wanting to buy a ticket will stand in line before the ticket booth as soon as the sale of tickets starts. They may even sleep in front of the ticket booth the night before to make sure they get a ticket when the booth opens in the morning. People in the front of the line are certain to get a ticket. Tickets are sold as long as they are available, according to the order of people waiting in the line. At some point, the maximum number of tickets will be sold and that is the end of it. Using the line, tickets are sold below the market price to people who are willing to wait in line and can take the time to do that. The price at which the tickets are sold is considered fair and not too high.

Using the waiting line mechanism instead of the market mechanism creates economic incentives for scalping. Why is that? The demand curve tells us what people are willing to pay for a ticket to a Rolling Stones concert. Serious Rolling Stone fans will be willing to pay a lot of money for a ticket. These fans want to pay much more than the market price $TP^\star$. Serious Rolling Stone fans can be found at the top of the demand curve as indicated in Figure 18.1. Less serious Rolling Stone fans can be found at lower parts of the demand curve. They also want to pay more than $TP^\star$, but not as much as the serious fans. When we use the market mechanism to allocate the seats, the result is that all those who are willing to pay at least the market price $TP^\star$ will get a ticket. When we use the waiting line, that is not necessarily the case. Using the waiting line to allocate scarce concert seats implies that those who are willing to spend the time get the tickets. The market mechanism allocates tickets to people willing to spend the money. When the waiting line is used, there will be serious Rolling Stone fans that did not have the time to wait in line but have the money and the desire to buy a ticket. And there will be people who had the time to wait in line but who are not such serious Rolling Stone fans and are willing to part with their tickets for a good price. There is plenty of opportunity for scalping. Scalping a ticket will increase the welfare of both the buyer and the seller.

It is very hard to conclude that laws against ticket scalping are anything but inefficient. Still, are there externalities great enough to make the laws efficient? As already noted, ticket scalping may prevent the distribution of tickets desired by the promoters and performers.[7] What would a Rolling Stone concert be like if everyone there were fifty-five years old and sat and clapped once in a while? To some extent, youthful excitement is part of the show.

---

7. In reality, charging less than market value for tickets may be a way to enhance a band's image as being not as profit-oriented as mainstream society.

A better, albeit less defined, possibility is that society in general has a moral reaction to ticket scalpers. To some, it just does not seem fair that tickets that appear to be priced and available to all end up in the hands of those willing to pay the most. We prefer the waiting line rationing system precisely to keep the price down. To some, it seems more "democratic," although in reality it is not since the opportunity cost of spending time in the line will vary greatly. Scalping is criminalized to enforce the lower price even though it technically means a less efficient allocation of tickets.

QUESTIONS FOR DISCUSSION

1. The *exclusionary rule* is a rule created by the U.S. Supreme Court. Under the rule, evidence obtained in an illegal search by the police may not be used in a trial even if it is completely reliable evidence. Do you think this rule fits with an approach to criminal law that is consistent with efficiency?

2. The chapter notes that criminal law is often used to control externalities. In the chapters on torts you learned that tort law is also about externalities and that it is possible for individuals to recover punitive damages. Why is criminal law necessary if there is a way to collect punitive damages under tort law?

3. Sometimes it is said that criminal law exists, in part, to prevent people from changing property rules into liability rules. Do you understand what this means? Explain.

4. Do you think victimless crimes exist? If so, name one. Is there any economic justification for criminalizing that activity?

5. Society aims to deter criminals by convicting them of their crimes and putting them in prison. Given this objective, why do we also observe civilian liability court cases in which the victims of the crime ask the judge to hold the criminals liable for the damage caused by the crime? Does this mean that deterrence from criminal law is insufficient?

CHAPTER NINETEEN

The Rational Criminal

I T MAY SURPRISE YOU THAT THE GOAL OF CRIMINAL LAW is not to eliminate all crime. First, that would be very costly— even more costly than the harm caused by some crime. Second, society actually condones some criminal conduct. For example, we generally approve when someone speeds to take an injured person to the hospital. Consequently, any policy toward crime involves a balancing process. It is probably best to view criminal law as a process of regulating behavior.

In order to know how to reduce crime, we have to know how we can influence individual criminal behavior. This chapter introduces the assumption of rational criminal behavior and the predictions flowing from this theory that help to measure the social costs and benefits of fighting crime. In the first section, the most elementary model of the rational criminal is explained. It leads to two important questions: whether all criminal acts can be classified as rational behavior, and what insights are to be gained from assuming rationality in crime. In the next section we will discuss answers to the first question. Following, we develop a more detailed model of the rational criminal and stress its usefulness in understanding criminal behavior. Policy implications of the model of the rational criminal are discussed in the fourth section. Finally, the last part of the chapter discusses attitudes toward risk. In Chapter 20, we start from the assumption of the rational criminal to discuss efficient levels of deterrence.

CRIME AS A RATIONAL PROCESS: THE SIMPLE MODEL

The basic economic assumption is that a criminal behaves rationally. He will commit a crime if his expected benefits outweigh his expected costs. Let us take the following everyday example of shoplifting. A student desperately needs an expensive economics textbook for his class. He is running short of cash and in the bookshop he sees a huge pile of the textbook he needs. He is thinking about stealing it— putting it under his coat and walking out of the shop. Rational behavior implies that when deciding whether or not to shoplift, he compares the benefits of stealing the book with the cost of maybe getting caught and being fined. The benefit, of course, is getting the book without having to pay for it.

The cost of shoplifting is an expected cost. It is not a sure cost, because it depends on the probability of getting caught. The student knows that not all shoplifters are caught. He has heard that lots of people get away with it. He has read somewhere that at most one in ten shoplifters are caught by the bookstore, reported to the police, and fined. So the expected costs consist, first of all, of the expected monetary cost: the probability of getting caught (in this case a probability of one out of ten) multiplied by the amount of the fine. But there might be other costs, such as the personal cost of feeling guilty or ashamed or the cost of being branded as a shoplifter and of social rejection by his peers. For major crimes, incarceration is another part of the expected cost.

The assumption of rational criminal behavior implies that this student contemplating shoplifting is making a mental calculation comparing the benefits of stealing the textbook with the expected cost of being fined and punished. If the benefits of stealing the book are greater than the expected cost, he will grab the book and walk out of the store. By doing that, he has intentionally harmed other people and has committed a crime.

CASE 19.1 **Deterrence and Rationality:** *Roper v. Simmons,* 543 U.S. 551 (2005)

One of the assumptions underlying the use of punishment is that individuals are rational. In criminal law, the rationality assumption is usually analyzed in terms of whether the defendant has *capacity*. In other words, can the defendant make the connection between unlawful conduct and its consequences? This is where the issue of insanity and other defenses arises. One issue is the age of the defendant. In *Roper,* the defendant participated in a murder at age seventeen and was convicted and sentenced to be executed at age eighteen. The technical argument was that execution amounted to "cruel and unusual punishment" in violation of the U.S. Constitution. A majority of the Court held that it was, due to the age of the defendant. The following excerpt illustrates the reasoning for accepting the argument that the defendant was not "rational" and the implications of that finding:

> Because the death penalty is the most severe punishment, the Eighth Amendment applies to it with special force. . . . Capital punishment must be limited to those offenders who commit "a narrow category of the most serious crimes" and whose extreme culpability makes them "the most deserving of execution." The death penalty may not be imposed on certain classes of offenders, such as juveniles under 16, the insane, and the mentally retarded, no matter how heinous the crime. These rules dictate the underlying principle that the death penalty is reserved for a narrow category of crimes and offenders.
>
> Three general differences between juveniles under 18 and adults demonstrate that juvenile offenders cannot with reliability be classified among the worst offenders. First, as any parent knows and as the scientific and sociological studies respondent and his *amici* cite tend to confirm, "[a] lack of maturity and an underdeveloped sense of responsibility are found in youth more often than in adults and are more understandable among the young. These qualities often result in impetuous and ill-considered actions and decisions." . . . It has been noted that "adolescents are overrepresented statistically in virtually every category of reckless behavior." Arnett, "Reckless Behavior in Adolescence: A Developmental Perspective," 12 Developmental Review 339 (1992). In recognition of the comparative immaturity and irresponsibility of juveniles, almost every State prohibits those under 18 years of age from voting, serving on juries, or marrying without parental consent.
>
> The second area of difference is that juveniles are more vulnerable or susceptible to negative influences and outside pressures, including peer pressure. This is explained in part by the prevailing circumstance that juveniles have less control, or less experience with control, over their own environment. . . .

The third broad difference is that the character of a juvenile is not as well formed as that of an adult. The personality traits of juveniles are more transitory, less fixed.

These differences render suspect any conclusion that a juvenile falls among the worst offenders. The susceptibility of juveniles to immature and irresponsible behavior means "their irresponsible conduct is not as morally reprehensible as that of an adult." Their own vulnerability and comparative lack of control over their immediate surroundings mean juveniles have a greater claim than adults to be forgiven for failing to escape negative influences in their whole environment. The reality that juveniles still struggle to define their identity means it is less supportable to conclude that even a heinous crime committed by a juvenile is evidence of irretrievably depraved character. From a moral standpoint it would be misguided to equate the failings of a minor with those of an adult, for a greater possibility exists that a minor's character deficiencies will be reformed.

Once the diminished culpability of juveniles is recognized, it is evident that the penological justifications for the death penalty apply to them with lesser force than to adults. We have held there are two distinct social purposes served by the death penalty: "'retribution and deterrence of capital crimes by prospective offenders.'" . . . As for retribution, we [have remarked] "[i]f the culpability of the average murderer is insufficient to justify the most extreme sanction available to the State, the lesser culpability of the mentally retarded offender surely does not merit that form of retribution." The same conclusions follow from the lesser culpability of the juvenile offender. Whether viewed as an attempt to express the community's moral outrage or as an attempt to right the balance for the wrong to the victim, the case for retribution is not as strong with a minor as with an adult. Retribution is not proportional if the law's most severe penalty is imposed on one whose culpability or blameworthiness is diminished, to a substantial degree, by reason of youth and immaturity.

As for deterrence, it is unclear whether the death penalty has a significant or even measurable deterrent effect on juveniles, as counsel for the petitioner acknowledged at oral argument. In general we leave to legislatures the assessment of the efficacy of various criminal penalty schemes. . . . Here, however, the absence of evidence of deterrent effect is of special concern because the same characteristics that render juveniles less culpable than adults suggest as well that juveniles will be less susceptible to deterrence. In particular, . . . "[t]he likelihood that the teenage offender has made the kind of cost-benefit analysis that attaches any weight to the possibility of execution is so remote as to be virtually nonexistent. To the extent the juvenile death penalty might have residual deterrent effect, it is worth noting that the punishment of life imprisonment without the possibility of parole is itself a severe sanction, in particular for a young person.

IS ALL CRIME RATIONAL?

The answer to this question is clearly "no." Committing crime involves more than the calculus of rationality. Some crimes stem from anger and frustration and occur without thought. A prime example of this is the *crime of passion* when a wife walks into the bedroom, finds her husband in bed with her best friend, and kills them both on the spot, or "road rage," when someone just freaks out and drives his or her car into someone else's car. For some crimes, such as rape, the assumption of rationality seems far-fetched, dead wrong, or even offensive. At the same time, society obviously needs to deter these crimes. We assume that there is some rational component even to the crime of rape. Otherwise rape is undeterrable.

There are many other explanations of crime that help us understand criminal behavior besides the economic assumption of rational behavior; understanding does not mean that we condone it. In the end, crime has a great deal to do with people's choices. There are sociological explanations that point to a criminal's possibly horrible childhood environment, to the company he keeps at present, or to cultural deviance and anomie. There are psychological and genetic explanations that point to genes, personal characteristics of criminals, or psychiatric problems (psychopaths). In fact, it may be that some people find some activities more attractive because they are criminal. Clearly, there is some truth in the various approaches to crime and criminals. Each of these explanations, including rationality, captures a part of the reality. They are all pieces of a large and complicated puzzle. There is no mega-theory that can fully explain and predict why certain individuals commit certain crimes.

It is sometimes said that if criminals were completely irrational, then no system of punishment would help to combat crime. Nothing would deter them. But even then criminal law and punishment has relevance for society. Two of the objectives of criminal law are retribution and isolation—which means to separate criminals from the rest of society in order to reduce the harm from crime. Even if criminals are all irrational, we can use economics to help us account for the costs and benefits of achieving these objectives.

If the assumption of rational behavior is only part of the explanation for crime, then why do we make this assumption? Clearly, the assumption fits some crimes—such as theft, drug trafficking, and fraud—better than others, but it seems likely that, except in the most extreme circumstances, most criminals will react to the probability of getting caught and to the punishment that might await them. In other words, regardless of the passion and irrationality involved in the crime, at least at the margin, more punishment would seem to make a difference. Granted, this difference may be small and other factors may dominate, but the rationality assumption is needed to complement the criminological, sociological, psychological, and genetic explanations.

LAW AND ECONOMICS IN ACTION 19.1

ECONOMIC ANALYSIS OF CRIME

The assumption of rational criminal behavior goes back to Jeremy Bentham. Bentham was an eighteenth-century utilitarian philosopher who in his essay titled "Principles of Penal Law" wrote: "the profit of the crime is the force which urges man to delinquency: the pain of the punishment is the force employed to restrain him from it. If the first of these forces be the greater, the crime will be committed; if the second, the crime will not be committed."[1] This quote appeared in an article by Erling Eide that provides a recent review of the relevant theoretical and empirical literature on the economic approach to crime.[2] Gary Becker has also written a classic article on the economic approach to crime.[3]

---

1. *Works*, 1 (1788), 1843, p. 399.

2. "Economics of Criminal Behavior" by Erling Eide (Chapter 8100 in Vol. 5, *Encyclopedia of Law and Economics*, ed. Boudewijn Bouckaert and Gerrit de Geest [Cheltenham: Edward Elgar, 2000], 307–344). Article from the *Encyclopedia of Law and Economics* can be downloaded from the web.

3. "Crime and Punishment: An Economic Approach," *Journal of Political Economy* 76, no. 2 (1968): 169–217.

THE RATIONAL CRIMINAL DEFINED

As already noted, in the most basic model of rational criminal behavior it is assumed that the criminal compares the benefits and expected costs of a crime that he intends to commit. In this section, we will discuss the various components of the benefits and costs of a crime. These benefits and expected costs can be affected by criminal policy. They are the tools for effective deterrence of criminal activities.

The Benefits

Benefits can be either tangible or intangible. Tangible benefits are, for instance, the amount of money or the stolen property in case of theft or robbery, the monetary gains from fraud and embezzlement or from trafficking drugs, the amount of ransom in abduction cases, or the fee the professional killer gets for killing someone. Often the benefits are intangible. Intangible benefits would include psychic benefits, such as the thrill of danger, approval from fellow criminals, retribution, or feeling good about having pulled it off. In the rest of this chapter and the next one on crime, in order to keep things simple, we will often assume that we can put a monetary value on the intangible benefits so that we can add them together and come up with a dollar figure.

The Private Costs

Private costs of crime are costs from the point of view of the criminal, as distinguished from the social costs of crime discussed in Chapter 18.[4] A distinction can be made between several kinds of private costs. First, there are what we could call the "professional" costs—expenditures the criminal needs to make in order to commit his crime. This could include material costs, such as a fast car, a gun, and a pair of black stockings (to pull over the head) for a bank robbery. Second, there are opportunity costs or income forgone. If a criminal can choose

---

4. Note that the private costs of criminals are part of the social cost. For instance, the income forgone by criminals as they busy themselves with unproductive criminal activities rather than productive labor is also income forgone to society and hence a social loss. As shown in the next chapter, social costs also include the costs to victims and to other members of society.

between a regular job and a career in crime, the income from the regular job is income forgone. Income forgone is the income he could have earned on the regular job had he not been involved in crime. There might also be psychic costs such as feelings of guilt, shame, anxiety, and fear.

Again, assume that we can monetize the psychic costs and add the various elements together to come up with a dollar value for the private costs.[5] If we call total monetary value of private benefits B and the total monetary value of private costs C, then the net benefit NB that a criminal derives from a crime is equal to the difference between his private benefits and costs:

$$\text{Net benefits} = \text{Private benefits} - \text{private costs}$$
$$NB = B - C$$

Expected Punishment

There is a second important cost element to consider: expected punishment. A rational criminal realizes that he might be caught and subsequently penalized for his crime. Expected punishment consists of two elements. The first element is the probability of getting caught and being penalized; the second element is the size of the penalty.

First, the police will not catch every criminal, so the probability of being apprehended will be smaller than one. But the police do catch some criminals, so the probability will be greater than zero. The same

---

5. The personal costs mentioned in this paragraph are certain costs or those that occur for sure when one decides to commit a crime. There are also costs that are uncertain because they depend on the probability of being found out, getting caught, and being convicted. These are called expected costs. Criminals might become stigmatized or even ostracized by society. In some cases, a known criminal might lose his voting rights or lose the right to participate in certain professions (somebody caught on a fraud charge can never become a banker). The conviction for a crime can be followed by a civil law case in which the victims claim damages and restitution. In a number of countries (such as the Netherlands) criminals might have their ill-gained profits and possessions impounded after being convicted as a criminal. The government will in this way try to make sure that the gains from criminal activities are taken away. These expected costs will enter the net benefit calculation in a way similar to that of the expected punishment, discussed in the next section. Expected costs are defined as costs in dollar terms multiplied by probability of punishment.

reasoning holds true for the probability of being convicted or penalized. Not all apprehended suspects are convicted, and not all convicted criminals are penalized. Hence the probability of conviction and punishment is also a number between zero and one. Assume that the probability of getting caught and apprehended for shoplifting is 0.20 (meaning that one out of five shoplifters is caught and handed over to the police). Assume that half of those apprehended for shoplifting are subsequently convicted and penalized. The combined probability is the product of these two probabilities—or the probability of punishment.[6] In the shoplifting case, this can be stated,

Probability of punishment for shoplifting = Probability of getting caught and apprehended × the probability of conviction

or

$$0.20 \times 0.50 = 0.10$$

This means that in one out of ten occurrences, a shoplifter is caught and punished.

Probabilities can be defined objectively or subjectively. Objective probabilities are the outcome of statistical measurements in which the number of times something happens (an apprehended shoplifter being fined) is counted and related to the total number of times it could have happened (total number of apprehended shoplifters, both fined and not fined). Subjective probabilities are estimates made by an individual whereby he makes a wild or educated guess as to what the

---

6. To simplify, we have combined the probability of being convicted and penalized into one probability number. In a more detailed model of rational crime, it might be appropriate to distinguish between many more probabilities. For instance, in the case of shoplifting, we could further distinguish between the probability of getting caught and the probability of being apprehended. Private security guards working in the shop often catch shoplifters, but they will not always call the police. Assume that the probability of getting caught by a private guard is 0.30 and that in only half of the cases the police are notified (probability is then 0.50). Not all apprehended shoplifters are convicted and not all convicted shoplifters are punished (they might get away with a reprimand). Assume that the probability of conviction after apprehension is 0.80 and the probability of being punished after conviction is 0.90. The combined probability of being caught, apprehended, convicted, and punished is then the product of all these probabilities: $0.30 \times 0.50 \times 0.80 \times 0.90$ which equals 0.108. Combining the probabilities as we do in this chapter does not change the arguments presented.

probabilities might be. These subjective probabilities, which are the estimates of the criminals, are the important ones for our theory.

Obviously, subjective and objective probabilities might differ. An optimistic criminal might think that the probability of punishment is much lower than it objectively turns out to be. He will be caught and fined more often than he expects. Eventually he will learn. A pessimistic criminal might assume a subjective probability that is higher than the objective probability. Because he will be deterred by his own pessimistic overestimate of the probability more than he would be if he knew the objective probability of apprehension, his error is in a way beneficial to society.

Why make a distinction between these different kinds of probabilities? Why make a distinction between the probability of apprehension and the probability of penalization?[7] As we will discuss in Chapter 20, the model of rational crime will be used to specify effective crime-fighting policies. Increasing the probability of apprehension and conviction will increase the costs of expected punishment; therefore, the number of people choosing to commit crimes will decrease. Looking at these probabilities from a policy angle, increasing the probability of apprehension is related to the efforts of the police system, and increasing the probability of penalization is related to the efforts of the prosecutorial and judicial systems.

The second element for the criminal is the size of the penalty.[8] The punishment can be either a fine or incarceration.[9] The fine is usually an amount of money to be paid. When a criminal is caught, the proceeds of his crime (the stolen property, the ransom in case of abduction) can sometimes be partly or completely retrieved. In those

7. And possibly other probabilities as explained in the previous footnote.

8. Individual rates of discount might be another element. The benefits from a crime usually occur immediately, whereas punishment might come much later in time. Individuals who value present things much more than things in the future are said to have a high discount rate for time. Criminals with a high discount rate will weigh the benefits arriving soon in time heavily and will discount (give less weight) to punishment in the distant future.

9. In many countries, criminals can also be ordered to spend a certain amount of time doing social duties such as helping in a community center or cleaning beaches. The analysis of the effect of this type of punishment runs more or less parallel to the analysis of incarceration.

cases, the criminal also loses (part of) the benefits of his crime. In the case of incarceration, the criminal cannot do his usual job while he is in jail and hence forgoes income that he otherwise would have earned. This income forgone can be used as a monetary equivalent for punishment. Suppose a criminal earns $50 a day. If he is convicted to 20 (working) days in jail, the income forgone is $50 \times 20 =$ $1,000.

Expected punishment (EP) is the combination of the probability of punishment ($Prob$) and the dollar value of the fine or of incarceration (F):

$$\text{Expected punishment} = \text{Probability of punishment} \times \text{the dollar value of the punishment}$$
$$EP = Prob \times F$$

For instance, if the probability of punishment for shoplifting is 0.10 and the fine for shoplifting is a $500 fine, then the expected punishment for shoplifting is

$$\text{Expected punishment for shoplifting} = 0.10 \times \$500 = \$50$$

Combining the Elements: Falling on *Hard Times*

If we combine all of these elements, we have the basic model of the rational criminal. Suppose a student of English literature is standing in a bookstore next to the shelf with British Classics and is considering stealing Charles Dickens's *Hard Times,* which he needs for class. The book is a beautiful leather-bound edition that sells at $59.95. The student experiences no psychic benefits or costs. There are no professional costs necessary for his intended crime nor any expected costs. The student is wearing a coat with pockets wide enough to make *Hard Times* disappear. The net benefit for the student if he decides to steal the book is

$$\text{Net benefits of stealing } Hard\ Times =$$
$$\text{Private benefits} - \text{private costs}$$
$$NB = B - C$$
$$NB = 59.95 - 0 = \$59.95$$

Assume that the probability of punishment for stealing a book from a bookstore is 0.10. The fine is $500. Hence the expected punishment for stealing the book is

$$EP \text{ bookstealing} = \text{Probability of punishment} \times \text{level of fine}$$
$$= Prob \times F$$
$$= 0.05 \times \$500 = \$50$$

The student will compare the net private benefits with the expected punishment. If the net benefit is higher than the expected punishment, the English student, as a rational criminal, will commit the crime. If the expected punishment is higher, the rational criminal will not commit the crime.

In the given example,

$$\text{Net benefit} > \text{Expected punishment}$$

$$\text{Private benefits} - \text{private costs} >$$
$$\text{probability of punishment} \times \text{fine}$$
$$\$59.95 - 0 > 0.05 \times \$500$$
$$\$59.95 > \$50$$

In this case, crime is profitable, and the English language student will steal the Charles Dickens book.

This example makes clear that as long as the left-hand side (the net benefits) is greater than the right-hand side (the expected cost of punishment), rational criminals will commit crimes. So to deter rational criminals from committing crime and hence reduce the crime rate, society should devise policies that decrease the net benefit of crime and/or increase the expected punishment.

POLICY IMPLICATIONS

The rational model of crime is basically a cost-benefit analysis. The benefits are compared with the costs. Policies that decrease the benefits of crime and increase the costs of crime will be helpful in reducing the crime level. How can we reduce the net benefit of crime? First, we can try to increase the private costs to the criminal. Households could, for instance, take more preventive measures (more locks on the doors and windows, alarm systems) to protect their property. These protective measures will increase the cost of theft and robbery. The criminal will need to invest more in professional costs. For example, in Amsterdam, where bike theft is endemic, there are many ways to keep a bike from being stolen. A bike owner can increase the number of locks on the bike from one to three (one for the front wheel, one for the back wheel—wheels are sometimes stolen separately—and one to chain the bike to a bike stand or a lamppost). Bikes can then be stolen only if the thief invests in large professional chain-cutters. Or people use only second-hand and downtrodden bikes with hardly any value for in-city bike trips, again reducing the net benefits of bike theft.

An important cost element for the criminal is forgone earnings— the income he could be earning on a regular job rather than in a criminal career. Clearly, those parts of the population who run the risk of becoming unemployed and staying out of work for a long period or who can only find unattractive, low-paying jobs have low costs of forgone earnings. In their circumstances, the trappings of a criminal career could appear very attractive.[10] Viewed in this way, a policy to combat unemployment or to upgrade the skills of workers with bad labor market prospects could, in a wider sense, contribute to less crime.

We have also mentioned possible psychic benefits and costs to criminals. Feelings of guilt and shame, for example, come about because the rational criminal finds himself in a situation in which he does not adhere to norms and expectations that society holds and that he has internalized.[11] Expressed in a positive way, an individual may feel strongly that it is his duty to adhere to societal norms. These nega-

---

10. Although as documented in a chapter entitled "Why Do Drug Dealers Still Live with Their Moms?" in *Freakonomics,* a book by Steven Leavitt and Stephen Dubner (New York: William Morrow, 2005), most drug dealers do not make much money, not even enough to live on their own.

11. Another way to model the importance of personal norms is by using the concept of preferences and utility levels for the income derived from crime. People will differ in their preferences for criminal activities depending on their adherence to societal norms and their own moral codes. In this model, we assume the rational criminal will choose between committing or not committing a crime depending on whether this maximizes his or her utility level. Suppose that before committing a crime, a criminal has income or wealth equal to W. His level of utility corresponding with this wealth or income level is $U(W)$. The utility function $U(W)$ does not have to be linear. Suppose that higher and higher levels of wealth or income give you a less than proportional increase in utility (100 dollars extra when you already have a billion dollars gives you less utility increase than 100 dollars extra when you have only a thousand dollars initially). With diminishing marginal utility of wealth, the utility function will be concave. Suppose that without committing a crime, a

tive guilt feelings or positive normative feelings about what a person "ought" to do are important. It is clear that at a simple level, the probability of getting caught and convicted is rather small for quite a number of crimes. On this basis, one would expect more crime to occur than is actually occurring. Most people have strong personal and ethical norms and will not even consider committing a crime or a felony even if expected punishment is very small or even zero.

Societal norms are not only passed on and instilled in the minds of children by their families but also by schools. In this wider sense, schooling could also be considered as part of a larger scheme to combat crime. Another possibility to consider is that strictly adhering to the law and the policies of apprehending, prosecuting, and convicting criminals might by itself improve the moral environment and thereby increase the strength with which ethical norms are held in society.

A high rate of recidivism is also in accordance with the model of rational choice. If the opportunities for an offender remain the same, and the net benefit of the same crime is still higher than the expected punishment, the degree of criminality will not decrease after a conviction. Recidivism is not necessarily a matter of erratic or ingrained behavior, but the consistent result of rational choice.

---

criminal has a wealth level W and derives utility from it equal to $U(W)$. This is his utility level without committing a crime. If the criminal decides to commit the crime, his expected utility level becomes $E[U \text{ (crime)}] = Prob \times U(W + NB - F) + (1 - Prob) \times U(W + NB)$, where $Prob$ is the probability of punishment, F is the fine, and NB is the net benefit from crime. If he gets punished, his wealth will be $W + NB - F$, and his utility level will be $U(W + NB - F)$. If he gets away with his crime without being punished, his wealth will be $W + NB$, and his utility level corresponding will be $U(W + NB)$. He will be punished with probability $Prob$ and escape with probability $1 - Prob$. He will commit a crime if utility without crime $U(W)$ is less than the expected utility from crime $E[U(\text{crime})]$. This modeling of the choice of the rational criminal is more general than the linear model we present in the text. We will come back to the utility function when discussing attitudes toward risk in the last section of this chapter. The specification we discuss here allows for making a distinction between individuals having different utility levels for legal income and illegally acquired income. Individuals with high moral codes will have higher utility from legal income. The qualitative predictions of this more general model are similar to the more simple model used in the text.

The main thrust of crime fighting is increasing the level of expected punishment. Crime does not pay when expected punishment is higher than net benefits. How can we increase expected punishment? There are many ways. We can either increase the probability of apprehension by increasing the size and effectiveness of the police force, or we can increase the probability of conviction by increasing the size and effectiveness of the judicial system. Finally, we can increase the level of the fines or the number of days of incarceration.

Expected punishment is the product of the probability of punishment and the size of the punishment. What is special about this equation is that the same dollar amount of expected punishment can be reached by either increasing the probability of punishment and at the same time decreasing the level of punishment or by decreasing the probability of punishment and increasing the punishment. Table 19.1 shows how five different combinations lead to the same expected punishment. In the first case, an expected punishment level of $50 is achieved with a quite small probability of punishment (0.5 percent) combined with a large ($10,000) fine. In the last case, a relatively high probability of punishment (50 percent) combined with a small fine of $100 leads to the same expected punishment of $50.

From the calculations in Table 19.1, it seems possible to trade off a decrease in the probability of punishment for an increase in the level of punishment and still keep the expected punishment constant. This is an interesting implication because, from the government's point of view, establishing a certain level of probability of punishment is much more expensive than imposing a fine. In general, an increase in the probability of punishment requires a larger budget for the requisite police force and judiciary system. Increasing the level of the fine can be done with the stroke of a pen (and much less government expense).

TABLE 19.1 Expected Punishment

PROBABILITY OF PUNISHMENT	PUNISHMENT ($)	EXPECTED PUNISHMENT ($)
0.005	10,000	50
0.025	2,000	50
0.05	1,000	50
0.10	500	50
0.50	100	50

There are, however, limits to trading off lower probabilities of punishment for higher levels of fines. The implications of this trade-off turn out to be awkward at some point. Suppose the government wants to achieve an expected level of punishment equal to $50 in the case of shoplifting. It could in principle attain this level of expected punishment by catching and convicting a single criminal and punishing him with an extremely high fine. This is awkward because it goes against our notion of what is fair and just. We expect the level of the fine to be in proportion to the severity of the crime. We could capture and convict only one in a million shoplifters (probability of punishment: 0.000001) and fine that one person $50 million. The expected punishment is still $50, the same as before, but clearly the fine is completely out of proportion to the seriousness of the offense. A fine this high would almost certainly violate the U.S. Constitution's prohibition of punishment that is *cruel and unusual*.

A second reason the government cannot increase the levels of fines indefinitely is that most criminals are not wealthy enough to pay a high fine—even if we confiscate all the criminal's income and assets. Hence, very high levels of fines are neither a sensible nor practical policy.

The government could substitute incarceration for monetary fines. Ideally, one could determine the cost to the criminal of a day in jail. This would include the opportunity cost of earnings lost plus some value attributed to the loss of freedom. Of course, jail does mean free room and board, and this would have to be accounted for. When all these factors are considered, suppose a value of not being in jail is $100 per day to the criminal. Suppose also that the fine that was originally intended (but which is much higher than all the wealth that the criminal possesses) is $100,000. In that case, the substitute punishment could be 1,000 days in jail. This sounds straightforward, but incarceration is much more costly for society; it requires investment in prison buildings and paying salaries to prison guards and wardens.

Given these limitations, the government will look for a sensible mix of policies to reduce crime. It will set monetary fines at rather low levels (mostly for minor crimes and misdemeanors) and it will set incarceration sentences for major crimes. It will also try to achieve an adequate level of probability of punishment. We will return to what constitutes an effective crime-fighting policy in Chapter 20.

THE IMPLICATIONS OF ATTITUDES TOWARD RISK

In the analysis of rational crime so far, we have implicitly assumed that the rational criminal is indifferent to the risks inherent in committing a crime. When the rational criminal is indifferent in this way, we say that he is being risk neutral.[12] For example, a person who is indifferent between getting a certain payment of $1,000 or a 0.5 probability of $2,000 and a 0.5 probability of 0 dollars also is said to be risk neutral.

In general, however, people value certainty over uncertainty, and if given the choice between $1,000 for sure and an expectation of $1,000, they will always prefer the $1,000 for sure. This is called risk aversion. A risk-averse person might even prefer $1,000 for sure over an uncertain expected income of $1,200 (for instance, through an uncertain income stream consisting of $2,000 with probability of 0.5 and $400 also with probability of 0.5). A risk-averse person is willing to accept a lower certain income level than a higher (uncertain) expected income level. The higher his level of risk aversion, the more difference he is willing to accept between the certain and the uncertain income.

The counterpart to a risk-averse person is a risk-loving or risk-preferring person. Risk-loving people like to take gambles. Intuitively, a risk-loving person prefers a lower uncertain expected income to a higher certain income because he gets additional utility from taking the risk; he gets a kick from taking a gamble.

When a rational criminal has to decide whether to commit a crime, he is comparing a certain situation with an uncertain situation. Assume a person considering committing a criminal act has a regular level of income of $1,000 a month. If he does not commit the crime, he just has this $1,000 for sure. If he decides to commit a crime, his income will be uncertain. If he does not get punished, his income is $1,000 plus the net benefit of his crime, say $200, a total of $1,200. If, how-

---

12. In terms of the more general model introduced in the previous footnote, risk neutrality implies that the expected utility of an uncertain event—the uncertain event being the probability of being punished or not) equals the utility of the expected benefit, that is, $Prob \times U(W + NB - F) + (1 - Prob) \times U(W + NB) = U[Prob \times (W - F) + (1 - Prob) \times (W + NB)]$.

ever, he gets punished, he is fined $100 (and assume for simplicity that his net benefit from crime is confiscated), which leaves him with a total income of $900.

Suppose now that in option A, the probability of punishment is 0.20. In that case, the expected income of committing the crime is $(0.80 \times 1,200) + (0.20 \times 900) = \$1,140$. Suppose that under option B, the probability of punishment is 0.80. The expected income of committing the crime will now be $(0.20 \times 1,200) + (0.80 \times 900) = \$960$. A risk-neutral person would always commit a crime in case A because the expected income of $1,140 is more than the certain income of $1,000 and he is indifferent to uncertainty. He neither likes nor dislikes it. A risk-neutral person will never commit a crime in case B because the certain income of $1,000 is higher than the expected income $960.

A sufficiently risk-averse person might not commit a crime in either situation. He will certainly not commit a crime in situation B (the uncertain income is lower than the certain income and on top of that he dislikes uncertainty). But he might not commit a crime in case A either because the higher uncertain income of $1,140 might not be sufficiently higher than the certain income of $1,000 to offset his dislike of uncertainty.

On the other hand, a sufficiently risk-loving person might always commit a crime. He will certainly commit a crime in case A. He might commit a crime even in case B. Although the expected income of $960 is lower than the certain income of $1,000, the difference of $40 might not outweigh the utility gain he gets from taking the gamble. He likes uncertainty enough to take that risk.

Taking into account the risk attitude and the risk aversion or risk-loving characteristics of prospective criminals changes somewhat the predictions we made above when we assumed that all prospective criminals were risk neutral. If prospective criminals are mostly risk averse, then fewer crimes will be committed, with the same levels of expected punishment, than in a population of risk-neutral prospective criminals. Risk-averse criminals will dislike the uncertainty and risk that comes with crime. Obviously, not all crime will disappear. Even in a population of risk-averse prospective criminals, the expected income from crime might be so high that it more than outweighs the disutility that comes with the risk and uncertainty of the criminal profession. If prospective criminals are mostly risk loving (which intuitively they might be), more crimes will be committed than in a population of only risk-neutral criminals.

Individual attitudes toward risk imply a different evaluation of the utility levels derived from increasing levels of income. Figure 19.1 shows the relationship between income and utility levels for three types of persons: a risk-averse person (panel A), a risk-neutral person (panel B), and a risk-loving person (panel C). We will use Figure 19.1 to illustrate the differences in evaluating the cost and benefits of crime for a risk-averse, risk-neutral, and risk-loving criminal.

In all three parts of the figure the level of utility increases with the level of income.[13] In the case of the risk-averse criminal, utility levels increase at a decreasing rate (concave curve in panel A); for the risk-neutral criminal, the increase is proportional (linear line in panel B); and the risk-loving criminal's income increases at an increasing rate (convex curve in panel C).[14] These differences in rate of increase are the graphic representation of the differences in attitude toward risk among the three types of criminals.

Now assume that without the crime, the criminals each have a certain income level of $1,000 and they each derive a utility level of a 100 out of that income. Suppose the criminal considers stealing a bike worth a $100. If he is not caught, that implies his income after the crime is $1,100. In all three cases, utility increases (albeit by different amounts). If he gets caught, he loses the bike and on top of that gets a $150 fine. This reduces his income to $850 and brings with it a reduction in utility.

In addition, assume that the probability of getting caught is 0.40 and that there are no costs involved in stealing the bike. The net benefit from stealing the bike is $100. The expected punishment is equal to 0.40 times the fine of $150 and the confiscation of the stolen bike worth $100. Hence, the expected punishment is $0.40 \times (\$150 + \$100) = \$100$. In this case, net benefit ($100) equals net punishment

---

13. Note that utility level numbers are fictitious numbers.

14. In this section, we use specific numbers to illustrate our arguments. The results that we derive are, however, of a general nature. The results we discuss are "driven" by the differences in the curvature of the utility functions in the three panels.

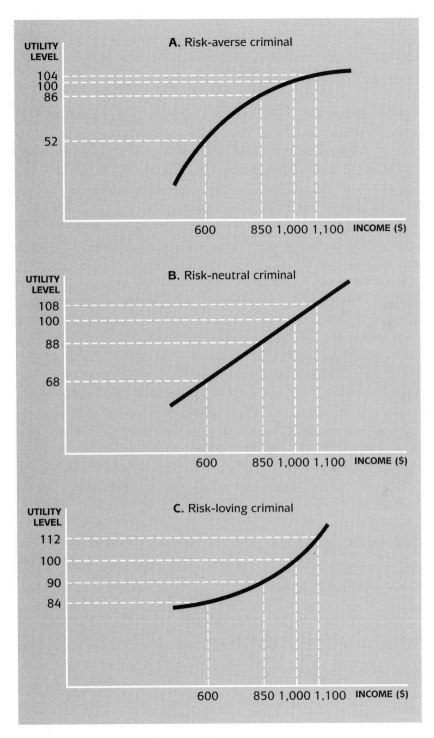

FIGURE 19.1 Attitudes Toward Risk

($100) and this crime does not pay. Another way of looking at this is that if he does not steal the bike, he does not lose or gain anything and has a certain income of $1,000. If he steals the bike, there is a 60 percent chance that he will not be caught or punished and will end up with an income of $1,100. But there is also a 40 percent chance that he will be caught and punished and in the end have an income of only $850. His expected income from the crime is $1,000—0.60 × 1,100 + 0.40 × 850. The expected income from crime is the same as his certain no-crime income. So why bother?

Let us now take the utility levels into account and see how this changes the analysis. From Figure 19.1, we can read the utility levels corresponding to the different levels of income. For instance, for the risk-averse person, the income level of $1,100 corresponds to a utility level of 104 and the income level of $850 corresponds to a utility level of 86. If he does commit the crime, he has a utility level of 86 with probability 0.40 (that is when he is caught and punished and ends up with $850 only) and a utility level of 104 (if he is not caught and has an income of $1,100). Hence, his expected utility of stealing is 0.60 × 104 + 0.40 × 86 = 96.8. This is what we calculated in the top left cell of Table 19.2 for the risk-averse criminal. Similarly, we calculated in the first column the expected utility level for the risk-neutral criminal and for the risk-loving criminal.

The expected utility level of the risk-neutral criminal from crime is 100. This is precisely the same as his utility from his certain income level of $1,000, which is also 100 (see panel B). A risk-neutral criminal is indifferent between a certain income of $1,000 and a risky expected income of $1,000 (0.40 × 850 + 0.60 × 1,100). But the

TABLE 19.2 Expected Utility

	PROBABILITY: 0.40 PUNISHMENT: $250	PROBABILITY: 0.80 PUNISHMENT: $250	PROBABILITY: 0.40 PUNISHMENT: $500
Risk averse	0.60 × 104 + 0.40 × 86 = 96.8	0.20 × 104 + 0.80 × 86 = 89.6	0.60 × 104 + 0.40 × 52 = 83.2
Risk neutral	0.60 × 108 + 0.40 × 88 = 100	0.20 × 108 + 0.80 × 88 = 92	0.60 × 108 + 0.40 × 68 = 92
Risk lover	0.60 × 112 + 0.40 × 90 = 103.2	0.20 × 112 + 0.80 × 90 = 94.4	0.60 × 112 + 0.40 × 84 = 100.8

risk-averse criminal, on the other hand, is not indifferent. His expected utility level from committing the crime is only 96.8. He derives less satisfaction from an uncertain income level (which is on average equal to $1,000) than from the same certain income level. The risk-loving criminal, on the other hand, gets an extra kick from his criminal activities. The uncertain criminal income level of $1,000 gives him more utility than the same certain no-crime income level. His expected utility level of stealing the bike goes up to 103.2. Hence, for the same probability of punishment and level of punishment, risk-loving criminals will commit crimes more often than risk-neutral and risk-averse criminals.

In the second column of Table 19.2, we doubled the probability of getting caught from 40 per cent to 80 percent while keeping the level of punishment intact. Expected income from stealing the bike now goes down to $900 (= .80 × $850 + 0.20 × $1,100). Clearly, the utility levels go down for all three types of criminals. Utility levels go down below the level of 100 corresponding to the no-crime certain income level of $1,000. Increasing the probability of punishment clearly works as a deterrent for crime in this case.

In the third column, we went back to the original punishment probability of 40 percent but now we doubled the total punishment from what it was in column 1 (i.e., $250) to $500. For the calculations in column 3, we assumed that when the bicycle thief gets caught, he loses the bike (= $100) and on top of that he gets a $400 fine. In this case, the expected income is 0.40 times $600 (if punished) plus 0.60 times $1,100 which is again $900 (same as in column 2). Compared with column 1, expected income goes down and hence utility derived from stealing the bike goes down for all criminal types with a doubled punishment in column 3.

The risk-neutral criminal is only interested in the level of income and not in whether it is certain or uncertain or what the source of uncertainty is. The expected level of income is 900 when we double the punishment probability (column 2) or double the punishment (column 3). He does not care. In both situations, the utility level corresponding to an income of $900 dollars is 92. But matters are different for the risk-averse and risk-loving criminals. In column 3, the risk-loving criminal derives a utility level of 100.3 from the uncertain income level of $900 resulting from crime, which is higher than the utility level of 100 he derives from his certain, no-crime income level of $1,000. Doubling the punishment level will not deter him from crime. On the other hand, looking back at column 2, doubling the punishment probability does deter him. In column 2, his utility level is only 94.4. One can conclude that a risk-loving criminal is more sensitive to a doubling of the probability of punishment than to doubling the punishment. This contrasts with the risk-averse criminal. If we compare his utility levels between column 2 and 3, we see that his utility level is lower when we double the punishment level (83.2 in column 3) compared to doubling the probability (89.6 in column 2). One can conclude that risk-averse criminals will be more deterred from doubling punishment than from doubling probability of punishment. For an intuitive explanation of this, we suggest the following. In the third column, we widen the spread between the two uncertain income levels to $600 and $1,100 from what it is in columns 1 and 2: $850 and $1,100. This wider spread increases the undesirable risk element for the risk-averse criminal and hence his utility goes down a lot in column 3.

To conclude, we have shown that when the population consists of risk-averse criminals, increasing the probability of punishment is less effective than increasing the level of punishment. If the population consists of risk-loving criminals, the reverse holds true. They are more likely to abandon crime if the probability of punishment is increased than when the level of the fine is increased.

CASE 19.2 **The Felony Murder Rule:** *Roary v. State of Maryland,* 867 A.2d 1095 (Maryland 2005)

One of the most controversial doctrines in American criminal law is the *felony murder rule.* It also can be connected to the assumptions we make about the attitudes of criminals toward risk. Basically, the rule is that if someone is killed in the course of a felony, it is murder. This may seem to make sense, but remember that murder usually requires that the criminal have some intent to commit murder. Otherwise the idea of deterrence seems to lose its connection to the crime. In addition, a felony can include things like conspiring with others to commit crimes that actually do not seem to pose much of a threat of physical harm. In other words, under the rule, one can be convicted of murder without intending to harm anyone and without having direct involvement in causing the harm. This may seem harsh, but is it possible that the ultimate outcome is desirable?

In *Roary*, the defendant participated in beating up a person who later died. The defendant's participation consisted of kicking the victim in the leg. Two other people dropped a boulder on the victim's head, and this resulted in the death. The question was whether Roary was guilty of murder since he was involved in a felony assault that eventually led to the victim's death. A majority of the Maryland court held that he was. The dissent in the case made the following argument that stresses the disconnection between the idea of deterrence and a death that was not intended. Note that the dissent quotes extensively from an article by a legal scholar:

> [T]he purported underlying purpose of the felony-murder doctrine, that of deterrence, is not furthered by permitting first degree assault to serve as a predicate felony. . . . The deterrence purpose underlying the rule has been described as follows by one commentator: "The primary justification offered for the contemporary felony-murder rule is deterrence. The doctrine is allegedly designed to save lives by threatening potential killers with the serious sanction for first or second degree murder. One deterrent argument holds that the threat of a murder conviction for any killing in furtherance of a felony, even an accidental killing, might well induce a felon to forego committing the felony itself Because it could lead to quite severe punishment, the risk averse might shy away from the entire felonious enterprise. Another argument, the more prevalent of the two main deterrent explanations of felony-murder, maintains that the rule is aimed at discouraging certain conduct during the felony, not the felony itself. The goal is to encourage greater care in the performance of felonious acts. Such care will lower the risks to human life and result in fewer deaths. Still another view suggests that felons who might kill intentionally in order to complete their felonies successfully will be discouraged by the rule's proclamation that the law will entertain no excuses for the homicide. Calculating felons will forego killing because of their awareness that the chance of constructing a defense that would eliminate or mitigate liability is virtually nonexistent and that, therefore, their likely fate is a murder conviction." James J. Tomkovicz, "The Endurance of the Felony-Murder Rule: A Study of the Forces that Shape Our Criminal Law," 51 Wash & Lee L. Rev. 1429 (1994). If indeed the purpose of the felony-murder rule is to deter accidental or

negligent killings, how then is the purpose furthered by finding murder when the defendant intentionally commits a dangerous and life threatening assault? Moreover, how is the purpose furthered when the rule is applied, as it must be under Maryland law, to an accomplice who may not have inflicted the harm personally, had no knowledge that the ultimate perpetrator had a deadly weapon, and had no intent to commit murder?

The application of the felony-murder rule and the extension of the doctrine to the case sub judice is particularly disturbing. [The] jury found that Roary did not intend to kill the victim, nor did he intend to inflict grievous bodily harm upon him. It is only by the application, and the extension thereof, of the felony-murder doctrine that Roary was convicted of murder.

What do you think? Do you agree that it makes little sense to find that a person did not commit murder and then convict that person of felony murder when he did not intend to commit murder? The author of the quoted article says that the extra punishment may cause the risk-averse person not to commit the felony in the first place. Do you agree?

WRAPPING UP

We can summarize our discussion of the rational criminal in a simple graph using the familiar instruments of demand and supply curves. It has been shown above that rational criminals will—given that everything else is kept constant—"demand" more crime if the expected punishment is lower. The expected punishment can be seen as the "price" a criminal will have to pay for committing the crime. The lower the price (i.e., the lower the expected punishment), the more crime will be committed. In Figure 19.2, we put the "price of crime" on the vertical axis and the number of crimes on the horizontal axis. Next, we draw the "demand for crime curve" as a downward-sloping curve. If the government, through its expenditure on the police force, the judiciary, and penal system, creates an expected level of punishment equal to A, the number of crimes committed will be C_A. If the government increases the expected level of punishment to B, the number of crimes will go down to C_B. How much expenditure the government should allocate to fighting crime will be discussed in Chapter 20 where we explain the choice of an optimal level of deterrence.

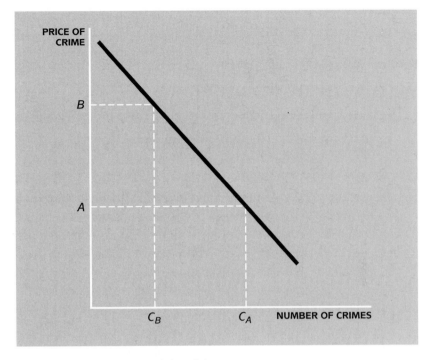

FIGURE 19.2 The Demand for Crime

QUESTIONS FOR DISCUSSION

1. The theory of the rational criminal predicts that if the difference between net benefits and expected punishment of a crime is high enough, everybody will become a criminal eventually. Or to be more concrete, if a person faces the opportunity to steal a lot of money with 100 percent certainty that nobody can discover who committed the crime, he or she will steal the money. Do you agree or disagree? Why?

2. In some countries, minor crimes are sometimes punished by sentencing the perpetrator to do community service such as helping in an old-age home, helping with the construction of a children's playground, or cleaning up beaches. How does this enter into the cost-benefit calculations of a rational criminal? Is it effective in reducing minor crimes? Why is it sometimes used to sentence well-known public figures such as media stars and sports figures?

3. Illegally downloading copyrighted music and movies from the Internet is a crime. It is stealing property. Yet people who would not consider stealing a book from a bookstore have been known to download illegally from the Internet. What is the rational cost-benefit calculation behind this behavior?

4. To deter crime, it is more effective to increase the probability of catching criminals than it is to punish them severely. Do you agree or disagree?

5. You have probably heard of plea bargains—when a defendant accepts a lower level of punishment to avoid a trial that may result in a higher level of punishment. It is possible, though that the trial could lead to an acquittal. Who is more likely to opt for a plea bargain—a risk-averse, a risk-neutral or a risk-loving person? Should punishment depend on how one feels about risk?

6. Reconsider the felony murder rule. The argument is that it makes risk-averse people less likely to commit crimes. Is it inefficient to have punishment that impacts people differently depending on their attitudes toward risk?

APPENDIX: A MORE GENERAL MODEL OF THE RATIONAL CRIMINAL

A more general way to model the behavior of the rational criminal that allows us to include the effect of personal norms and predilections is by using the concept of preferences and utility levels for legal and illegal income.[15] People will differ in their preferences for criminal activities depending on their adherence to societal norms and their own moral codes. In this model, we assume the rational criminal will choose between committing or not committing a crime depending on whether this maximizes his or her utility level.

Introducing Utility

Suppose that before committing a crime, a criminal has income or wealth equal to W. His level of utility corresponding with this wealth

15. Gary Becker started the modern approach to the economic modeling of crime in his article titled "Crime and Punishment: An Economic Approach."

or income level is $U(W)$. The utility function $U(W)$ does not have to be linear. Suppose that higher and higher levels of wealth or income give you a less than proportional increase in utility: $100 extra when you already have a million dollars gives you less of a utility increase than $100 extra when you only have $1,000 initially. This is the property of diminishing marginal utility of wealth or income. With diminishing marginal utility of wealth, the utility function will be concave. To illustrate this property, let us assume that the utility function $U(W)$ is a simple square root function with the following functional form: $\sqrt{x}$. This function looks like Figure 19.A1.

From this graph, one can read that when x equals 4; $\sqrt{4} = 2$ and when $x = 9$; $\sqrt{9} = 3$. In this appendix, we replace x with wealth W and this will be our utility function:

$$U(W) = \sqrt{W}$$

Doing this, we assume that we can "translate" a person's wealth levels into utility levels using the square root. The level of utility should

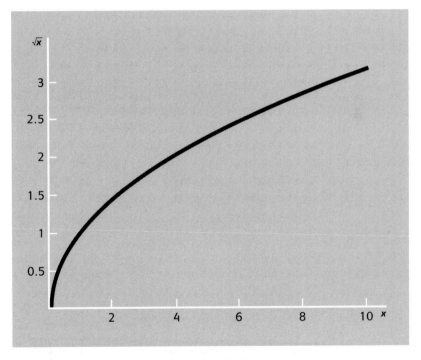

FIGURE 19.A1 Diminishing Marginal Utility

TABLE 19.A1 Marginal Utility and Wealth

WEALTH	TOTAL UTILITY	MARGINAL UTILITY
1,000	31.62	
1,100	33.17	1.55
1,000,000	1,000	
1,000,100	1,000.05	0.05

be seen as an index or an indicator, the more the better. If it is help-ful, you can also measure the level of utility in abstract units that you could call "utils." Because the slope of the concavely shaped function in the graph diminishes at higher levels, a utility function in the form of a square root exhibits diminishing marginal utility of wealth. We illustrate this property in Table 19.A1 where we compare the increase in the utility level of adding an extra $100 to somebody possessing $1,000 and someone with a million dollars. We assume that both per-sons have the same square root utility function to translate wealth into utility (or maybe it is the same person being poor when he has only $1,000 and rich when he has a million).

A person with $1,000 has a utility level of 31.62 (= $\sqrt{1,000}$). If he gets an additional $100, his utility level increases to 33.17 (= $\sqrt{1,100}$). The increase in utility, called the marginal utility of the extra $100 is 1.55. If a millionaire gets an additional $100, his utility level increases from 1,000 to 1,000.05 only. His marginal utility is only 0.05, which is less than the 1.55 of the poor person who had $1,000 initially. This is the property of diminishing marginal utility of wealth or income. As we get richer, we still become more happy or satisfied (or whatever utility stands for), but to a smaller degree.[16]

A Criminal's Utility Trade-off

Suppose that without committing a crime, a criminal has a wealth level W and derives utility from it equal to $U(W)$. This is his utility level without committing a crime. If the criminal decides to commit a crime, his expected utility level becomes

---

16. For those who know about derivatives, a concave function has a positive first derivative and a negative second derivative. This holds true also for the first derivative of the square function: $\frac{1}{2}x^{-\frac{1}{2}} > 0$ being positive and the second deriv-ative: $-\frac{1}{4}x^{-\frac{1}{2}} < 0$ being negative.

$$E[U \text{ (crime)}] = Prob \times U(W + NB - F)$$
$$+ (1 - Prob) \times U(W + NB)$$

Where *Prob* is the probability of punishment, *F* is the fine and *NB* is the net benefit from crime. Because we have probabilities in the formula, we define the utility level as the expected utility level $E[U(\text{crime})]$. If he gets punished, his wealth will be $W + NB - F$, and his utility level will be $U(W + NB - F)$. If he gets away with his crime without being punished, his wealth will be $W + NB$, and his utility level corresponding to this will be $U(W + NB)$. He will be punished with probability *Prob* and escape with probability $1 - Prob$. He will commit a crime if utility without crime $U(W)$ is less than the expected utility from crime $E[U(\text{crime})]$; that is, when

$$E[U(\text{crime})] > U(\text{no crime}) = U(W)$$

Let us illustrate this using the square root utility function. Suppose the prospective criminal has initial wealth (W) equal to \$1,000. As we calculated above, the utility level corresponding to this amount of wealth is 31.62. This person is contemplating stealing a book worth \$100. In terms of our formula above, that is the net benefit of crime *NB*. The probability of catching a shoplifter is one out of ten or $Prob = 0.10$. How big should the fine *F* be to deter this criminal? This can be calculated using our model. This person will commit a crime if

$$0.10 \times U(1,000 + 100 - F) + 0.90 \times U(1,000 + 100) > U(1,000)$$
$$0.10 \times U(1,100 - F) > U(1,000) - 0.90 \times U(1,100)$$
$$0.10 \times \sqrt{(1,100 - F)} > \sqrt{(1,000)} - 0.90 \times \sqrt{(1,100)}$$
$$\sqrt{(1,100 - F)} > 10(31.62 - 0.90 \times 33.17)$$
$$\sqrt{(1,100 - F)} > 17.67$$
$$1,100 - F > (17.67)^2 = 312.23$$
$$F < 787.77$$

This person will commit a crime if the fine is less than \$787.77. You can check this if you plug in this value for the fine in the first line and see if the inequality holds.[17]

---

17. There is a slight rounding-off error because we worked with two decimal digits only. Also, in the way we set up the problem, we assumed that the criminal gets to keep the book even after he is punished. If that is not the case, the fine would be \$100 less. Or, put differently, the fine of \$787.77 might include the value of the book.

Suppose the probability of getting punished can be doubled and becomes 0.20 instead of 0.10. Does this mean the fine can be halved as in the linear case we used in the Policy Implications section of this chapter? After doing the calculations it can be determined that with prob = 0.20 the fine F should be minimally $453.82. This is higher than $393.88 which would be the half of the previous fine of $787.77. The intuition behind this is that one has to "hit" a person harder with diminishing marginal utility of wealth or income in money terms to get a high enough reduction in utility terms.

Risk Attitudes

This modeling of the choice of the rational criminal is more general than the linear model we present in the text of Chapter 19. The specification we discuss here allows for making a distinction between individuals having different utility levels for legal income and illegally acquired income. Individuals with high moral codes will have higher utility from legal income. The qualitative predictions of this more general model are similar to the more simple model used in the text.

We come back to more general utility functions when discussing possible attitudes towards risk of prospective criminals in this chapter. An aversion towards risk taking can be expressed in the form of a utility function with diminishing marginal utility of wealth or income, such as we used in this appendix. Risk-loving can be formulated by using a form for the utility function with increasing marginal utility. Risk neutrality implies constant marginal utility.

In terms of the general model introduced here, risk neutrality implies that the expected utility of an uncertain event (the uncertain event being the probability of being punished or not) equals the utility of the expected benefit:

$$Prob \times U(W + NB - F) + (1 - Prob) \times U(W + NB)$$
$$= U\,[Prob \times (W + NB - F) + (1 - Prob) \times (W + NB)]$$

This is a property that does not hold true for the (nonlinear) square root function. As can easily been shown using, for instance, the following example $W = \$1,000$; $NB = \$100$; $F = \$500$ and $Prob = 0.10$:

$$0.10 \times \sqrt{600} + 0.90 \times \sqrt{1,100} \neq \sqrt{(0.10 \times 600 + 0.90 \times 1,100)}$$
$$0.10 \times 24.49 + 0.90 \times 33.17 \neq \sqrt{1,050}$$
$$32.30 \neq 32.40$$

But it does hold true for a utility function that is just a linear transformation of the level of wealth or income, such as for instance $U(W) = a + bW$ or $U(W) = cW$. Assume that $U(W) = \frac{1}{2}W$. Utility levels are just half of the wealth levels. It is not hard to see now that with such a utility function,

$$Prob \times U(W + NB - F) + (1 - Prob) \times U(W + NB) = U\,[Prob \times (W + NB - F) + (1 - Prob) \times (W + NB)]$$ holds true:

$$Prob \times \tfrac{1}{2}(W + NB - F) + (1 - Prob) \times \tfrac{1}{2}(W + NB) = \tfrac{1}{2}\,[Prob \times (W + NB - F) + (1 - Prob) \times (W + NB)]$$

You should be able to show that the same property holds true for a slightly more general linear utility of the form $a + bW$, such as, for instance, $20 + \frac{1}{2}W$.

CHAPTER TWENTY

Efficient Levels of Deterrence

WOULD IT BE POSSIBLE TO CREATE A SOCIETY WITH-out crime? Would it be sensible? To answer these questions, let's start with murder. Murder is a hideous crime, and ridding society of murder would certainly be a blessing. Murders happen for all kinds of reasons, at all kinds of places, and at all times. If society wanted to prevent any murder from happening at all, it would have to expand its police force and its judicial system and prison capacity enormously so as to create a near-certainty that killers would be caught and receive stiff punishments. This would hopefully scare every individual with the slightest inkling of maybe murdering somebody into not committing any murder at all ever. If this were successful and every murder were deterred, the police force and legal system would never actually have to perform. The level of deterrence would be so effective and pervasive that no murders would be committed. But the enormous police force and judicial system would have to be there as an ever-present threat, an effective warning that nobody would get away with murder. To achieve zero murders, society would probably have to be transformed into a police state, with a police officer at every corner of the street, lots of preventive body and home searches, wire-tapping, and so on: a level of police activity so intensive and disturbing that it would grossly invade the privacy of citizens. This regime would use an enormous proportion of the public budget, but it might just be possible to create a society without murder (or, for that matter, without any crime).

One important reason this is not a sensible policy has to do with the opportunity cost of all those dollars spent on preventing every murder. By pouring lots of public money into preventing death by murder, the government has to withdraw resources from other life-saving policies such as public expenditure on road safety, combating contagious diseases, or funding cancer research. The opportunity cost of saving a life by preventing a murder might be another life lost in a traffic accident or through an awful disease. By putting all its money into avoiding murders, the government might unwittingly allow deaths to happen on the road and in hospitals. It is like deciding that dying from a road accident or from an awful disease is of less importance than being murdered. The government's budget is always limited; it must choose where to spend money and where not to. In the end, society will still have traffic deaths and people dying from terminal diseases, and there will be murders, but the government's money will have been spent as efficiently as possible to avoid deaths wherever they occur with the limited means available.

Determining the governmental crime budget is also very much a political decision. Different political parties have different views on how important fighting crime is and on how tough a stance the government should take with respect to criminals. Political parties make choices as to how the budget should be spent. They also have different views on where the responsibility of the government lies and on how much citizens are expected to protect themselves (by installing alarm systems, putting more locks on doors, hiring security agents, etc.). When different administrations gain political power, the approach to crime and hence the budget allocated to crime changes. There is also a great deal of difference between societies in their approaches to crime.

In this chapter, we concentrate on the economic approach to spending government money on deterring crime. Given that it is not sensible to have a level of deterrence that eradicates all crime, the question becomes, What is the efficient level of deterrence? In addition, what is the lowest-cost method of achieving that level?

In the first section, we begin by describing the economic approach to determining the optimal level of crime. Unlike Chapter 19, in which the perspective was that of the individual rational criminal, here the focus is on society more generally. The basic approach is one in which steps to deter crime should be taken as long as the benefits (in terms of crimes prevented) exceed the costs (in terms of enforcement and punishment). The analysis is complicated by the fact that there are two basic forms of punishment: fines and imprisonment. From an economic standpoint, the most obvious difference is that imposing fines costs society very little compared to imprisonment. Offhand, one could draw the conclusion from this huge cost difference that if fines and imprisonment have the same deterrent effect on criminals, it would be optimal to use only fines for punishment. As we will discuss in the second section, this conclusion is not completely off track but not completely correct, either. There are good economic reasons to include imprisonment in the optimal package of punishment.[1]

Another complicating factor is that not all criminal conduct is treated the same. Very low levels of punishment are typically associated with crimes that are easy to detect or unlikely to cause great harm. In effect, some "crimes" may be economically justified depending on the context. A policy about crime has both a macro and a micro element. At the macro level, we must decide how much to invest in fighting crime in general. At the micro level, a decision must be made about how to allocate the crime budget among individual crimes.

Defining optimal crime policy in terms of deterrence only, as we will do in most of this chapter, is incomplete. As you have seen, punishment is also handed out to criminals for other reasons such as retribution, rehabilitation, and isolation. We discuss the limitations of a "deterrence only" crime policy in the concluding section of this chapter.

OPTIMAL LEVEL OF DETERRENCE: A COST-BENEFIT ANALYSIS

The Macro View

We begin by comparing the cost of crime to society with the cost of deterrence. Effective deterrence reduces the crime level in society,

---

1. See A. Mitchell Polinsky and Steven Shavell, "Public Enforcement of Law," *Encyclopedia of Law and Economics,* vol. 5, ed. Boudewijn Bouckaert and Gerrit de Geest (Cheltenham: Edward Elgar, 2000), 307–344, for an extensive discussion of these issues.

and every crime avoided is a benefit. The cost of crime and the cost of deterrence are illustrated in Figure 20.1. The costs are shown on the vertical or y-axis. This is either the cost of deterrence or the cost of crime. Reduction of the cost of crime can also be seen as a benefit for society. For simplicity, we assume that costs can be measured in dollars. The horizontal or x-axis shows the amount or level of crime going from zero crime to very high levels. Reading the x-axis from right to left shows the level of deterrence in terms of reduction of the crime level.

Curve *B* in Figure 20.1 is the social cost of crime. We have drawn it as increasing rapidly. This reflects the probably realistic assumption that more crime causes increasingly more harm to society. In effect, ten crimes are more than twice as costly to society as five crimes. This means that curve *B*, which has an upward slope, becomes steeper

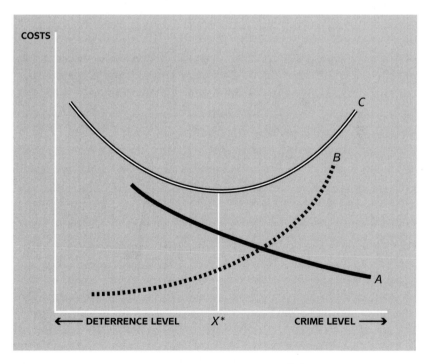

FIGURE 20.1 Costs and Benefits of Crime and Prevention

at higher levels of crime.[2] A few crimes could be considered regretful but a fact of life in society whereas higher crime rates become much more worrisome and cause harm not only in physical and material terms but also in emotional terms. As crime rates continue to increase, the social fabric of society might fall apart and complete chaos could take over. You can see that the curve is also a way of presenting the benefits from deterring crime. The more crime deterred, the greater the benefits.

Curve *A* represents the costs of deterrence. It is easiest to understand this curve by going from right to left (i.e., for increasing levels of deterrence or decreasing levels of crime). Start at the right. At that point, there is a lot of crime in society and many criminals. The government is spending very little to fight crime. Withdrawing resources from other uses where they are plentiful does not entail large opportunity costs. A reasonable assumption might also be that it will be relatively easy to catch a criminal and punish him or her when crime levels are high. At high levels of crime, the resources used in fighting crime have a low opportunity cost and are readily adaptable to fighting crime. Each unit of crime prevented will cause this curve to increase as we go to lower levels of crime. The curve increases as we move to the left, increasing the level of deterrence, and going to lower and lower crime levels. As we approach the left of Figure 20.1—and hence a society with hardly any crime at all—it becomes expensive to find and eliminate the last few violators.[3] It is easy to catch a thief when there are a lot of them; it is hard to catch the one and only thief who is still running free. Also, as crime is reduced to lower and lower levels, resources that have a higher and rising opportunity cost must be diverted to fighting crime. That is, in a nutshell, what the increas-

2. The social cost of crime fighting includes the costs incurred by government agencies to combat crime as well as by citizens who install security devices and businesses that hire security services to protect their premises. The discussion in this chapter concentrates on the governmental outlays of combating crime. The decisions of households and firms to invest in private crime protection depend on the level of deterrence provided by government agencies but may also be required by insurance companies.

3. In Figure 20.1, the lines are not drawn up to the "extreme" positions of either zero crime levels or the position where society is completely criminal. Neither will presumably ever occur.

ing curvature—reading it from right to left—of curve A expresses. The higher the level of deterrence, the higher the costs of deterring.

Curve C is the vertical sum of curves A and B. For each level of crime, it gives the sum of the costs of crime to society and the costs of deterrence. Curve C is high for low crime levels because, in those regions, the cost of deterrence will be relatively high. It is also high for high levels of crime because that is where the harm caused by crime is at its highest. The lowest point on curve C will be somewhere between these two extremes. The lowest point is the point at which the total cost of crime to society is at its minimum. The total cost of crime to society is the sum of the cost of prevention and deterrence plus the cost of crime itself. This point is labeled $X^\star$ in Figure 20.1. This point establishes both the "optimal level of crime" and the "optimal level of deterrence."

From the standpoint of efficiency, it does not make sense to reduce crime to zero. An all-out war against drugs cannot be justified on economic grounds alone. It is not efficient to go below the optimal level $X^\star$ because going to lower levels of crime will increase the costs of deterrence more than it reduces crime's harm to society. In terms of the curves in the figure, to the left of $X^\star$ curve A increases faster than curve B decreases. Nor is it efficient for crime levels to be higher than $X^\star$ because the harm from crime increases faster than the cost of deterring it. Note that in our analysis, $X^\star$ is not only the optimal level of crime but also the optimal level of deterrence.

You can also understand this result by relying on marginal analysis. The slope of curve B is the marginal cost of a unit of crime. The slope measures the marginal increase in cost when crime increases with one unit. In Figure 20.2, we have drawn the marginal cost of deterrence curve as A_1, and the marginal cost of crime curve as B_1. For convenience, we have drawn these lines as straight increasing or decreasing lines. When drawing the cost of crime curve B in Figure 20.1, we assume that increasing crime levels lead to ever-increasing costs for society. This assumption implies that the marginal cost of crime B_1 is increasing as we move from left to right, to higher and higher levels of crime. Conversely, B_1 can also be interpreted as the marginal benefit of crime deterrence. If we read Figure 20.2 from right to left—that is, in terms of increasing levels of deterrence—we see that the marginal benefits of crime B_1 become smaller and smaller for higher levels of deterrence.

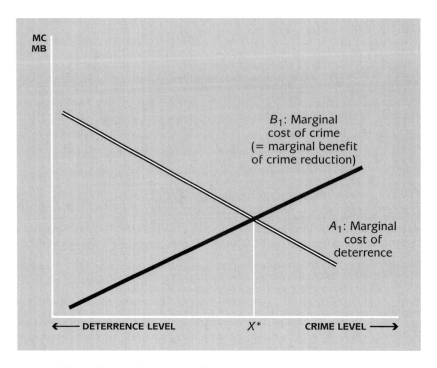

FIGURE 20.2 Costs of Crime and Deterrence: A Marginal Approach

Similarly, when drawing the cost of deterrence curve A in Figure 20.1, we assume that the opportunity cost increases at an increasing rate as we move into higher levels of deterrence, from right to left into lower and lower crime levels. This explains why the marginal cost of deterrence line A_1 in Figure 20.2 is increasing from right to left.

Society will want to invest in crime prevention as long as the marginal cost of the harm prevented exceeds the marginal cost of deterrence.[4] It is important to remember that crime is reduced as you move from right to left on the graph. As we move from high levels of crime to lower levels (from right to left), the marginal cost of deterrence

---

4. Total harm is an increasing function of the level of the crime rate x, that is, $h(x)$ and the cost of deterrence is a decreasing function of x, that is, $d(x)$. Then minimizing total cost: $h(x) + d(x)$ implies $h'(x) = d'(x)$ or when marginal social harm is equal to marginal cost of deterrence. The optimal level $x^\star$ can be solved from this equality and the optimal level of deterrence would then be $d(x^\star)$.

increases but is lower than the decreasing cost of crime (the difference between A_1 and B_1) until we reach point $X^\star$. At this point, it is inefficient to attempt to reduce crime any further because the marginal cost of an extra unit reduction of crime below $X^\star$ is higher than the additional cost of crime to society. Another way of explaining the same point is by interpreting curve B_1 as the decreasing benefit of deterrence curve (going from left to right). As we deter more and more crime (starting from a high level) and we move into lower and lower crime levels, the marginal benefit of each extra unit of crime deterrence is higher than the marginal cost of deterrence (B_1 is higher than A_1) until we come to optimal crime level $X^\star$. If we decrease the crime level below the optimal point $X^\star$, the marginal benefit of crime deterrence goes below the marginal cost of crime to society (B_1 is below A_1).

It might be hard to accept the fact that the economic analysis of crime leads to the conclusion that there is some sort of "optimal level of crime" that is positive (or an optimal "level of deterrence" that is less than 100 percent). Even though economic analysis allows for all kinds of harm caused by crime—monetary costs, nonmonetary costs such as bodily harm or psychological trauma, and indirect costs such as the insecurity resulting from living in an area with high crime rates—there is ultimately an optimal crime level. This is because deterrence requires using society's resources, which have opportunity costs. The money that is being spent on police and prisons could be spent instead on education and health care. The cost of deterrence (curve A in Figure 20.1) is a reflection of these opportunity costs. It makes sense to spend an additional dollar on deterrence as long as this additional dollar "buys" a reduction in harm that is worth more than a dollar (or at least equal to a dollar). As soon as we buy less than a dollar's worth of harm reduction, it is better to spend that dollar on other important policy objectives, such as improvement in health care, where we can maybe achieve more than a dollar's worth of better health.

Still, the economic approach to the optimal crime rate is restricted because it considers only the deterrence effect. It neglects other considerations for punishing criminals such as retribution, rehabilitation, and isolation. We will come back to these issues at the end of this chapter.

The Micro View

From the point of view of society—the macro view—the crucial issues are the harm done to society and the cost of avoiding that harm. The goal is to achieve an efficient level of deterrence in which an extra dollar spent on deterring crime yields (at least) a dollar reduction in the harm caused by the crime. You may wonder how this translates to decision making by each individual—the micro view. Consider this example. Stealing a fairly new fifteen-speed bike is worth $1,000 to the owner and also to the thief, and the probability of apprehending and punishing a bike thief is 25 percent. What is the optimal level of punishment for this crime? It would be a $4,000 fine because we should make expected punishment at least as large as the net benefit ($1,000) to the thief. If we set the punishment for bike theft at $4,000 and the probability of apprehension and punishment is 25 percent, then the expected punishment for the rational criminal is 0.25 times $4,000 or $1,000.

If we know the net benefit of a crime and the probability of apprehension and punishment, then the optimal level of punishment can be calculated as the amount of harm divided by the probability of apprehension and punishment (1,000 divided by 0.25). Put differently, if the level of harm is h and the probability of detection is p, then the optimal punishment is h divided by p or h/p.

As we saw in Chapter 19, the rational criminal will compare the net benefits that he receives from stealing the bike (which is the value of the bike for him minus his "professional" costs such as buying a pair of pliers to cut the lock) with the expected punishment. If his net benefits are smaller than this expected punishment, he will not commit the crime. Setting the level of punishment at $4,000 will deter all crimes by criminals for whom the level of net benefits from stealing is less than or equal to $1,000. In this way, we are avoiding all bike thefts that harm society to the amount of $1,000—which is what we wanted to avoid in the first place.

You should note that this does not eliminate every bicycle theft, nor would we want it to. Assume that a father must take his very sick child to a nearby hospital. As he carries the child in his arms, he sees the bike—the only means of transportation available at the moment—standing against the wall. In desperation, he jumps on the bike and rushes to the hospital with the child in his arms. The net benefit for him of stealing this bike and saving his child's life is far greater than the $1,000 damage he causes to society. In this case, we would talk about an *efficient* crime. The net benefit to the thief is higher than the harm done to society. The fine of $4,000 does not deter the worried father from stealing, but that is the result we want in this particular case because it adds more benefit to society (the life of a child saved) than it causes harm. That is what we mean when we say it is efficient to steal the bike. In effect, there are efficient levels of many crimes, and the trick is to set the "price" (expected punishment) equal to the harm to society.

Although it is hard to imagine that public officials engage in a refined analysis to determine the efficient level of different crimes, much of criminal law in practice does seem to reflect an economic analysis. Serious crimes are punished severely because of the serious social harm. We want to make sure that the rational criminal commits the crime only if the benefits are very great. For example, murder is punished very severely, but we do not punish the person who finds it necessary to take the life of someone else in order to save his or her own. This, of course, is self-defense, and the benefit to the person committing the killing is obviously very high.

At least in theory, there are efficient levels of even very harmful crimes. Still, when you think about some crimes—rape, child abuse—it is hard to see them as ever being efficient. In a sense, the efficient level is zero if we compare the cost to society and the benefit to the individual. But even here, an economic analysis is involved. In theory, we could devote enough resources to stop all rapes, but it would be extremely expensive and consume resources that could be employed to create even greater benefits elsewhere. Still, it is disconcerting to think in terms of efficient levels of very harmful crimes. It may be more comforting to say that these crimes are permitted to continue because eliminating them would cause more harm in terms of forgone opportunities than the harm of the crimes themselves. This does not make them efficient in terms of a comparison of the criminal's benefit to the harms caused to society. It just becomes even more inefficient to eliminate the inefficiency.

THE COST OF ADMINISTERING PUNISHMENT

As shown in the previous section, the optimal level of deterrence is set at the point where the total cost to society (crime and deterrence cost) is at its minimum. In addition, the key to punishment is to set it to deter inefficient but not efficient crimes. An issue that is implicit in each of these considerations is how to achieve the best level of deterrence at the lowest cost. The total deterrence budget can be spent in many different ways. Rational criminals are deterred by a package consisting of a probability of punishment and a level of punishment— the expected punishment—and these two elements are the most important items of the crime-fighting budget.

Expenditures on Creating a Probability of Punishment

The key to deterrence policy is to achieve an objective probability of punishment that corresponds with the subjective probability in the minds of rational potential criminals. Professional and hardened criminals usually know quite well the risks they are running. This probability of punishment is determined by, first, the level of expenditure on the police force and, second, by the level of expenditure on the judicial system. For convenience, we assume that the greater these expenditures, the greater the probability of punishment. The degree to which the probability of punishment increases for every extra dollar spent will depend on the efficiency of the police and the judicial system.

CASE 20.1 Expected Levels of Punishment and the Constitution: *Solem v. Helm*, 463 U.S. 277 (1983)

One of the things stressed in the text is the comparison of expected benefits and expected punishment. The same level of expected punishment can be achieved with high probabilities of relatively low levels of punishment or low levels of relatively severe punishment. As a high probability of catching and convicting criminals can be expensive, the more efficient choice may be to catch very few criminals and punish them severely. This case suggests there is a limit on just how far such an analysis can be taken. In this case Helm, the defendant, had been in several scrapes with the law in the early 1970s. Then, in 1979, he wrote a bad check for $100. Under South Dakota law dealing with repeat offenders, he was sentenced to life in prison. He appealed that this amounted to cruel and unusual punishment in violation of the United States Constitution. The Supreme Court agreed. Part of the Court's reasoning was as follows:

> The constitutional principle of proportionality has been recognized explicitly in this Court for almost a century. In the

leading case of *Weems v. United States,* 217 U.S. 349, 30 S.Ct. 544, 54 L.Ed. 793 (1910), the defendant had been convicted of falsifying a public document and sentenced to 15 years of "cadena temporal," a form of imprisonment that included hard labor in chains and permanent civil disabilities. The Court noted "that it is a precept of justice that punishment for crime should be graduated and proportioned to offense," and held that the sentence violated the Eighth Amendment. The Court endorsed the principle of proportionality as a constitutional standard. . . .

There is no basis for the State's assertion that the general principle of proportionality does not apply to felony prison sentences. In sum, we hold as a matter of principle that a criminal sentence must be proportionate to the crime for which the defendant has been convicted.

When sentences are reviewed under the Eighth Amendment, courts should be guided by objective factors that our cases have recognized. First, we look to the gravity of the offense and the harshness of the penalty. Second, it may be helpful to compare the sentences imposed on other criminals in the same jurisdiction. Third, courts may find it useful to compare the sentences imposed for commission of the same crime in other jurisdictions.

Since this case was decided, the issue of what constitutes "cruel and unusual" punishment has been hotly contested among members of the Supreme Court. See *Harmelin v. Michigan.*[5] Some of the debate takes place in the context of capital punishment. Although *Solem* has not been expressly overruled by the Court, a majority of its members now favor a test of "grossly disproportionate" over a test of "disproportionality." What impact does this have on the likelihood of an economically sensible approach to punishment?

Expenditures on Imposing a Level of Punishment

The other element in the formula of expected punishment is the choice of whether to use fines or incarceration. There are some administrative costs to imposing a fine, but its costs are far less than those of incarceration. In addition, a fine that is paid generates income for the government. Still, this income is far from sufficient to cover the costs of fighting crime.

---

5. 501 U.S. 957 (1991).

The far greater costs of maintaining a prison system include not only direct costs such as upkeep and maintenance of prison buildings, salaries of wardens, and costs of clothing and food for the inmates but also indirect costs such as income and production forgone by the inmates and the effects on their families. Sometimes inmates do productive work while in prison, but the value they create for society is generally lower than what they would produce in a regular job.[6]

LAW AND ECONOMICS IN ACTION 20.1

MAGNITUDES OF CRIMINAL INVOLVEMENT

"The participation of American men in crime is staggering. Consider first the number of men convicted of a crime and sent to prison or jail. In 1993, 910,000 were in state or federal prison; an additional 440,500 were in jail, for a total of 1,350,000 incarcerated. With a male workforce of 69.6 million or so, this is one man incarcerated for every 50 men in the workforce! This proportion is approximately the same as the share of long-term unemployed men on the dole in many western European countries."

Reference: Richard Freeman, "Why Do So Many American Men Commit Crimes and What Might We Do about It?" *Journal of Economic Perspectives* 10 (1) (Winter 1996): 26.

The third option, community service, is more expensive to administer than imposing a fine, but less than a prison term. This option is not discussed below. As you will see, an optimal allocation of the budget for deterrence requires that we first use fines to the maximum possible level and only then decide on prison terms. If community service was taken into account, we would still use punishment by fine to the maximum first and then choose between community service and imprisonment.

There are also crime-fighting costs to innocent citizens. Innocent people can be stopped and searched by police who are tracking down a criminal. Privacy can be invaded, and citizens doing jury duty also

---

6. Note that in some countries there are laws in place that restrict prison labor from being used productively (often passed at the behest of unions).

incur costs. The judicial system is not perfect, and sometimes innocent citizens are apprehended and even convicted. These judicial errors are not only costly for the persons involved but also for their families, their employers and—if they have their own business—for the employees working for them.

Selection of Punishment

This section addresses the basic choice between fines and imprisonment. Clearly this could be expanded with some interesting extensions, such as how optimal enforcement differs between strict liability and fault-based liability and between act-based sanctions and harm-based sanctions. Other possible extensions are the issue of self-reporting and of increasing levels of punishment for criminals who commit several harmful acts, for example kidnapping and killing the kidnapped victim (this is called *marginal deterrence*).[7]

Consider a very simple case. Increases in the probability of punishment are increasingly costly for society. Assume that all crimes can be dealt with by imposing monetary fines and that imposing monetary fines entails no costs whatsoever. What would the optimal punishment be in this case? Very simply, a combination of very low probabilities of punishment combined with a tremendously high level of fines.

Suppose the social harm caused by bicycle theft is $1,000. In this simple world, we would deter bicycle theft by creating a very low probability of detection of 0.000025 (25 in a million), and imposing a fine equal to $4,000,000. The expected punishment would in this case be $1,000, equal to the harm caused. This policy does not make much practical sense. To start with, it does not seem fair to punish a thief who stole a bike with the enormous fine of $4,000,000. Also, most bicycle thieves do not have the resources to pay a $4,000,000 fine. Even if they have the resources, criminals often refuse to pay the fines, and we have to resort to other measures. There is clearly a limit to the level at which we can set fines, a limit that is roughly determined by the wealth of the criminal. This is why fines are, generally speaking, used in the case of less serious crimes. Suppose the

---

7. See Polinsky and Shavell, "Public Enforcement of Law," for a discussion of these extensions.

probability of punishment is set at 25 percent, and the resource level of criminals is at most $10,000. This implies that fines are effective for crimes that cause a level of harm up to $2,500. To illustrate, take this formula:

Optimal level of punishment
= Harm divided by probability of punishment

and replace "optimal level of punishment" with "maximum amount of punishment by fine," we can derive the maximum harm that can be deterred by fines as

Maximum harm = Maximum amount of punishment by fine ×
probability of punishment

Or in our example:

Maximum harm = $2,500 = 10,000 × 0.25

In this case, only those crimes that cause $2,500 or less worth of harm can be effectively deterred by fines. Any crime more harmful than that will mean that a prison term or a combination of fine and prison term will be necessary.

The difference between fines and imprisonment creates something of a dilemma. Fines are less expensive but only effective for crimes that are less serious. Imprisonment is preferable for more serious crimes but is far more costly. One way to overcome this problem is to maintain the same level of expected punishment by increasing prison sentences and lowering the probability of apprehension and conviction. This means fewer people in prison for longer time periods and less spent on apprehension and conviction. Even here, though, there are limits. In the same way that monetary wealth limits fine levels, people have only one lifetime to spend in prison. Thus, a sentence of 100 or 150 years is like fining a poor person $500,000. Plus, at least in the United States, the constitutional limit on cruel and unusual punishment has to be taken into account. Since the prison sentence side of the expected punishment calculation can only be stretched so far, that leaves the need to imprison more people. This not only raises the costs of prisons but also the costs of apprehension and conviction. What this ultimately means is that it may be more than four times as expensive to deter crimes giving rise to $100,000 harm than it is to deter $25,000 crimes. The result is an economic bias away from punishing more serious crimes. It is bit of a generalization but, in a sense, very serious crime may be more likely to be profitable for the criminal.

CASE 20.2 **Fine and Imprisonment:** *United States v. Turner*, 998 F.2d 534 (7th Cir. 1993)

Fines and imprisonment are both forms of punishment. If everything else were equal, fines would be preferable because they are less expensive to administer. Another possibility would be to imprison criminals and require them to pay the expenses. In Turner, the defendant falsely filed for a tax refund. Although he could have been fined, the judge felt he could not pay a fine. Instead the judge sentenced him to "work release" and required him to pay the state's cost of the program which was calculated to be $2,700. His attorney appealed. The decision is of particular interest because it was made by Judges Posner and Easterbrook, two of the most economically oriented federal judges.

> Sentencing Guidelines [federal guidelines for punishment] prescribe fines for most federal offenses. Each offense level corresponds to a range of fines. In addition to the fine derived from the table, "the court shall impose an additional fine amount that is at least sufficient to pay the costs to the government of any imprisonment, probation, or supervised release ordered." § 5E1.2(i) Dale Turner contends that this additional fine is unauthorized by statute and in any event may not be imposed if the judge determines that the defendant is unable to pay the base fine.

★★★

> Three courts of appeals have addressed the question whether § 5E1.2(i) is valid. Two have held that it is, and one that it is not. The third circuit concluded that the Sentencing Commission exceeded its authority in promulgating § 5E1.2(i) because measuring a fine by the costs of confinement does not reflect any of the statutory objectives of sentencing. Yet Congress told the Commission to consider not only "the nature and degree of the harm caused by the offense" but also "the deterrent effect a particular sentence may have on the commission of the offense by others". These instructions track the criteria addressed to judges in the bench to impose sentences that "reflect the seriousness of the offense" and "afford adequate deterrence to criminal conduct". The Guidelines call for longer

sentences as the harm caused by the offense rises; longer sentences (or sentences in more secure custody) are more costly; thus the costs of confinement rise with the seriousness of the crime, and a fine based on these costs therefore reflects the seriousness of the offense. Moreover, higher fines are more potent deterrents to crime. Section 5E1.2(i) increases the fine, and therefore increases deterrence. . . . [T]he rationality of the approach cannot be doubted. The costs of incarceration do not precisely reflect social loss and deterrence, to be sure, but the Constitution does not require a close match between the gravity of the offense and the penalty meted out.

According to the third circuit, "there is no reason to believe that assessing the costs of imprisonment (in addition to other fines) deters criminal conduct". . . . This is equivalent to asserting that higher fines do not increase deterrence, a proposition that leaves us flabbergasted. The system of penalties under the Guidelines is constructed on the belief that higher fines, and longer sentences of imprisonment, are more effective deterrents. A large body of evidence supports this intuition. . . . A carefully thought out theory of criminal penalties proposed by Professor Gary Becker—a theory that was cited when Becker received the 1992 Nobel Prize in Economics—includes the costs of incarceration (and the other costs of the criminal justice system) as part of the socially optimal punishment for crime. See Gary S. Becker, *Crime and Punishment: An Economic Approach,* 76 J.Pol.Econ. 169 (1968). . . .

★★★

The district judge stated that Turner could not pay any fine imposed under § 5E1.2(c). Yet the judge immediately added: "The defendant does have some capacity to earn income; consequently, I do not excuse the cost of community confinement." This suggests that the judge may have been asking whether Turner could pay $100 or more immediately, rather than whether he could pay the § 5E1.2(c) fine in installments. If, as the judge stated, Turner can pay $2,700 in installments, then he can pay a fine calculated under § 5E1.2(c). And if Turner cannot pay such a fine, then he cannot be expected to pay anything computed under § 5E1.2(i).

The tension between the judge's treatment of the § 5E1.2(c) fine and the § 5E1.2(i) fine makes it prudent to return this case for further proceedings. On remand the district judge shall establish a new fine using the approach to § 5E1.2 that we have described. Because the United States has not filed a cross-appeal, the total fine imposed on remand may not exceed $2,700 in present value.

In the example above, we fixed the probability of punishment at 25 percent. However, when deciding on the optimal deterrence system, the probability of punishment is a policy variable that has to be set. In general, we are looking for a deterrence system consisting of probability, monetary fines, and imprisonment—each with different levels of cost attached to it. Defining an optimal deterrence policy means that we have to balance these different cost levels against each other and come up with a package that is the least costly. It turns out that there is no simple formula to describe the optimal levels of probability, level of fines, and length of prison terms.

Individualized Punishment

Regardless of our efforts to get the most out of our enforcement dollars, a couple of factors stand as barriers that cannot be overcome. These are factors that prevent us from *individualized* punishment. Suppose the bike thief in the example discussed above causes $1,000 of social harm when he stole the bike, but he can sell the bike for only $100 because people are wary of buying bikes with "unknown origins." Also assume that he incurred no cost to steal the bike, so his net benefit of stealing the bike is $100. If the probability of detection is still 25 percent, we could deter this particular thief for this particular theft by setting the level of punishment at $400 (100 divided by 0.25). In other words, a $400 fine would do the job as effectively as a $4,000 fine. The importance of this point may not be clear until you realize that if the issue were the length of a prison sentence it would mean a shorter (and much less expensive) sentence. We would still deter only crime that is inefficient, and crimes that are efficient would still occur. It is, of course, almost impossible to know what the individual net benefit for each thief and each theft are, so in general we cannot use net benefit as a guide for setting punishment. Instead, we set the punishment at social cost, which may be unnecessarily expensive. This does not mean that we "overdeter," but it does mean that more may be spent than necessary.

The idea of setting expected punishment to fit each crime and each criminal is clouded by another problem. What we have implicitly been assuming until now is that rational criminals are risk neutral. This means that they would be indifferent between a 0.25 probability combined with a $4,000 fine and a 0.000025 probability and a $4,000,000 fine. After all, the expected fine is $1,000 in either case. If, however, criminals are risk averse, the fact that they are running a risk causes them disutility. The level of expected punishment does not have to be as high for risk averse as for risk-neutral criminals to achieve the same level of deterrence (see the end of Chapter 19 for an explanation of this). If the population of criminals were risk averse, we would not have to use high fines to create the same level of deterrence. However, the reverse would hold true if the population of criminals consisted of mostly risk-loving individuals. In that case, we would have to increase the expected level of punishment. If criminals are like most people, they are risk averse, which means we could lower the level of punishment below the social cost of the crime. Again, this refinement might mean we could save on the cost of achieving optimal deterrence. The problem, again, is that the cost of refinement probably exceeds the savings that may be involved.

OTHER CONSIDERATIONS

As explained above, one could probably say that the economic analysis of the optimal deterrence system is biased toward the use of fines as a punishment method because it is, on average, less costly than imposing prison sentences. However, there are other considerations that would argue for the use of prison sentences more often than an economic analysis would initially indicate. To the extent that these considerations are valued by society, the economic case for imprisonment—even on a cost-benefit basis—becomes more compelling. These considerations are retribution, rehabilitation, and incapacitation. Each of these considerations is discussed briefly below.

Retribution

Denial of freedom is seen by society as a just form of retribution for crime, and presumably society derives benefits from seeing criminals punished with prison terms. However, it is difficult to quantify these benefits. The benefits depend in some way on societal norms, which differ between countries and vary between political systems and ethical beliefs. Regardless, it is clear that they play an important role in all penal systems, which means that even as an economic matter, incarceration itself creates benefits that must be included in the cost-benefit analysis.

Rehabilitation

It can be argued that imprisonment provides the criminal with something valuable. It might make him see the error of his ways. It is doubtful whether that will work for hardened criminals, but there was a time in the history of the United States during which the possibility of rehabilitation was put forth as one of the principal purposes of incarceration. Now we more frequently think of prisons as places where criminals learn how to be more effective criminals. Still, there is often counseling and job training in prison, and some marketable skills in honorable professions can be learned. The point is that a comprehensive evaluation of the optimal way to respond to criminal acts would require accounting for the possibility that prison, as opposed to fines, has a transforming effect.

Isolation

While they are in prison, criminals cannot commit crimes, which is the main benefit of isolation. Criminals are removed from society and put in an environment where they can do much less harm. If sanctions do not deter, isolation provides a strong reason to put criminals in jail. If that is the case, how long should we keep criminals in prison? Again, we can build an efficiency argument for this by comparing the costs of detaining a criminal with the harm he would cause to society if he were free on the streets. As long as the expected harm exceeds the cost of their imprisonment, they should remain in prison. Isolation should be used for hardened criminals whose net harm is relatively high and for repeat offenders whose probability of committing crimes again is high. As criminals get old and sick and as the probability of committing crimes reduces with age and deterioration of health, these factors become less important.

QUESTIONS FOR DISCUSSION

1. Suppose the cost of deterring crime is constant for all levels of crime. In terms of Figure 20.2, this assumption implies that marginal cost curve A_1 is a straight horizontal line at some given level of cost.
   a. Assume that this straight marginal cost of deterrence line is everywhere above B_1 the marginal cost of crime curve (marginal benefit of crime deterrence curve): what is the optimal level of crime?

b. Assume that this straight marginal cost of deterrence line is everywhere below B_1 the marginal cost of crime curve (marginal benefit of crime deterrence curve): what is the optimal level of crime?

c. Is the assumption of constant marginal costs of deterrence realistic?

2. What happens to the optimal level of crime (deterrence), $X^\star$ in the notation of this chapter? Use Figure 20.2 to answer these questions.

a. If crimes get more vicious and hence the marginal cost of crime increases in society?

b. If police and other staff members of the legal system get substantial wage increases and hence the marginal cost of deterrence increases?

3. Plagiarism is an increasing problem at universities: Students are handing in term papers that are largely or totally copied from the Internet and claim it is all their own original work.

a. Formulate an efficient policy to deter plagiarism optimally.

b. Would you tolerate some level of plagiarism?

4. Discuss: Suppose bicycle thieves think that the probability of getting apprehended and punished is only 10 percent, whereas it is really 20 percent. How does that effect the optimal deterrence policy? Similarly, if bicycle thieves are very pessimistic and think the probability of getting apprehended and punished is 30 percent, whereas in reality it is only 20 percent, how does this effect the optimal deterrence policy?

5. Any level of criminal punishment is permitted as long as it is not grossly disproportionate to the crime committed. In tort cases, punitive damages may not include amounts for harm to people other than those who are parties to the lawsuit. Which of these is more consistent with an economic approach to punishment?

CHAPTER TWENTY-ONE

Empirical Evidence

I N THE PREVIOUS CHAPTERS, WE DEVELOPED A THEORETI-
cal model of the rational individual criminal and used the predictions of this model to develop a model of deterrence for optimal crime-fighting policy. At the heart of this model is the hypothesis
or theoretical prediction that rational criminals will commit fewer
crimes if the probability of being apprehended and punished and the
severity of punishment are increased. In this chapter, we will present
empirical evidence on whether these theoretical predictions are valid
in the real world. The statistical evidence involves a number of steps.

In the first section we review the main theoretical predictions that
come out of the model of the rational criminal. These are the predictions that we will attempt to test and measure using empirical data
and statistical techniques. In the second section we explain in straightforward terms what we mean by *statistical evidence*. The third section
analyzes the main results of the relevant empirical literature and
focuses on the measured effects of probability and severity of punishment. It turns out that the empirical evidence is not always perfect
and that there are some weaknesses. In the fourth section we discuss
criticism of statistical testing. The last section concludes this chapter
and this unit with a discussion of how statistical evidence can be used
in the formulation of crime policy.

PREDICTIONS

In Chapter 18 on the rational criminal, we assumed that a criminal considers the costs and benefits of committing a crime. On the cost side of his balance sheet is the expected punishment, which consists of two elements: the probability of punishment times the severity of punishment (such as amount of the fine or number of days in prison). From the policy point of view, increasing expected punishment is an instrument to combat crime. Increasing expected punishment for different crimes would in theory imply a reduction in crime. How much an increase in expected punishment would decrease crime is a matter for empirical measurement.

A rational criminal is assumed to make a comparison between the costs and benefits of a career in crime versus a "straight" career. In other words, it is not as simple as evaluating the benefits of criminal behavior. The rational person/criminal will also evaluate the prospects of legal behavior. Thus, ultimately, the amount of crime is a function of variables that affect both the criminal life and the "straight" life. There are quite a number of variables that might have an influence on the choice of a rational individual when choosing between a legal and a criminal job. Let us review some of those. Suppose the economy is booming, employment is growing, and hence good legal job opportunities with attractive incomes become more available. This might have a negative effect on crime. An increase in unemployment can come about because there are fewer job openings than job seekers. Persistent and structural unemployment can create a situation in which there is always a lack of good legal job opportunities; such a situation makes it harder to get a "straight" job and could be correlated with higher levels of crime. An increase in income differences that leaves more people below the poverty line and puts more people in the top 10 percent could increase the likelihood that some people commit crimes. If there are more people living in poverty, the difference between legal income opportunities and criminal income will grow and this might, for some of them, be sufficient reason to commit a crime. At the same time, it could be said that the increase in wealth at the top of the income distribution creates more opportunities for crime. So one would expect increasing inequality to have a positive effect on the crime rate. Finally, when private citizens and businesses spend more on protecting their properties by installing burglar alarms or hiring security services, the burden of a criminal will increase and the expected returns of crime will diminish. Therefore, increasing private expenditures on crime prevention and protection will have a negative effect on the crime rate.

From the theoretical model of the rational criminal explained in the previous chapters and from the previous examples, we can deduce the following theoretical predictions or hypotheses, which we should test empirically:

- A higher probability of apprehension, conviction, and punishment will reduce crime.
- More severe levels of punishment will have a negative effect on crime.
- An increase in or an improvement of legal income opportunities will reduce crime.
- An increase in or an improvement of illegal income opportunities will increase crime.
- More pronounced income differences will increase crime.
- Higher unemployment leads to more crime.

An important aspect of the theory of the rational criminal is that we are assuming that preferences are constant. We are assuming that the criminal is always weighing costs and benefits in the same way. Put differently, the cost and benefit items may change, but the individual weighing process remains the same. When making predictions based on the theory of the rational criminal, we are assuming that the opportunities for crime or for legal income becomes either better or worse. Given the preferences of the population, an improvement in the opportunities for crime or a worsening of legal income opportunities will entice more people to choose crime. If presented with lots of attractive job openings, more people will choose a legal job. If the labor market situation worsens and unemployment increases, some people who previously chose legal income might now consider committing a crime. They still have the same preferences as before, but their choice alternatives have changed and hence they might make a different choice.

In reality, preferences are not always constant. To begin with, preferences differ between people. People weigh costs and benefits differently. For instance, crimes are committed more than proportionately by young males. Part of the explanation is clearly that the legal opportunities offered by society to young males—certainly less educated young males—are few, and illegal opportunities are plenty. So part of the explanation for why some of them choose crime is because the income from crime is higher for them than what they could make in a legal job. But part of the explanation is probably that the preferences of young males are different from the preferences of older people. Young males might, for instance, be more willing to take risks or be more attracted to the excitement of criminal gangs.

Individual preferences are also influenced by social norms that can also change over time. For example, the female crime rate is increasing. Part of the explanation might be that the preferences of females are changing because the norms as to what women should or should not do in society have changed. People might have different preferences when they belong to a society in which the majority of the population is churchgoing and adheres to strict moral norms as compared to a secularized and more anonymous society.

To make things even more complicated and less predictable, law itself may influence norms. For example, in quite a number of cities, many pedestrians do not wait until traffic lights turn to cross the street. Some citizens still wait until the light turns green; they have internalized the norm that one should wait for a traffic light. It is clear, however, that as more and more people stop obeying traffic lights, the number of "good" citizens will dwindle. The disappearing norm will in the end change the decision of even the most law-abiding citizen. The reverse is also true. If the police decide to put an end to this crossing at a red light and, regularly and for a long period, an officer is posted nearby to hand out tickets and fines, then slowly the social norm of waiting for green might be restored. This mechanism comes into play when the police apply it to crimes such as shoplifting and drug dealing. In these cases, the effect of crime fighting is felt not only through the increase of probability of punishment and the severity of punishment, but over time also through changes in the norm and the preferences of rational people. People will again internalize the norm that shoplifting is bad and fewer people will choose to do it. In some sense, this impact of crime fighting on changing norms and changing preferences strengthens the prediction of the rational criminal. But in another sense, the prediction works less through the expected punishment effect than through the effect on the social code. The mechanism whereby upholding the law may eventually restore the old norm does not always work. Once social norms pass a tipping point (this could be, for instance, the point at which the majority of the population does not obey the norm any longer) attempts at legal enforcement will certainly not always restore the old norms.

TESTING (CRIMINOMETRICS)

What we want to find out most of all from empirically testing the theoretical predictions of the rational crime model is whether expected punishment has a significant deterrent effect on crime and, if so, how large that effect is. There are statistical techniques available to do just that. In this section, we will first present the basic principles of these statistical techniques so that you can understand what they are. We will use the statistical measurement of the effect of expected punishment as an example throughout this section. Measuring the effects of other possible determinants of crime such as unemployment and income inequality proceeds along similar lines.

Statistical measurement of the effect of something on something else is sometimes very straightforward. Suppose you want to know whether a particular fertilizer makes the grass grow faster. What you do is divide your lawn into two parts. On one part you apply the fertilizer and on the other you don't. Next you take a chair, watch the grass grow, and measure the grass in each plot at regular intervals. If the grass grows faster on the fertilized part of your lawn, your statistical test is positive. This is the simplest statistical test possible because what you are testing is simple (fertilizer versus no fertilizer). Also, we have implicitly assumed that the two halves of your lawn are—apart from the fertilizer—completely similar. Statistical tests become more complicated if you want to test for the effect of different amounts of fertilizer (going from a little bit to very much) or when you combine different amounts of fertilizer with different amounts of water. The statistical test becomes even more complicated if the two halves of the lawn are not exactly the same. Suppose one part is open to the sun and the other part is under the trees or one part of the lawn is a favorite spot for all the neighborhood cats. Shade, sunshine, and frolicking cats also have an effect on how fast the grass will grow. In order to isolate the effect of the fertilizer on the grass, you have to control for the effects of shade, sunshine, and cats. Statisticians have developed methods that allow you to measure the effect of different amounts of fertilizers in combination with different amounts of water while at the same time controlling for the other effects like those of hours and amount of sunshine and number of frolicking cats. A statistical technique that is often used to measure the individual size of the effect of different determinants is called regression analysis.

Let us illustrate this technique using the famous example of an empirical study done by Isaac Ehrlich on the whether capital punishment has a deterring effect on the number of capital murders.[1] Ehrlich used information on the number of capital murders committed in the different states of the United States. He also had a measure of the probability that murderers got caught and punished in each of the different states and knew whether a state applied capital punishment or not. The effect of the probability of punishment for capital murder and the effect of the probability of capital punishment itself on the occurrence of capital murders are, of course, the variables of interest for our model of the rational criminal (in this case "the rational murderer"). But because the number of murders in any given state is also influenced by other factors such as the level of urbanization (there are presumably more murders in urban than in rural environments) and the age distribution (a state with a relatively young population will probably have more murders than a state with a relatively old population), Ehrlich controlled for these variables.

---

1. The original article "The Deterrent Effect of Capital Punishment: a Question of Life and Death" by Isaac Ehrlich appeared in the *American Economic Review* (June 1975): 397–417. The article raised a lot of criticism from other researchers. Some of the criticism had to do with the statistical techniques used. Isaac Ehrlich redid the same study using different statistical techniques in an article titled "Capital Punishment and Deterrence: Some Further Thoughts and Additional Evidence" in the *Journal of Political Economy* (August 1977): 741–788. In his article, he confirmed his previous results but did not completely succeed in quieting all criticism. See also Law and Economics in Action 21.1.

What he estimated was the following relationship:

Number of capital murders in state $i = a_0 + a_1$ (probability of punishment in state i) $+ a_2$ (state i has capital punishment) $+ a_3$ (level of urbanization of state i) $+ a_4$ (percentage of young people living in state i) $+ a_n$ (other relevant characteristics of state i) $+ \epsilon_i$

This is called the regression equation. On the left-hand side is the variable to be explained—in this case the number of capital murders in a state. On the right-hand side are the explanatory variables. These are measured for each state i of the United States. These are the variables that have an effect on the variable to be explained. Finally, there is what is called the "error term" designated as ϵ_i. The "error term" is a stand-in for all other variables that can have an influence on the variable to be explained; that is, the number of capital murders in state i, but which are left out of the regression equation either because we do not want to measure them or because we can't measure them. There are still hundreds of variables that can have an influence on the number of murders in a state such as the climate, the number of guns, and social tension. We do not or cannot measure them all and hence we represent these unmeasured effects with the symbol ϵ_i. Furthermore, we assume that some of these left-out variables have a positive effect while others have a negative effect on the number of murders in the state and that all these positive and negative effects together average out to zero. Using state data on the explanatory variables and the statistical technique of regression analysis, Ehrlich estimated a value for the "a"s in the regression equation—the coefficients of the regression equation. The coefficients of interest are of course a_1 and a_2. Coefficient a_1 is an indication of the size of the effect of the probability of punishment on the number of capital murders, and coefficient a_2 is an indication of whether the use of capital punishment in a state had a deterrent effect on the number of capital murders.

Isaac Ehrlich found that both a_1 and a_2 have a significant negative effect on the number of capital murders in a state. In this sense, his empirical model confirmed empirically what the model of rational crime predicted theoretically. His result on coefficient a_2 especially was a hotly debated issue. Ehrlich found empirically that when a state used capital punishment, the number of capital murders was reduced significantly compared to states that did not have capital punishment. Capital punishment is an issue that has many deep moral, philosophical, and social dimensions, and Ehrlich was criticized because he dealt with the issue in a single cold statistical dimension.

Using regression analysis, Ehrlich also found that urbanization and the presence of young people increased the number of capital murders in a state (the coefficients a_3 and a_4 were both significantly positive). The coefficient a_0 is called the intercept term. There is always a given number of murders that happen—think about murders committed during interpersonal disputes and noncontemplated crimes of passion—that cannot be explained by anything rational and are not deterrable. The intercept term captures this number.

The coefficients in the regression equation (the "a"s) are statistical estimates. Something is a statistical estimate if it is not completely certain. To summarize the level of uncertainty that is connected with a statistical estimate, statisticians have developed a test that tells you whether a coefficient is significantly different from zero. If a coefficient (such as the coefficients a_1 and a_2 in Ehrlich's regression equation) is significantly different from zero, it means that there is only a 5 percent chance that it could be equal to zero.[2]

LAW AND ECONOMICS IN ACTION 21.1

EIGHTEEN FEWER MURDERS

In a recent article in the *American Law and Economics Review*, the original Ehrlich study was revisited using recent, county-level, post-moratorium data. The data set covers 3,054 counties for the 1977–96 period in the U.S. The authors estimated a system of regression equations in which they explained the probability of arrest for murder, the probability of death sentence, the probability of execution and the effect of these probabilities and other variables on the county murder rate. They carefully analyzed the sensitivity of the estimation results to different specifications of

---

2. This is called a 95 percent level of confidence. In statistical terms, it implies that one can be confident that there is a 95 percent chance that the coefficient is not zero. It is also possible to define 90 percent or higher confidence levels. The lower the level of significance, the weaker, however, is the strength of the statistical relationship.

the regression equations using different cuts of the data sets. They used a panel data set, which has data on each county for a number of years. Their results show that the county murder rate was significantly and negatively influenced by the three probabilities of arrest, sentence, and execution. They also found significant positive effects for the percentage of males and African Americans. A higher National Rifle Association (NRA) presence, measured by NRA membership rate, seems to have a similar murder-increasing effect.[3] Their main finding is that capital punishment has a deterrent effect. Each execution results, on average, in eighteen fewer murders—with a margin of error of plus or minus ten.

Reference: Hashem Dezhbakhsh, Paul H. Rubin, and Joanna M. Shepherd, "Does Capital Punishment Have a Deterrent Effect? New Evidence from Postmoratorium Panel Data," *American Law and Economics Review* 5, no. 2 (2003): 344–373.

The data that Ehrlich used for his regression analysis are state-level data. These are called cross-section data. He basically took a cross section of the different states of the United States at a certain point in time. It is also possible to have time series data.

In a study of the Netherlands, Van Velthoven and Theeuwes collected information on the crime rate in the Netherlands for each year between 1950 and 1996.[4] They also had information on the average yearly probability of punishment and on the average level of fines and of days of imprisonment. And they had information on variables such as age, rate of unemployment, inequality of income distribution, and so on in each year. They also found that the probability of punishment and the level of punishment had a significant negative effect on the crime rate in the Netherlands. They found that the crime rate was lower the higher the probability of punishment, the higher the level of the fines, and the more days of imprisonment. Although these vari-

---

3. Note, however, that a higher NRA (National Rifle Association) presence may be caused by a higher crime rate or a higher murder rate, so the direction of causation is not necessarily as interpreted in the text box.

4. Ben Van Velthoven and Jules Theeuwes, *De ontwikkeling van de criminaliteit in Nederland tussen 1950 en 1996* (The development of the crime rate in the Netherlands between 1950 and 1996) (Amsterdam: Justitiele Verkenningen, 1998).

ables are significant and hence confirm the expectations of the theory of the rational criminal, they are not sufficient to explain most of the change in the crime rate in the Netherlands over time. Variables that had much more influence on the evolution of the crime rate included, for example, the increasing rate of secularization and increasing divorce levels over time. Secularization and divorce rates are variables that can be seen as capturing the changing social norms in Dutch society.

ESTIMATES/RESULTS

In the last few decades, quite a number of regression equations explaining crime rates for different sorts of crimes have been done in different countries using cross-section and time series data. Erling Eide and Richard B. Freeman provide thorough international summary surveys of this empirical literature.[5] Most of the empirical studies find a rather negative effect on the crime level of the probability of punishment and of the severity of punishment (level of the fine, length of days in prison). In quantitative terms, the effect of the probability of punishment is "larger" (more negative) than the effect of the severity of punishment. This implies that crime policies that create a higher probability of being caught and punished are more effective in combating crime than policies that increase fines and incarceration.

LAW AND ECONOMICS IN ACTION 21.2

CRIMINAL PROCEDURE AND CRIMES

People who are accused of crimes are protected from arbitrary actions by authorities. No doubt you have seen movies and TV shows in which those arrested are "read their rights." One such right is that any evidence that is collected in violation of reasonable expectations of privacy of the accused cannot be used against that person. This is called the exclusionary rule. It does not matter if the evidence is actually accurate—like drugs found on a drug dealer. If it was collected unlawfully, it is excluded. This is a fairly

---

5. Erling Eide, "Economics of Criminal Behavior," Chapter 8100, in *Encyclopedia of Law and Economics*, Vol. 5, ed. Boudewijn Bouckaert and Gerrit de Geest (Cheltenham: Edward Elgar, 2000), 345–389; Richard B. Freeman, "Economics of Crime," in *Handbook of Labor Economics*, Vol 3 (Amsterdam: Elsevier, 1999).

controversial rule, and some claim it means criminals go free. What it does in terms of the model we have been discussing is to lower the level of the expected punishment. In the April 2003 issue of the *Journal of Law and Economics* Raymond Atkins and Paul Rubin report on a test of whether the exclusionary rule leads to higher levels of crime. Their conclusion is that it does. Before you decide this is unequivocally a bad thing, consider this. The purpose of procedures that protect criminals is to guard against the conviction of those who are innocent. In order to fully evaluate the exclusionary rule, we also would have to know how many innocent people might have gone to jail if the rule did not exist.

Reference: Raymond Atkins and Paul Rubin, "Effects of Criminal Procedure on Crime Rates: Mapping Out the Consequences of the Exclusionary Rule," *Journal of Law & Economics,* 46, no. 1 (2003): 157–80.

When average income levels are used as explanatory variables for crime, the results can go either way (some studies find positive effects, others find negative effects, a lot don't find any effect at all).[6] Only a few studies can make a distinction between available average level of legal and illegal income. In one study, Richard Freeman found that the average level of legal income has a negative effect on crime (higher legal income levels keep youngsters away from crime) and the average level of illegal income has a positive effect.[7]

Indicators of income inequality are not always significant. One would expect that with large income differences, crime is a rewarding activity for low-income groups that may steal from the very rich. Estimates vary across studies. Some studies do find a positive effect on the crime rate of a higher inequality level.[8] In most studies, a higher level of unemployment will correspond to higher crime levels. Most studies also find that the presence of young males and ethnic minorities has a positive effect on the crime rate.

6. A positive effect means that the variable moves in the same direction. With a negative effect, they move in opposite directions.

7. Richard B. Freeman, "Why Do So Many Young American Men Commit Crimes and What Might We Do about It?" *Journal of Economic Perspectives* 10, no. 1 (1996): 25–42.

8. Such as Freeman, "Why Do So Many Young American Men Commit Crimes" and Van Velthoven and Theeuwes, *De ontwikkeling van de criminaliteit.*

ABORTION AND THE CRIME RATE

The idea may be uncomfortable, but how about the idea that legalized abortion lowers the crime rate? This was the conclusion of economists John Donohue and Steven Levitt. In fact, they claim that one-half of the drop in crime can be traced to legalized abortion. Their studies show that crime rates began falling in the United States exactly eighteen years after the U.S. Supreme Court ruled in *Roe v. Wade* that states could not have laws prohibiting abortion. In fact, crime rates dropped earlier in states that permitted abortion before the Supreme Court decision. Donahue and Leavitt theorize that abortions are more frequently performed on mothers who are unwed, uneducated, and poor—factors that tend to give rise to high crime rates. So, however you feel about abortion, what do you think?

Reference: John J. Donohue III and Steven D. Levitt, "The Impact of Legalized Abortion on Crime," *Quarterly Journal of Economics,* 116 (no. 2) (May 2001): 379–420.

METHODOLOGICAL PROBLEMS AND CRITICISM

In general, the empirical studies confirm the theoretical expectations of the theoretical model of the rational criminal. This does not mean, however, that these empirical results are without problems. A lot of things can go wrong in the use of statistical techniques. For example, when researchers use aggregate time series data (for instance, yearly observations on the national crime rate, the average probability of punishment, the national unemployment rate), they often encounter the problem of spurious correlation. Spurious correlation means that aggregate time series data usually move up and down in unison just because they are all aggregate data. There are, over time, consecutive periods of economic upturns and downturns and these make all aggregate variables go up and down in unison. That means that there is always some correlation between aggregate data, but this correlation is spurious in the sense that it is always there and does not explain anything specific. Statistical techniques are available to correct for spurious correlation and to reveal the "real" correlation.

Cross-section data such as those Ehrlich used in his studies have other problems. Some states might experience high crime rates (lots of capital murders) and because of that they institute capital punishment. States with fewer capital murders do not see the need for capital punishment. In that case, the direction of causality goes from crime to severity of punishment. In his first study (1975), Ehrlich assumed that the causality went from punishment to crime levels. There are statistical techniques that allow for both causality directions at the same time, and in his more recent studies (1977) Ehrlich applied these techniques (and still confirmed his original results on the negative effect of capital punishment on crime).

Finally, there are substantial measurement problems on the side of the variable to be explained. Often, crime rates are underreported and hence the variable that is measured and explained in crime regression underestimates the real amount of crime. If the proportion of underreporting is always the same, then the statistical damage is not as bad as when the proportion of underreporting varies all the time. Some researchers try to correct for underreporting by using information on data from victimization studies, which always find higher crime rates than the officially reported data.

Finally, the variables that we measure in crime regression are often an approximation of the variables that we want to study. For instance, an important variable such as social norms or changes in social norms are impossible to measure. Approximating this variable with, for instance, the divorce rate or secularization rate is sensible but not perfect. Even the murder rate, which is an important variable to be explained in Ehrlich-type regressions, is not measured perfectly. The measured murder rate contains murders that may not be deterrable, such as nonnegligent manslaughter and nonpremeditated crimes of passion. It is hard, if not impossible, to separate deterrable and nondeterrable murders.

APPLICATION

The results of the empirical investigations presented in this chapter can and are used for policy decisions. This is borne out by the considerable public attention that Ehrlich's work on capital punishment has received. The Solicitor General of the United States, for example, introduced Ehrlich's findings to the Supreme Court in support of capital punishment (*Fowler v. North Carolina*).

Another interesting policy application is for prediction purposes. The research department of the Ministry of Justice in the Netherlands has developed and estimated an extensive crime model in which the evolution of different crime rates, apprehension rates, conviction rates, and punishment rates (for fraud, theft, murder, etc.) are estimated. This "criminometrical" model is used to generate predictions of future crime rates together with a prediction of future needs for expansion (or contraction) of the police force and of the judicial and penitentiary system. One of the results of this statistical model is a prediction of how many prison cells the Netherlands might need in the next five to ten years, given the prediction of future crime rates for this period. This prediction information is then used in the decision to build or to mothball prison cells in the years to come. It should be added that this systematic approach does not always work perfectly. There is at present a shortage of prison cells in the Netherlands.

QUESTIONS FOR DISCUSSION

1. The essential explanatory variables in a regression with number of crimes as the variable to be explained are probability of punishment and severity of punishment. As explained in the text, this type of regression has been estimated in several countries. Although the regression coefficients (the "α"s) for the probability of punishment and for the severity of punishment are usually significant in all country regressions, the coefficients differ among countries. They are larger in one country than the other. What could explain these differences?

2. Suppose you want to explain the number of shoplifting crimes in U.S. shopping malls. You have data on the number of shoplifters caught for each shopping mall in the United States. How would you specify the regression equation? Which explanatory variables would you like to insert on the right-hand side of the regression equation?

3. In this chapter, when reviewing the empirical evidence, we noted that most of the empirical studies find a significant negative effect

on the crime level of the probability of punishment and of the severity of punishment. In quantitative terms, the effect of the probability of punishment is "larger" (more negative) than the effect of the severity of punishment. Discuss what this implies for effective deterrence policies.

4. In their article titled "The Impact of Legalized Abortion on Crime" (see Law and Economics in Action 21.3), John Donohue and Steven Levitt formulated the hypothesis they wanted to test empirically as follows: "Legalized abortion may lead to reduced crime either through reduction in cohort size or through lower per capita offending rates for affected cohorts." Explain and discuss these two channels whereby more abortions might lead to lower crime rates some eighteen years later.

Economics
of Litigation

CHAPTER TWENTY-TWO

The Value of a Case

THROUGHOUT THIS BOOK, IT HAS BEEN IMPLICIT that parties who are victims of a tort, a contract breach, an antitrust violation, or some other source of damages will collect from the party responsible for the *wrong*. That supposition involves a huge simplification. Unless the party committing the wrong immediately concedes that he or she is responsible, produces a checkbook, and writes a check to the victim, the injured party will have to retain an attorney and sue or at least threaten to sue the other party. This can be a very expensive proposition. Consequently, no matter how wronged or indignant an injured party may feel, there is a point at which the ultimate positive outcome, if any, of pressing a claim must be considered. More specifically, the focus is on the value of a case.

The analysis of the value of a case requires one to view the *case* or the *claim* as an asset. This asset can be employed to produce income or some other benefit. For example, the objective may be to stop the offending behavior of others, ranging from playing loud music to discrimination. The present value (PV) of that expected net outcome is the value of the case. In summary form, the value of a case can be expressed as

$$V = PV \text{ (expected recovery)} - PV \text{ (expected costs)}.$$

This simple formulation contains a tremendous amount of information. The purpose of this chapter is to examine the factors that go into determining the value of a case.

Before going into those details, you might ask why the value is so important. First, if litigants are rational, it makes little sense to press a claim if V is less than or equal to zero. This could be the conclusion one comes to after one visit to an attorney. The attorney may explain that your damages are so low or the probability of winning is so remote or the expected costs are so high that V is zero or less.

Perhaps more important is the role the value calculation plays in settlement. Currently about 95 percent of cases are settled without a trial. You can view a settlement as involving a sale by a plaintiff of his or her cause of action. Thus, even if the value of the plaintiff's case exceeds zero, the defendant may offer more than the estimated value. If so, it is rational to settle. Critical to settlement is that the parties be roughly in agreement on the value of a case or that the defendant place a higher value on the case than the plaintiff. The details of the settlement possibility will be discussed in Chapter 23. Finally, determining V may also have another purpose. Parties who bring "frivolous" lawsuits and their attorneys can sometimes be liable to opposing parties. A negative value may be a step in determining whether a suit is frivolous.

In this chapter, we cover these steps in some detail. The first section explores the factors that determine the expected recovery. Next we focus on the expected costs of litigation. The last section adds some of the many possible refinements to the model.

CASE 22.1 A Market for Legal Services? *Hughes v. Joliet Correctional Center,* 931 F.2d 425 (7th Cir. 1991)

People without legal training usually have a good sense of when they have been "wronged." They are likely to be far less adept at knowing the *value* of their case. Typically, that requires a trip to an attorney. Attorneys, thus, both assess the value of cases and are attracted to cases of high value. This connection is expressed in this excerpt from an opinion by Judge Richard Posner. The case itself dealt with the complaint of a prisoner who alleged that malpractice in a prison hospital amounted to cruel and unusual punishment. The relevant issue in this case dealt with the decision of a judge not to request an attorney to assist the plaintiff. The court found that the judge should have requested an attorney for the plaintiff but in the process Judge Posner observed:

One could of course question the necessity of courts' ever *providing* counsel to indigent plaintiffs in cases that if meritorious promise a substantial recovery of damages. Such cases should be attractive to tort lawyers, who can be hired on a contingent-fee basis by an indigent plaintiff. Why should government intervene, even to the limited extent of merely "requesting" a private lawyer to take on the case for free, if the market can be relied on to supply legal services to those indigents whose legal rights have actually been violated? If Hughes has been crippled for life as a result of the defendants' deliberate indifference to his medical needs, he should be able to obtain a substantial award of damages with which to compensate a privately retained lawyer; and perhaps from his failure to have retained a lawyer we should infer that his case probably is not as strong as it looks on the basis of the incomplete record to date. On the other hand, maybe it is unrealistic to attribute to prisoner Hughes sufficient sophistication to have realized that he ought to make efforts to retain a lawyer on his own, rather than simply ask the district judge to do it for him. We need not resolve the question, as our quarrel with the district judge is that she should have considered Hughes's request in light of the particulars of his case rather than simply deny the request in accordance with a general policy. We conclude that his suit was dismissed prematurely.

Having a case of high value and knowing it are different things. Obviously, the connection may involve a problem of transaction costs. Do you think lawyer advertising is likely to close this gap? Even for prisoners?

EXPECTED RECOVERY: THE STANDARD ANALYSIS

Expected recovery (*ER*) can be expressed as

$$(P \times Award) + (1 - P) \times 0$$

where P is the probability of obtaining a favorable verdict that will withstand any possible appeal. As a recovery may not occur for months or years, this amount must be reduced to present value.[1] In addition, the term *award* should be viewed as having a broad definition. We all tend to think in terms of the award as a monetary recov-

---

1. In some instances, however, a court will allow the plaintiff to recover interest on the damages from the time of the harm to the trial.

ery roughly equal to damages suffered. In fact, the award can be in the form of an injunction or some other ruling that vindicates hard-to-quantify values. Still, at some level, a litigant must decide what the award or victory is worth and compare that with the costs of the effort.

Obviously, the higher the expected recovery, the more likely it is that V will have a positive value. It may make sense to pursue an action with a low probability of recovery if the possible damages are high. Similarly, a high probability of recovering modest damages may result in an attractive case. Interestingly, the legal system plays a major role in providing an incentive for some potential litigants. As you have seen, in some torts cases, punitive damages are available. In antitrust cases, plaintiffs stand to recover actual damages multiplied by three. In effect, in an antitrust claim

$$ER = (P \times 3 \times Damages) + (1 - P) \times 0$$

On the other hand, punitive damages are not available in an action for breach of contract. All other factors being equal—and certainly they are not—one would expect litigation efforts and resources to be drawn toward the types of actions in which the legal system provides a "boost."

Perhaps the most important and sometimes controversial way in which the expected recovery can be increased is by use of a *class action*. In a great many instances, each person who is damaged by the actions of another will have only minor losses and V will be low not simply because the expected recovery is low but because the recovery will be offset by expected costs. A class action allows plaintiffs to combine their damages into one total amount. A good example would be an antitrust case in which each buyer from a group of firms engaged in price fixing may have paid only $5.00 more than the competitive price. Obviously, this is small potatoes (if each consumer buys the product only once in a lifetime, not if you buy it every day) and not worth being pursued by any one victim. On the other hand, if there are one million victims who can combine into a "class," damages are equal to $5 million and expected recovery increases.

EXPECTED COSTS

An assessment of expected costs is substantially more difficult than the analysis of the expected award. This complexity stems from two sources. First, a litigant may incur many types of costs. It is tempting to think in terms of attorneys' fees alone but there may also be expenses for expert witnesses, travel, postage, photocopying, materials, and so on. Just as important, a lawsuit may take up a substantial amount of the litigants' time. The opportunity costs associated with lost work time or even leisure should not be ignored.

More troublesome in terms of calculating expected costs is the variety of ways these costs may be paid for. For example, in an antitrust case a winning plaintiff's reasonable attorneys' fees will be paid for by a losing defendant. In addition, parties to a contract may include a term about the allocation of legal fees should a dispute arise. States have various rules about which types of costs will be paid by the losing party. In some foreign jurisdictions, attorneys' fees are paid by the losing party. There is no generalized rule for all cases, but whatever the expected costs are, they must be subtracted from the expected award to arrive at V. If the costs are predictable and the party pays only his or her costs, the determination is simple (for simplicity reasons we ignore present value notation):

$$V = \text{Expected award} - C \text{ (expected cost of litigation)}$$

On the other hand, if some portion of the costs are recoverable from the losing party,

$$V = \text{Expected award} - [O + (C_1 - pC_1) + (1 - p)C_2]$$

where C_1 are the costs of the plaintiff and C_2 are the costs of the defendant. As you can see, under the unrealistic assumption that there is a 100 percent chance of the plaintiff winning, all of his costs will be paid by the defendant and the plaintiff will pay none of the defendant's costs. This assumes a 100 percent cost shift, which may not be realistic.

An additional matter complicating an expected costs determination is the widespread use of contingent fees. A contingent fee is an arrangement under which the attorney representing a plaintiff agrees to accept as payment a percentage of any recovery and to forgo payment if there is no recovery. This does not mean that a plaintiff incurs no costs. Generally, there will be costs other than attorneys' fees that a litigant will incur. In this situation,

$$V = .66 \text{ expected award} - \text{expected costs}$$

where .33 is the contingent fee, P is the probability of winning, and A is the award. Expected cost in this formulation does not include the plaintiff's attorney fees. Instead the award itself is reduced. The losing plaintiff may still incur other costs, including some of the defendant's costs.

All these factors should suggest to you very clearly that the value of a case is influenced by many factors that are not related to the merits of the claim or the amount of the harm caused. Public policy, like the trebling of damages and the award of attorneys' fees in antitrust claims, and private contractual arrangements between the parties or between a party and his or her attorney are critical determinants. A number of other important refinements increase the reality of the model.

REFINING THE MODEL

Incremental Analysis

In a sense, the idea that you determine the value of a case at the outset is misleading. As you would expect, the process of discovering the value of a case is an unfolding one and each step involves a marginal analysis. In fact, it may not be until *discovery,* a procedure in the case during which the sides exchange information, that you will have some concrete idea about the value of your case.

As an example, suppose you slip and fall and are injured in a grocery store. It may occur to you that the store should pay for your medical bills. Your first decision is whether to invest the time and incur the costs of seeing an attorney. Even at this stage, at least intuitively, you compare costs and benefits. From this point on, your decisions become more educated, but each step that involves additional expense involves marginal analysis. For a fee, the attorney may agree to write a letter to the store indicating that you would like the store to pay for damages. If the store refuses, there will be another decision about whether to file a claim. At some point, the store may offer to settle the case and you will have to compare the settlement offer with the costs and benefits of continuing. If you lose, you may eventually have to decide whether the cost of an appeal is justified by the marginal benefit. In most, if not all, instances, the initial valuation of a case will involve some guesswork about the two possible roads that a case can develop in the future.

Expected Damages and the Level of Litigation

As the model suggests, the value of a case is directly related to the size of the award and the probability of recovery. Obviously, when damages are low, one would expect few lawsuits because low recoveries are unlikely to cover court fees and even modest attorneys' fees. From this you may infer that as the stakes get higher, the number of litigated cases will also rise. It is important to recall three fairly obvious points. First, it takes two to make a lawsuit. Second, potential defendants can avoid the damages if they do not cause harm to others. Third, as a defendant's potential damages go up, the motivation to take action to avoid the harmful event also increases.

You can understand this by thinking in terms of our basic model of supply and demand as depicted in Figure 22.1. Suppose the demand (D) here is for bicycles. Suppose further that the manufacturer is faced with a choice about the strength of the metal used to attach the pedals. A lower grade metal may give way once in a while

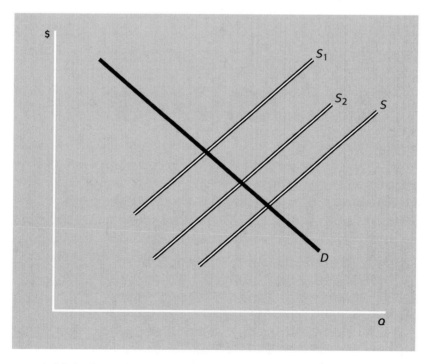

FIGURE 22.1 The Impact of Increased Production Costs

resulting in injury to the rider. If the lower grade metal is used, supply will be S. Forecasters report that use of the lower grade metal will mean lawsuits and possible liability to those injured. The cost of the harm and the expense of lawsuits will be internalized moving supply to S_1. Manufacturers may look for substitute measures to avoid these expenses much like a manufacturer might look for a less expensive input. One possibility is the use of higher grade metal. If this is less expensive than the lawsuits, the new supply curve will be S_2. In effect, the threat of liability will set into motion a series of reactions that will lead to product improvements. What this means is that as potential expected awards increase, one might actually find fewer lawsuits. The idea is fairly simple. When potential damages are high, product improvements or even more careful behavior become better substitutes for the expenses and potential liability of lawsuits.

Repeat Players

When thinking about potential plaintiffs and defendants, it may be tempting to view the expected recovery as a zero-sum game. That is, whatever is awarded to the plaintiff is the amount lost to the defendant. If this were the case and if the plaintiffs and defendants estimate similar costs, V would be the same regardless of the side of the case one is on. As you will see, this has important implications for settlement. There is an important reason that estimates of V and, in particular, the expected award may not be the same for the plaintiff and the defendant. One or both of the parties may be what are known as *repeat players*. To understand why, remember that the expected award is the amount the plaintiff stands to gain if victorious. From the defendant's perspective, this can be slightly different. Obviously, the defendant pays the plaintiff's damages and the defendant's *award* is the liability avoided. The liability avoided with respect to one single plaintiff may not represent the total potential losses associated with losing the case or the gain from winning. In fact, losing a case may set a precedent that opens the door and makes it easier for future plaintiffs to recover. Thus, a party is not merely attempting to win a case but to have a longer-run impact on the course of the law.

A simple example may be useful here. You may have heard of or remember reading in Chapter 18 about the lawsuit by a woman who had been burned when coffee she bought at McDonald's spilled and scalded her. Suppose her damages were equal to $40,000 and that is the amount she will enter into her calculation of V. On the other hand, McDonald's may realize that if it loses the case a precedent may be set about the legal liability it incurs as a result of hot coffee spills. More specifically, a ruling by a court that people scalded by hot coffee are contributorily negligent and not permitted to recover would be very valuable to McDonald's. This is because McDonald's is a repeat player. While the burn victim has but one case to litigate, McDonald's could find itself faced with the same issues and possible liability in case after case.

The consequence of a loss in one case will increase the likelihood of a string of cases with the ultimate damages exceeding $40,000. In short, McDonald's V may greatly exceed the V for the $40,000 plaintiff. When this happens there can be two outcomes. First, the defendant may be more flexible with respect to settlement. The defendant may prefer that there not be a judicial statement made on the critical issue of contributory negligence. Second, because of the higher expected award, McDonald's can invest far more in the lawsuit than the plaintiff before V becomes negative. In effect, the parties are litigating about two different matters. The plaintiff wants to recover for a single incident of harm. The defendant is effectively defending against a number of instances of harm. In our McDonald's hypothetical, this is accomplished by obtaining a holding that people who spill hot coffee are ultimately responsible for their own injuries.

The discussion above focuses on the defendant as the *repeat player*. Can a plaintiff be a repeat player? The simple answer is yes, but generally it is less likely for plaintiffs to be repeat players. A successful plaintiff, especially in a milestone case in which the law may shift, is subject to something like free-riding problems. For example, suppose in our McDonald's hypothetical the harm to the burn victim is $40,000. For a plaintiff to win a case in which it is determined that serving hot coffee that is above a safe temperature is negligent may open the door to a multitude of additional lawsuits against the defendant. Unless the plaintiff is able to internalize some part of the benefit a victory will mean for others, the plaintiff may invest no more than $40,000. While McDonald's will internalize the benefits of a possible victory far in excess of $40,000, the individual plaintiff will not.

Again, this is not to say that the defendants are the only repeat players. It is possible for plaintiffs to repeatedly litigate in order win a breakthrough case. Similarly, defendants can be subject to free riding. For example, the benefits of a decision that hot coffee burns are a result of contributory negligence will accrue to restaurants generally. Still, the repeat player matter is most likely to come up when a relatively large corporation selling to the public finds that it is possibly liable to a number of potential plaintiffs.

There are a couple of factors that create in plaintiffs a repeat player-like effect. One of these, discussed above, is a *class action*. This permits plaintiffs to combine resources to fund a lawsuit and to internalize the benefits. The other possibility is punitive damages. As you may recall from Chapter 18, the economic theory of punitive damages would permit a plaintiff to recover the full amount of a defendant's wrongdoing. This has an effect similar to allowing a plaintiff to internalize the benefits to other possible plaintiffs.[2] As it turns out, judicial limits on punitive damages mean that a single plaintiff may not be able to collect an amount equal to the damages to all plaintiffs but even some punitive damages will mean that plaintiffs will begin to take on repeat player characteristics.

Finally, the repeat player phenomenon can be found on the plaintiff's side if one focuses on attorneys as opposed to clients. There are economies of scale associated with developing an expertise in a particular field. An attorney who is known for successfully pursuing a particular type of claim or for causing courts to look favorably on a novel legal theory may find clients lining up for his or her assistance. Each client's investment will still be limited by the expected award. On the other hand, each dollar spent will have greater impact if it is spent on retaining an attorney who has himself or herself repeatedly tried a certain type of case.

CASE 22.2 Fees and Incentives: *Kirchoff v. Flynn,* 786 F.2d 320 (1986)

This chapter and the next focus on the "case" as something that has value and can, in effect, be "sold" in the form of a settlement.

---

2. It is not the same because subsequent plaintiffs may still recover an amount equal to their damages.

In this excerpt, many of the relationships between attorneys' fees and strategy are discussed. First, some background: The case involves Mr. and Mrs. Kirchoff. Mrs. Kirchoff was out walking one day with two dogs and a parakeet. She was arrested for feeding pigeons and allowing her dogs to roam without a leash. Mrs. Kirchoff did not cooperate and was taken to jail, but first the two dogs and the bird were taken to her home where the police ran into Mr. Kirchoff and a fight resulted. Eventually, the police were sued for assault, battery, false arrest, and malicious prosecution under the Civil Rights Act (section 1988). The Kirchoffs turned down a settlement offer for $42,000 and eventually were awarded $25,000 by a jury. This case dealt with the issue of attorneys' fees.

The Kirchoffs had a contingent fee agreement with their attorney under which he would have received 40 percent or $10,000. Unlike the usual private tort action, this amount was to be paid by the city since under the Civil Rights Act, the plaintiff is to recover the full amount of the award. The attorneys argued, however, that they were entitled to more, having spent 332 hours on the case at $150 per hour for a total of nearly $50,000. The appellate court found that the award of $10,000 awarded by the trial court based on the contingent fee contract was inappropriate. The reasoning will assist you in understanding the impact of different types of fees.

> A court awarding fees under § 1988 is supposed to compute the "market rate" for the attorneys' work and assess that reasonable fee against the defendants. . . . [T]he rate should "simulate the results that would obtain if the lawyer were dealing with a paying client." The district judge thought that 40% of the award is the "market rate" for cases of this type; it was, after all, the rate the Kirchoffs themselves negotiated. What could be a better gauge of the market than an actual transaction in it?

The court goes on to explain why the contract is not satisfactory.

> In ordinary tort litigation the contract fixes entitlements. If the plaintiff recovers $25,000, the lawyer gets $10,000 and the plaintiff $15,000. The plaintiff, with money on the line, takes care when negotiating. The Kirchoffs' contract is not about the disposition of their money. As the district court said, the (or a) policy behind § 1988 is to ensure that the plaintiffs keep the whole recovery. So in negotiating a contract such as this, the

Kirchoffs were dickering about the defendants' money, not their
own. . . .

One logical response would be to say that 40% is the
customary fee in tort litigation in which plaintiffs *are* looking out
for their own wallets, and the bargains these other plaintiffs
strike offer vicarious protection to defendants in cases under
§ 1988. A court need only match these private bargains to arrive
at the "market rate." This would be too facile, however, because
the risks plaintiffs face in § 1983 litigation are greater and the
rewards smaller. A § 1983 case is not like [other] litigation, in
which all but a few defenses have been stripped away. . . . A
plaintiff suing the police may encounter juries sympathetic to
the defendants—more sympathetic, anyway, than juries are apt
to be when the defendant is a deep-pocket corporation in a
products liability . . . suit. When the plaintiff wins on the
merits, the jury may treat the defendant as having shallow
pockets. . . . Litigants under § 1983 therefore have a harder
time on the merits, and recover less when they win, than
plaintiffs in much other tort litigation. The observation that a
contingent fee of $1/3$ or $2/5$ of the recovery fetches adequate
counsel . . . in products liability suits therefore does not
demonstrate that the same percentage is the "market rate" in
riskier, lower-stakes litigation under § 1983.

The market for legal services uses three principal plans of
compensation: the hourly fee, the fixed fee, and the contingent
fee. The contingent fee serves in part as a financing device,
allowing people to hire lawyers without paying them in advance
(or at all, if they lose). It also serves as a monitoring device. In
any agency relation, the agent may pursue his own goals at the
expense of the principal's. A fixed fee creates the incentive to
shirk; a lawyer paid a lump sum, win or lose, may no longer
work hard enough to present his client's case. Fixed fees
therefore are used only in cases where the client can monitor the
results and the lawyer's work (did the lawyer secure the divorce
or not?) or where the client (or the client's general counsel) is
sufficiently sophisticated to assess what the lawyer has
accomplished.

An hourly fee creates an incentive to run up hours, to do too
much work in relation to the stakes of the case. An hourly fee
may be appropriate where it is hard to define output (in
litigation, for example, the outcome turns on the merits and not
simply the lawyer's skill and dedication), so the hourly method
measures and prices the inputs, the attorney's hours. Again,

however, it is necessary to monitor the lawyer's work. The general counsel of a corporation or a sophisticated client may measure inputs well, but in litigation under § 1988 the plaintiff usually has little ability to monitor and also has little incentive to do so, knowing that the defendant will pay the bill. So the court rather than the plaintiff must do the supervision.

To sum up: the district judge was entitled to compute the attorneys' fee in this case as a percentage of the total award. The court was mistaken, however, to lift that percentage out of the contingent fee contract. The 40% was to be a minimum, not a cap. The contract was not bargained between the lawyer and the real parties in interest—the defendants. It also may not provide the percentage that is used in similarly risky tort litigation with moderate stakes.

Fee Arrangements

Earlier in our analysis, the importance of different fee arrangements on V was noted. The most interesting and controversial topic on the cost side of the analysis is contingent fees. To be sure, a contingent fee has a "bounty hunter" feel about it since the attorney has a personal financial interest in the outcome of the case. Your response might be, "Doesn't an attorney have a financial interest in every case?" The answer is "yes and no." Losing cases is bad for business and any attorney who is known for his or her victories in the courtroom is likely to be in greater demand. On the other hand, an attorney who charges by the hour is paid the resulting fee whether he wins or loses, whereas the contingent fee attorney depends on victories for his or her livelihood.

More interesting is the way contingent fees may affect V, the likelihood of filing an action, and the relationship between the parties. If attorneys observe their ethical commitments, the same effort will be put forth on behalf of an hourly client and a contingent fee client. The difference between a contingent fee arrangement and an hourly billing system is reflected in Figure 22.2. The vertical axis is the legal fee (either hourly or contingent) and the horizontal axis is the expected award. *SF* on the graph shows the legal fee under a standard hourly fee arrangement. It slopes upward to suggest the likely but not certain possibility that more hours will be spent on cases involving higher

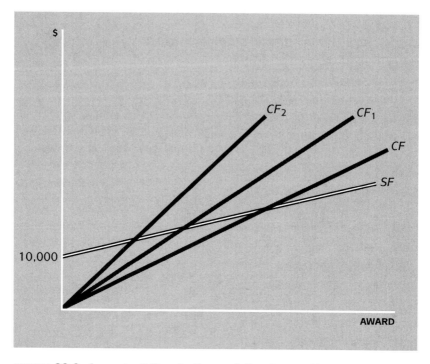

FIGURE 22.2   Impact of Hourly Fee and Contingent Fee

expected awards. The *y* intercept is at $10,000, suggesting that there is a minimum fee one can expect to incur just to commence a case. The intercept of a contingent fee will be at zero and the slope will depend on the percentage of the fee and the probability of a favorable outcome. *CF*, *CF*₁, and *CF*₂ represent three contingent fee possibilities. For example, *CF* could represent a 33 percent fee in the context of a case with a 60 percent chance of victory. *CF*₁ and *CF*₂ could represent 40 percent and 50 percent contingent fees, respectively. What is clear is that expected fees will be different depending on the fee arrangement.

It is also likely, as illustrated in the graph, that as the expected return increases, the contingent fee increases faster than hourly fees and will eventually exceed hourly fees. This is not mathematically necessary because a case with a low enough probability of success may have a slope that is even less than the slope of the hourly fee curve. Still, the more likely case is one in which the contingent fee curve slope exceeds the slope of the hourly fee curve. For example, in a case with an expected award of $10,000, the plaintiff would be better off entering into a contingent fee arrangement. When the expected award is $100,000, the opposite is true and the plaintiff would be better off contracting for an hourly fee.

The implications of these differences are important. First, V will vary—not on the basis of the claim or even on the basis of expected award—but on the payment agreement between the client and the attorney. Second, in many instances, the cost to the client who selects a contingent fee arrangement will be higher than the cost if the client selected an hourly payment schedule. It may occur to you that the fee arrangement alternatives have the effect of steering relatively less affluent clients to what may be the more expensive fee arrangement. For example, a person of moderate means may not be able to come up with the $10,000 but be able to afford an expected contingent fee of $15,000—because the latter involves no fee if there is no recovery. While it may be true that the less affluent or the more risk averse will select the more expensive route here, it is probably not accurate to regard this as something that decreases the likelihood of an action. For many people, the alternative of a seemingly less expensive hourly fee payable—win or lose—is not an option.

The choice of fee arrangement may also introduce biases into the attorney's effort and into the decision making about whether to pursue an action. An attorney who is paid by the hour may not be as careful about the amount of time devoted to a case and may be willing to overstate the likelihood of a favorable outcome because the costs of his or her efforts are fully shifted to the client.

The contingent fee attorney enters into more of a partnership with the client because success for the client means success for the attorney. At the same time, the attorney's goals may be different from the client's. The client is focused exclusively on maximizing the size of the award. The attorney is focused on maximizing the *difference* between his or her share of the award and the costs of pursuing the action. A consequence of this is that an attorney may refuse to take a contingent fee case even if V is positive. This is because the expected award may exceed expected costs but one-third of the expected award (the contingent fee) may *not* exceed costs. Another way to maximize the difference between the fee and the cost could be to minimize costs. This is called the "shirking" problem because the agent (the attorney), in maximizing his or her own profit, does not act in a way that maximizes the result for his or her client.

A final type of fee arrangement deserves brief mention. Sometimes an attorney will charge a flat fee for each service. For example, there could be a charge for filing the claim, taking a deposition, drafting a memorandum, and so on. Here you can see that the temptation will be to minimize the time spent on each task. What you should begin to see is the broad impact of fee arrangements on V. Fee arrangements obviously influence the level of expected costs. In more subtle ways, the fee arrangement may also have an impact on the probability of success.

Frivolous Claims

It is important to distinguish between a low-value case and a case that produces a net social loss. Many cases—indeed, some very important cases—may be those that have a low probability of succeeding or for which the monetary outcome is modest. Cases that cause shifts in the law are often characterized by low value but are often pursued nonetheless. The focus of these cases may be to redefine property or other rights. Any value for the plaintiff follows from this shift in the law. But in this case, there is also a value to society that is not internalized by the plaintiff. In these cases one sometimes sees organizations (such as trade unions, civil liberties organizations) subsidize the plaintiff.

On the other hand, even a fairly simple case can be expensive for the parties. This results in the potential for extortion by either side. For example, a plaintiff could file a claim that he knows is false but which will cause the defendant to incur $10,000 in expenses and then offer to settle with the defendant for $5,000. Or a defendant, knowing that any effort to deny liability is a farce, may threaten to force the plaintiff to go through a lengthy and expensive trial as a means of convincing the plaintiff to settle for less than actual damages.

These possibilities raise the issue of *frivolous* claims. The way the law discourages these claims is by sanctioning attorneys and parties who assert claims or defenses that have no reasonable basis in law or fact.[3] In other words, a frivolous claim involves elements of dishonesty, deception, or sloppiness.[4] The economic reason for penalizing those asserting such claims is obvious. Frivolous claims amount to little more than an effort to use the legal system to extort a redistribution. The impact of the redistribution on overall welfare is unknowable because it involves an interpersonal comparison of utility. What is known is that the redistribution can be costly and, thus, a net loss. Any "value" a frivolous claim has is by virtue of the loss that can be imposed on the opposing party, not the consequence of a shift in the law or a definition of rights.

LAW AND ECONOMICS IN ACTION 22.1

WHAT GOOD WAS LAW SCHOOL?

The behavior that results in the sanctioning of attorneys or parties typically must be quite extreme. For example, in a recent Mississippi case the plain-

3. The mechanism for sanctions is usually Rule 11 of the Federal Rules of Civil Procedure which provides as follows:

Representations to Court. By presenting to the court (whether by signing, filing, submitting, or later advocating) a pleading, written motion, or other paper, an attorney or unrepresented party is certifying that to the best of the person's knowledge, information, and belief, formed after an inquiry—reasonable under the circumstances—

(1) it is not being presented for any improper purpose, such as to harass or to cause unnecessary delay or needless increase in the cost of litigation;

(2) the claims, defenses, and other legal contentions therein are warranted by existing law or by a nonfrivolous argument for the extension, modification, or reversal of existing law or the establishment of new law;

(3) the allegations and other factual contentions have evidentiary support or, if specifically so identified, are likely to have evidentiary support after a reasonable opportunity for further investigation or discovery; and

(4) the denials of factual contentions are warranted on the evidence or, if specifically so identified, are reasonably based on a lack of information or belief.

(c) Sanctions. If, after notice and a reasonable opportunity to respond, the court determines that subdivision (b) has been violated, the court may, subject to conditions stated below, impose an appropriate sanction upon attorneys, law firms, or parties that have violated subdivision (b) or are responsible for the violation.

4. A. Mitchell Polinsky and Daniel L. Rubinfeld, "Sanctioning Frivolous Suits: An Economic Analysis," *Georgetown Law Journal* 397 (1993).

tiff (Eatman) was involved in a twelve-car pile-up. Her attorney wrote to the city of Moss Point, Mississippi, claiming that the city was liable because the person striking Eatman was a city employee who was driving a city car on city business at the time of the collision. In general, employers are liable for their accidents caused by their employees. Moreover, it makes sense to involve employers when possible as they are likely to have "deeper pockets" than employees. In this case, however, the city quickly determined that the employee was on vacation at the time and using his own car. Moreover, no one from the city was involved at all. Nevertheless, the plaintiff sued the city. Evidently, the only thing the plaintiff and her attorney "knew" at the time of filing the action was that the defendant was an employee of the city. The suit was quickly dismissed and the city requested that the plaintiff's attorney be sanctioned for filing a frivolous claim. The court applied the following standard: "[A] pleading or motion is frivolous within the meaning of Rule 11 only when, objectively speaking, the pleader or movant has no hope of success." The telling exchange at the sanction hearing went like this:

> BY THE COURT: Well, what have you got to show that the City of Moss Point has anything to do with it?
> BY MR. ALTMAN [Eatman's attorney]: At this point, we don't have anything, other than what we have in the police report.
> BY THE COURT: Which is what? That just shows that's where he worked.
> BY MR. ALTMAN: That's correct, Judge.
> BY THE COURT: It doesn't say anything else.
> BY MR. ALTMAN: That's correct.

In short, the attorney appeared to take a stab in the dark in an effort to name the city as a defendant. The sanction imposed by the court was that the Altman was required to pay the city's legal fees.

Reference: Eatman v. City of Moss Point, 809 So.2d 591 (Miss. 2000).

QUESTIONS FOR DISCUSSION

1. Sometimes you hear of people pressing legal claims *on principle.* Does this mean that the value of the case analysis is irrelevant?

2. Can you give an example of a suit that may have great value but no action is taken because of free riding? How does a class action help overcome this problem?

3. The case excerpt discusses hour rates, fixed fees, and contingent fees. What types of cases are most appropriate for each fee structure?

4. Suppose a firm goes into the investment business except that it buys your "case." That is, you go to an agent who assesses your claim and offers to pay you a flat fee for the case. The agent then hires attorneys who try the case and the investment company keeps the profit. Can you think of any economic objection to this?

5. Suppose an attorney files a frivolous claim. Do you think the punishment of being required to pay the opposing party's legal fees is a sufficient deterrent? Why or why not?

CHAPTER TWENTY-THREE

The Economics of Settlements

D ESPITE WHAT YOU MAY INFER FROM TELEVISION AND movies, very few legal disputes actually end up in a courtroom. In fact, most reliable research on the matter indicates that at least 95 percent of the parties to a dispute end up settling their cases. This chapter is devoted to the economic explanation for why settlement is the norm and the theories that attempt to explain why some cases do not conform to this norm.

This is an important inquiry for reasons that may not be readily obvious. As you know, the common law is judge-made law. Judges typically make law when they write opinions.[1] But it is not as though a judge can wake up in the morning and decide that he or she would like to adjust the law with respect to torts or contracts and then issue an opinion. Instead, judges write opinions only when deciding specific cases, and only about 5 percent of possible cases actually make it to trial. Even fewer make it to an appeal, the context in which an opinion is typically written. These then become the contexts in which new law is formed or old law reinforced. What this means is that legal scholars spend a fair amount of time trying to determine whether cases

---

1. To some extent, law is made when judges have the discretion to hear a case on appeal. Leaving a lower court opinion intact can be interpreted as approval of the law applied in that case.

that are tried have certain characteristics in common. The possibility that the selection of cases for trial determines the evolution of law will be covered in the next chapter.

The first section is devoted to the reasons that settlement is so common. The reasons that cases do not settle are reviewed in the second section.

WHY SETTLE?

The easy answer to "why settle?" is because it increases the utility of both parties. This is easy to understand when you realize that a settlement is actually a contract. The plaintiff is the seller and the defendant is the buyer. The plaintiff sells his or her right to sue to the defendant. From our analysis of contract law, you know that contracts are made when there is a surplus available that the parties can share. In a simple example, I may have a BMW that I value at $25,000. You think the car is wonderful and would pay up to $30,000 for it. There is a $5,000 surplus and the decision on a price somewhere between $25,000 (the lowest I will take) and $30,000 (the most you will pay) has the impact of dividing that surplus.

This may not seem at first impression to fit the model of a lawsuit. Where is the opportunity to share a surplus? The opportunity comes, for the most part, from the benefit of avoiding a trial and all the expenses leading up to trial. For example, suppose I crash into your car and the damage is $10,000. There is some question, however, about whether I am at fault, and that is, in effect, what the trial will determine. You begin by calculating the value of your case. You decide the probability of winning is 60 percent and the cost of the trial is $2,000. The expected value of the case is, therefore, $4,000 (60% × ($10,000) − $2,000. As you know from Chapter 22, as defendant I too will be involved in calculating my expected loss. Thus, I may also decide that you have about a 60 percent chance of winning and that the costs to me will be $2,000. My expected loss will be $8,000 (60% × $10,000) + $2,000.

As plaintiff, you would be willing to sell your right to sue me for anything over $4,000. Similarly, I would be happy to buy my way out of this predicament for anything less than $8,000. This creates a range of $4,000, much like the $5,000 range in the contracts example above.

In effect, litigation costs can be avoided if the parties settle. They do this by negotiating over the amount saved. The higher these costs, all else being held equal, the higher the likelihood of settlement. From a slightly different perspective and as the figures here suggest, cases will settle because the expected gain to plaintiffs is typically less than the expected loss to defendants.

Now that you understand the basic model, there is some important fleshing out to do. The first step in this process concerns the costs of settlement. In the example, when the $4,000 range is established, it is the sum of the plaintiff's and defendant's litigation expenses. This probably overstates the actual range. First, a fair amount of litigation expense may be incurred before a settlement is arrived at. Thus, the more precise analysis is one that describes the range as *expected remaining litigation expenses*. On the eve of a trial, after a great deal of preparation and travel, the litigation expenses remaining to be saved will be smaller than at the outset of the dispute.

The settlement range may be further narrowed by the fact that there are transaction costs of arriving at a settlement. If there are several potential litigants, there can be difficulties in coordination. In addition, there will be expenses associated with research and the actual negotiation. Thus, the settlement range is actually the remaining cost of litigation minus the remaining transaction costs of settlement. Although it is possible, it will be rare that this figure is not positive.

A second qualification of the model deals with the possibility that the parties are risk averse. In our example, the bargaining range is $4,000. Does that mean that the plaintiff would never accept less than $4,000 and the plaintiff would never pay more than $8,000? Probably not. For example, suppose the defendant offered the plaintiff $3,950 to settle. This would be compared to an expected outcome of $4,000 which includes a 40 percent probability of not recovering at all. A risk-averse plaintiff may regard a certain $3,950 as more attractive than $4,000 that includes a 40 percent chance of no recovery. The same analysis can also be applied to the defendant, who might prefer to pay $8,050 rather than take the *risk* of paying $10,000 in damages. The point is that the range within which to find settlement can probably be stretched a bit further than that described by the expected gain and loss. The more risk averse the parties, the further the stretch. You should not infer from this that the parties will be equally flexible due to risk aversion. An individual, for example, may be quite concerned about the risk. A corporation that is involved in litigation all the time and has significant resources may be less risk averse, reasoning that the losses and wins will balance out.

A third factor leading to settlement is mutual lack of confidence of the parties in the strength of their cases. Again, go back to our simple numerical example in which both parties think there is a 60 percent chance that the plaintiff will prevail. Suppose, however, that the plaintiff is worried about the merits of his or her case and thinks the probability of prevailing is only 50 percent. On the other hand, the defendant, also being pessimistic, believes there is only a 30 percent chance that he or she will prevail. If you recalculate the value of the case to the plaintiff, it is now $3,000.[2] The defendant now sees the expected loss as $9,000.[3] As you can see, the range within which a settlement may occur—even aside from risk aversion—has expanded to $6,000.

The size of the legal fees also has an impact on the probability of settlement. In effect, the higher the fees, the more the parties can save by settling. In Chapter 22, we saw that under some conditions, both parties' legal fees or other expenses are paid for by the losing party. In other situations, the legal fees are paid only by the plaintiff if his or her attorney wins the case. Because these fee arrangements can have an impact on the value of a case, they will also have an impact on the range within which a settlement is possible.

Take a case arising from the same event. The probability of a victory by the plaintiff is 50 percent and the damages are $20,000. Both parties agree on this. The expected award is $10,000. The defendant's legal expenses (net of settlement costs) are fixed at $2,000, meaning that the defendant would pay up to $12,000 to settle the case. Also assume the plaintiff has a contingent fee agreement under which the legal fees are 33 percent of any award. Now the value of the case to the plaintiff is $0.5(20,000) - 0.5(0.33)(20,000)$ or $6,666. The expected attorney's fees are $3,333. The settlement range will be between $6,666 and $12,000.

2. 50% of ($10,000) − $2,000 = $3,000.
3. 70% of ($10,000) + $2,000 = $9,000.

Ultimately, the impact of the contingent fee, as opposed to a fixed fee, on settlement will be influenced by what the attorney would have accepted as a fixed amount. That is impossible to know without knowing the complexity of the case and the hours likely to be devoted to it. There is, however, another way to approach the question. Suppose after assessing the value of the case from a contingent fee perspective, the attorney is asked what he or she would accept in the form of a certain fee. In all likelihood, the attorney would have accepted a fixed amount less than $3,333. This is because attorneys, like most people, are generally risk averse. In this context, a certain amount of say, $3,000, could easily be preferred to a 50 percent chance of $6,666 and a 50 percent chance of zero. From this perspective, the generalized effect of contingent fees would appear to increase the likelihood of settlement by making the settlement range broader than it would be if the fee agreement were not contingent on outcome.

Another fee possibility is that the loser pays all the expenses of both parties. Here again, assume the case involves $20,000 in alleged damages and a 50 percent probability that the defendant will be found liable. The fixed costs of litigation in excess of settlement costs is $2,000 for each party. The value of the case to the plaintiff will be 0.5(20,000) − $2,000 or $8,000. For the defendant, the value of avoiding the action is 0.5(20,000) + $2,000 or $12,000. The settlement range will be $4,000—from $8,000 to $12,000. Now suppose the rule is that the loser pays all fees. At first, this appears to be the same outcome as our initial example. For the plaintiff the value is 0.5(20,000) − 0.5(4,000), again $8,000. The value of avoidance to the defendant will again be $12,000 − 0.5(20,000) + 0.5(4,000). The settlement range is $4,000 and the expected legal fee is $2,000.

There is, however, a difference between both the $8,000 and the $12,000 expectations based on the riskiness of the legal fees. Again, under the fixed fee in which both parties pay their own $2,000 legal fees, there is no risk—win or lose, the cost is the same. Under the alternative, the expected $2,000 fee is the combination of a 50 percent probability of paying nothing and a 50 percent probability of paying $4,000. Again, most people are risk averse and will pay something to avoid the uncertainty. "Paying" in this context means the defendants could be more generous with settlement offers and plaintiffs willing to take less. In effect, both parties would be purchasers from the other of "insurance" against the zero or $4,000 risk. The overall impact will be to expand the settlement range. The greater the legal fees, in any given context, the greater the expansion. Obviously, the policy that the loser pays the costs of both sides is one that encourages settlement over litigation.

Settlement is greatly encouraged when there is asymmetry in expected gains and losses with the defendant's calculations of likely losses exceeding the plaintiff's gains. A more detailed look at asymmetry is discussed below, but for now one particular form of asymmetry fits nicely within the model as explained so far. In our simple model, the parties agreed on the measure of damages and the probability that the plaintiff would win. This is the zero-sum model in which the plaintiff's winnings are the defendant's losses. In Chapter 22 we noted that this is not always the case. In some instances, a plaintiff may have a relatively modest claim. For the plaintiff to prevail, however, the court may be required to adopt a change in the law that will favor that plaintiff as well as others.

In Chapter 22, we discussed the McDonald's case in which McDonald's coffee scalded a customer. In that case, suppose the damages to the plaintiff were $40,000 and the probability of prevailing was only 25 percent. The cost for both sides might be $5,000. The value for the defendant is $5,000. If, in the course of the litigation, the court adopts a new rule that stands up on appeal, servers of hot coffee like McDonald's may be faced with a number of other potential plaintiffs. Thus, while the probability of losing is only 25 percent and the expected loss in this case only $5,000, McDonald's or a similar defendant may pay in excess of that amount to avoid the case altogether. Strategic considerations in this context, however, can also cut the other way. It may eventually occur to McDonald's that it is not a good idea to settle with each burn victim/plaintiff because those settlements will add up. It may, at some point, be more cost-effective to stop a parade of settlements and to litigate the matter. In this instance, the potential defendant compares the relative costs and benefits of a repeated settlement strategy to a "hard-nosed" litigation policy. The larger point, however, is that the repeat play effect can have an enormous impact on whether settlement occurs.

ENCOURAGING SETTLEMENT

The fact that most lawsuits are settled is not merely the result of rational negotiation over litigation costs that can be saved. Laws that have an impact on legal fees can also have this effect. Take a look at these statutes from the State of Florida (Florida Statutes 768.79):

OFFER OF JUDGMENT AND DEMAND FOR JUDGMENT

(6) Upon motion made by the offeror within 30 days after the entry of judgment or after voluntary or involuntary dismissal, the court shall determine the following:

(a) If a defendant serves an offer which is not accepted by the plaintiff, and if the judgment obtained by the plaintiff is at least 25 percent less than the amount of the offer, the defendant shall be awarded reasonable costs, including investigative expenses, and attorney's fees, calculated in accordance with the guidelines promulgated by the Supreme Court, incurred from the date the offer was served, and the court shall set off such costs in attorney's fees against the award. When such costs and attorney's fees total more than the amount of the judgment, the court shall enter judgment for the defendant against the plaintiff for the amount of the costs and fees, less the amount of the award to the plaintiff.

(b) If a plaintiff serves an offer which is not accepted by the defendant, and if the judgment obtained by the plaintiff is at least 25 percent more than the amount of the offer, the plaintiff shall be awarded reasonable costs, including investigative expenses, and attorney's fees, calculated in accordance with the guidelines promulgated by the Supreme Court, incurred from the date the offer was served.

(7)(a) If a party is entitled to costs and fees pursuant to the provisions of this section, the court may, in its discretion, determine that an offer was not made in good faith. In such case, the court may disallow an award of costs and attorney's fees.

(b) When determining the reasonableness of an award of attorney's fees pursuant to this section, the court shall consider, along with all other relevant criteria, the following additional factors:

1. The then apparent merit or lack of merit in the claim.
2. The number and nature of offers made by the parties.
3. The closeness of questions of fact and law at issue.
4. Whether the person making the offer had unreasonably refused to furnish information necessary to evaluate the reasonableness of such offer.

5. Whether the suit was in the nature of a test case presenting questions of far-reaching importance affecting nonparties.
6. The amount of the additional delay cost and expense that the person making the offer reasonably would be expected to incur if the litigation should be prolonged.

Under the statute, either party may make an offer to settle the case. If the offer is declined and was fairly close to the outcome of the case, that party has its legal fees paid by the other party. How does this affect settlement negotiations?

WHY NOT SETTLE?

As the analysis above suggests, settlement is almost the norm and there are good economic reasons for this. Given that transaction (settlement) costs are almost always lower than the cost of litigating a case, what accounts for cases going to trial? Actually, a number of factors contribute to the inability to agree on a satisfactory settlement.

Asymmetrical Expectations

As you read above, asymmetry in expectations can be one of the most important factors limiting settlement. Of course, asymmetry can run either way. As long as the plaintiff's expected gain is less than the defendant's expected loss, settlement is likely. Quite the opposite is true when the imbalance runs the other way. For example, if a plaintiff's expected value is $20,000 and the defendant's expected loss is $10,000, a settlement is not likely, simply because neither party sees the settlement as in its self-interest. This type of asymmetry may be the result of different estimates of damages, the plaintiff's probability of success, or expected costs.

As the percentage of cases settled indicates, wide disparity in these estimates is not common. When there is disparity, it is more likely to be the result of different views of the two factors that are critical in the outcome of a case: What are the facts and what is the law? Take a simple example of when a car collides with the rear end of another car. The case involves two components. The first is the law in respect to rear-end collisions. When it comes to the law, competent attorneys interpreting statutes or common law in the vast majority of instances will be in general agreement on the legal rule to be applied—which is that the driver of the car rear-ending the other is liable. On the other hand, there may be greater disagreement about the facts of a case. The parties may disagree about which car was moving at the time. Both parties are 100 percent sure of their positions. Unless the attorneys can convince each party that the jury is as likely to believe one party as the other, this case may not settle.

Disagreements about the law can be dealt with by legal research. Disagreements about the facts are often settled through a process of discovery—a formal period during the litigation process in which the parties exchange information. To understand how discovery may hasten settlement, consider a typical antitrust case in which a plaintiff claims that two suppliers have agreed to increase the prices he pays for a raw material. As you may know, when competitors agree on prices, they violate the antitrust laws. That is the legal or easy part. The hard part is showing as a factual matter that the parties actually did agree. During discovery, the plaintiff may be permitted to see all of the written exchanges between the two firms and to interview the parties in the firms in charge of pricing.[4] As this process continues, the parties may begin to reach consensus on the facts of the case. For example, the plaintiff may not be able to find any indication in the writings that the firms had communicated with each other at all. In addition, all the people interviewed may consistently deny there was an agreement. Or the result of discovery may go the other way. A number of documents may be found that suggest the parties were in regular contact on price. In either case, the parties begin to see the facts of the case in a similar light and the likelihood of settlement will increase.

You should not infer from this analysis that a persistent disagreement about the facts of a case will mean that there will be no settlement. Remember, the potential for settlement comes from the costs of trying a case. For example, suppose a plaintiff is 70 percent sure that the facts and law favor his side of the case on a $100,000 claim and the cost of litigation for the plaintiff is estimated at $25,000. The

---

4. This takes place during a *deposition* in which attorneys pose questions to possible witnesses.

defendant is equally sure of prevailing (70%) and faces a similar cost. The value of the case to the plaintiff is $45,000 and the value of the expected loss to the defendant is $55,000. The outcome is that there is a $10,000 settlement range even though the parties have irreconcilable views of the merits of the claim. As explained above, risk aversion may expand this range even further.

Bilateral Monopoly

Bilateral monopoly is a condition under which there is only one buyer and one seller in a market. The view expressed here of the plaintiff as seller of a claim and the defendant as buyer sets up a bilateral monopoly. In a bilateral monopoly, both parties may realize that both would be better off if an exchange were to take place but become bogged down in bargaining over the gains from the exchange. Above you learned that the gain or settlement zone is the difference between litigation and settlement costs. Suppose this creates a zone so that the plaintiff is better off with any amount over $10,000 rather than litigating and the defendant is better off paying any amount under $20,000. We have settlement zone of $10,000 but the parties may dig in. The question then is what "price" will be determined within this range. The plaintiff may be determined to take no less that $16,000 and the defendant says any amount over $12,000 is too much. Both parties have an incentive to bluff and claim that they could not settle for anything other than the amount that allows them to capture most of the benefit of the settlement. Some people view this standoff as a type of transaction cost that may impede or even prevent an agreement from being reached. In a litigation setting with various deadlines, it may be that the time for settlement will pass before the bargaining process is concluded. You should note also that the longer the bargaining process continues, the more litigation costs are likely to be incurred. This means that available gains from settlement dwindle as the parties proceed along the course to trial.

Similar to this is the possibility that a party will not accept a settlement within the settlement range in order to create a reputation it feels will inure to its benefit in future cases. A reputation of being hard-nosed, determined, or aggressive may mean that future opposing parties lower their expectations about what to view as a reasonable outcome.

Human Factors

A number of subjective factors may come into play in determining the size of the settlement range and whether the parties are able to agree on a point within that range. To understand the importance of this, recognize that the model of settlement presented here is based on a belief that individuals are motivated by maximizing their financial outcome and, at a more subtle level, that people presented with the same empirical or objective evidence will process it and apply it the same way in their settlement efforts. Under this theory, the most compelling explanation for nonsettlement, other than high settlement costs, is that one or both parties has made an error. In a sense, trials are accidents because the expected outcome for both parties is almost always less when there is litigation than when there is a settlement. This is the essence of a theory proposed by George Priest and Benjamin Klein in their path-blazing 1984 study of cases that did not settle.[5]

Human beings do not always act in the manner that economic theory suggests and when human nature deviates, it can create some asymmetries that interfere with settlement. One study suggests that two factors play a role in creating barriers to settlement.[6] One is self-serving bias, especially when a litigant's self-image is on the line. For example, consider an auto accident that has implications for the driving skills of each party. An admission of the weakness of one side of the case and the strength of the other side is also a commentary on relative driving skills. In a sense, the estimated outcome, case value, and settlement range may be affected by self-serving biases. The same study also suggests that maximizing pecuniary outcome may not be the same as maximizing utility. More specifically, a person derives utility from a sense of being treated fairly. Experiments have shown that at times individuals will pass up offers that would increase their material well-being if the offer offends their sense of fairness.[7]

---

5. George L. Priest and Benjamin Klein, "The Selection of Disputes for Litigation," *Journal of Legal Studies* 13 (January 1984): 1.

6. See George Loewenstien, Samuel Issacharoff, Colin Camerer and Linda Babcock, "Self-Serving Assessments of Fairness and Pretrial Bargaining," *Journal of Legal Studies* 22 (January 1993): 135.

7. You can read more on this in Chapter 30 (available online).

Related to this are instances in which people litigate over things as a matter of principle. These types of actions can involve relatively petty squabbles such as the exact location of a property line. In other cases, the issues may involve emotionally or morally charged matters. For example, people may litigate over child custody, the right to express themselves, and whether they are permitted to observe certain religious rituals. Recently, a case involving the permissibility of including "under God" in the Pledge of Allegiance made its way to the U.S. Supreme Court. Settlement in these cases is unlikely for two reasons. First, they are often about "rights" and it is hard to fashion compromise outcomes that have any value to the parties in terms of vindicating their claims. Second, it is hard to determine the value of these cases and compare the values of the competing parties. Since it is expensive to pursue virtually any action, the ceiling value of these cases can be as high as all the resources available to the parties. But the salient feature is that these suits are not about maximizing pecuniary gain.

LAW AND ECONOMICS IN ACTION 23.2

CAN'T WE ALL JUST GET ALONG?

You have probably heard that the Japanese avoid open disputes. Disputes are, in effect, a symptom of disharmony and the cultural bias is in favor of encouraging harmony. It stands to reason, then, that settlement would be the norm in Japan and that the reason for this could be traced to a different cultural perspective on disagreement and litigation. In a 1989 study published by the *Journal of Legal Studies,* Mark Ramseyer and Minoru Nakazato put some of these notions to a test. Remember, the general idea would be that settlement is common because harmony is an important element in a person's utility function. An alternative hypothesis might be that the Japanese settle because they are able to agree quite readily on who is liable. As you know from the text, this is more likely when there is little uncertainty in the law. Another explanation would be that litigation is so expensive in Japan that the settlement range is very broad. Interestingly, these two possibilities suggest general explanations for the same outcome. On the one hand, the Japanese settle more because the courts are clear about who the likely winner is. On the other hand, the Japanese settle because attempts to litigate entwine the parties with an inefficient, time-consuming, and expensive court system. Ramseyer and Nakazato found that the Japanese tend to litigate less (although not less than many other countries) but seemed no less motivated by a desire to be compensated. In effect, parties did not fail to make claims and did not seem to settle for less or pay more to avoid violating a norm of harmony. As for the alternative ways in which the court system may play a role, the authors concluded that settlement was the outcome of a system that was working very effectively to narrow the range of uncertainty about how a case was likely to turn out.

Reference: Mark Ramseyer and Minoru Natazato, "The Rational Litigant: Settlement Amounts and Verdict Rates in Japan," *Journal of Legal Studies* 18, no. 2 (1989):263.

Some Empirical Evidence

The Priest-Klein theory of settlement suggests that when parties do not settle, it would generally be the result of irrationality or error. Error here does not mean that one party or the other is careless or incompetent, but that the parties are unable to reach a sufficient consensus about the value of the case to permit an agreement that avoids the heavy costs of litigation. In these instances, the plaintiff or the defendant or both are unrealistically optimistic about the value of the case and the settlement range is erased. When you think about it, this seems more likely to occur when cases are close ones. The more the law and facts favor one party or the other, the more likely there is to be a settlement range within which the parties can agree. When it is fairly obvious who the likely winner and loser will be, it makes little sense to incur litigation costs in order to find out. Thus, the Priest-Klein theory suggests that the most frequently litigated cases are ones that are close calls. This theory is more likely to hold when the trial is a zero-sum proposition. As already discussed, when the winner's gains are not the same as the loser's losses, the likelihood of settlement declines.

One implication of this theory is that trial outcomes should be about 50–50 in terms of favoring plaintiffs and defendants. Deviations would be explained, for the most part, by uneven stakes. This theory has been repeatedly tested over the last twenty years and the results vary. One over-arching question is whether a finding that cases tend to go one way or another actually confirms the theory. Could there be other reasons for trial or settlement other than the rational-zero-sum model?

One of the more intriguing efforts at testing the theory was undertaken by Gross and Svyerud.[8] One finding was that the validity of the 50 percent theory varied depending on the type of litigation. Plaintiffs are more likely to be successful in commercial litigation than in personal injury claims. In addition, the authors found that when plaintiffs must pay for trial costs in advance as opposed to relying on contingent fees, there is a greater tendency to settle and to have a higher win rate when they do take their cases to trial. This outcome fits nicely with the variables explored here. A litigant who must pay, win or lose, is going to lower his or her settlement demand and take great care in choosing which cases to try. These factors cut the other way when a contingent fee is involved.

Another finding was that when one party will lose more at trial than the other will win, the number of trials decreases but the win rate for defendants increases. Again, this fits with what you would expect. When defendants will lose more than a plaintiff will gain, the settlement zone will expand. Cases that are selected for trial will be those in which the defendant is fairly confident of success. This finding is also consistent with the notion that repeat litigants are more likely to prevail. Not only do these litigants enjoy economies of scale in trial preparation, their motivation to win may be fueled by knowing that their implications of a loss may far exceed the benefits to a single winner.

As an overall matter, when all the relevant variables are accounted for, the process of settlement conforms generally to what economic models would predict. Large litigation costs, like transaction costs, channel parties to alternative means of achieving their ends. The resolution of disputes is no exception. In fact, as an overall matter, not only do parties settle rather than litigate, but the last thirty years have seen a huge upswing in the market for private means of resolving disputes. Increasingly, parties turn to mediation and arbitration as means of reducing the costs of resolving their differences.

8. Samuel R. Gross and Kent D. Svyerud, "Getting to No: A Study of Settlement Negotiations and the Selection of Cases for Trial," *Michigan Law Review* 90 (1991): 319.

QUESTIONS FOR DISCUSSION

1. Very often when parties settle a lawsuit they agree not to disclose the terms of a settlement. Is there an economic rationale for this?

2. Class actions are lawsuits often involving thousands of plaintiffs with relatively small claims. The claims are joined together and the members of the class are represented by attorneys who typically have contact with very few, if any, of the plaintiffs. With court approval the attorneys can settle the cases for the clients. Do you see any basis for requiring judicial approval of these settlements?

3. Settlement is most likely to occur when parties agree on the likely outcome of a lawsuit. What would be wrong with a process that required parties, before a trial, to hire a jointly agreed-upon legal expert to tell them how the case is most likely to turn out?

4. Does it make sense to prohibit settlement when litigation involves a principle? Isn't society as a whole relying on people who litigate about freedom of speech or religion or similar matters not to be "bought off"?

CHAPTER TWENTY-FOUR

The Evolution of Law

W HEN YOU THINK ABOUT LAW, YOU MIGHT IMAG-
ine parties going to court with the hope that the court
will apply *existing* law and declare a winner. Sometimes
the law is court-made (common law) and sometimes it is made by
legislators. In both cases, though, judges do far more than simply settle disputes according to existing standards. In some cases, courts
interpret statutory law or even common law when those sources of
law are not sufficiently clear to cover every eventuality. In other cases,
courts may also change the law through both subtle interpretations
and stark declarations. In effect, the law evolves to fit modern society and new information. Sometimes the long-run implications of this
potential change are more important to the parties than their fate in
individual cases.

Changes in the common law, however, are not always easy to predict and may occur slowly. The reason has been discussed in the last
two chapters. Judges only get to write opinions when a case actually
goes to trial. Yet 95 percent of disputes are settled out of court. In
effect, changes in the common law come about when judges have a
rare opportunity to comment (write opinions) in the context of a very
small sliver of the actual disputes that exist at a particular time. Moreover, it's not up to judges to determine which cases are chosen for
their commentary; it is the parties themselves who make this decision.
This all leads to a very important question that has intrigued scholars for the last forty years: Do the cases that parties choose to try and

even press to appeal share common characteristics that are somehow different, at least in some respects, from the general run of cases? If so, how do these cases set the path along which the law evolves?

This chapter is devoted to the theory that legal rules produced by the common law tend to be efficient. Put differently, as time passes, the changes in the law are in the direction of more efficient rules. The first section describes the economics of this process and the next examines the limitations of the theory. Finally, the last section reviews recent changes in the law to determine whether those changes are consistent with the evolutionary theory.

THE EVOLUTIONARY PROCESS

The theory of how law evolves to become efficient was pioneered by Paul Rubin and George Priest.[1] In broad terms, the theory is that parties are more likely to go to trial rather than settle when an inefficient rule is involved. Because judges are more likely to be reviewing inefficient rather than efficient rules, changes in the law, on average, will be in favor of efficiency. Once a rule is changed from inefficient to efficient, it becomes less likely to be challenged again.

So, how does this work? Let's take a relatively simple numerical example. Suppose you own a chain of grocery stores and once in a while someone slips on spilled milk or water on the floor. The current rule is that you are liable for any injury resulting from falls inside your stores. On average you have one slip a month that costs an average of $20,000 for a total annual average of $240,000. You pay the damages because you have discovered that it would cost you $300,000 a year to hire extra personnel to patrol the aisles constantly in search of spills. On the other hand, most of the spills could be avoided if customers were a little more careful—by walking a little slower and thus adding some time to their shopping trips. The total value for customers of the lost time per year is $60,000. As you know from reading this book or just common sense, a rule that requires you to pay $240,000 a year for damages that could be avoided for $60,000 is inefficient.

---

1. Paul H. Rubin, "Why Is the Common Law Efficient?" *Journal of Legal Studies* 6 (January 1977): 51; George L. Priest, "The Common Law Process and the Selection of Efficient Rules," *Journal of Legal Studies* 6 (January 1977): 65.

To understand why you would be inclined to go to trial, suppose someone slips and falls on a very obvious wet spot on the floor and claims damages of $40,000. The trial would cost you $5,000. Now consider the outcome if you do go to trial. First, note that you must figure you are likely to lose the case, but since there is always a chance that the court may change the rule, the probability of winning is not zero but 25 percent. Without regard for the benefits of a rule change, the value of the case to you is a loss of $35,000 [(0.75 × $40,000) + $5,000] and you appear to be prepared to settle for anything less than that. On the other hand, there is a 25 percent chance that the court will alter the rule so that you will save $240,000 in just the first year. This changes things dramatically. Thus, even for one year, the expected outcome of trying the case is $25,000. [0.25($240,000) − 0.75($40,000) − $5,000]. In effect, because you have a chance to get a very favorable change in the law, you are not interested in a settlement. In fact, you may be willing to pay $25,000 or more not to settle because if the law changes in your favor, you won't have to pay damages ever again.

Now look at this from the point of view of your customers and, to make the point, assume that somehow all your customers are united in their interests.[2] If the case goes to trial, the expected value of the case, assuming the cost to them is also $5,000, is $25,000 [(0.75) $40,000 − $5,000]. But, if they go to trial, there are dangers. There is a 25 percent chance that the court will change the rule and that, as a group, they will have to incur the cost of avoiding the slips.[3] From the customers' perspective, the overall expected outcome of a trial is $10,000 [0.75 ($40,000) − 0.25($60,000) − $5,000]. Presumably they would have to receive more than this to settle the case.

Why is the case worth so much less to the plaintiffs here? The reason should be obvious. If they lose, the law does change, but the consequences to them are modest compared to the gain to the defendant. More important, suppose the parties attempt to settle the case. The

2. This might be the case if the customers formed a buying coop in which cost reductions were shared by all. You will understand the importance of this assumption as you read on.

3. Do you understand why they would choose to avoid the slips rather than to incur the $20,000 cost each time a slip occurs?

defendant, hoping for a change in the rule, is eager to try the case because even with only a 25 percent chance of winning, the expected outcome is worth $25,000. In effect, the defendant would have to be paid that amount not to defend the case in court. This is unlikely since the plaintiffs require at least $10,000 not to try the case. It would be irrational for either party to settle at a price the other party would find acceptable. This case will go to trial.

You can now switch the numbers and see that if the rule were efficient in the first place, the parties would not go to trial. Again, assume the probability of a rule change is 25 percent. When the consumer suffers a $40,000 fall, the value of the case is $5,000. [(0.25($40,000) − $5,000]. Even accounting for a rule change, the value is $20,000 [0.25($60,000) + 0.25(40,000) − $5,000]. A settlement offer above that amount will keep the case out of court.

Now think about the defendant/grocery store. It has only a 25 percent chance of losing but the consequences are severe: It loses the case and the rule it favors. The outcome of a trial is a loss of $65,000. [0.25($40,000) + 0.25($240,000) + $5,000)]. Avoiding a trial for anything less is a better position to be in. In short, the plaintiffs are better off with settlement in excess of $20,000 and the defendant is better off settling the case for anything less than $65,000. The case will settle without a court getting the chance to change the rule.

The analysis suggests that courts are more likely to be presented with cases that involve inefficient rules. Conversely, cases involving efficient rules are more likely to settle. Obviously, in the model, there are several important variables. An important one is the difference in the costs of the efficient and inefficient rule. The greater the difference, the more likely there is to be a trial. Another factor is the likelihood the court will alter the rule. If there is very little chance, the probability of a trial is less—which makes sense because even if the rule is very inefficient and the probability of a rule change is zero, there is no expected gain from the change. Obviously as the probability gets higher, the expected gain also increases. Finally, in our example, the cost of litigation to each party is $5,000. As these costs increase, the likelihood of litigation declines. You can think of the litigation cost as the transaction cost of changing the rule. As the costs go up, parties are likely to buy less of this "service."

Thus, the crucial first step in the evolutionary theory is that the cases governed by inefficient rules are more likely to make it to court. You may ask, What happens when they get to court? Why do they become efficient? Do judges know an efficient rule from an inefficient rule? The answer may be that it does not matter. Suppose a judge decides the cases entirely randomly.[4] Even on that basis, some rules will shift categories from inefficient to efficient. Those rules then become less likely to be litigated. In effect, the universe of efficient rules gradually increases while the universe of inefficient rules gradually decreases.

A CLOSER LOOK AT THE THEORY

The above model involves the assumption that both parties have something to gain from having a rule that favors one of them. Suppose only one party or neither party cares about the rule itself but only about the outcome of the immediate case.[5] In short, only one party or neither party goes to the step of determining the benefits of a rule change. If only one party cares about the value of the rule, it is likely that this party will bring the case to trial even though the change it seeks may not be to an efficient rule. This is because the relative efficiencies of the two rules will not be compared. In effect, the advocate for the efficient rule is not present to defend it or to promote a change to the rule. If neither party has a stake in the rule as opposed to the outcome in a particular case, the law is unlikely to change at all. The case will settle or not settle based on what the current rule is and not on the willingness of either party to advocate changing the rule.

Under certain circumstances, it seems likely that the evolutionary theory works. Certainly, the decision to enter into litigation is made with the belief that it is better than the alternative. When there is a chance of avoiding expenses not just in a pending case but in future cases as well, the attraction of litigation is even greater. On the other hand, as noted above, sometimes one or both parties will be unmoved by the efficiency of a particular rule. When this happens, inefficient rules may stay that way and even more inefficient rules be advocated.

Why would a party not be interested in a change from an inefficient to an efficient rule? One reason is that legal decisions and rules have a public goods character. As you will see, this possibility can

4. See Priest, "The Common Law Process," 70–71.
5. See Rubin, "Why Is the Common Law Efficient?" 54–56.

wreak havoc on the "evolution to efficient rules" theory. First, remember what public goods are. They are goods that result in benefits to people other than those who produce them. In short, those who invest in the goods are unable to fully internalize the benefits. Now reconsider our example, but this time assume that you do not own a chain of grocery stores but only one. Once in a while someone slips and falls and you are liable for $40,000. This happens about once every other year. In our example, you were able to capture the benefits of a rule change because, by owning a chain of stores, the damages to be avoided, and thus the benefits to you of a rule change, were relatively high. Now, however, a change in the rule would be of much more modest benefit to you. Most of the benefit would be captured by the owners of other stores.[6] In a sense, they would be free riding on your effort to change the rule. If you are unable to capture all the benefits of a change, your motivation may decline so much that it simply is not rational for you to invest in the change. You should note that this does not mean the rule is efficient. It just means that no single party benefits sufficiently to mount a challenge to the rule.

The free-rider analysis could also account for the possibility that some rules will actually change from efficient to inefficient. Remember the decision to litigate was not based directly on the concept of efficiency. Instead, both parties simply examined the benefits of litigating an issue—as opposed to settling—and elected to litigate. The decision is based on the so-called bottom line, not a quest for efficiency. In our example, we might start with an efficient rule, the benefits of which are shared by many unrelated store owners. The cost to be avoided by the customers is $50,000 per year. If a slip and fall occurs and the consumers are again viewed as a single entity, the gain from a rule change is the damages collected on the case at hand plus avoiding expenses of $50,000 a year. Each store owner may not be willing to pay enough to convince the customers, as group, to settle. As a consequence, it is the efficient rule that is challenged.

This is certainly not to say that free-riding problems stand in the way of every possible rule change. In the model we have examined, if a party internalizes the benefits of an inefficient rule while those

---

6. See Gordon Tullock, "Public Decisions as Public Goods," *Journal of Political Economy*, 99 (1971): 913.

favored by an efficient rule are scattered, the general conclusion is that the case will settle and the inefficient rule will persist. But this is not always the case. A number of factors may come into play to ensure that the case still is heard. Sometimes the party decides to play hardball and not settle or to settle only at a price that is unacceptable. In other situations, the bilateral monopoly structure of settlement negotiations may mean that the parties find themselves in a trial when both would have been better off by settling. Once the issue is before the court, the rule may be changed to the efficient one. On the other hand, since the failure to settle is not the result of the inefficiency, it is just as likely that efficient and inefficient rules will be litigated. In effect, these are the instances in which the parties are in court because of poor communication or asymmetrical information.

CASE 24.1 An Evolutionary Case: *Escola v. Coca Cola Bottling Co. of Fresno,* 150 P.2 436 (Cal. 1944)

It is difficult to test the evolutionary theory of law as originally expressed. As a general matter, however, changes in the law toward more efficient standards probably have less to do with case selection than with some level of economic intuition exercised by judges. A case commonly viewed as instrumental in the development of products liability law is *Escola v. Coca Cola,* a 1944 case in which the plaintiff, a waitress, was injured by an exploding Coke bottle. The majority of the court found the bottler liable, applying a negligence standard. Justice Traynor's concurring opinion in which he reasons that strict liability is the appropriate standard is viewed as signaling a movement in tort law in that direction. According to Justice Traynor:

> I concur in the judgment, but I believe the manufacturer's negligence should no longer be singled out as the basis of a plaintiff's right to recover in cases like the present one. In my opinion it should now be recognized that a manufacturer incurs an absolute liability when an article that he has placed on the market, knowing that it is to be used without inspection, proves to have a defect that causes injury to human beings. . . . Even if there is no negligence, however, public policy demands that responsibility be fixed wherever it will most effectively reduce the hazards to life and health inherent in defective products that reach the market. It is evident that the manufacturer can anticipate some hazards and guard against the recurrence of

others, as the public cannot. Those who suffer injury from defective products are unprepared to meet its consequences. The cost of an injury and the loss of time or health may be an overwhelming misfortune to the person injured, and a needless one, for the risk of injury can be insured by the manufacturer and distributed among the public as a cost of doing business. It is to the public interest to discourage the marketing of products having defects that are a menace to the public. If such products nevertheless find their way into the market it is to the public interest to place the responsibility for whatever injury they may cause upon the manufacturer, who, even if he is not negligent in the manufacture of the product, is responsible for its reaching the market. However intermittently such injuries may occur and however haphazardly they may strike, the risk of their occurrence is a constant risk and a general one. Against such a risk there should be general and constant protection and the manufacturer is best situated to afford such protection.

What do you think is the efficient rule—negligence or strict liability? How could it make a difference in the level of care exercised by the bottler? Does this case fit the evolutionary theory of cases that are unlikely to settle finding their way to court? Wouldn't the bottler have far more to lose by a finding of negligence or strict liability than the plaintiff stood to gain?

Similarly, class actions, which allow parties to combine relatively small claims, and punitive damages, may offset the impact of free riding. These cases may find their way to a court because the gain to plaintiffs is magnified. Once there, inefficient rules may be changed to efficient ones (or vice versa). You should note, however, that the efficient rules flowing from these cases will be relatively unstable. This is because the magnifying effect may be temporary. In the future, it may be advantageous for a party able to internalize the benefits of an inefficient rule to try the case against a party unable to internalize all the gains of protecting the efficient rule.

EVALUATION AND EXAMPLES

It is important to focus on what the evolutionary theory of law says. The theory is not that the law is efficient. The theory is one that seeks to explain the mechanism through which efficient rules are established.

The idea is that inefficient rules are more frequently challenged. Testing whether the theory is accurate with respect to this mechanism is difficult if not impossible. For example, in his seminal work, *The Economic Analysis of Law,* Judge Richard Posner makes the case that a great deal of the common law is already efficient. If he is right, and most people agree with him at one level or another, one would expect few challenges to the current rules themselves. That is, one would expect to see few changes in the common law because efficient rules are less frequently challenged. This does appear to be the case, but then, it is the nature of the common law to change slowly. In addition, as the analysis above indicates, current rules may have great staying power because they are efficient *or* because those benefiting from even inefficient rules are better able to internalize the benefits of those rules than those who favor the counter rules. Thus, little can be determined by observing that most common law rules seem stuck in place.

Another approach to examining the validity of the theory is to review changes that have occurred in the common law. Here, too, it is hard to find sufficient evidence to affirm or reject the theory. For example, in the field of contract law, the most radical change in the last century was the widespread acceptance of the doctrine of promissory estoppel. As you may recall from Chapter 10, when applying promissory estoppel, a court enforces a promise by one party when another party reasonably relies on that promise even when no exchange is involved. In other words, they enforce "free" or "gratuitous" promises. This was a change from the traditional approach of enforcing promises only when they were part of an exchange. In that chapter, we also identified reasons that a rule favoring routine enforcement of gratuitous promises is likely to be efficient. Whether there was an evolutionary factor at work is a different question.

For the most part, a study of the development of the doctrine does not reveal the types of economic factors that are needed for the evolutionary model to work. More specifically, those cases are always or nearly always populated by litigants who were unlikely to be able to internalize the gains from the rule change itself. In order for the internalization to take place, a party would have to anticipate promises being made in the future on which it would rely only to discover the promise is then broken. To be sure, this is an unlikely position for most to anticipate. On the other hand, some of the early cases leading to promissory estoppel involve educational institutions that rely on many gratuitous promises and are able to internalize the economic advantages of a rule change as opposed to simply the benefits of a favorable outcome in a single case.[7] In short, these parties seem to fit the evolutionary model. This lends support to the evolutionary theory but does not prove it. For example, while institutions receive many promises and are able to internalize the gains of a rule change, those making promises may make them only occasionally and have little opportunity to internalize the benefits of a rule permitting promise breaking. This is not to say that promissory estoppel is inefficient. Instead, even if it is, we cannot determine whether its establishment is a result of a fair economic contest between those benefiting from two opposing rules.

A similar change has taken place with respect to the condition of property that is purchased or rented. The conventional rule was strictly "buyer beware." A tenant or renter who moved in and found rats or termites or poor construction generally had no recourse. This was not necessarily an inefficient rule. People moved less frequently than they do today. They tended to move shorter distances and to stay longer. They were likely to know the risks of different types of housing in the community and how to avoid those risks and the reputation of the owner or lessor. As people became more transient, moved longer distances, had less prior connection to the area, and stayed shorter time periods, the older rule became inefficient. The inefficiency stems from the fact that the cost of information about the property and the steps necessary to guard against catastrophic losses would be far higher to the newcomer than to the owner or lessor. Many states have adopted an implied warranty of habitability, which means that the seller or lessor is liable if the housing turns out to be seriously defective. As with promissory estoppel, the law has changed, but one would be hard-pressed to show that the evolution was a result of the process described earlier in this chapter.

Changes in products liability law can be added to promissory estoppel and implied warranties of habitability as an instance in which the law has taken a turn to greater efficiency. Clearly, many of the harms

---

7. *Allegany College v. National Chautauqua County Bank of Jamestown*, 159 N.W. 173 (1927).

caused by defective products can be avoided less expensively by manufacturers than by poorly informed buyers. On the other hand, even if the rule has become efficient, whether it got that way through the process suggested by the evolutionary theory is not clear. Manufacturers have a far greater ability to capture the benefits of a rule that is inefficient than disconnected consumers have to capture the benefits of an efficient products liability rule. This would suggest that the movement to a more efficient rule cannot be traced to a comparison of the gains and losses to the parties.

If the theory does not work every time or even rarely, what accounts for the selection of cases and the tendency toward the adoption of efficient rules? As you saw in Chapter 23, there are many reasons that cases do not settle without trial. Not all of these are the result of an existing inefficient rule. Once these cases make it to a court, it is possible—even likely—that judges adopt rules that make intuitive sense and reflect a fair amount of subtle economic reasoning.

LAW AND ECONOMICS IN ACTION 24.1

GRASSROOTS ECONOMICS

The evolutionary theory seeks to explain why inefficient rules become the subject of judicial decisions, but it does not explain why a judge would choose one rule over another. It is possible, as Richard Posner has noted, that efficient rules often are just intuitively correct or the product of common sense. Here is an excerpt that seems to support this point. Written in 1969—before the economic approach to law had an impact—the court displays its reasoning in adopting an implied warranty of habitability in a case in which a lessor rented commerical property that flooded whenever it rained:

> It has come to be recognized that ordinarily the lessee does not have as much knowledge of the condition of the premises as the lessor. Building code requirements and violations are known or made known to the lessor, not the lessee. He is in a better position to know of latent defects, structural and otherwise, in a building which might go unnoticed by a lessee who rarely has sufficient knowledge or expertise to see or to discover them. A prospective lessee, such as a small businessman, cannot be expected to know if the plumbing or wiring systems are adequate or conform to local codes. Nor should he be expected to hire experts to advise him. Ordinarily all this information should be considered readily available to the lessor who in turn can inform

the prospective lessee. These factors have produced persuasive arguments for reevaluation of the Caveat emptor doctrine and, for imposition of an implied warranty that the premises are suitable for the leased purposes and conform to local codes and zoning laws. *Reste Realty Corp. v. Cooper,* 251 A.2d 268 (1969).

So what do you think? Do you think the court senses that a change has occurred in society that makes it more efficient for the owners and lessors of property to attend to any defects? If you do, you would be among those who feel economic analysis takes place at least at an intuitive level because a great many opinions reflect the same reasoning found here.

One area in which the evolutionary theory has promise involves laws that govern large commercial relationships. Here the parties may be able to internalize the gains from rule changes to affect their litigation decisions. The area of antitrust law seems to fit the model. Most of what we regard as antitrust law is found in the Sherman Act of 1890 and the Clayton Act of 1914. The actual statutes are, however, very general and for all practical purposes antitrust law is judge-made. One particular instance may be especially on point. The courts have adopted two sets of antitrust rules. Some practices by firms are per se unlawful. They are illegal without a detailed analysis of their actual economic impact. Other practices are determined to be unlawful only after an actual comparison of the anticompetitive effects with possible procompetitive effects.

In 1967, the Court adopted a series of per se rules that many commentators thought made little economic sense.[8] One of these rules prohibited manufacturers from selling to a retailer and then restricting the geographic area within which the retailer could sell. This was a practice manufacturers used to avoid having two or more retailers who were selling the manufacturer's goods competing with each other. At one level, the impact of these requirements was anticompetitive. On the other hand, the objective of the manufacturer could easily be to avoid free riding between retailers. For example, without the restriction, any retailer who invested significant sums in promoting the man-

---

8. *United States v. Arnold, Schwinn & Co.,* 388 U.S. 365 (1967).

ufacturer's products might find another retailer taking advantage of that investment. The overall impact would be that all retailers would be reluctant to invest heavily in efforts to sell the manufacturer's products. This reluctance could then hurt the manufacturer's efforts to compete against other manufacturers. In effect, the per se rule may have promoted competition among retailers of the same brand while stifling competition among manufacturers of different brands. You should also recall that the per se rule allows for no exceptions. This means even restraints that might increase competition and increase consumer welfare were unacceptable.

In 1977, the Supreme Court reversed itself and declared that manufacturer restraints on the areas of operation by retailers would be assessed under the rule of reason.[9] In other words, the Court recognized that these restraints could have both procompetitive effects and anticompetitive effects and opted to allow these effects to be balanced. There can be little doubt that the change by the Court involved substituting an efficient rule for an inefficient one. Under the rule of reason, competitive impact and impact on consumer welfare would be assessed on a case-by-case basis.

Like changes in the common law, a change in the interpretation of antitrust law does not come about unless parties are willing to litigate the issues. In the context of the restraints on reselling retailers, there can be little doubt that manufacturers were likely to internalize substantial benefits from a rule change. And as it turns out, the firm leading the charge to change the rule was a relatively small firm that thought it could become a competitive force if it could promise its retailers that they would be protected from free riding by other retailers. These benefits would be reaped across the United States. The retailer objecting to the rule change was much more limited in its operation and stood to gain less from maintaining the per se rule than the manufacturer would derive from the rule of reason.

This scenario seems to track the evolutionary model fairly closely. First, the existing rule that allowed for no judicial consideration of the procompetitive effects of manufacturers' restraints was almost certainly inefficient. The only way it would not be inefficient would be

9. *Continental T.V., Inc. v. GTE Sylvania*, 433 U.S. 36 (1977).

if those types of restraints are nearly always harmful to consumers. That, however, was not the case. Thus the rule precluded the examination of restraints that might turn out to increase competition. A firm that was able to internalize the benefits of a rule change was motivated to litigate the matter. The development falls short only in the sense that there were potential free riders on both sides of the case. In other words, many manufacturers stood to gain from the Court's reversal but did not participate, and many retailers who stood to lose by virtue of the rule change also stood on the sidelines. Thus, while it seems extremely likely, it cannot be determined with 100 percent confidence that refusal to settle and the movement of the dispute into the court system was strictly the result of the rule's inefficiency.[10]

Ultimately, it is impossible to prove the evolutionary theory. One can only give examples that go either way. It is probably easy to find examples that seem to confirm the theory, but they may not actually confirm it if the choice of the efficient rule was not the result of the process described here. For example, a judge may just prefer an efficient rule and select it. In addition, it is hard to know what constitutes an efficient rule when values like "fairness" or "justice" are litigated.

QUESTIONS FOR DISCUSSION

1. Can you think of any law that has changed in your lifetime? What inspired that change?

2. Suppose the Supreme Court eventually overturns its decision in *Roe v. Wade* that gave women the right to have abortions. Could you interpret *Roe v. Wade* as having been "inefficient," with those challenging it as having more to gain by a change in the law than those opposing its reversal have to lose?

---

10. More recently, the Court changed its mind about a rule stating that it was per se unlawful for a manufacturer to place a maximum price at which retailers can resell the manufacturer's output. A convincing case has been made that this too was an evolutionary movement to a more efficient rule. See Roger D. Blair and John E. Lopaka, "Albrecht Overruled—at Last," *Antitrust Law Journal* 66 (1998): 537.

3. Because corporations are likely to be repeat players, isn't law likely to continually evolve in their favor? Are the changes "efficient"?

4. Obviously legal changes are not limited to judge-made law. Do you think legislative changes requiring greater mileage standards for automobiles, safer working conditions, and the elimination of discrimination are also representative of an evolutionary process?

Behavioral Issues

CHAPTER TWENTY-FIVE

Behavioral Assumptions and Related Questions

O NE OF THE MORE FASCINATING CHALLENGES ASSO-
ciated with applying economics to law stems from the
assumption that people are rational maximizers of self-interest. This is especially important when economics is applied to behavior and decisions of individuals when these have legal consequences,
such as breaching a contract, harming another person, polluting, committing a crime, and the like. Is the assumption that rational individuals maximize their own interests when they break a contract or
commit a crime appropriate? In the first section of the chapter we
look at what the *rational self-interest* assumption means. We explore
the implications of this assumption for the application of economics
to law in the next section. The question is whether there are "wrin-
kles" in law that make the assumption less appropriate than it would
be otherwise. In the third section *rationality* is compared to *capacity*,
the concept in law that is closest to rationality. The fourth and fifth
sections are devoted to empirical findings that are inconsistent with
the rational self-interest assumption. Finally, in the last part we ask
how much we can infer from the choices people make. This may seem
like an odd question, but remember that economics is about expressing preferences, and it is assumed that we know the preferences of
people by looking at their choices.

Much of what you will read in the following pages suggests that there is some slippage between the *rational self-interest* assumption and actual behavior. In many cases, this may be unimportant. You should understand, however, that even when this slippage exists, it is not a criticism of economics or economists. The starting point for virtually any science is to make simplifying assumptions, and economists do not try to conceal the assumptions they make. To go beyond the baseline *rational self-interest* assumption is certainly something that economists have done but, as a general matter, this raises issues better addressed by psychology or even biology.

When the assumption of rational self-interest was introduced into economics by Adam Smith, it was not his objective to give an accurate description of human behavior. Smith was interested in social outcomes. He wanted to show that even when individual persons acted only in their rational self-interest, this would nevertheless lead society to an optimal level of social welfare.

THE RATIONAL MAXIMIZER OF SELF-INTEREST

The assumption that people are maximizers of self-interest is probably not something you labored over in prior economics courses. Exploring it in some detail becomes important, though, when applying economics to law. Implicitly, the assumption of rationality is linked to the idea that people try to maximize something. The most important element of rationality is that, as a general matter, people make consistent choices. For example, if your objective is to maximize your wealth, you are unlikely to both work hard and to pour money into the ocean. The more formal way of expressing rational behavior is to say that rational people must not violate the rule of transitivity. As an example, if you like apple pie more than pecan pie and pecan pie more than rhubarb pie (and who doesn't?), you cannot also like rhubarb pie more than apple pie. That would violate the axiom of transitivity. You will see below that in recent years economists have begun to seriously question whether the rationality assumption is accurate.

You may think that rationality, as indicated by consistent choice, is a pretty easy standard. On the other hand, do you always really know what you want? Are you always capable of defining what the alternatives are? Are you completely informed about the characteristics and qualities of each of the alternatives? Can you always rank them? Are we really capable (intellectually, emotionally) of making all the necessary calculations to figure out what rational choice is in a situation of uncertainty and lack of information? The point is that a great deal of behavior may be irrational because of the difficulty of achieving perfectly consistent choices. Interestingly, even irrational behavior may be rational if the costs of determining what is rational outweigh the benefits.

If the idea is that individuals make consistent choices to maximize something, the question then is, What do they maximize? The economist's assumption is that the object of that maximizing behavior is self-interest. This does not mean that everyone is struggling every day to become as wealthy as possible. It is likely that self-interest includes more than wealth. There is, however, a more complicated question here that may have implications for the application of economics to law. The question is whether, aside from mistakes, a rational person ever acts in a way that is not self-interested. One way of looking at this question suggests that to be rational is also to be self-interested. The reasoning goes like this: Whatever you do, you do it because you prefer that choice to any other. To make choices that are the ones you prefer is to act in self-interest. This assertion may or may not be accurate. The argument, however, is nonfalsifiable, meaning that it holds true under all possible circumstances. If there are no circumstances under which the assertion can be shown to be false, it also cannot be proven to be true and must be accepted as a matter of faith.

Those who accept the idea that to be rational is to be self-interested must sometimes explain behavior that seems to be inconsistent with self-interest. For example, why would you ever leave a tip in a restaurant to which you know you will never return? Or why vote when the expected benefit from voting—the probability of affecting the outcome times the benefit to you if you do—is likely to be less than the cost of traveling to the polls? Why contribute to charity? For the economist who believes it is impossible to be rational and not self-interested, the explanation is that you do these things because they result in increases in utility. Sometimes it is called "psychic income." There is always enough psychic income to make every decision rational and self-interested.

SELFISH GENES

The complexity of the concepts of altruism and self-interest are explored in an evolutionary context in a fascinating book, *The Selfish Gene*, by Richard Dawkins. An example of altruism would be the unconditional love of parents or siblings or the warning call of certain birds, which alerts the flock to danger but attracts the predator's attention to the individual. Since evolution will favor those individuals that behave in ways that allow them to pass on their genes, it makes no sense for individuals in a herd or group to put themselves at risk for the good of the group—genes that guide such behavior should disappear as these animals die out from their actions, and the selfish animals live. Evolution works on an individual level, not a group one, and individual animals would seem to gain no gene-passing advantage by behaving altruistically. Dawkins shows, in a number of examples from aggression to family planning, how completely selfish choices will actually lead to stable outcomes, including herding behavior, that make individual animals appear to be altruistic when they are actually maximizing their own gene-based self-interest. For example, the altruism of relatives is explained by the fact that families share a high percentage of genes, so the helpers are often helping their own genes get passed on by saving members of their family. The bird's warning call, which has evolved to make it very difficult to tell which bird makes the call, is explained by an evaluation of its choices. If the bird simply flies away and hides without making the warning call, then it will lose the protection of the flock. If it stays with the flock and doesn't make the warning call, the flock won't hide, and the predator may still eat it. Thus, its best choice is to risk calling attention to itself, warning the flock, and then hiding with the other birds.

Reference: Richard Dawkins, *The Selfish Gene* (New York: Oxford University Press, 1976; 30th Anniversary ed. 2006).

Some economists, most notably Nobel Prize winner Amartya Sen, believe that non-self-interested choices are possible. For example, he distinguishes between cases in which one is motivated by sympathy and those in which one is motivated by commitment.[1] Suppose you see a homeless person and it makes you sad. If you give him money,

1. See Amartya Sen, "Rational Fools: A Critique of the Behavioral Assumptions of Economic Theory," *Philosophy and Public Affairs* 6 (1977): 317.

you are motivated by sympathy, and the gift is consistent with self-interest. On the other hand, if your motivation is more like, "People should not be homeless, because it is morally wrong," but you feel no particular angst or sadness upon seeing a homeless person, a contribution is consistent with commitment, which, according to Sen, involves "counter-preferential choice."

Obviously, the question of whether every choice is motivated by self-interest cannot be empirically decided one way or the other. And, ultimately, the answer to this question may not be that important. On the other hand, as you will see, when economics is applied to law, the possibility that self-interest and rationality are separate can have important implications.

BEHAVIOR AND LAW AND ECONOMICS

This discussion of the concept of self-interest may seem a bit tedious and unnecessary. On the other hand, it may have very practical implications if you believe, as many seem to, that law has moral implications. To understand why, consider the effort by the highly respected economist Robert Cooter to explain exactly what his behavioral assumption is. In an article written in 1984, he begins with the usual stipulation that he is assuming people are "rationally self-interested." He then goes on to define "rational self-interest" as *excluding* "someone who acts from a sense of duty or obeys the law out of respect."[2] You can see how this aligns with the idea that counter-preferential choice is possible. The idea is that I obey the law because I *should*, but if whatever is illegal were not against the law, I would do it. Perhaps you feel this still means self-interest is at work but, as you will see, even this introduces a practical problem.

To illustrate how this complicates matters, consider the case of marijuana smoking. It may seem a bit unusual, but one could actually determine the demand for marijuana in a given market for a given price at a given time period. Suppose we examine this demand in a market in which marijuana is legal and plot the outcome, giving us D_1 in Figure 25.1. Now, suppose there is a vote to make marijuana illegal, and all those caught buying, selling, or using marijuana pay a

2. Robert Cooter, "Prices and Sanctions," *Columbia Law Review* 84 (1984): 1523.

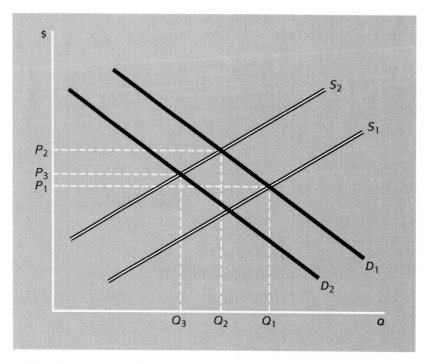

FIGURE 25.1   Supply, Demand, and Legal Change

fine. As a result, the suppliers of marijuana will find it harder to supply and will also include the expected fine in their selling price. The supply curve shifts from S_1 to S_2. Consumers on the demand side are faced with a higher price and their first response will be to demand less marijuana. The new market equilibrium is price P_2 and quantity Q_2 where demand curve D_1 and the new supply curve S_2 intersect. Price has increased (it was originally P_1) and quantity decreased (it was originally Q_1).

On the other hand, your self-image may be that you are a law-abiding person, and your natural inclination is not to break the law. Perhaps illegal activities are less enjoyable, and the guilt you feel makes the whole experience less fun. The point is that rather than move you to a new point on the original demand curve, the impact may be to shift the curve to the left as depicted by D_2.[3] If that happens, the mar-

3. This assumes, of course, that the guilt factor offsets the increased demand by those who like "guilty pleasures."

ket equilibrium is at the intersection of D_2 and S_2. The equilibrium quantity decreases even further to Q_3, and the new price P_3 is not as high as P_2.

There are two perspectives you might adopt to understand why the impact could be to move demand to D_2. First, you could view it as buying a different product altogether. In other words, a change in the law has changed the qualities of the product. Before it was "law-abiding without guilt," and now it is "illegal marijuana." Although it is technically incorrect to put the demand for two different products on the same axis, the point remains valid. The second perspective is that your taste for marijuana has changed. It no longer satisfies whatever need you had as much as it once did. In effect, changes in law may alter not just the choices that are in your self-interest, but also the way in which you derive utility from your choices (your utility function) may change.[4]

You will recall that any demand curve is accurate only as long as tastes remain fixed. This is usually put in terms of exogenous and endogenous influences. The assumption is that taste and preferences are determined exogenously and set the position of the demand curve and that price is endogenous and explained by the intersection of demand and supply. In that case, a change in price results in movements up and down the demand curve (in Figure 25.1, the new supply curve S_2 moves along demand curve D_1 and the new intersection determines the new market price). The implications of Sen's writings and of the marijuana example, however, are that law may have an impact at both levels. In other words, changes in the law—say a stiffer fine for some unlawful activity—may have an impact on both demand and the position of the demand curve (through its effect on changing preferences) and on quantity demanded (through its effect on price). The impact on the curve itself would be the result of the moral element of law. The curve shifts if someone obeys the law out of a sense of duty or obligation. This does not mean that the assumption that tastes and preferences are fixed is improper when economics is applied to law. Rather, as with all assumptions, you should be conscious of what has been eliminated from the analysis.

---

4. The analysis could be reversed. Perhaps illegality makes marijuana more attractive because it involves an element of rebellion. In that case, the demand curve would shift to the right after marijuana becomes illegal.

The complexity that this separation of effects introduces can be understood by thinking about one of the things economists do—predict the outcome of policy shifts. Return to the example of marijuana as a product and again start from the position in which it is legal (in Figure 25.1, that is, with demand curve D_1 and supply curve S_1 and with price P_1 and quantity Q_1). Now suppose, based on your analysis of criminal law, you decide that it is better to discourage marijuana use and you aim at a decrease in the quantity traded on the market from Q_1 to Q_2. By studying the relationship between demand and supply and price and quantity in the past, you discover a relationship like the one shown in by S_1 and D_1 in Figure 25.1. You decide that if you make marijuana illegal and make sure that there is a certain probability of getting caught and being fined (see the chapters on criminal law), the supply curve will shift upward from S_1 to S_2 along demand curve D_1 and a price increase from P_1 to P_2 will yield the desired decrease from Q_1 to Q_2. But what you have not taken into account is that the action of making marijuana illegal also has moral significance for consumers and shifts the demand to D_2. The new level of marijuana traded on the market is Q_3, and you have overshot the mark.

LAW, RATIONALITY, AND CAPACITY

Another thing that you should understand about applying economics to law is that those who analyze behavior in the context of law do not typically think in terms of rationality. Economists are free to invoke the rationality assumption because it is a simplifying starting point for the descriptions and predictions that follow. The alternative assumption of irrationality would render most economic studies meaningless. Law, because it deals more directly with human behavior, is more reactive and individualized in its perspective. This means that those who actually make and interpret laws do not have a refined notion of what it means to be rational. As you saw in the context of contract law and criminal law, the concept that is closest to rationality in legal settings is *capacity*. Capacity is often broken down into two categories: cognitive and volitional. Cognitive capacity means the ability to recognize the consequences of one's actions. Volitional refers to the ability to control what one does. For example, a very old person may not possess the cognitive capacity to understand that if he or she spends the last bit of savings there will be nothing to live on. A person who lacks volitional capacity may understand that excessive drinking or gambling is bad but be unable to stop. The consequence of lacking capacity in law is usually that the person is not held responsible for his or her actions. The most publicized versions of this are cases in which someone breaks the law but is not punished because he or she was insane.

The question to consider is whether capacity and rationality are different and, if there is a difference, whether this difference is relevant to the application of economic analysis to law. Capacity and rationality overlap a great deal. In fact, in many instances when courts speak in terms of capacity, they probably mean "capacity to make rational decisions." This is not, however, always the case, and there are important distinctions between capacity and rationality. First, when economists say *rational*, they mean in the scientific sense—principally adherence to the axiom of transitivity. *Capacity*, as used by courts, is far more a function of political, cultural, and religious factors. Second, economists use the notion of rationality as a means of setting bounds on their analysis. Courts examine evidence as it relates to specific individuals in order to determine whether they should be held accountable for their acts.

This second distinction may not seem important to you, but it is crucial because it allows courts to make what are essentially normative distinctions. For example, courts tend to find that a person lacks capacity if he or she engages in behavior that falls outside social norms. Obviously, this is not the test of rationality for an economist. In addition, capacity is often used as a tool for correcting an injustice. It is not uncommon for a court to find that someone who entered into a very one-sided contract lacked capacity. The point is that while irrational behavior may be a sign of a lack of capacity, the two concepts cannot be viewed as interchangeable.

The relationship between capacity and rationality is illustrated by a 1993 U.S. Supreme Court decision.[5] In the case, a person shot and killed three people and was apprehended. Afterward, he pled guilty and elected to act as his own attorney even though he had no legal

---

5. *Godinez v. Moran*, 509 U.S. 389 (1993).

training and was entitled to the assistance of an attorney even if he could not afford one. After being sentenced to death, he claimed that he was not *competent* to make the decision to plead guilty or to act as his own attorney and that the sentence should be thrown out. From the standpoint of rationality, you might say that the defendant violated the axiom of transitivity. More specifically, if his desire was to avoid conviction and the death sentence that followed, the consistent course of action would have been to plead innocent and rely on an attorney. Thus, if the Court used rationality as a standard, the prisoner *might* have had his sentence reversed. The Supreme Court, however, did not consider the question of rationality directly. Instead, it looked at whether the convicted person was able to understand his choices and their consequences.

You may want to note that even though the decisions of the prisoner may seem to you to be irrational, they might not be. For example, a severely guilt-ridden person with little to live for might prefer a death penalty to life in prison and realize that pleading guilty and not consulting an attorney would be the best way to get to that outcome. The point is that the decision of a court will very often be consistent with the outcome it would have reached had it used a rationality standard. Still, the analyses can be quite different.

CHALLENGES TO RATIONAL SELF-INTEREST

Wealth and Endowment Effects

The question of whether people are actually rational is an important one in any area of applied economics, and the application of economics to law is no different. Predicted outcomes may be wrong if people do not behave rationally. One of the more interesting phenomena that seems to put rationality in question is that if a person currently possesses something, he or she tends to attribute greater value to it. You may recall this issue from your study of the Coase theorem in Chapter 6. For example, suppose you see an autographed copy of your favorite novel in a rare bookstore. The price is $100 and you do not buy it. Now suppose someone gives the book to you as a gift and then a friend visits you, sees the book, and offers you $100 for it. You say no. How can you both value the book at more than $100 and value it at less than $100? A great deal of empirical work suggests that the pattern of attributing greater value to something when you own it as opposed to when it is owed by someone else is not uncommon. On the other hand, are you irrational because what you seem to be saying is that $100 is more valuable than the book, which is more valuable than $100?

In fact, it is probably not accurate to conclude that these preferences are indicative of irrationality, because the example involves comparing choices after changing something that has an impact on your preferences. In this case, it is whether you own the book. This is, however, a bit of a problem because some applications of economics to law involve attempts to determine who attributes greater value to something, and experiments show that the valuation can change based on the way the question is framed.

Most of the studies on this "framing" phenomenon can be traced to a path-breaking article by Nobel Prize winner Daniel Kahneman and co-author Amos Tversky.[6] In the article, they explain and present empirical evidence of "prospect theory."[7] One of the findings is that people change their valuation of different alternatives depending on the starting point. For example, a person with $1,000 may value a $10 gain differently from a person with $5,000. Accordingly, "value should be treated as a function of the asset position that serves as a reference point, and the magnitude of the change . . . from that reference point."[8]

The impact of the reference point on the ordering of choice has proven to be pervasive. In some instances, the reasons are obvious. For an economist to take seriously that you value something by a certain amount, you must actually be able to spend that amount. Claiming that something is worth $20 to you when you do not have $20 carries no economic significance. If you already own an asset, you are more likely to actually be able to back up your claim of *value*. Thus,

6. Framing can also have a literal interpretation. For example, you may respond differently to what is essentially the same question depending on how the question is asked. For example compare "Do you support our troops and loved ones in the military overseas?" as opposed to "Are you in favor of maintaining military bases in foreign countries?"

7. Daniel Kahneman and Amos Tversky, "Prospect Theory: An Analysis of Decision under Risk," *Econonemetrica* 47, no. 2 (1979): 263.

8. Kahneman and Tversky, "Prospect Theory," 277.

those who already own the asset are likely to be able to claim they attach a higher value to it. This phenomenon is called the *wealth effect*. The wealth effect does not contradict the rationality assumption but can make the application of economics to law more complex.

The most interesting aspect of the wealth effect is that it can be unrelated to actual wealth. In other words, individuals do change valuation depending on the reference point, but the reference point has nothing to do with differences in ability to pay. As an example, think about this experiment.[9] A group of people were gathered together and brought into a room. As each one entered, he or she was given either $3 or a ticket to a raffle. The terms of the raffle were explained to the group. It was for coupons redeemable for books worth $70 or $50 in cash. At that point, the participants were permitted to exchange what they were given. Those who received $3 were permitted to buy raffle tickets for that amount. Those who possessed raffle tickets could sell them for $3. Since they all heard the same information about the raffle, you would expect that a consensus would have formed about whether the raffle was a good gamble based on the expected value of winning. This would be the probability of winning times the value of the prize. Thus, in the experiment, if the expected benefit were $4, one would expect all those receiving $3 to trade it for a ticket, and if it were worth less than $3, one would expect people to sell their raffle tickets.

In fact, 82 percent of the participants who received tickets elected to keep them. And 64 percent of those who had received $3 elected to keep the money rather than trade it for a ticket. In other words, whatever objective value the raffle had, it was perceived differently by the participants. This is very much like the wealth effect but receiving the $3 or the raffle ticket in the initial allocation seems very unlikely to determine the ability of the participants to pay. Instead, what seems to be at work is something more like an *endowment effect*, meaning that simple possession of something determines how much one values it. More generally, one's perception of value is a function of a reference point.

9. Jack L. Knetsch and J. A. Sinden, "Willingness to Pay and Compensation Demanded: Experimental Evidence of Disparity in Measures of Value," *Quarterly Journal of Economics* 99 (1984): 507.

At one level, these findings suggest that the economist's assumption of rationality is inaccurate. This does not mean that the assumption should not be made. It simply means that one must be conscious of the possible implications of the inaccuracy. At another level, it is not clear that the studies actually refute the rationality assumption at all. As already noted, changing reference points involves altering the starting point from which consistent preferences may then be formed. It is not a refutation of rationality to find apparent inconsistencies when reference points are altered.

Regardless of how one feels about wealth and endowment effects, they are probably more important when economics is applied to law than to economic theory generally. As already noted, some of those who apply economics to law have taken the normative position that legal rights, like the right to a piece of property, should be allocated to those who value them the most as indicated by a willingness and ability to pay. This, in turn, means deciding who actually does value a specific right the most. What the wealth and endowment effect tell us is that those who favor this normative position must consider the reference point when determining value.

Ultimatum Games

One of the more intriguing areas of research leading economists to question the rational self-interest assumption involves experiments with what is called the ultimatum game. The game works like this. Groups of participants who are strangers are divided into pairs. One member of the pair, person 1, is given a sum of money and told that he can share the money with the other party, person 2, and that both parties may keep their shares if person 2 approves. Person 1 gets one try and the parties are not permitted to communicate. If you were in the position of person 1, you might be tempted to give person 2 nothing or just a penny or two. Your thinking would be that even if you are completely selfish, person 2 is no worse off and, with a penny, he or she would be better off. So why would he or she deny approval and deprive both of you of any part of the $10? Rational self-interest would seem to require accepting any amount.

Put yourself, though, in the position of person 2. If person 1 gave you 2 cents, how would you feel? If you said "unhappy," you are apparently in the company of most participants in the experiments. In the ultimatum game, very low or zero allocations by those in the role of person 1 are routinely rejected, meaning that both parties receive nothing. Put differently, the rejecting party would rather take nothing than a nominal part of the initial amount. Perhaps sensing this, those in the role of person 1 routinely allocate significant portions of the original amount to their partners. It is important to note that rejection cannot be rationalized by saying it is a step in a strategic process designed to assure a higher share the next time around. There is no next time.

LAW AND ECONOMICS IN ACTION 25.2

PERSPECTIVES ON SHARING

In "Giving According to Garp: An Experimental Test of the Consistency of Preferences for Altruism," James Andreoni and John Miller report that individuals seem to have fairly consistent or rational preferences for fairness. This means that it may be possible to economically model this fairness preference and sidestep some of the criticisms of economics' *rational maximizer of self-interest* assumption. Interestingly, the experimenters found that subjects' fairness preferences fell into or close to three groups: selfish, in which the person maximizes his or her own return; Rawlsian, in which the reward is divided evenly; and Utilitarian, in which the reward is maximized regardless of the recipient. To give an example of how these preferences might work, consider the following game. The subject gets forty tokens and may pass or keep as many as he or she likes. If the tokens are worth $1 each whether they are passed or not, then the selfish person will keep all forty, the Rawlsian will keep twenty and pass twenty, and the Utilitarian can actually do anything because the total payoff will always be $40. Now, however, let's assume that the tokens are worth $1 if they are kept and $3 if they are passed. The selfish person will keep all forty, and the Rawlsian will keep thirty and pass ten, so that each person will get $30. The Utilitarian will actually pass all of the tokens, maximizing total payoff at $120.

Reference: James Andreoni and John Miller, "Giving According to Garp: An Experimental Test of the Consistency of Preferences for Altruism," *Econometrica* 70 (2002): 737–53.

There are many variations on the ultimatum game. It has been played in a variety of countries to test the outcomes in different cultural settings and the results are generally the same. One thing that seems to change the outcome is providing information that leads the parties to believe that person 1 "earned" the right to be the initiating party. In these instances, a very uneven division is more likely to be seen as acceptable. Interestingly, in a similar game called the "dictator game," person 2 has no power to reject or deny a gain to both parties. One might expect completely selfish behavior in these instances by the player in the position of person 1. In fact, even in these games, many players elect to share.

Probably the most important question in the context of the ultimatum game is whether the outcomes would hold if the amounts at stake were significantly higher. When pots are low, like $10, a player in the position of person 2 may feel no qualms about rejecting a 10 percent share of $1. Suppose the pot were $100,000. Would you reject a 10 percent share of $10,000? Experiments at this level have not been conducted. A few years ago, however, the game was played with students with pots of $100, and the result were generally the same as those observed with smaller amounts.[10]

The ultimatum game is often regarded as a test of rationality, and the results are interpreted as refuting the rationality assumption. The point is that if one prefers more wealth to less, how can it be rational to reject even a small share of the pot if it is offered? Put differently, if you would bend over to pick up a dollar on the street, isn't it irrational to reject the dollar if offered in the ultimatum game? At a simplistic level, this does seem to be irrational, but what the ultimatum game really tells us is that the dollar in the street is not the same as the dollar in the ultimatum game. The test, therefore, is not a very good one for assessing rationality. What the ultimatum game does indicate is that people possess a sense of justice or fairness and they are willing to pay, in the form of rejecting low offers, in order to either communicate or maintain that sense of fairness. Just how much this sense of fairness is worth is difficult to say.

10. Elizabeth Hoffman, Kevin McCabe, and Vernon Smith, "On Expectations and Monetary Stakes in the Ulitmatum Game," *International Journal of Game Theory* 25 (1996): 289–301.

The importance of this sense of fairness is starkly illustrated in a game devised by Richard Thaler. The question posed to subjects was expressed like this:

> You are lying on the beach on a hot day. All you have to drink is ice water. For the last hour you have been thinking about how much you would enjoy a nice cold bottle of your favorite brand of beer. A companion gets up to go make a phone call and offers to bring back a beer from the only nearby place where beer is sold (a fancy hotel) [a small run-down grocery store]. He says that the beer might be expensive and so asks how much you are willing to pay for the beer. He says that he will buy the beer if it costs as much or less than the price you state. But if it costs more than the price you state he will not buy it. You trust your friend, and there is no possibility of bargaining with the (bartender) [store owner]. What price do you tell him?[11]

In the experiment, subjects who were the given the fancy hotel version of the question reported a median price of $2.65. Subjects given the run-down store version reported a median price of $1.50. Here again, something appears to be amiss with respect to rationality. Given that it is the same beer with the same thirst-quenching potential, how can it be worth both $2.65 and $1.50 at the same time? Clearly, what has worked its way into the decision is some sense of what is a fair price.

Whether these experiments suggest that people are irrational or can be explained by the fact that people attribute value to feeling they have been treated fairly is probably not important. The more important question is whether these observations are relevant when one applies economic analysis to law. The answer is, unfortunately, that the phenomenon is likely to be relevant sometimes but it is not always easy to tell when. One can imagine cases in which it could be very important. For example, you were briefly introduced in Chapter 11 to the idea of an *efficient* contract breach. Because courts determine the damages one must pay for breaching a contract, they in effect set the price for a breach of contract. The theory, as you saw, is that this price should be set so that breaches occur only when making the

---

11. Richard H. Thaler, *The Winner's Curse: Paradoxes and Anomalies of Economic Life* (Princeton, N.J.: Princeton University Press, 1992), 21–49.

breach is efficient. Now return to the idea that individuals possess a sense of fairness that can be expressed in a monetary equivalent. Also, consider that many people view breaking a promise as being unfair or unkind and will make a sacrifice to avoid doing so. The challenge for a court in pricing contract breaches is how to factor the value of fairness. The same type of problem may arise when the law responds to any action that has an interpersonal impact.

WHAT TO MAKE OF CHOICES

One very important aspect of law that is considerably out of sync with economics is how to react to choices people make. There are actually four related questions. The first is whether some choices are somehow qualitatively different from others. For example, is the choice by a not-very-intelligent and poorly educated person to eat an unhealthy diet different from the choice of a well-educated person to buy a product after a great deal of research? The second is whether choices reveal preferences. Even rational people with well-defined preferences may fail and make a wrong choice when attempting to express that preference. The third is how to respond to the possibility that some people may wish they had different preferences. Finally, do choices reveal preferences when they are instantly regretted?

The Quality of Choices

On the first of these issues, the position of economics is clear. There are no judgments made about why a choice is selected. Whether the market is for sex, cigarettes, or yogurt, economists report on quantities and the variables that may determine the quantity demanded. In matters of preferences, modern economics has little to say. This is quite different from law, which actually delves into the determinants of preferences and makes qualitative distinctions. Consider the famous case of the dancing lessons from Chapter 9.[12] In that case, a woman who was recently widowed attended a dancing school and was sold a few lessons. After several more visits and evidently a fair amount of smooth talking, she purchased enough dance lessons in advance to keep her dancing for most of the rest of her life. An economist studying the

12. *Vokes v. Arthur Murray Inc.*, 212 So.2d 906 (Fl. 1968).

demand for dancing lessons would simply record the price of the lesson and the quantity demanded. In the real case, however, a court actually found that the dance studio went too far in its sales tactics and permitted the buyer to avoid the contract. In other words, the court allowed her to get out of the contract even though the salesperson at the dance studio had not broken the law. In fact, a great deal of law is devoted to assessing the *legitimacy* of how choices are made. Legal doctrines like duress, undue influence, mistake, misrepresentation, and unconscionability are frequently used as means of what amounts to assessing the quality of choices. This is not to say that economics or law employs the preferable perspective. Each discipline simply takes the point of view that is consistent with its principal use.

Do Choices Reveal Preferences?

The second question is more complicated. If the goal is to maximize efficiency, however measured, it is important that choices actually reveal preferences. In the case of economic analysis, these choices are expressed in markets or by voting. It is important to remember, though, that it is not the preference but the expression of that preference that is of primary interest to economists. Thus, as you know, the most heart-felt "preference" that is not backed by dollars in the relevant market or a vote at the right time and place goes unregistered. When the expression does occur, the assumption is that it lines up with the preference backing it. Paul Samuelson coined the phase "revealed preferences" to describe this phenomenon.

Despite a general reliance on the idea that preferences are revealed, most economists would agree that there are at least two related instances in which this might not occur. One is when the potential for free riding exists. This is sometimes also referred to as the "chicken game." It works like this. Suppose there is a fence between your property and that of your neighbor. The fence is dilapidated and would cost $500 to replace. You would pay $500 for a new fence if you had to, but you hope your neighbor will also notice the fence and replace it himself. You would also be willing to split the cost of the fence. Your preferences, ranked in order of most preferred to least preferred, look like this:

1. Neighbor repairs fence
2. You and neighbor share fence repair for $250

3. You repair fence yourself for $500
4. Neither you nor neighbor repairs fence.

If you engage in the chicken game, you will not repair the fence yourself and you might even tell your neighbor that you have no interest in the fence in hopes he will relent and repair it. Economists, looking no further than your actions, would conclude that at a price of $500, the quantity of fence you demand is zero. That is correct, but is it correct to say that the choice you made accurately reveals your preference when it comes to the fence? The point is that when free-riding opportunities arise, there are temptations to not reveal preferences. Note that if your neighbor acts the same way you do, the fence will never get repaired and the outcome is the worst possible.

This phenomenon explains why governments supply some goods. For example, you might be willing to pay $100 in taxes to have more police protection. But if your neighbor pays the $100 you can free ride. If you and your neighbor both conceal your preferences, there will be no police protection although you both value it sufficiently for it to be allocatively efficient for more police protection to be produced. Goods characterized by free riding and allocatively inefficient levels of output are called public goods and are frequently supplied by the government.

The second possibility occurs if you are involved in another type of strategic situation. You may be familiar already with the prisoner's dilemma, but a review may nonetheless be useful.[13] The standard formulation is that two people are caught committing a crime and are questioned about it before they can confer. Each prisoner is then approached by the prosecutor with a deal. If she confesses and the other prisoner does not, she will go free and the other prisoner will go to prison for twenty years. If they both confess, both will go to jail for ten years, and if neither confesses, they both will escape with three-year sentences. The possibilities are expressed in Figure 25.2.

The best outcome would be for both parties to refuse to bargain, resulting in a three-year sentence each. On the other hand, if one prisoner takes the risk of not confessing and her counterpart does con-

---

13. The prisoner's dilemma is a basic form of strategic interaction (or lack of interaction). Strategic interactions are dealt with in game theory. We applied game theory to legal questions in the appendix to Chapter 13.

		B's Strategy	
		Confess	Do not confess
A's Strategy	Confess	10 / 10	20 / 0
	Do not confess	0 / 20	3 / 3

FIGURE 25.2 The Prisoner's Dilemma

fess, then the strategy of not cooperating backfires and the nonconfessor goes to prison for twenty years. Given this outcome, the choice is likely to be to confess, and when both parties do this they receive sentences of ten years each. In fact, this is the rational outcome for each prisoner if she is acting independently. On the other hand, if there were some way to solve the dilemma, the prisoners could cooperate in order to arrive at the three-year sentence.[14]

There is a great deal of empirical evidence that individuals, especially when they play the game repeatedly, are able to solve the prisoner's dilemma. The problem for those merely observing the behaviors is that the solution requires both players to act in a manner that appears not to be in their self-interest. In effect, they reveal one thing in the hope of achieving another. The trick in assessing preferences is to know when this is occurring.

LAW AND ECONOMICS IN ACTION 25.3

ACHIEVING COOPERATION

One of the most important explorations of the prisoner's dilemma is Robert Axelrod's *The Evolution of Cooperation*. He describes the best strategies to employ when playing the game and the implications this has for cooperation in real-world settings. Axelrod argues that individuals acting in their

14. See Amartya Sen, "Behavior and the Concept of Preference," *Econometrica* 40 (1973): 241.

own self-interest will learn to use and benefit from cooperative behaviors emphasizing reciprocity so long as they have many chances to interact, and therefore a reason to maintain cooperative behavior. The strategy is called "tit for tat" and consists of cooperating on the first move and making the same choice as the other person did on the previous move. He applies this theory to the development of altruistic behavior in animals and evolution, but he also shows how the prisoner's dilemma model and the same reasoning can be applied to everything from politics to social structures. One interesting example of cooperation in a seemingly impossible setting is the "live and let live" system that occurred in the trenches in World War I, in which soldiers on both sides would often intentionally miss their targets so long as the other side continued to do so as well. Axelrod also gives advice to players of the prisoner's dilemma game as well as to policymakers and reformers who want to create an environment of reciprocity to maximize benefits for everyone.

Reference: Robert Axelrod, *The Evolution of Cooperation* (New York: Basic Books, 1984).

In both the chicken game and the prisoner's dilemma, the problem is that individuals deliberately conceal (chicken game) or cannot communicate (prisoner's dilemma) about their preferences. Entire branches of economics are designed to study these phenomena, and very sophisticated methodologies are employed to break through the concealment. As a discipline, law has never been as wedded to the idea that choices reveal preferences. And, like economics, law allows for and responds to instances in which this is not the case. Those who apply economics to law are generally on solid footing when they assume choices reveal preferences, but it is important to know about the instances in which this is not the case.

Preferences for Preferences

The third area in which one needs to look behind expressed preferences is when individuals claim to want to have different preferences. This may sound like a strange idea, but consider the person who really likes to gamble but votes to have gambling banned in his or her community. This idea may even extend to various addictions or eating disorders. In these instances, people claim that if they could choose their preferences, they would choose different ones. Gauging preferences by observing choices is still accurate, but it does not pick up on the possibility that these individuals think they would experience higher levels of utility if some of their current preferences did not exist.

Before moving to the question of whether economics or law should pay much attention to the preferences-for-preferences possibility, it is important to note that not all wished-for preferences go completely unexpressed. As already noted, sometimes people vote in a manner that appears to be inconsistent with preferences expressed in the market. A fascinating branch of economics is devoted to examining choices made in a political context in which the supply and demand for laws is studied. In these markets, votes are spent rather than money. Obviously these are not markets for preferences per se but sometimes the laws people vote for are ones that require them to act as though their preferences were different.

One interpretation of the possibility that people do one thing and vote to be forced to not do it is that they are irrational. Why vote to prohibit something you do when it is legal? In actual fact, this is probably not irrational at all. A person who enjoys gambling might rank his preferences like this:

1. Gambling is legal for responsible people like me.
2. Gambling is illegal for all.
3. Gambling is legal for all.

That person may wish that somehow gambling could be regulated so that only responsible people would be permitted to gamble. The next preference is to make gambling illegal not just for himself but also for all people. This preference can only be expressed in political markets and does not conflict with "buying" gambling in the market by going to a casino. This is not inconsistent with the third choice of "If gambling is legal, I will gamble." Thus, to some extent, the appearance of having a preference for preferences is actually a function of the distinction between ordinary markets and political markets. It is also possible that people express different types of preferences in different markets. Kenneth Arrow has made the case that market transactions are a function of "tastes" while voting is more a function of "values."[15]

---

15. Kenneth Arrow, *Social Choice and Individual Values*, 2nd ed. (New York: Wiley, 1963).

Although there are a number of ways to explain and reconcile instances in which choices seem inconsistent with preferences, a small group of cases remain in which people seem to want to be different. Alcoholics and drug addicts invest huge sums in efforts to change their demand for alcohol and drugs. People with various other dependencies may also wish they could change and express a different set of preferences. Because economics is essentially descriptive and cannot describe what is not expressed in political or conventional markets, these possibilities are not of great importance.

On the other hand, a good deal of law seems to be shaped by the consideration of preferences that are not revealed readily in choices. Sometimes this takes place on a large scale like government attempts to assist those who would like to stop alcohol or drug use. In other instances, the recognition of a choice that is inconsistent with a preference takes place in individual cases. For example, a person who makes a contract while under the influence of drugs or alcohol may not be held to that contract. The reasoning is that the preference expressed by that party is not his or her "real preference." In other instances, people do things that seem out of character: What is done does not reflect the person's general values. For example, courts have considered something called the battered spouse defense when battered spouses turn on their tormentors and kill them. The accused offers a defense—an argument that she should not be punished—that as a battered spouse she saw no other way to escape the violence. Often battered spouses say they would like to leave the tormentor but cannot. In other words, the preference is to leave but the choice does not reveal that preference.

The relevance of this for law is pretty clear. One of the goals of criminal law is to prevent people from harming each other. Thus, in the context of spouses who kill spouses, it is important to be able to assess the likelihood that the spouse will kill again and the best way of preventing it. The spouse who aspires to be able to leave should the situation arise again might be treated most efficiently by a judicial response that allows the underlying preference to be expressed. This could entail counseling rather than imprisonment.

Regret

A distinction between choice and preference may arise in instances in which people regret decisions they have made. Economics does not pay a great deal of attention to these instances. From an economic perspective, the preference expressed after a high-pressured sales pitch is just as much a preference as any other. And there is truth to that insofar as whatever the reason and no matter how temporary, it was the preference at that instant. Similarly, in law, the person who makes what turns out to have been a bad decision or experiences what is sometimes referred to as "buyer's remorse" generally has no recourse.

There are some cases in which the law does, however, seem to take regret into account. Law has a doctrine called *undue influence* that means basically that one party has influenced another so much that the second party's preference has been overridden. These are not cases in which one person threatens another with harm. Instead, these are cases in which there is almost a badgering quality to the interaction. Often the badgering takes place at an inappropriate time or place. The idea is that what is expressed is not really the badgered party's preference but that of the person doing the pressuring. This ideal that one can pierce choice and somehow assess people's true preferences can be seen in requirements that individuals be permitted a "cooling off" period before permanently committing to a position.

This chapter suggests, as did Chapter 1, that those who specialize in economics may have a different approach to law from the approach of those who do not specialize in economics. Principally, this difference stems from the assumptions that economists must make in order to engage in a meaningful and useful analysis. You have seen this throughout this book, whether in the context of contracts, criminal law, or even marriage. On the surface, it appears that those who deal with law do not make assumptions but react to actual behavior. In fact, every decision in law or in broader policymaking involves an expectation of the consequences of that decision, and that involves an assumption of how people will react. Thus, there are assumptions underlying law as much as there are assumptions underlying economics. The question is whether the assumptions are the same and if they are accurate.

QUESTIONS FOR DISCUSSION

1. Do you agree that in order to apply economics to law, one must assume that people do not act out of a sense of duty or obligation?

If those people are excluded and some people do obey the law out of a sense of duty, how does this alter the analysis?

2. In law, the idea of what it means to be insane or to lack capacity can change from time to time. You have seen these ideas in the context of contracts and criminal law. Rationality, on the other hand, seems to have a standard definition. Should law adopt the concept of rationality as its standard of capacity in the context of criminal law and contracts?

3. One of the things that has been discovered is that women are more generous than men when playing the ultimatum game. Supposedly, though, both men and women are rational. Can you think of any way women might be treated differently from men by the courts?

4. In making policy, should the focus be on what people say they want or what they do? For example, people say they want to lose weight but then eat jelly doughnuts. In public policy decisions about how to make people better off, doesn't this mean subsidizing the consumption of jelly doughnuts rather that touting the benefits of "healthy" eating?

5. Assume that smokers when making the decision to start smoking are rational and also knew that smoking would probably lead to lung cancer. Quite a number of them develop lung cancer. Does it make sense to require the cigarette manufacturer to pay damages to smokers (or their families)? What if smokers insist that they would rather not smoke?

Index